8-23

Lidia's
Italian Table

Lidia's Italian Table

Lidia Matticchio Bastianich

Edited by Christopher Styler

Photography by Christopher Hirsheimer

William Morrow and Company, Inc. New York

Library of Congress Cataloging-in-Publication Data

Bastianich, Lidia Matticchio.
    Lidia's Italian table / Lidia Matticchio Bastianich.—1st ed.
        p.   cm.
    Includes index.
    ISBN 0-688-15410-7
    1. Cookery, Italian.   I. Title.
TX723.B32   1998
    641.5945—dc21   98-2949
                                                    CIP

Printed in the United States of America

First Edition

7   8   9   10

BOOK DESIGN BY RICHARD ORIOLO

www.williammorrow.com
www.lidiasitaly.com

I would like to dedicate this book to my first grandchild, my little angel, Olivia Anne Bastianich.

Olivia dearest, the foods, flavors, and stories in this book are those of your family and of your heritage; they are your roots. May the sentiments and love with which they were written accompany you through your life. You are the future which reflects the past.

Love,
Noni

To Deanna, my lovely daughter-in-law, and my son, Joseph: Thank you for this precious gift.

To my daughter, Tanya, and my huggable Roman son-in-law, Corrado: I have more stories and recipes for when you bless me with your children.

You, my children, are the sun on the horizon that lights my day and the stars in the night that show me the way.

Love,
Mom

Dear Chris:
This book is the first solo flight for me. I am not a writer by profession, but a chef who is passionate about food and loves to share it with diners, readers, and viewers.

There is one person who was by my side from page 1 to the end. He tested every recipe, corrected my grammar and spelling, and shifted and added words whenever necessary to capture my thoughts. I feel Chris Styler has become part of my family with this project and it is with him that I share this book. I couldn't have done it without you. Thank you for everything.

Contents

Acknowledgments

Lidia's Italian Table was created with love, passion, and help from my dear friends, family, and colleagues. Included in the cast of characters was my hardworking recipe tester, editor, and television kitchen coordinator, Christopher Styler, whose organization and attention to details is unsurpassed. I also want to thank my producer, Geoffrey Drummond, and director, Bruce Franchini, along with the entire production staff, who spent three weeks with me in my home coaching me, laughing with me, and becoming part of my family. In addition, it was fun and gratifying to watch them all become grappa connoisseurs. I thank Pam Hoenig, my editor, for her attention and support throughout the entire project. I also thank my agent, Jane Dystel, for guiding me through it all.

My mother, Erminia, and Gianni Bencina were, as always, by my side and very supportive. I couldn't have done it without them. I would also like to thank my son, Joseph, and the staff of Felidia, Becco, and Frico Bar. Their professionalism and management skills allowed me to take time away from the restaurants and devote it to the book and the television show. To my kitchen staff, especially executive chef Fortunato Nicotra and pastry chef Eileen Guastella, I am forever grateful. They kept the fires at Felidia burning during my absence. My office staff—Shelly Burgess, Magdalena Spirydowicz-Tulipan, and Miguelina Polanco—were by my side through the entire production of the television and book. I am so grateful to them for everything they did for me during this exciting time. Many thanks to Patricia Brown and John Brady for the work that they did during the initial stages of the book and show and for their support, friendship, and advice throughout its finish.

I am very grateful to my sponsors, Banfi Wines and Colavita USA, for everything they have done for me and to the following people for providing products for the show and book—we couldn't have done it without you: Ceramica in New York City for the beautiful and authentic Italian table top and accessories; Villeroy & Boch for the elegant plates, platters, glasses, and silverware; Le Creuset and Meyer Farberware for supplying cookware; Adria Hotel in Bayside, New York, for allowing our production crew to stay with them; Gourmet Garage, New York City, for the generous food donations; the Consorzio di Parmigiano-Reggiano for the donation of my favorite cheese; the Blue Ribbon Fish Company for fabulous fresh fish and shellfish; Clarence House in New York City for their fine linens; the Keil Brothers in Bayside, New York, for their generosity in supplying beautiful plants and trees for the set; and Accent on Flowers for contributing plants.

In addition to writing about food, I also have a passion for reading about it. As a result, my library is quite extensive, and there are a number of books that I constantly consulted while writing this work. I'd like to give credit to them too: Emilia Valli's *La Cucina Friuliana* (Padova: Franco Muzzio, 1992); Mady Fast's *La Cucina Istriana* (Padova: Franco Muzzio, 1990); Maria Stelvio's *Cucina Triestina* (Trieste: Stabilimento Tipografico Nazionale, n.d.); Harold McGee's *On Food and Cooking* (New York: Charles Scribner's Sons, 1984); Frances Bissell's *The Real Meat Cookbook* (London: Chatto and Windus, 1992); Vincenzo Buonassisi's *La Cucina Degli Italiani* (Milano: Idealibri, 1988); Reay Tannahill's *Food in History* (New York: Stein & Day, 1973); Time-Life's *The Good Cook Series* (New York: Time-Life Books, 1980); Anna Gosetti della Saldi's *Le Ricette Regionali* (Milano: Casa Editrice Solares, 1967)—and my own *La Cucina di Lidia* (New York: Doubleday, 1990).

Introduction

What is life's recipe? What shapes our thinking and our philosophy, forms our habits, stimulates creativity, and drives our passion? What ingredients does love require, what spice does joy need?

Let me invite you on a journey with me from my childhood through my formative years and beyond to see how my love for food and my desire to share it have developed. In these pages, I talk about the growing of food, the harvesting and enjoyment of food, and the preparation, storing, drying, curing, and preserving of food. Each season has its distinct colors, flavors, and aromas—I still vividly remember my early food experiences, which gave way to my lifelong love affair with Italian food. I would like to share these experiences with you.

I was blessed with a very serene and secure childhood in Pola, a town on the peninsula of Istria, which juts into the northernmost arm of the Adriatic Sea, where I was raised under the loving guidance of my parents and maternal grandparents. Their lives were devoted to the growing and preparation of food, some of which they served in their *osteria*—a collection of tables and chairs set up in the courtyard in front of their house. On rainy days, the tables moved indoors, to the *cantina* (wine cellar).

I turned eleven years old during the aftermath of World War II and the coming of Communism to Istria, which had been given to Yugoslavia after Italy's defeat. My world was overturned. My parents decided to flee Istria and settle in Trieste, a border city populated by many political refugees like us coming back to Italy. We were taken in initially by my great-aunt Zia Nina. Then, like many refugees, my parents decided to move to a refugee camp, where we awaited an opportunity to emigrate.

And what a wonderful opportunity it was for me at twelve and for my brother, Franco, at fifteen to come to America! My mother, Erminia, my father, Vittorio, Franco, and I became acclimated to American life within a year.

Throughout my school years, I loved the sciences—especially biology—but I slowly found myself gravitating towards food. My part-time and summer jobs were always food-related. If I started working in a bakery as a salesgirl, I would end up in the back baking bread; if hired as a hostess in a restaurant, I would end up in the kitchen making salads.

For my sixteenth birthday, some of my new friends in Astoria, New York, decided to have a birthday party for me. They hired a young man named Felice to play the accordion at the party. Talking to Felice, I realized we had a lot in common: He too had emigrated from Istria to the United States to avoid the Communist regime after the war and he had also been working in restaurants since his arrival. We became friends and, eventually, through Felice's persistence and frequent visits to my house, more than friends. In 1966, we married. Two years later we had our first child, a son, Joseph. In 1972, one short year after the opening of our first restaurant, Buonavia, in Forest Hills, came our daughter, Tanya.

By now my passion for food was full-blown. I had taken courses in food anthropology and the science of food and was going regularly to Italy to gain experience by working in the restaurants, wineries, *salumerie,* and *pasticcerie*. I still make these "learning trips" when I go to Italy—there is always something wonderful to taste and something new to learn.

About nine years after we opened our first restaurant, we launched another, Villa Secondo, also in Queens. Even with two successful restaurants, I still yearned to move to Manhattan. In 1981, we sold both our restaurants in Queens and opened Felidia on East 58th Street in midtown Manhattan. Today, Felidia is going stronger than ever and is still the epicenter of all my activities.

My son, Joseph, graduated from Boston College in 1989 and went on to work as a bond trader on Wall Street. But Joseph, like me, soon realized that his passion was food and cooking. He went to Italy for a year and apprenticed in restaurants and wineries; then he came back to work with us at Felidia. In 1992, he opened Becco Restaurant on the popular Restaurant Row—West 46th Street in Manhattan's theater district. Becco was followed in 1995 by Frico Bar restaurant, only a few blocks away on West 43rd Street. In between the start-ups of the two restaurants, he became a husband to our lovely daughter-in-law, Deanna Damiano, and recently a father to Olivia, our little angel.

Tanya always showed artistic leanings. She graduated from Georgetown University in 1993 and went on to get her Ph.D. in Renaissance art history from Oxford University in 1998. She married Corrado Manuali, a huggable Roman, and moved to Prato, a town just outside Florence. Tanya and Shelly Burgess, her peer from Syracuse University, have taken the idea of my food learning trips, added the benefit of their artistic experience, and are now running a company called Esperienze Italiane, which leads guided food, wine, and culture tours to different parts of Italy.

Grandma Erminia, my mother, who made all of this possible, still lives with us. Through all the long nights I worked at the restaurants, she was there to take care of our home and of Tanya and Joseph while they were growing up.

Our family has been through a lot together, but when we are all gathered around Lidia's Italian table, I know everything will be fine forever. The thread of food and cooking that winds through my family helps keep us together, no matter how physically far apart we may be at times. Since this thread is so important to my life and my family, I wanted to tell you a little bit about my history. Now I will let my recipes and food tell the rest of the story.

May you receive and enjoy these recipes with the love with which they were written, and may they give much pleasure and enjoyment to you, your family, your friends, and your life.

Ingredients

Throughout the book I emphasize the importance of the quality and authenticity of raw ingredients when preparing Italian food. The following products are the cornerstones of Italian cuisine, and understanding them is a must—knowing how to buy them, store them, and use them is the basis of Italian cooking.

Parmigiano-Reggiano

If there is one product that has carried the flag of Italian cuisine around the world, it is Parmigiano-Reggiano, from the region of Emilia-Romagna in central Italy. The king of Italian cheeses in flavor and in size—a "wheel" weighs about sixty pounds—

Parmigiano-Reggiano is made from 100 percent cow's milk and has a finely grained texture and a golden straw-yellow color. Its aroma of cream and butter with herbal overtones is complex and rich.

Parmigiano-Reggiano is produced under very strict guidelines and must be aged for at least one year before it is put on the market. This young cheese is used in most pasta dishes and other cooking. Older cheese—aged up to two years—has a much more pronounced and complex flavor and is darker yellow with a more crumbly texture. It is an excellent appetizer served with a sparkling wine, such as Prosecco, or a wonderful way to finish a meal and a good bottle of Barolo.

For authenticity, look for the words *Parmigiano-Reggiano* embossed around the entire surface of the rind. Most specialty food stores and many national supermarket chains carry authentic Parmigiano-Reggiano.

To serve the cheese on its own as a separate course, break off one-inch chunks with the tip of a knife or a short-handled knife with a spade-shaped blade made specifically for that purpose; avoid slicing the cheese, as it crumbles easily. To serve grated Parmigiano-Reggiano with pasta, risotto, or soups, grate it at the last minute—grated cheese loses aroma and flavor quickly. Store the cheese, wrapped tightly in plastic wrap, in the refrigerator.

Olives and Olive Oil

(Olive ed Olio d'Oliva)

To me, the olive tree signifies life and eternity and is imbued with a sense of spirituality. Maybe it is because throughout my life olive oil has been so important, so respected, and so truly appreciated. I have memories of it being consumed with reverence.

My paternal grandparents had groves of olive trees. I don't remember my Grandma Francesca—she passed away before I had an opportunity to know her—but a few of my younger years were spent with Grandpa Tonin. Like my family he lived in Busoler, on the other side of town from my maternal grandparents, Nonna Rosa and Nonno Giovanni, with whom I spent a lot of time.

Nonno Tonin would take me for walks through his olive trees, and I remember the shimmering, silvery green leaves and the clusters of olives looking so delicate—some vibrant green with purple speckles and some completely deep purple. The trunks of those olive trees, however, were not delicate—they looked to me like the gnarled faces of old men in pain. Whenever I had to pass the olive groves at night during my visits with Nonno Tonin, I had images of those old men in the trees chasing me.

Five years ago, I planted three hundred and fifty olive trees in Busoler in memory of my grandparents and in honor of the land they loved and worked with such dedication. When I visit now, the land is alive, the olive trees are smiling and waving in the breeze, and I swear I can see my grandparents working the fields.

Olive oil is the basic element of my cooking, as it is of the entire Mediterranean Basin. As far back as I can remember, the harvest of the olives took place in the cold months of late November or early December. The women harvested olives from the branches that were reachable from the ground with the help of a ladder and a *tela,* or cloth, that was spread around the base of the olive trees to catch the olives that fell to the ground. The men climbed into the higher branches to gather the hard-to-reach olives. There always seemed to be a sense of urgency in harvesting the olives. When I was young, I thought that was because of the cold weather, but I have come to learn that olives have to be milled as soon as possible after they are harvested to produce the best oil. If left in storage, the olives begin to ferment and the quality of the oil suffers.

As I recall, Dignano—a small town next to Pola—was the location of the communal olive oil mill. There were two huge cylinders of stone that, when pulled by donkeys, rolled around and around over a wide stone base. Olives were layered over the base stone and, as the donkeys circled the base, the stone cylinders crushed the olives to a paste. A metal drain spout ran from the press, channeling the free-flowing oil into a container. The pulp was then collected and put into large, double-thick filters made of jute that were shaped like life preservers or car tires. These were stacked one atop the other on a wooden pole. Turning the lever on top of the pole slowly applied pressure to the filters, gently squeezing as much oil as possible from the olive pulp. When all the oil had been extracted using this method, hot water was applied to loosen any olive oil still lodged in the paste. The taste memory of hot crusty bread dunked in this freshly pressed olive oil is a flavor reference that I carry with me. I search for that flavor in every olive oil I taste and use.

Today, the process of making olive oil remains basically the same, except that machines, mills, and centrifuges do the job that stone, donkeys, and people used to do. The grade of olive oil that appears on its label is based on its residual oleic acid; generally speaking, the less acidic an olive oil is, the higher its quality. These are not arbitrary designations; the International Olive Oil Council is responsible for setting these guidelines and monitoring them. Olive oil labels can be tricky to read, but here are a few things to look for:

- Extra Virgin is from the first cold pressing of olives and has no more than 1 percent oleic acid.

- Virgin Olive Oil, also from the first cold pressing, contains from 1 to 3.3 percent oleic acid.

- Olive Oil is virgin olive oil with an acidity level of higher than 3.3 percent that has been chemically refined to remove impurities and excess acidity and has had some virgin oil added to it to replace flavor and color removed during refining.

- Olive-Pomace Oil is the oil extracted from olive pomace (crushed olives) with the help of solvents, which is then blended with virgin olive oil.

- Olio Novello is newly pressed olive oil—usually less than two months old—and is just beginning to come to the States. In Italy, it is quite traditional, and a seasonal cuisine is built around it, usually in the month of December. You might want to ask your specialty food store to carry some. It will be vibrant green, murky, very vegetal, and fresh. It is excellent drizzled over soups—or use it to make bruschetta or to dress seafood, greens, and steamed vegetable salads.

All olive oil is best when used within a year after pressing, although under certain circumstances it can age well for up to two years. As olive oil ages, its flavor becomes milder and less herbal. To keep olive oil, transfer it to small bottles that seal tightly and store them in a dark, cool place. Being of an unstable molecular composition, olive oil oxidizes quickly and, if left in contact with air for long periods of time, will become rancid.

There is olive oil produced all over the Italian peninsula, starting with the northernmost region Lombardia that surrounds Lake Garda. I love the oil from this region—it is very gentle and has a mild herbal aroma with a mild, nutty finish. I use it as a condiment sprinkled over fish carpaccio, steamed vegetables, and light salads. Ligurian olive oil is also gentle but a bit more herbaceous and aromatic; it has a mild sweetness and, as Liguria is the birthplace of pesto, it is, of course, the oil best suited for pesto and herbal infusions. I use it in fish salads and tossed salads and as the base for other fish preparations. I also like to drizzle it over just about any fish dish right before serving.

Tuscan olive oil is hearty and packed with flavor. Its peppery finish goes wonderfully with beans, dense soups, roasts, and slabs of grilled *Bruschette* (page 21). Most of the Italian wine producers in Tuscany also produce olive oil. In fact, there is a new *consorzio* (syndicate) of oil producers in Tuscany in the Gallo Nero zone of Chianti. This *consorzio*—Olio Extra Vergine di Oliva Terre del Chianti Classico—will guarantee that the oil is just from that region. There is also a *consorzio* called Laudemio of about twenty-five olive oil producers who bottle olive oils of extremely high quality under their own strictly enforced controls. All Laudemio oils are packaged in the same narrow eight-sided bottle with the Laudemio name, but each producer has its own label, which features the name of the *azienda,* or agricultural firm. These are expensive oils but, in most cases, a truly superior product.

The region of Umbria produces an oil that is very herbal with a buttery, nutty finish—delicious for *frittate,* hearty mushroom dishes, and preparations using the black truffle from Norcia and the white truffle from Acqualagna. It is also excellent for risottos and braised meats.

Puglia is located in the heel of Italy. After the Pianura Padana, the fertile planes of the Po River, Puglia is the largest breadbasket of Italy. Fields of durum wheat and endless groves of olive trees dress the countryside. It is a magnificent region, studded by ornate baroque churches of local limestone, which is soft when mined and excavated but hardens with time and takes on a golden yellow hue that, in the light of the setting sun, is mystifying.

In Puglia, the olives ripen under intense summer sun that lasts well into the fall. The oil made from these olives has a lot of flavor and, with the new technology, a lot of elegance. I use

Pugliese olive oil for most basic cooking: braising, vegetable preparations, and soup. Sicilian oil is similar to the Pugliese oil and has lots of herbal flavors that can go a long way.

In our restaurants—Felidia, Becco, and Frico Bar—we always have plenty of these regional olive oils on hand. Seasoning a finished dish with the perfectly complementary oil is like pairing the right wine with a carefully prepared dish.

Truffles
(Tartufi)

The white truffle (*Tuber magnatum*) is one of the most exquisite of all Italian food products. Deceivingly, it looks like a potato, and it can vary in size from that of a hazelnut to an orange to the very rare prize of a truffle the size of a grapefruit or larger! At their best, white truffles should be hard to the touch, as crisp as a turnip, and as smooth and round as possible. The ideal size is that of an egg. The aroma should be sharp and intense: If there is a truffle in the kitchen, you should smell it as you walk through the door. True appreciation of white truffles comes from the olfactory pleasures they provide us. The musky smell of the woods, leaves, and mushrooms is unique and provocative, and once you are lucky enough to encounter it, it will be recognizable to you forever.

The white truffles from the city of Alba in the region of Piedmont are the most prized, although white truffles are also found in Acqualagna in the Marche region and in Istria. They grow on the roots of chestnut, linden, and hazelnut trees in clayish soils. The *tartufai,* or truffle hunters, keep the locations of these trees guarded since the truffles grow in the same place every year. The foraging is done in the dusky light of the early morning hours with the help of dogs. Swine were also used widely at one time, but they would eat their find if the truffle hunters were not quick enough to snatch them away. Dogs, on the other hand, are content with a small reward after each find. Once the dog has located the tuber and excitedly begins to dig with his paws, the truffle hunter takes over and continues to dig cautiously with a hoe, then packs the precious find in a burlap bag.

The dogs used by the *tartufai* are usually hunting dogs and are trained while still young. Newly trained truffle hounds can fetch a pretty penny—from $2,000 and up. Considering that the price of white truffles can range from $700 to $2,000 per pound, depending on quality and availability, the price for the hunting dog is within reason. And while this price may sound exorbitant, an ounce of truffle is enough to shave over four portions of risotto—and the experience is singular.

White truffles are highly seasonal—they become available in mid- to late October and are at their best in mid-November to mid-December. In January, their brief season is finished.

Today the essence of the truffle can be enjoyed in the kitchen year-round by using truffle oil, truffle paste, whole truffles in brine, truffle butter, and truffle "flour." Most of these products are quite good and can be used independent of fresh truffles to add flavor and aromas to pastas, risottos, soups, meats, and sauces. However, for extra-flavorful results, use one of these products along with fresh white truffles—for example, finishing a risotto with a little truffle oil before shaving truffles over it.

Fresh truffles can keep for up to ten days if you follow this procedure: Wrap them individually in a paper towel, then store them in an airtight container filled with rice in the refrigerator. The rice will absorb the aroma of the truffle and make a delicious risotto thereafter. Change the paper towel daily.

The white truffle is not meant to be cooked—it is best enjoyed shaved tissue paper–thin over pasta, risotto, eggs, meats, and salads with a palm-size device made specifically for the purpose. Careful—these truffle shavers are extremely sharp! If you don't have a truffle shaver, use the coarsest side of a box grater—the side you would use for grating carrots. To prepare a truffle for shaving, first brush any dirt from the surface of the truffle with a stiff brush. To make the truffle easier to deal with at the table, you may shave off any rough or protruding parts beforehand into the dish you are cooking. Then shave the truffle over each plate, letting the heat of the food release the aromatic molecules, which the diner then delightfully inhales. My absolute favorite way to enjoy truffles is to shave them over soft scrambled eggs—preferably fresh from the farm—that have been cooked in extra virgin olive oil. In its simplicity, this dish is one of the most sensuous meals you'll ever have.

Porcini
(Boletus edulis)

Porcini mushrooms are an absolute Italian favorite and are used extensively—in both their fresh and dried form—in the Italian cuisine. Porcini were considered a delicacy by the ancient Romans and were found throughout medieval times at banquets and papal tables.

Porcini are found in limited quantities in the late spring and early summer, but the more abundant harvest comes in the fall—especially September and October. Foragers find porcini in dense woods, usually under chestnut, oak, beech, and pine trees. The mushroom's common name, *porcino*, derives from its looks—round and pudgy like a piglet, or *porcellino*.

The best fresh porcini for sautéing or sauces are the smaller, firm ones with round and fat stipes (stems) and caps that slightly overhang the pores. Larger porcini with longer stipes and caps that have started to open are excellent for grilling whole. The important qualities in fresh porcini of any size are a firm, smooth cap, firm white stems, and honey- to lemon-colored pores located under the cap. Toward the top of the stipe, where it is connected to the cap, there is a white net of membranes. When cut, the meat of fresh porcini should be solid and white. In older porcini and porcini that are not cooked within a few days of gathering, the caps can become slimy and flaccid and the pores begin to turn green and also become slimy. If this is the case with your porcini, scrape out the pores with a teaspoon before slicing or cooking them.

To clean porcini, cut off the woody, dirty base of the stipe, then, with a dry or damp towel, clean the cap and the stipe. It is usually not recommended to wash porcini in water unless they are excessively sandy.

If the porcini mushrooms are small and compact, leave the caps and stipes together and cut them lengthwise into slices; if larger, remove the cap and slice the stipe and cap separately length-wise into ⅛- to ¼-inch-thick slices. Porcini are quite perishable, so use them as soon as possible after buying or gathering them.

To store porcini in the refrigerator, line a baking sheet with paper towels and spread them so that air can circulate around, then cover the mushrooms completely with a dry kitchen towel. If they are very fresh, they will keep for two to three days.

Dried sliced porcini—usually labeled "*Boletus*" or "*Boletus edulis*"—are intense in flavor, are available year-round, and keep well for months. They are an excellent way to add concentrated mushroom flavor to simmered dishes, risottos, and sauces. When buying dry porcini, look for large whole slices of mushrooms that are pale in color with a brownish delineation where the pores meet the cap. All porcini, especially the dried ones, are susceptible to larvae, so check that there are none in the packet. Smell the packet—the aroma is the best indication of what you are buying. Porcini should have an intense chocolaty mushroom smell, pleasant and complex.

A little will go a long way with dried porcini mushrooms—what you don't use, keep tightly sealed in a dark, cool place; you can also freeze them.

In most cases, dried porcini are soaked to reconstitute them and maximize the flavor. Place the required amount of dried porcini slices in a heatproof bowl and pour over them enough hot liquid, such as stock or water, to cover them completely. Let them steep for twenty to thirty minutes, until they are fully softened. Drain the porcini and reserve the soaking liquid—it is very flavorful. (All of the recipes in this book that call for dried porcini use the soaking liquid in the dish.) Feel the porcini; if they are gritty, rinse them briefly but thoroughly under cold water and pinch or cut off any tough bits. Chop the porcini according to the recipe. When you use the steeping liquid, be sure to pour off the liquid slowly, leaving the last few tablespoons, which contain the sediment, behind or, better yet, strain the liquid through a coffee filter or a sieve lined with a double thick-ness of cheesecloth.

Porcini paste is also very useful in flavoring your Italian recipes. You can buy porcini paste in jars or, more economically, make it yourself from dried porcini.

Porcini Paste

MAKES ABOUT 1 SCANT CUP

1 ounce (about 1 cup) dried porcini mushrooms
1 cup water
¼ cup extra virgin olive oil, plus more for storing the paste

In a small saucepan, bring the porcini and water to a boil. Cover the saucepan and boil for 5 minutes. Cool completely and drain the porcini, pressing the mushrooms firmly to extract as much of the liquid as possible. Strain the cooking liquid through a coffee filter or a sieve lined with a double thickness of cheesecloth and reserve it. If the porcini feel gritty, rinse them briefly under cold water. Pinch or cut off any tough parts of the porcini and discard. Place the mushrooms in a blender and blend at low speed. With the motor running, gradually pour in the cooking liquid. Add ¼ cup of the oil slowly and continue blending until the mixture forms a smooth paste, stopping once or twice to scrape down the sides of the blender jar.

Transfer the paste to a small glass jar and smooth the top into an even layer. Pour enough olive oil over the paste to completely cover. The porcini paste will keep for up to 4 weeks in the refrigerator or up to 3 months in the freezer.

Tomato Paste
(Concentrato di Pomodoro)

Tomato paste is made by dehydrating ripe cored and seeded tomatoes, either by simmering them for a long time or—as it is done in Southern Italy—by spreading a very smooth puree of cooked tomatoes out on a wooden board to dry in the sun. The mixture is turned and spread out again several times a day for several days until it dries into a paste.

In both cases, the result is a very dense puree with an intense flavor of tomato with low acidity and a high sugar content. American tomato paste usually comes in small six-ounce cans, while the Italian imports come in toothpaste-like tubes. I prefer the Italian for its flavor and storage ease. Keep either in the refrigerator after opening. Since tomato paste is not used in large quantities, but rather by the teaspoonful or tablespoonful, it is most likely you will have some of the canned tomato paste left after opening the can. Transfer the remainder to a small glass or plastic container, top it with a light film of olive oil, and refrigerate it. Stored like this, it will keep for two months; left uncovered, it will dry out or get moldy.

Tomato paste is used in cooking to bring that extra kick of tomato flavor to the finished dish. I use it in soups, and it is especially good when making sauces with game meats such as venison, pheasant, quail, or boar. I even use it when roasting. Try adding a tablespoon or two to the pan gravy—it will add color and flavor. Remember that tomato paste is best when cooked for longer periods of time in the preparation—thirty minutes or more. It is not an ingredient that you can add at the last minute.

Hot Peppers
(Peperoncino, Peperoncini Ciliegia, e Peperoncini Sigaretta)

There are a few types of *peperoncini* (hot peppers) used in Italian cooking, especially in the southern regions of Abruzzo, Calabria, Basilicata, Campania, and Puglia, where they are most popular.

The hot pepper most commonly used in Italian cuisine is the *diavolillio*. It is similar to the cayenne pepper that came from Central and South America, and in its dried form is known simply as *peperoncino*. It is available either whole or in its crushed form. The crushed form, which is the most typically used, contains both the flesh of the dried pepper and its seeds, which are the major source of piquancy. A pinch of *peperoncino* goes a long way when added to sautéing vegetables or a pot of soup. Whole dried *peperoncini* are sometimes simmered in vegetable dishes, pasta sauces, or soups and are removed afterward.

Peperoncino is also found milled into a fine powder, which, in this country, is called cayenne. *Peperoncino*, either whole, crushed, or milled into cayenne, should be bright red—a brownish color indicates that the *peperoncino* has been sitting around quite a while.

The other two types of hot peppers—*peperoncino ciliegia* (cherry pepper) and *peperoncino sigaretta* (bird peppers)—used in Italian cooking are either fresh or bottled in oil and vinegar. The smaller bird peppers are usually used whole, while the larger cherry peppers are usually cored and cut into smaller pieces. Use the fresh peppers in recipes for braised meat, fish, or vegetables. Those preserved in a brine-vinegar solution are especially good for meat preparations, particularly pork or chicken.

In any of its forms, *peperoncino* is very stimulating to the digestive process and can be a tonic and a purge for the system.

Salt
(Sale)

Salt is one of the most common ingredients in a kitchen, readily available, not expensive, and used in almost every cooking preparation. Salt in the kitchen is important both as a flavoring agent and as a preservative.

It was not always so—salt was once a highly prized commodity. Salt was an important source of tax revenue for kings, since it was considered a product of the earth. It contributed to the popular discontent that led to the French Revolution, and the objection by the Tuscans to paying *la tassa di sale* (salt tax). Their resentment is still evident today in their saltless bread.

In my cooking, I prefer to use sea salt that is made by natural evaporation from sea water or mined from large deposits—usually a remnant of a salt lake. Sea salt comes in different grades of coarseness. Grains of fine crystal sea salt, white in color, are the size of fine bread crumbs. I use it for dishes that require very little cooking time or in cold dishes. It is also the salt used to dress salads, to season meats and poultry when grilling or sautéing, or when you need to add that last pinch of salt to a dish. For preparations that require a long cooking time, such as braising, boiling pasta, soups, or sauces, I prefer the coarse crystal sea salt or rock sea salt, which is grayish in color—it has a much more pronounced flavor of the sea. I also use coarse or rock sea salt to cure meats or marinate meats or vegetables.

"Table salt" is a fine-grain salt with additives that keep it free-flowing, and "iodized salt" is table salt with added iodine. Both are commonly used and perfectly fine for any preparation. But when I can't find sea salt, I prefer to use kosher salt, which is coarse in texture and contains no added ingredients other than salt.

Salt needs to penetrate evenly into every product that you cook. Be especially attentive when you cook meat or fish—salt it lightly in its raw stage so that the salt will permeate it while cooking. Then taste and make adjustments along the way, as I describe in most of my recipes.

Salt fried foods with fine salt immediately after they have been fried so that the heat will melt the salt and let it permeate the food. When boiling vegetables, add a little salt to the water, and also season them with salt as soon as you drain them. Pasta water should always be salted before adding pasta. When cooking dry legumes, do not add salt initially; it will prevent them from becoming completely tender. Add salt only during the last ten minutes of cooking.

Wine

(Il Vino)

At the Italian table wine is food—it is as necessary as bread to complete an Italian meal. Ever since I can remember as a child in Busoler, wine was on the table when we ate—even as children we drank *bevanda,* water tinted with wine.

Now wine has become much more for me. It is the element that fulfills and completes my meals and the meals that I serve at our restaurants. In our restaurants, the extensive collection of wines represents all of the regions of Italy and its artisans—the Italian wine producers. At Felidia, we are the repeat winners of the *Wine Spectator*'s Grand Award Winning Wine List, meaning that we have one of the best wine lists in the world. We accept that honor with pride because wine is that important to us. Our son, Joseph, and Dan Perlman, the sommelier at Felidia, carry on this tradition in unison.

Italy is the largest producer of wine in direct proportion to its size. It is also the largest producer in the diversity of wines it produces. The whole Italian peninsula, rich with hills and mountains, enjoys the Mediterranean climate. Its diversity lies in the different intensity of the sun, from the cooler north, which yields a wine rich in perfumes that is elegant, fresh, and vivacious, to the intense sun of the south, which yields pronounced, intense wines and some of the best sweet dessert wines on the peninsula. In between, there lies a myriad of wonderfully delicious and different wines.

When traveling through the regions of Italy to discover its art and savor its food, you should also seek out the diversity of its wines. Italy's popular culture is a mosaic of different dialects, regional cuisines, and products. Wine, like the dialects, is part of that popular culture, and reflects the soul and the way of life of the people who produce the wine.

The pairing of food and wine can be a pleasurable experience of choice and experimentation at a happy table, and it can be programmed, preplanned, and researched, an experience that can take on the intensity of true artistry.

The principles and reasons behind the pairing of food and wine are certainly many and, depending on which direction taken, the pairing will be different.

A traditional pairing is to pair the local food to the local wine. This has been done for centuries and it works. There is nothing better than a glass of Tocai Friulano with prosciutto di San Daniele, or a risotto with truffles paired with a good Barolo from Piemonte, or a roasted pork served with Cannonau from Sardegna, or *cantucci* dunked in Vin Santo.

There can be poetic reasons and romantic reasons for pairing food and wine; the reason could exalt a special food and find a supporting wine or to feature a great wine and use food as the pedestal. But in most cases, harmony between food and wine is what we look for. An equilibrium between the two should exist so that one doesn't smother the other, but enjoyed together they are both better.

Many books have been written on the subject and listings and tables have been created, but when I pair food with wine I look for the most intense qualities of one or the other and then try to bring them into balance. For example, if there is a fatty component in the food, then an acidic wine will balance it. If there is an intense complexity of herbs and spices with meats, then a complex red will counterbalance that complexity. If there is a pristine fresh fish preparation, then a crisp, fruity aromatic white will do. With a robust tomato pasta sauce, a robust fruity Chianti will be just fine.

Do not amplify or accentuate the same dominating qualities in food by choosing a wine with the same qualities. You can work backward if you have good wines in your cellar, then choose the food to complement them. Of course, the better the food, the better the wine and the better the experience.

To do a just pairing, you need to have tasted the wine before so that you can best match it. Can wine be enjoyed without premeditation of food? Yes—I love a good Brunello with a hamburger.

The Italian depth of wine needs a forum of its own, but here I will share with you some of the wines that I enjoy and serve with my food—may they bring you closer to the flavors of *Lidia's Italian Table*.

Typically in Italy with hors d'oeuvres and antipasti, sparkling or white wines are served as an aperitif. Prosecco di Conegliano-Valdobbiadene is one of those sparkling aperitifs. In Italy today, it is in vogue to begin the meal with a glass of Prosecco or spumante; in fact, most restaurants will serve it immediately as the customer is seated. Some good producers are Zardetto and Vincenzo Toffoli.

Prosecco is a lightly sparkling wine which is predominantly made from prosecco grapes but Chardonnay or Pinot Bianco can be added. Golden yellow in color, it has an aroma of apples, honey, and acacia flowers. It is dry but quite inviting, with a pronounced but balanced acidity. I would serve it with most of the *antipasti* in this book, especially with the Tuscan beans and caviar bruschetta.

Today, Italy is producing some excellent sparkling wines, specially from the Franciacorta area in Lombardy. Vinified in the traditional *metodo champenoise,* they usually are vivacious and bubbly with a pleasant, balanced acidity and the mellow flavors of yeast. Sparkling wine is excellent with crustaceans, and it also makes an excellent companion to prosciutto. Some of my favorite producers are Bruno Giacosa, Bellavista, Ferrari, Castello Banfi, and Ca' del Bosco.

White wines such as Tocai or Ribolla Gialla—two grapes indigenous to Friuli—are vinified into wonderful wines that are excellent served with the first course or fish dishes. Tocai, the wine of the Friuliani, is poured *sfuso,* or from the barrel in local osterias and trattorias of the region. It is a dry wine, fruity, aromatic, and has almond overtones with a balanced acidity. Prosciutto di San Daniele or a Montasio cheese frico served with Tocai is as Friulian as it gets. Tocai is also wonderful with fish salads and grilled fish preparations such as the Grilled Calamari Strips, Stuffed Squid with Borlotti Beans, and Whole Roasted Striped Bass. Ribolla Gialla is one of my favorites; it is very aromatic, dry with a subdued acidity, but very vivacious and fresh. It is excellent with vegetables or fish soups such as the Broccoli and Shrimp Soup and Crabmeat and Skate Soup. Some good producers are Borgo Conventi, Pra di Pradis, Marco Felluga, Gravner, Radikon, and Girolamo Dorigo.

Pinot Grigio is not an indigenous grape of Italy but the popularity of Pinot Grigio is international. Several regions in Italy produce Pinot Grigio, but some of the best is vinified in Friuli. The Pinot Grigio from Friuli is aromatic and has a high acidic finish; it's bright and refreshing. It pairs exceptionally well with complex and fatty foods and is excellent with Scallops Baked in Their Shells, Simply Braised Octopus, Pan-Roasted Monkfish with Thyme, Potatoes, Leeks, and Truffle Oil, and Lobster in Zesty Tomato Sauce. It is also excellent with Roasted Chicken with Pomegranate and Griddle-Crisped Spring Chicken. Some of my favorite producers are Schiopetto, Borgo Conventi, Livio Felluga, and Villa Frattina.

Sauvignon and Chardonnay are wines which are produced more and more by Italian producers today, trying to satisfy the global demand for them. There are some excellent Chardonnays produced by major producers in Italy which in style are ideal for Italian food. Some good Chardonnay producers are Dorigo and Jermann from Friuli, Regaleali from Sicily, Colli Amerini from Umbria, and Castello Banfi from Tuscany. A good Italian Chardonnay is excellent with Shrimp Risotto, Vermicelli with Green Beans and Shellfish, Spinach and Leek Gnocchi Roll, Grouper in White Sauce, Swordfish in Sweet-and-Sour Sauce, and Chicken Bites with Sausages in a Vinegar Sauce. Sauvignon is excellent with Pan-Roasted Monkfish, Grouper in White Sauce, Sea Conch Salad, and Mussels in Saffron Broth. Some of the good Sauvignon producers are M. Schiopetto, Radikon, Gravner, Antinori, and Miani.

The "Pigato" by Abbona, a white from Liguria, is excellent with pesto, Spaghetti with Shrimp and Basil Sauce, Sea Conch Salad, and Razor Clams in Broth. Fiano di Avellino, a white from Campagna by Mastroberardino, is a crispy, dry white wine that is complex and has almond overtones. It is a wine that is wonderful served with vinaigrettes or with dishes that contain vinegar like *Puntarelle* and Anchovy Salad, red cabbage and shrimps, and braised peppers with anchovies. Fiano di Avellino is also a good accompaniment for pasta and risotti, especially with Fusilli with Fresh Spinach and Ricotta and Linguini with Mussels and Zucchini with its Flowers.

Some of the wines I enjoy most are *uvaggi*—blends of white or red. An *uvaggio* is a blend of different varietals vinified by the producer into one wine which reflects the producer's style and capabilities. I remember my maternal grandfather, Giovanni, every season vinifying one blend of white varietals and one blend of red varietals; that was his production, and it was good wine. He made only two wines. Some of my Friulian favorite white wine *uvaggi* are Terre Alte by Livio Felluga, Roncuz by Russiz Superiore, Vintage Tunina by Jermann, Cervaro della Sala by Antinori, and Luna dei Feldi by Santa Margherita.

Terre Alte is a blend of Sauvignon and Chardonnay. I enjoy it very much with Swordfish in Sweet-and-Sour Sauce, Scallops Baked in Their Shells, Lobster in Zesty Tomato Sauce, Seared Rabbit Loin over Arugula with Truffle Dressing, Seared Marinated Breast of Chicken with Tomato and Basil, and Roasted Kid Goat. Roncuz by Russiz Superiore is a blend of Chardonnay, Sauvignon Blanc, Riesling, and Ribolla Gialla. I would serve it with Swiss Chard and Vegetable Crostata, Bollito Misto, Fillet of Halibut with a Savory Tomato Sauce, and Capellini with Sea Urchins. Vintage Tunina, a blend of Chardonnay and Sauvignon and very aromatic in flavors of pears and honey, is excellent with Veal Chops with Spinach and Pecorino Romano, Veal in Guazzetto, Roasted Veal Shanks, Chicken Bites with Sausages in a Vinegar Sauce, and Braised Rabbit in Balsamic Sauce. The Cervaro della Sala, a blend of Chardonnay and Grechetto, I serve with Malfatti with Shellfish and Istrian Wedding Pillows. Luna dei Feldi, a blend of Chardonnay, Muller Thurgau, and Traminer, is very good with Pan-Roasted Monkfish with Thyme, Potatoes, Leeks, and Truffle Oil and Lobster in Zesty Tomato Sauce.

With chicken dishes such as Griddle-Crisped Spring Chicken, Country-Style Spring Chicken with Olives and Potatoes, or Roasted Chicken with Pomegranate, I would serve a good Chianti, which traditionally is made predominantly of the Sangiovese grape with some Canaiolo, Trebbiano, or Malvasia, although today the blend varies considerably. Chianti, when good, is velvety with lots of fruit, yet light and dry with a balanced acidity. Some of the good producers are Fontodi, Querciabella, Isola e Olena, Monsanto, Castello di Ama, Ruffino, Antinori, Castello Banfi, and Badia a Coltibuono. Chianti is one of the most versatile Italian reds and accompanies a wide range of foods from soups to pasta to risotto to fowl, veal, and game. A Chianti will be especially good served with Mushroom and Potato Soup, Risotto with Squash, Risotto with Squab, Creamy Risotto Milanese Style, Pappardelle with Quail in Guazzetto, Squash-Filled Ravioli with Marjoram Sauce, Garganelli with Rabbit in Guazzetto, Merlot-Braised Chicken Thighs, Veal Ossobuco with Barley Risotto, Veal Scallopine with Tomato and Basil, Veal in Guazzetto, Spicy Seared Veal Kidneys, Calf's Liver Venetian Style, and Minute Steak as Served in Trieste.

Another Tuscan red is Brunello di Montalcino, which is made from 100 percent Sangiovese Grosso varietals. It is a full-bodied wine that is aged in oak for several years and has lots of elegant fruits with a balanced acidity. It almost has an air of nobility about it. I would serve it five years or older with Braised Rabbit in Balsamic Sauce, Roasted Loin of Pork Stuffed with Prunes, Veal Ossobuco with Barley Risotto, and Roasted Kid Goat. Some of the good Brunello producers are Lisini, Fattoria dei Barbi, Castello Banfi, Soldera, Val di Suga, and Col d'Orcia.

There are also Supertuscans, a sample being the blend of the Sangiovese grape and Cabernet Sauvignon or Cabernet Franc. Although these wines can vary according to producers and blends, a Supertuscan is a big wine with lots of fruit and evident but balanced tannins. It is a wine that harmonizes well with dishes like Pheasant in Guazzetto with Gnocchi, Risotto with Squab, Roasted Veal Shanks, Veal in Guazzetto, Gnocchi with Venison Stew, Wild Boar Braised in Barolo, Roasted Guinea Hen with Balsamic Glaze, Roasted Veal Shanks, Veal Ossobuco with Barley Risotto, and Braised Venison with Polenta. Some of my favorite Supertuscans are Summus by Castello Banfi, Tignanello by Antinori, Cabreo by Ruffino, Cepparello by Isole e Olena, Luce by Frescobaldi, and Mondavi and Flaccianello della Pieve by Fontodi.

With game dishes and intense dishes, there are Barolo and Barbaresco from Piedmont that are made from the Nebbiolo grape but in different localities.

Barolo, which is a big red with elegant aromas of roses and violets, has a pronounced undertone of the grape and tannins that are very much in balance. Barolo is wonderful with Braised Lamb Shanks in Guazzetto, Braised Beef in Barolo Wine, Risotto with Squab, Polenta as Served in Piedmont, Polenta, Gorgonzola, and Savoy Cabbage Torte, Garganelli with Pheasant in Guazzetto, and Roasted Loin of Pork Stuffed with Prunes. Some of my favorite producers are Ceretto, Vietti, Clerico, Gaja, Bruno Giacosa, Prunotto, Valentino, Fratelli Dogliani, and Paolo Scavino.

Barbaresco is its more elegant cousin, fruity and bold but with an elegance and silkiness to it. I would serve it with Gnocchi with Butternut Squash Sauce, Pappardelle with Quail in Guazzetto, Risotto with Shavings of White Truffle, Risotto with Squab, Polenta Nest with Truffled Egg, Seared Lamb Chops with Rosemary and Mint Sauce, and Roasted Kid Goat. Some of my favorite producers are Cigliutti, Gaja, Bruno Giacosa, Produttori del Barbaresco, Vietti, and Pasquero Elia.

There are some red uvaggi (blends) hailing from other regions of Italy that are my favorites. Il Roncat by Giovanni Dry, a blend of Schiopettino and Refosco from Friuli, is excellent with Istrian Wedding Pillows, Gnocchi with Sage Sauce and Dry Ricotta, and Ricotta Gnocchi with Radicchio Trevisano. Granato by Azienda Agricola Foradori from Trentino Alto Adige is made from sixty-year-old vines. It is very good served with Roasted Veal Shanks, Veal Chops with Spinach and Pecorino Romano, Calf's Liver Venetian Style, and Braised Lamb Shanks in Guazzetto. Il Baciale' by Giacomo Bologna from Piedmont is a superb blend of Barbera and Pinot Nero and is excellent with Risotto with Shavings of White Truffle, Risotto with Squab, and Garganelli with Pheasant in Guazzetto. Colle Picchioni by Paola di Mauro from Lazio is a blend of Merlot and Cabernet Sauvignon and is excellent with all lamb dishes and spicy pork chops.

The Cannonan by Sella e Mosca from Sardegna goes well with Malloreddus with Sausage and Tomato Sauce, Roasted Kid Goat, and Seared Lamb Chops with Rosemary and Mint Sauce. I also enjoy tremendously the Montepulciano d'Abruzzo by Emidio Pepe from Abruzzo, a true traditionalist in wine production. His wine is excellent served with Spinach and Leek Gnocchi Roll, Gnocchi with Butternut Squash Sauce, Veal Ossobuco with Barley Risotto, and Roasted Veal Shanks.

The production and enjoyment of Italian dessert wines spans the whole peninsula. In Piedmont, the Moscato—a very aromatic and slightly bubbly white—is wonderful with Ricotta-Filled Strudel. The Picolit from Friuli, of very limited availability but extraordinary in floral intensity and flavor with a balanced acidity, is excellent with Baked Crepes with Ricotta, Angels' Kisses, and Apple Strudel. The Torcolato by Maculan from the Veneto, with complex flavors of apricots and acacia, is superb served with the Blueberry Apricot Frangipane Tart. The Vin Santo from Tuscany is excellent paired with Easter Bread. Malvasia delle Lipari, an exceptional product from the Aeolian islands, has an intense aroma and flavor of dried apricots and figs—it is splendid with the Blueberry Apricot Frangipane Tart. Most of these wines can be enjoyed in leisurely after-dinner conversation with some biscotti or, as they are called in Italy, *vini da meditazione*—wines to sip slowly and meditate on the sweetness of life.

Grappa

Grappa is a favorite Italian drink. It is distilled from grape pomace—the skins, seeds, and stems that are left after the juice is drawn off for winemaking. Grappa has been drunk in Italy since the Dark Ages, when feudal lords gave the pomace left after wine making to the serfs who worked their land. From these humble beginnings, grappa has become quite a sophisticated drink—you can find grappas made from individual grape varietals, grappas from specific regions of Italy, and most grappas today are packaged in collectors'-quality glass bottles.

I witnessed grappa making during my childhood in Busoler. Good grappa is made immediately after the grapes have been crushed, when the pomace is still fresh and juicy. The result is a drink of intense flavor, with a pungent bite.

Conventionally, grappa is served as an after-dinner drink, either alone or with espresso. If you pour the grappa directly into the espresso, you are making a *caffè corretto,* or "corrected coffee." Grappa also makes a wonderful aperitif, served either at room temperature or directly out of the freezer. Whichever way you serve it, you can increase your enjoyment by infusing the liquid with fruits and herbs. These flavors temper the harshness and bite of the grappa.

The first step in savoring grappa is to choose a grappa you like. Good grappa is not cheap; prices begin at twenty dollars and can go up to forty dollars plus for a 750-ml bottle. If you have a favorite wine, select a grappa made from the same grape varietal—the varietal should be listed on the label. Many of the grapes used to make grappa are Italian in origin, such as verduzzo, picolit, and moscato; other grapes include merlot and chardonnay.

Next, select an appropriate glass. I prefer a tulip-shaped glass so the alcohol can softly carry a concentrated essence to the nose and palate. When drinking grappa, first enjoy its vibrant scent, redolent of its grape varietal. Then take a sip and let it coat your mouth. Swallow. Then partially open your mouth, take a slow breath, and you will feel the flavors come alive. The alcohol's pristine quality and the intense momentary palate stimulation create grappa-drinking pleasure.

Infusing grappa is a simple process. The ingredients are few—grappa, the flavoring elements, and, perhaps, a little sugar. Quart-size glass canning jars with hinged or screw-top lids lined with a rubber seal are good containers. Cheesecloth and a bowl are the only other necessary equipment. The most important element is time.

Measurements are relatively unimportant when you make an infused grappa. You can make flavored grappa in larger quantities than outlined below, with as many or as few flavoring agents as you like. When using fresh fruit, I like to fill the jar with fruit and pour in enough grappa to cover, which produces a very flavorful drink.

The use of sugar is a matter of taste. I strongly recommend using sugar with very tart fruits like cherries and raspberries. I like all my infusions—even the herbal ones—with a touch of sweetness, so I almost always use one or two tablespoons of sugar, depending on the fruit's sweetness, for every cup of grappa. However, grape-infused grappas require less sugar or none at all, and dried fig grappas never need additional sweetening.

Steep the grappa with the flavorings for anywhere between eight days and four months. Depending on the recipe, this should happen in either a well-lit place or a dark place that is warm or at cool room temperature. (By Mediterranean standards, "room temperature" is between 55° and 60°F.) Sunny windowsills are the best warm, well-lit places; inside a kitchen cabinet near the stove is good when the grappa needs to be warm and dark. If the recipe requires the grappa to be "room temperature," just make sure it's not in direct sunlight and that the room isn't warmer than 60°F. A basement should do fine.

A progress check is needed every few days as the grappa steeps. Because alcohol is volatile, it may begin to evaporate if your seal is not tight, and the grappa level may decrease. Top off with fresh grappa as necessary.

After steeping, filter the liquid and age the grappa according to the directions for each recipe. To filter, drape a piece of cheesecloth over a bowl and pour in the grappa. Gather the cloth's ends and lift it from the bowl to remove the solids from the grappa. (If you use fruit infusions, and the fruit appears to be in good shape, you can eat it as a heady dessert.) After filtration, you can transfer the grappa to a decorative bottle for display as it continues to age.

You can age infused grappa indefinitely. The following recipes' time periods are the minimum needed to create a properly flavored drink. As the grappa continues to age, it will mellow, lose some of its edge, and acquire a "rounder" flavor.

Grappa di Lamponi (Raspberry Grappa) Fill a 1-quart jar with washed raspberries, 1 cinnamon stick, 4 cloves, and ¼ cup sugar. Pour in grappa to cover. Seal and store in a warm, dark place for 3 weeks. Filter as described above and age at room temperature for 1 month or more before serving. If you like, serve the grappa with a few fresh raspberries in each glass.

Grappa di Ficchi Secchi (Dried Fig Grappa) Fill a 2-quart jar two-thirds full with dried figs and pour in grappa to cover. Seal and steep for 2 months in a warm, dark place. The figs are delicious to eat; filtering is unnecessary. No further aging is necessary before serving fig grappa.

Grappa di Camomilla (Chamomile Grappa) Combine 2 cups loosely packed dried chamomile flowers (available at health food stores and tea shops), 3 cups grappa, and 3 to 6 tablespoons (to your taste) sugar in a 1-quart jar. Let it steep in a sunny spot for 3 weeks, shaking the bottle about twice a week to redistribute the ingredients. Filter as described above and age at room temperature for 2 months or more before serving.

Grappa di Miele (Honey Grappa) Gently warm 4 cups of grappa in a heatproof glass container placed in barely simmering water. Watch the heat carefully; you don't want the grappa to evaporate. Add ¼ to ½ cup good-quality honey, depending on the preferred sweetness, and stir until completely melted. Cap the jar and let rest for 4 months in a cool, dark place, shaking the bottle twice a week. Filter as described on page 16. No additional aging is needed before serving honey grappa.

Grappa di Menta Peperita (Peppermint Grappa) Combine 30 fresh peppermint leaves, ¼ cup to ½ cup (to your taste) sugar, and 4 cups grappa in a 1-quart jar. Cover and let rest in a sunny spot for 5 days. Move the grappa to a cool, dark place and let it steep for another 3 days. Filter as described on page 16 and age for 1 month or longer.

Grappa di Rosmarino (Rosemary Grappa) Combine ½ cup fresh rosemary leaves, ¼ cup sugar, and 4 cups grappa in a jar. Cover and steep for 4 weeks in direct sunlight. Filter as described on page 16 and age at room temperature for 2 months or longer.

Grappa di Ciliegie o Uva (Cherries or Grapes in Grappa) This recipe is a little different. Instead of filtering, the fruit and grappa are served together, preferably in a brandy snifter. It makes a particularly wonderful after-dinner digestif.

Clip the stems of firm, plump cherries or grapes to ⅛ inch. Fill a jar with the fruit, measure in grappa to cover, and add 1 or 2 tablespoons (to your taste) sugar for every cup of grappa. Leave the jar loosely covered and let the grappa steep in direct sunlight for 1 week. Cover the jar tightly and move it to a shady spot. Steep for 3 months, away from strong light.

Appetizers

Antipasti

*A*ntipasto means "before a meal." The dishes that make up this introduction to a meal are a very important part of the Italian meal sequence. An antipasto course can be any assortment of cold or hot dishes served at the beginning of the meal. That sounds simple, but the beauty of a good antipasto lies in the diversity of the dishes and their ability to stimulate the palate in preparation for the meal to come.

The quantity of *antipasti* served at the table has changed throughout the ages. Traditionally, they may have contained more dishes than we are likely to see today in a whole meal. In today's contemporary Italian cooking, small tasty portions are the norm. An antipasto course can feature salads, vegetable dishes, marinated fish—preserved in salt or served as carpaccio—raw, salted, or smoked meats, prosciutto, *insaccati* (cured meats in casings), cheeses, *bruschette, focaccie*, and pastry-based filled offerings, such as *crostate*. In Italy, the antipasto always takes on seasonal tones by reflecting the products that are at their peak at that time of year.

I especially love preparing an antipasto buffet for a festive meal—the guests are usually numerous and the pace of the meal is lengthy, so a large array of different preparations is appropriate. Sometimes for a dinner of twelve I prepare up to twenty or more different *antipasti*. If you decide to do this, give your guests at least an hour to enjoy the antipasto, then segue into the rest of the meal with a light, clear soup as a first course. This sequence is very traditional in Italy.

The different foods that make up an appealing buffet are very important, but very personal. I like a mixture of vegetable dishes, salads, cheese, *affetati* (cold cuts and dry sausages), and other meats and fish. I like at least half of the *antipasto* buffet to be made up of vegetable dishes and salads; the rest can be equally divided among seafood, cured meats, and fish. The high vegetable and salad ratio is very Italian, and it keeps the dinner light. With regard to the temperature of the dishes, I like most of my *antipasti* to be cold or at room temperature, with a few hot dishes to round out the variety. If you are entertaining, these cold dishes can be prepared and arranged on platters beforehand, leaving a lot less work to do when you serve them. Whatever dishes you choose, look for a variety of color, flavor, texture, and temperature—that is the only real rule in serving an *antipasto* buffet.

Grilled Country Bread

▣ Bruschette ▣

Bruschette means "little burnt ones"—a reference to these grilled slices of country bread that are sometimes charred around the edges. What goes on top of these slices of oil-and-garlic-rubbed toasts is limited only by your imagination. Any vegetable, any fish, any legume or meat can become a topping for *bruschette*. The toppings that follow this recipe for the toasts are four of my favorites.

You can successfully prepare *bruschette* on a charcoal grill, in a stovetop grill pan, or even in a very hot oven. The edges of each slice of bread should be very crisp—even a little burned in places—and the centers should be toasted but not dried out. Choose a loaf of dense-textured, flavorful bread that is about five inches across for *bruschette*. If your loaf is much larger than that, cut the slices in half before grilling them.

MAKES 6 TOASTS

Prepare a charcoal fire or heat a grill pan over medium heat for 5 minutes. Grill as many of the bread slices as will fit in a single layer, turning them only once, until they are golden brown and crispy, even slightly charred around the edges, 3 to 5 minutes total, depending on the intensity of the heat. Remove the *bruschette* from the grill and brush them lightly with olive oil. Rub the garlic clove lightly over one side of the bread to flavor it.

> Six ½-inch-thick slices firm, country-style Italian bread
> Extra virgin olive oil
> 1 large garlic clove, peeled

Alternatively, the *bruschette* can be prepared in the oven. Preheat the oven to 450°F. Arrange the bread slices in a single layer and bake until golden brown and crispy around the edges, 6 to 8 minutes. Brush with olive oil and rub with the garlic clove as described above.

Serve the *bruschette* as soon as possible after toasting, with the topping of your choice.

Bruschetta with Dinosaur Kale

Bruschetta con Cavolo Nero

Dinosaur kale, also called black kale, has darker, crinklier, almost scaly leaves than regular kale. If you can't find it, use regular kale instead. I find my dinosaur kale at New York City's Union Square Greenmarket. Slice the reserved stems crosswise and cook them in garlic-seasoned oil as a side dish, or stir them into a vegetable soup.

MAKES 6 SERVINGS

½ pound dinosaur (black) or green kale

3 tablespoons extra virgin olive oil

2 garlic cloves, crushed

¼ cup thinly sliced onions

Salt

Pinch of peperoncino (crushed red pepper)

Bruschette (page 21)

Separate the kale into leaves and remove the thick stem from the center of each leaf. Shred the leaves ¼ inch wide. Wash the leaves thoroughly and drain them well, preferably in a salad spinner. Reserve the stems for another use.

In a medium-size skillet, heat the olive oil over medium heat. Add the garlic cloves and cook until golden brown, stirring, about 2 minutes. Add the onions and cook until wilted, about 2 minutes. Add the kale, season lightly with salt, and add the peperoncino. Reduce the heat to low and cook the kale, stirring often, until very tender, about 30 minutes. If the kale begins to stick to the skillet, add a tablespoon of water and continue cooking.

Meanwhile, prepare the *bruschette*. Adjust the seasoning, divide the kale evenly among the *bruschette*, and serve immediately.

Bruschetta with Tomato and Tuna

Bruschetta di Pomodoro e Tonno

I prefer tuna packed in olive oil—which is usually darker and more flavorful—for this dish. If you cannot find it, or if you prefer the milder flavor, use chunk light tuna, packed in oil or water, as you prefer.

MAKES 6 SERVINGS

Crumble the tuna into a large mixing bowl and add the tomatoes, onion, olive oil, peppers, and about three quarters of the basil leaves. Season with salt and toss well. Let stand while you prepare the *bruschette*.

Spread the tuna mixture over the *bruschette* and sprinkle with the remaining shredded basil. Serve immediately.

One 6-ounce can tuna packed in olive oil, drained
2 medium-size ripe tomatoes, cored, seeded, and cut into ⅓-inch cubes
½ medium-size red onion, thinly sliced
2 tablespoons extra virgin olive oil
6 Tuscan hot peppers in vinegar, drained, seeded, and chopped, or ¼ cup chopped pimientos in vinegar
8 fresh basil leaves, washed, dried, and shredded
Salt
Bruschette (page 21)

Prosciutto and Fig Bruschetta

Bruschetta di Prosciutto e Ficchi

Prosciutto is a salted and air-cured ham with a wonderfully rich flavor that is meant to be enjoyed without much embellishment. Therefore, buying the best-quality prosciutto is of the utmost importance.

The authentic Italian prosciutto that is available in the United States comes from two regions of Italy—prosciutto di Parma, from the Emilia-Romagna region, has a crown embossed on its rind, and prosciutto di San Daniele, from Friuli, has a ham embossed on its rind. Look for these symbols to ensure authenticity. Prosciutto should have a bright rose-pink color with a complex sweet and savory aroma. Get your prosciutto from a source that sells a lot of it, and buy it sliced thin and as close to the time of consumption as possible. Store the prosciutto tightly wrapped in the refrigerator, but let it stand at room temperature for 10 minutes before serving.

MAKES 6 SERVINGS

10 to 12 ripe fresh green or black figs
Bruschette (page 21)
6 to 8 long, thin slices prosciutto di San Daniele or prosciutto di Parma, or as needed
Freshly ground black pepper

Wipe the figs clean with a damp cloth or paper towel. Slice them crosswise into ⅛-inch-thick rounds.

Prepare the *bruschette*.

Cover the *bruschette* with overlapping fig slices. Drape the prosciutto to cover the figs. Grind some black pepper over the prosciutto and serve immediately.

Bruschetta with Tuscan Beans and Caviar

Bruschetta di Fagioli Toscani e Caviale

Ricchi e poveri (rich and poor) meet in this dish to create a very tasty, elegant, and mellow flavor.

MAKES 6 SERVINGS

Place the beans in a medium-size bowl and pour in enough cool water to cover by 4 inches. Soak the beans in a cool place for at least 8 hours, or overnight.

Drain the beans and place them in a large saucepan. Pour in enough cold water to cover generously and add the bay leaves and garlic cloves. Bring the water to a boil over high heat. Adjust the level of heat to a simmer and cook the beans until tender, 30 minutes to 1 hour.

Drain the beans. Remove the bay leaves and garlic and toss the beans while still warm with the olive oil. Let them stand, tossing occasionally, until lukewarm. Gently fold in the caviar until it is evenly dispersed. Season with pepper and, if necessary, salt.

Meanwhile, prepare the *bruschette*.

Set the *bruschette* on a plate, divide the bean mixture evenly among the slices, and decorate with the mâche. If desired, place the mâche in a small bowl, drizzle lightly with olive oil, add lemon juice to taste, and toss gently before placing on the *bruschette*.

½ pound dried cannellini (Tuscan white beans) or other small white beans such as baby limas or Great Northern, picked over and rinsed

2 fresh or dried bay leaves

2 garlic cloves, crushed

3 tablespoons extra virgin olive oil, plus more for dressing the mâche, if desired

4 ounces good-quality caviar, such as beluga, osetra, or American sturgeon

Freshly ground black pepper

Salt, if necessary

Bruschette (page 21)

Mâche leaves or other small, tender salad greens, washed and well dried, preferably in a salad spinner (see Note on page 38)

Fresh lemon juice (optional)

Fava Bean Puree with Dandelion Greens

🔒 Puree di Fave con Cicoria 🔒

This is a traditional Pugliese dish—Puglia is the heel of the Italian "boot," where vegetables reign in the kitchen. Silvery olive trees cover the hillsides and endless plains of golden durum wheat stretch from the Adriatic to the Ionian seas. Olive oil, pasta, vegetables, and fish—what a wonderful list of ingredients Pugliese cooks enjoy. Some of the most pristine and intense Italian food I have ever eaten was in Puglia. This recipe is from Concetta Cantoro, who, with her husband, runs Trattoria Casareccia—an extension of their home in Lecce. This dish makes a wonderful appetizer as is or served with some prosciutto and pecorino cheese.

MAKES 6 SERVINGS

For the beans

2 quarts water
½ pound dried split fava beans (about
    2 cups), picked over and rinsed
1 teaspoon salt, plus more if needed

For the greens

3 quarts salted water
1 pound young dandelion greens, chicory,
    or escarole (see Note)

For the croutons

2 cups ¼-inch cubes day-old country bread
    with crusts removed
2 tablespoons extra virgin olive oil

To finish the dish

5 tablespoons extra virgin olive oil
4 garlic cloves, crushed
Pinch of peperoncino (crushed red pepper)
Salt

In a 4- to 5-quart pot, bring the 2 quarts water, beans, and 1 teaspoon salt to a boil. Adjust the heat to a simmer, cover the pot, and simmer until the beans are tender, about 40 minutes.

In a separate large pot, bring the 3 quarts of salted water to a boil. Stir in the greens and cook until tender, about 10 minutes for dandelion greens, 20 minutes for chicory or escarole. Drain well and set aside.

While the greens are cooking, prepare the croutons. Preheat the oven to 350°F. Place the bread in a bowl and drizzle with the olive oil. Toss well. Spread the bread cubes in an even layer on a baking sheet and toast, stirring occasionally, until golden brown, about 12 minutes.

Uncover the pot of fava beans and continue cooking, stirring often to prevent sticking and to break up the beans, until the beans are very tender, the water has almost completely evaporated, and the mixture is coarsely mashed, about another 20 minutes. Cover the pot and set aside.

In a large skillet, heat 2 tablespoons of the olive oil over medium heat. Add the garlic cloves and cook, stirring, until golden brown, about 2 minutes. Add the drained greens and the peperoncino and season with salt. Cook, uncovered, until the water clinging to the greens has evaporated, about 5 minutes.

Return the fava bean mixture to low heat. Stir in the remaining 3 tablespoons olive oil. Remove the bean mixture from the heat and season with salt if necessary. Fold in the croutons until evenly distributed. Serve the fava bean mixture and braised greens side by side.

Note: If using dandelion greens, cut off the roots and separate into individual leaves if necessary. Trim them of any tough stems and discard any discolored leaves. If using chicory or escarole, cut the head in half and cut out the center core to separate into individual leaves. Cut the escarole lengthwise into 2-inch-wide strips. Whatever type of greens you are using, wash them well, as they can be quite sandy.

Baked Onions with Butternut Squash Filling

Cipolle Ripiene di Magro

This antipasto is also very good served as a side dish with roasts, especially if you spoon some of the roasting juices over the onions. A plate of these onions looks beautiful on a buffet table too, and they can be prepared in advance and popped into the oven along with the roast.

MAKES 6 SERVINGS

2 tablespoons red wine vinegar

2 tablespoons salt, plus more for seasoning the filling

6 medium-size (about 3½ inches in diameter) onions, either yellow or red or a sweet variety, such as Vidalia or Maui Sweet

1 pound peeled, seeded, and diced (½-inch) butternut squash (about 3½ cups)

¼ cup finely diced mostarda di Cremona (see Note on page 302), with syrup

¼ cup fine plain dry bread crumbs

1 large egg

½ teaspoon freshly grated nutmeg

Freshly ground white pepper

5 tablespoons unsalted butter, melted

6 amaretti cookies, finely crumbled (about ¼ cup)

For the sauce

1 cup heavy cream

1 cup Chicken Stock (page 80) or canned low-sodium chicken broth

½ cup freshly grated Parmigiano-Reggiano cheese

½ cup chopped fresh chives

Fill a large (4- to 5-quart) pot halfway full with water. Add the vinegar and the 2 tablespoons salt and bring to a boil. Meanwhile, peel the onions, leaving them whole and the root ends completely intact.

Add the onions to the water, cover the pot, and cook until the onions are half-cooked—a paring knife inserted into the onions should meet only a little resistance—about 25 minutes. Don't cook the onions until they are completely tender, or they will fall apart during stuffing and further cooking. Drain the onions and let stand until cool enough to handle.

Meanwhile, in a large saucepan of boiling salted water, cook the squash until completely tender, about 10 minutes. Drain the squash thoroughly.

Pass the squash through a food mill fitted with the fine disc into a large mixing bowl. (Alternatively, force the squash through a coarse sieve using the back of a large spoon or a ladle.) You should have about 2 cups puree. Measure out one third of the squash and set aside. Add the *mostarda* and syrup, the bread crumbs, egg, and nutmeg to the remaining squash, mix together well, and season to taste with salt and pepper.

Preheat the oven to 400°F.

Cut off about ½ inch of the top—opposite the root end—of each onion. Carefully remove the center of each onion, leaving two or three outer layers intact for filling. (This will be easiest if you hold the onion securely in one hand and scoop underneath the sections you want to remove with a soup spoon. Rotate the inner sections to free them.) Spoon the seasoned squash mixture into the onions, dividing it evenly.

In a small bowl, stir 2 tablespoons of the melted butter and the crumbled cookies together until blended, and spoon the mixture over the onions. Brush an 11 × 8-inch baking dish with 1 tablespoon of the remaining butter and place the onions in the dish. Spoon the remaining 2 tablespoons butter over the top of the onions. Bake until the onions and filling are browned, about 40 minutes.

Meanwhile, in a medium-size saucepan, combine the reserved squash puree, the cream, and chicken stock. Bring to a boil over medium heat. Adjust the heat to a gentle boil and boil until the sauce is syrupy, about 10 minutes. Stir in the grated cheese and bring back to a boil. Pass the sauce through a fine sieve and keep warm.

To serve, divide the sauce among serving plates. Place the onions over the sauce and sprinkle the onions and sauce with the chives. Serve immediately.

Tomato Tart with Pecorino Romano

Crostata di Pomodoro al Pecorino Romano

This is a good antipasto dish or cut into smaller pieces, it can be served as an hors d'oeuvre. Think of the shell as a base and fill it with whatever the season offers, such as a lavish assortment of mushrooms, a mosaic of zucchini and asparagus, or something as simple as potato or squash.

MAKES ONE 10-INCH TART; 6 SERVINGS

For the crust

2 cups unbleached all-purpose flour

¼ teaspoon salt

½ cup (1 stick) unsalted butter, cut into 8 pieces

¼ cup (½ stick) unsalted margarine or ¼ cup solid vegetable shortening, cut into 4 pieces

Grated zest (yellow part only, without the underlying white pith) of 1 lemon

1 teaspoon chopped fresh thyme leaves or ½ teaspoon dried thyme, crumbled

4 to 6 tablespoons ice water

For the filling

¼ cup extra virgin olive oil

2 cups sliced (½-inch-thick) leeks (white and light green parts only), well washed and drained

Salt and freshly ground black pepper

1 cup shredded Pecorino Romano cheese

2 tablespoons chopped fresh oregano leaves

2 medium-size ripe but firm tomatoes, cored, cut in half, and sliced ¼ inch thick

Sprigs fresh oregano (optional)

Make the crust. In the work bowl of a food processor fitted with the metal blade, combine the flour and salt. Add the butter, margarine, lemon zest, and thyme. Pulse until the mixture resembles very coarse meal, about 10 seconds total. Sprinkle ¼ cup of the water over the flour mixture and process just until incorporated. The dough should just hold together in the bowl, but not be wet or sticky. If it doesn't hold together, add enough of the remaining ice water a little at a time, processing very briefly after each addition, until the dough is the proper consistency. Turn the dough out onto plastic wrap and knead it lightly into a ball. Wrap the dough securely and chill for at least 1 hour, or up to 2 days.

On a lightly floured board, roll out the dough to a 12-inch circle about ⅛ inch thick. Fold the dough circle in half and place over half of a 10-inch tart pan with a removable bottom. Unfold the dough and gently press it into the corners and up the sides of the pan. Trim the overhanging dough to an even ¼ inch. Fold the overhanging dough over between the dough and the sides of the pan to form a lip of double-thick dough around the edge of the crust. Press a slightly smaller empty tartlet pan on top of the dough to prevent the crust from puffing up while baking. (Alternatively, you can line the dough with aluminum foil and fill the crust with two cups uncooked rice or beans, spread into an even layer.) Chill the tart shell for at least 30 minutes, or up to 4 hours.

Preheat the oven to 375°F.

Prepare the filling ingredients. In a medium-size skillet, heat 2 tablespoons of the oil over medium heat. Add the leeks and cook, stirring often, until tender, about 10 minutes. Season the leeks with salt and pepper and set aside. In a small bowl, toss the grated cheese and oregano together and set aside.

Bake the weighted tart shell for 15 minutes. Carefully remove the inner tart pan or aluminum foil and weights. Prick the bottom and sides of the crust at ½-inch intervals with a fork and return the tart shell to the oven. Bake until light golden brown, another 15 to 20 minutes. Remove and let cool completely. (Leave the oven on.)

Spread the leeks in an even layer over the bottom of the tart shell. Arrange the tomato slices, overlapping them slightly in concentric circles on top of the leeks. Season the tomato slices with pepper and drizzle with the remaining 2 tablespoons olive oil. Sprinkle the grated cheese mixture over the tomatoes. Bake the tart until the cheese is light golden brown, about 15 minutes.

Serve warm, decorated with sprigs of fresh oregano, if desired.

Braised Peppers with Anchovies

P e p e r o n i a l l ' A c c i u g h e

This dish is wonderful hot, but even better at room temperature and therefore great for parties as it can be prepared up to a day in advance.

MAKES 6 SERVINGS

12 whole salt-packed anchovies or ¼ cup
    anchovy fillets, drained
2 garlic cloves, crushed
5 tablespoons extra virgin olive oil
¼ cup (½ stick) unsalted butter
3 tablespoons milk
4 meaty yellow bell peppers (about
    1½ pounds), quartered and seeds and
    stems removed

If you are using salt-packed anchovies, rinse them well under cold running water and scrape the silvery skin off with the back of a paring knife. Remove the heads and tails, then pull the fillets away from the center bones. Scrape the fillets clean.

Combine the anchovy fillets and garlic and chop together until minced.

In a large skillet, heat the olive oil and butter together over medium heat. Add the anchovy-garlic mixture and cook, stirring constantly, until golden, about 4 minutes. Reduce the heat to low and stir in the milk. Add the peppers and stir to coat. Simmer the peppers, basting constantly with the pan juices, until tender, about 20 minutes. (If the peppers begin to stick, cover the skillet for 4 to 5 minutes, then uncover and continue cooking.) Serve hot or at room temperature.

Prosciutto di Parma "Purses"

Fagottini di Prosciutto di Parma

Cook these "purses" just long enough to brown them. Overcooking will make them salty and, as prosciutto di Parma is a carefully cured product, it doesn't need to be cooked to be rendered edible. When buying the prosciutto, ask for slices from the widest part of the ham, which will measure about eight by four inches.

MAKES 20 PURSES

Bring a large skillet of water to a boil and add the chives. Stir, separating the chives gently, just until they turn bright green, about 5 seconds. Transfer them with a slotted spoon to a bowl of cold water and let stand for a few seconds to stop the cooking. Remove the chives and drain them on paper towels.

> 20 sturdy fresh chives, each at least
>   5 inches long
> 10 thin slices prosciutto di Parma, each
>   about 8 × 4 inches
> About ½ cup freshly grated Parmigiano-
>   Reggiano cheese
> 2 tablespoons unsalted butter
> Ripe figs, cut into quarters, or thin wedges
>   ripe cantaloupe or honeydew melon

Cut the prosciutto slices crosswise in half to make pieces that measure about 4 inches square. Place 1 teaspoon grated cheese in the center of each square. Gather the edges of the prosciutto up over the cheese to form a "purse" with a rounded bottom and ruffled top, pinch the prosciutto firmly where it is gathered, and tie a chive around this "neck."

In a large, preferably nonstick, skillet, melt 1 tablespoon of the butter over low heat. Add half of the purses and cook, shaking the skillet very gently occasionally, until the undersides of the purses are golden brown, 3 to 4 minutes. Transfer to a plate. Add the remaining tablespoon butter and cook the remaining purses in the same manner. Serve with fresh figs or ripe melon wedges.

Fried Dough with Prosciutto

Gnocco Fritto con Prosciutto

This is a typical way to serve prosciutto around Modena. They also turn the fried dough into a sweet dish by drizzling some honey and powdered sugar over the rounds of fried dough while they're still hot.

MAKES 6 SERVINGS

One ⅗-ounce package fresh yeast or one
   1-ounce package active dry yeast
1 cup warm (about 100°F) milk
1 tablespoon extra virgin olive oil
1½ cups sparkling mineral water or
   club soda
4 cups unbleached all-purpose flour, plus
   more for kneading by hand
1 teaspoon salt, plus extra for final salting
3 cups vegetable oil, for frying
12 thin slices prosciutto

In a heavy-duty mixer fitted with the dough hook, combine the yeast, milk, and olive oil. Mix at low speed until the yeast is dissolved. Add the mineral water, 4 cups of the flour, and the salt. Continue mixing at slow speed, stopping to scrape down the sides of the bowl, until the dough is very smooth and elastic, about 10 minutes.

(Alternatively, you can mix the dough by hand: Stir the yeast, milk, and olive oil together in a small bowl until the yeast is dissolved. Place 4 cups of the flour and salt in a large bowl. Make a well in the center of the flour and pour in the mineral water and the milk mixture. With a fork, gradually incorporate the dry ingredients into the liquid. Continue stirring until the dough becomes too stiff to mix with a fork. Work the remaining flour into the dough with your hands just until a rough, firm dough is formed. Shape the dough into a rough ball and set it aside. Clean and dry your hands thoroughly. Knead the dough on a lightly floured surface until it is very smooth and elastic, about 10 minutes; flour your hands and the work surface as necessary to prevent the dough from sticking.)

Wrap the dough in a damp kitchen towel and let rest for 15 minutes.

Divide the dough into four equal pieces. On a lightly floured surface, roll out one piece of dough ¼ inch thick. With a 2-inch round cookie cutter, cut the dough into circles (cut the rounds as close together as possible to reduce the amount of scraps) and set them aside. Repeat with the remaining dough pieces. Knead the dough scraps into a smooth ball and let stand for 15 minutes before rolling and cutting into rounds.

Meanwhile, in a large, deep skillet, heat the vegetable oil to 350°F. (A small piece of the dough should give off a lively sizzle when dipped in the oil.) Add about one third of the dough circles (don't crowd them) and fry until they puff up, about 1 minute. Continue frying, turning often with a long-handled fork to cook the rounds evenly, until golden brown on all sides, about 3 minutes. Drain on paper towels and repeat with the remaining dough circles.

Sprinkle the fried dough lightly with salt and serve warm alongside the prosciutto or drape the prosciutto over the hot *gnocco fritto.*

Buffalo Mozzarella Poached in Tomato-Basil Sauce

Mozzarella di Bufala con Salsa di Pomodoro Tiepida

This is a winter dish that features the flavors of the summer salad everyone loves—*insalata caprese*, made with slices of fresh mozzarella and tomatoes and seasoned with fresh basil. This is a nice dish for company—the sauce can be made ahead and the mozzarella poached in the sauce just before serving.

MAKES 4 SERVINGS

7 tablespoons extra virgin olive oil

3 garlic cloves, crushed

2¼ teaspoons kosher salt

Freshly ground black pepper

2½ pounds ripe plum tomatoes, cored

1 medium-size onion, minced

12 bocconcini (about ¾ pound; see Note), drained

16 fresh basil leaves, washed and dried

Country-style bread, toasted, or *Bruschette* (page 21)

In a small bowl, stir together 3 tablespoons of the olive oil, the garlic cloves, ¼ teaspoon of the salt, and pepper to taste. Let stand for 30 minutes.

Meanwhile, bring a large pot of water to a boil. Add the tomatoes and cook for 5 minutes. Drain well. Pass the tomatoes through a food mill and set aside. (Alternatively, let the tomatoes cool slightly and slip off their skins. Place the peeled tomatoes in a food processor and process, using quick on/off motions, until the tomatoes are smooth.)

Place the remaining ¼ cup olive oil in a large, wide pot over medium heat. Add the onion and cook, stirring, until softened, about 5 minutes. Add the tomatoes, the remaining 2 teaspoons salt, and pepper to taste. Adjust the heat to a simmer and cook, stirring occasionally, until the sauce is slightly reduced, about 20 minutes. Place the bocconcini in the simmering sauce; the balls should be no more than halfway submerged. If not, transfer the sauce to an appropriate-size pot. Remove the pot from the heat and let stand for 10 minutes.

Meanwhile, chop 8 of the basil leaves and cut the remaining 8 leaves crosswise into thin strips.

Remove the bocconcini from the sauce, being careful not to splash the tops of the balls with sauce. Stir the chopped basil into the sauce and scrape it into a serving bowl of about the same size as the pot. Place the mozzarella back in the sauce. Stir the basil strips into the garlic oil and spoon the mixture over the mozzarella. Serve at once with toasted slices of good country-style bread or *bruschette*.

Note: Bocconcini—literally, "mouthfuls"—are small balls of fresh mozzarella that measure about 1½ inches in diameter and weigh about 2 ounces each, although they can vary in size. If you cannot find them, cut larger balls of fresh mozzarella in half and place them cut side down in the sauce to poach them.

Grilled Calamari Strips

Calamari alla Griglia

For best results, use young calamari that are no longer than 3½ to 4 inches. When calamari are young and tender, cooking time should be minimal. Fishermen in the Adriatic eat freshly caught young calamari raw, with just a squeeze of lemon. This dish makes a wonderful main course too.

MAKES 4 SERVINGS

1 pound calamari (squid) with body sacs no longer than 3½ to 4 inches, cleaned and skinned according to the directions on page 315

4 garlic cloves, sliced

2 tablespoons extra virgin olive oil

1 tablespoon chopped fresh thyme leaves

Pinch of peperoncino (crushed red pepper)

Salt and freshly ground black pepper

¼ cup chopped fresh Italian parsley leaves

Assorted salad greens, washed and dried (optional; see Note)

Cut the bodies of the calamari open along one side so they lie flat. If necessary, scrape the inside clean with the back of a knife. In a large bowl, combine the garlic, olive oil, thyme, peperoncino, and a pinch each of salt and pepper. Add the calamari bodies and tentacles and toss well. Let stand at room temperature for 30 minutes, or cover and refrigerate for up to 1 day.

Heat a griddle or large, heavy nonstick skillet over medium heat for 5 minutes. Add as many of the calamari pieces as will fit in a single layer. As the calamari cooks, they will roll into tight cylinders. Cook, turning occasionally, until the calamari are golden brown in places and tender, about 5 minutes. Transfer to a plate as they are cooked and add the remaining calamari pieces to the griddle as room becomes available.

Sprinkle the cooked calamari with the chopped parsley and serve over greens as a first course, or with toothpicks for spearing as a passed hors d'oeuvre.

Note: If you decide to use the greens, dress them lightly with olive oil, a squeeze of lemon juice or a dash of red wine vinegar, and salt and freshly ground black pepper.

Bread and Tomato Salad

Panzanella

Prepared traditionally, this recipe was very humble, with only a few simple ingredients. It was made by soaking sliced day-old bread in water, then draining the bread and seasoning it with salt, pepper, and olive oil before topping the salad with cubes of ripe tomato and shredded basil leaves. The version I share with you here is somewhat different, made with onions—red onions or even sweet onions like Vidalia are best—and it makes an excellent appetizer. You can serve it on its own, or with mozzarella or prosciutto, or, for added complexity, seared shrimp. It is also delicious when served with grilled meats or poultry.

MAKES 6 SERVINGS

In a large bowl, toss the bread, tomatoes, onions, and shredded basil leaves together until well mixed. Drizzle the olive oil and vinegar over the salad and toss to mix thoroughly. Season to taste with salt and pepper and let stand for 10 minutes before serving. Decorate with sprigs of fresh basil.

1 pound 2-day-old country-style bread, crusts removed and cut into ½-inch cubes (about 8 cups)

2 pounds ripe tomatoes, at room temperature, cored, seeded, and cut into ½-inch cubes (about 4 cups)

1 cup diced red onion

12 fresh basil leaves, washed, dried, and shredded, plus fresh basil sprigs for garnish

5 tablespoons extra virgin olive oil

3 tablespoons red wine vinegar

Salt and freshly ground black pepper

Puntarelle and Anchovy Salad

Insalata di Puntarelle

Puntarelle is a member of the chicory family. It abounds in Puglia, where it is known as *catalogna*. It has a slightly bitter (*amarognolo*) finish and is very herbal and refreshing. The season for *puntarelle* is late spring and early summer. In the United States, it is sometimes available in specialty vegetable stores. If you can't find *puntarelle*, try this recipe with frisée or chicory.

MAKES 4 SERVINGS

1 pound puntarelle, frisée, or chicory

¼ pound dried small white beans, such as cannellini or Great Northern, picked over and soaked in water to cover overnight

2 tablespoons extra virgin olive oil

2 tablespoons red wine vinegar

Salt and freshly ground black pepper

4 anchovy fillets, finely chopped

Clean the *puntarelle*. Separate the outer green leaves from the center and cook in boiling water until soft. Drain well. Cut the center tips into fine strips (2 × ¼ inch) and let stand in ice water for 2 hours. Meanwhile, drain the beans and transfer them to a 3- to 4-quart saucepan. Pour in enough cold water to cover the beans generously. Bring to a boil, adjust the heat to a simmer, and cook until the beans are tender, about 40 minutes.

Mix the oil and vinegar together in a small bowl and season with salt and pepper. Cut the boiled green leaves in half and place them in a medium-size bowl. Add the cooked beans and half of the dressing. Toss well.

In a separate bowl, toss the drained *puntarelle* tips, the anchovies, and the remaining dressing together. Serve the two salads side by side on salad plates.

Tuna, Capers, and Warm Potato Salad

Insalata di Patate con Capperi e Tonno

Pantelleria is an island halfway between Sicily and the northern shore of Africa. It is an arid island, but what does grow there is intense in flavor. Some of the best Italian *passito* wines—those made from grapes that are partially dried on the vine and sometimes further dried on straw mats in the *cantina* (wine cellar)—such as Bukkharam by Marco de Bortoli, come from there.

The capers of Pantelleria are the absolute best. Capers are the aromatic white-pink flowers of *Copparis spinosa*, a trailing prickly plant that grows on walls and stones. In springtime, the unopened buds of these flowers are picked and preserved by either pickling them in brine or salting them. The smaller the bud, the more intense the flavor and the more precious the merchandise. Capers have been used to season food in the Mediterranean Basin from antiquity.

MAKES 6 SERVINGS

Preheat the oven to 400°F. Bake the potatoes directly on an oven rack until very tender when pierced with a knife, about 40 minutes. Remove and let stand just until cool enough to handle. (Alternatively, cook the potatoes in a large saucepan of boiling salted water until tender, about 30 minutes.)

Meanwhile, in a medium-size mixing bowl, stir together the tomatoes, onion, basil, oil, and vinegar until blended. Season to taste with salt and pepper and set aside.

With a paring knife, using a kitchen towel to protect your hand from the heat, peel the potatoes and cut them into ½-inch-thick slices. In a large mixing bowl, toss the potatoes with the tuna and its oil. Add the capers and tomato-basil dressing. Toss well, adjust the seasoning, and serve.

3 medium-size baking (Idaho) potatoes, scrubbed

2 medium-size ripe tomatoes, cored, halved, and cut into ¼-inch-thick slices

½ medium-size red onion, thinly sliced

6 fresh basil leaves, washed, dried, and thinly shredded

¼ cup extra virgin olive oil

3 tablespoons red wine vinegar

Salt and freshly ground black pepper

One 6-ounce can tuna packed in olive oil

½ cup small (nonpareil) capers in brine, preferably from the island of Pantelleria, drained

Frico—The Dish That Gave Birth to a Restaurant

A *frico* is a very typical Friulian dish made by cooking Montasio cheese in a skillet until it melts and becomes golden brown and crisp. Fricos can be left unfilled and served as an hors d'oeuvre or stuffed and served as a first course, or, with a nice green salad, as a main course. Traditionally, fricos are filled with boiled potatoes and onions, but we are constantly inventing new fillings at our restaurant Frico Bar on 43rd Street and 9th Avenue in New York City. Stuffed fricos are so popular there that we make five to six different versions daily. The fillings on pages 45–48 are four of my favorites.

Here are a few things to keep in mind before making your first frico:

1. Read the recipe through carefully before you begin. Fricos are quite easy to make, but until you become familiar with the process, you will need to pay careful attention to how the cheese is behaving. Make one or two of the cheese crisps before attempting any of the filled fricos that follow.

2. Montasio cheese is a Friulian cheese made from 100 percent cow's milk. A whole wheel of Montasio weighs about twelve pounds. After four months of aging, Montasio is relatively soft and mild—that is when it is best for making fricos. When aged for six to twelve months, it is somewhat drier and sharper and makes a nice table cheese. Aged for over twelve months, it is quite sharp and makes a good grating cheese. Although it is not quite the same, you can substitute Asiago cheese for Montasio.

3. A small (4- to 5-inch) nonstick skillet is perfect for making fricos. With more than one skillet, you will cut the time it takes to make four fricos. But here's a little tip: Don't start more than one frico at one time. They will be easier to deal with if you stagger the starting times.

4. A heatproof rubber spatula is the ideal tool to work with if you are making fricos in a nonstick skillet. Metal spatulas can scratch the nonstick surface and don't adapt well to the sloped sides of the skillet. Regular rubber spatulas may not stand up to the heat.

5. The trick to making good fricos is the heat. The level of heat must be high enough to crisp the cheese but not so high that the frico turns too dark. If the heat is too low, however, the cheese will melt completely before it crisps up.

Montasio Cheese Crisp
🔒 Frico di Montasio 🔒

This is the basic unfilled frico that gets quite crisp when it cools to room temperature. If you like, drape the frico hot from the pan over the handle of a wooden spoon suspended between two cans. It will cool in the shape of a taco shell and, when filled with a salad of lightly dressed baby greens, makes a spectacular first course. Made smaller—the size of a chocolate chip cookie—and draped over a spoon, these are a wonderful hors d'oeuvre. Serve these fricos as they do in Friuli, with a glass of chilled white Tocai Friulano.

MAKES 4 CRISPS

Preheat the oven to 250°F.

½ pound Montasio cheese, rind removed (or about 6 ounces trimmed) and coarsely shredded (about 2½ loosely packed cups)

To cook the fricos in a skillet: Place a 4- to 5-inch nonstick skillet over medium-low heat and heat until a shred of the cheese begins to sizzle 2 to 3 seconds after it hits the pan. Scatter one fourth of the cheese in an even layer over the bottom of the skillet. Let the cheese cook without disturbing it or moving the pan until the fat that separates from the cheese begins to bubble around the edges, about 3 minutes.

At this point, shake the skillet gently to free the cheese crisp from the bottom of the pan. If it sticks, let it cook for a minute or two more, then try again. If the crisp is still sticking in places, carefully work a heatproof rubber spatula under the crisp to free it. After 6 to 7 minutes total cooking time, the underside of the crisp should be an even golden brown and the crisp should slide very easily in the pan. Slide the crisp onto a small plate, then invert the crisp back into the skillet. Cook the other side as you did the first.

Slide the crisp out onto a baking sheet and keep it warm in the oven while cooking the remaining fricos. Pat the fricos with paper towels before serving.

To cook the fricos on a griddle: Heat a cast-iron or other heavy, stick-resistant griddle over medium-low heat until a shred of the cheese begins to sizzle 2 to 3 seconds after it hits the surface of the griddle. Using one fourth of the cheese for each, form as many circles about 4 inches in diameter as will fit on the griddle without touching. Cook as described above, simply flipping the crisps with a metal spatula when the underside is golden. Fricos cooked on a griddle will require about 10 minutes total cooking time.

Filled Montasio Cheese Crisp

Frico Ripieno

MAKES 4 SERVINGS

Filling of your choice (recipes follow)

1 pound Montasio cheese, rind removed
(about ¾ pound trimmed) and coarsely
shredded (about 5 loosely packed cups)

Tender young salad greens, washed and
dried (optional; see Note)

Prepare the filling of your choice. Preheat the oven to 250°F.

To cook filled fricos in a skillet: Place a 4- to 5-inch nonstick skillet over medium-low heat and heat until a shred of the cheese begins to sizzle 2 to 3 seconds after it hits the pan. Scatter one eighth (about a generous ½ cup) of the cheese in an even layer over the bottom of the skillet. Arrange one fourth of the filling of choice over the cheese and press it very gently into an even layer. Sprinkle another generous ½ cup of the cheese over the filling in an even layer. Cook until golden brown and crisp on both sides as instructed on page 43. Filled fricos require a little extra care when removing them from the pan and turning them. Slide the crisp out onto a baking sheet and keep it warm in the oven while cooking the remaining fricos.

Pat the fricos dry with paper towels, cut in half, top with dressed greens if you like, and serve.

To cook filled fricos on a griddle: Heat a cast-iron or other heavy, stick-resistant griddle over medium-low heat until a shred of the cheese begins to sizzle 2 to 3 seconds after it hits the surface of the griddle. Using one eighth of the cheese for each, form as many circles about 4 inches in diameter as will fit on the griddle without touching. (If this is your first time making filled fricos, you may want to make six slightly smaller fricos on the griddle; they will be easier to flip.) Fill and cook as described above, simply flipping the crisps with a metal spatula when the underside is golden. Filled fricos cooked on a griddle will require about 12 minutes total cooking time. Serve as described above.

Note: If you decide to use the greens, dress them lightly with olive oil, a squeeze of lemon juice or a dash of red wine vinegar, and salt and freshly ground black pepper.

Potato-Onion Filling

Ripieno di Patate e Cipolle

MAKES ENOUGH FILLING FOR 4 FRICOS

In a pot large enough to hold them comfortably, cook the potatoes in boiling salted water to cover until tender but still firm—the skin should be unbroken—about 25 minutes. Drain the potatoes and let stand just until cool enough to handle.

> **2 medium-large baking (Idaho) potatoes (about 1 pound), scrubbed**
> **2 tablespoons extra virgin olive oil**
> **1 cup thinly sliced onions or scallions (white and light green parts only)**
> **Salt and freshly ground black pepper**

Peel the potatoes and cut them into ¼-inch-thick slices. In a large skillet, heat the olive oil over medium heat. Add the onions and cook, stirring occasionally, until softened, about 4 minutes. Add the sliced potatoes and cook, gently turning the potatoes occasionally, until golden, about 8 minutes. Season with salt and pepper.

These next three fillings start by making the above Potato-Onion Filling recipe. While the potatoes are cooking, prepare the remaining ingredients for the filling, then simply fold the two together.

Potato and Mushroom Filling

Ripieno di Patate e Funghi

MAKES ENOUGH FILLING FOR 4 FRICOS

Potato-Onion Filling (page 45)
2 tablespoons unsalted butter
2 garlic cloves, crushed
½ pound mixed mushrooms, cleaned
(see Note on page 63), and sliced
Salt and freshly ground black pepper
2 tablespoons chopped fresh Italian parsley
leaves

Prepare the potato-onion filling.

While the potatoes are cooking, prepare the mushroom mixture: In a large, heavy skillet, heat the butter over medium heat until foaming. Add the garlic cloves and cook, stirring, until golden, about 2 minutes. Add the mushrooms, season with salt and pepper, and cook, stirring, until all the liquid has evaporated and they begin to sizzle. Remove the skillet from the heat, remove the garlic cloves, and stir in the parsley.

In a large mixing bowl, gently stir the potato-onion filling and mushroom mixture together until combined.

Potato and Crabmeat Filling

Ripieno di Patate e Granchio

MAKES ENOUGH FILLING FOR 4 FRICOS

Prepare the potato-onion filling.

Pick over the crabmeat, removing any pieces of shell or cartilage. In a large mixing bowl, stir the potato-onion filling, crabmeat, and chives gently together until blended. Season with salt and pepper.

Potato-Onion Filling (page 45)
1 cup jumbo lump or lump crabmeat or diced (½-inch) cooked lobster meat or shrimp
¼ cup chopped fresh chives
Salt and freshly ground black pepper

Sausage and Broccoli di Rape Filling

Frico con Salsiccia e Broccoletti

MAKES ENOUGH FILLING FOR 4 FRICOS

Potato-Onion Filling (page 45)

2 tablespoons unsalted butter

2 garlic cloves, crushed

1 cup sweet Italian sausage (about 2 links), casings removed, or 6 ounces bulk Italian sausage meat

Pinch of peperoncino (crushed red pepper)

Salt and freshly ground black pepper

2 cups coarsely chopped broccoli di rape (florets, leaves, and thin stems only), washed and dried

Make the potato-onion filling.

In a medium-size skillet, melt the butter over medium heat. Add the garlic cloves and cook, turning once or twice, until golden, about 2 minutes. Add the sausage meat and peperoncino and season lightly with salt and black pepper. Cook, stirring to break up the sausage, until the meat is browned, about 10 minutes.

Stir the broccoli di rape into the skillet and reduce the heat to low. Cover and cook until the broccoli is wilted and tender, about 5 minutes. Drain off any excess fat and remove the garlic cloves.

In a large mixing bowl, fold together the potato-onion filling and sausage mixture until blended.

Soups

Minestre, Zuppe, e Brodi

I remember my grandmother Rosa telling me often how fortunate I was. While ladling out a sausage with my *pasta e fagioli,* she would explain that when she was my age, the flavor of meat in her *minestra* would have come from a prosciutto bone that was borrowed from the neighbors and then returned.

Those people may not have had abundance, but they surely knew the warmth of friendship and had a true understanding of the importance of community during trying times. Indeed, whenever I complained about something, my grandmother would reiterate, *"O mangia questa minestra o salta fuori di questa finestra"* ("Either eat this soup or jump out of this window"); in other words, "Take it or leave it." My late father, Vittorio, expected soup with just about every meal, with the exception of times when pasta or risotto took its place, so I learned early on how to prepare it.

When we came to the United States in 1959, I was twelve years old, and we lived in Astoria, Queens. My mother worked in North Bergen, New Jersey, and often she would come home from work late; therefore, I was in charge of supper. Of course, she would prepare the basics the night before, but I was responsible for cooking the soups. My mother assembled all the ingredients in the soup pot in the refrigerator and left me with the instructions: Add water up to the handles; keep the lid on; when it begins to boil, lower the flame to a simmer; and always skim regularly. Or, if it was a bean-based soup, the beans would get soaked overnight, and I would have to change the water and then proceed.

My brother, Franco, and I would do our homework while the *minestra* was perking away. Our cousins Louis and Marie lived two doors down from us in the same apartment building, and we kept both our doors open so Marie could keep an ear out for us. While we studied, the aroma of the *minestra* traveled down all four flights from our apartment. On some nights I was busy or careless and would forget to stir the *minestra,* and sometimes the potatoes and beans would be scorched. My mother could tell from the first floor and would rush to investigate the pot as soon as she came in, with her coat still on.

I love soup. To me it represents the heart of the household, especially on cold winter days. To come home and see the windows *appannate* (glazed with steam), to have the aroma of *pasta e fagioli* greet you at the door, means you know you will be comforted from the inside out as you sit down for dinner.

Soups have humble roots and a noble tradition in Italian cuisine. Sometimes considered the food of the poor, soup can be a meal in itself, and still often constitutes the main meal of the day for rich and poor alike. Soup was the one meal that could be left simmering for hours while the women did their work in the fields, in the farmyards, or in the house.

Soups are also known as the food of restoration—from the penicillin-like properties of chicken soup to the stomach-settling quality of vegetable soup to strength-giving bean soup. As Louis P. DeGouy declares in *The Soup Book,* published in 1949, "Soup is cuisine's kindest course. It breathes reassurance, it steams consolation, after a weary day it promotes sociability . . . there is nothing like a bowl of hot soup, its wisp of aromatic steam making the nostrils quiver with anticipation."

Hot or cold soups play a major role in the kitchen in every season, and because every food group can be used in making soups, it is the most versatile course for cooks. Italian cuisine is one of the richest and most varied in its collection of soups, partly because of the wide availability of different vegetables, legumes, and grains. There are three basic categories of soups served on the Italian table: *minestra, zuppa,* and *brodo.*

Minestra

Minestra is a soup dense with vegetables, legumes, and tubers to which either rice or some sort of pasta has been added. *Minestra* is also a synonym in Italian for the course that follows the antipasto; thus pasta and risotto served in that sequence are considered *minestra*.

The word *minestra* comes from *minestrare* (to administrate) and most likely derives from the fact that the *minestra*—which represents the entire meal in many cultures, especially throughout the Mediterranean—was portioned out by the authoritative figure in the family.

A *minestra* can be categorized or grouped by the ingredients that go into its base preparation: bean and potato, potato and carrot, or fish and vegetable. In the recipes that follow, I have given you the base preparations for each of these three groups, plus two variations. Once I lead you through the base preparations, I am confident that your imagination and what you have on hand will have you cooking your own variations in addition to mine.

Each of the *minestre* starts with *il trito*—the chopping together of aromatic vegetables and herbs and the fat that will be used in cooking the soup. During the winter months, my grandmother used the belly fat of the pig she had cured (pancetta) and had hanging in the *cantina* (cellar). She would chop the fresh rosemary, garlic cloves, and pancetta with a cleaver that she periodically submerged in the boiling *minestra*. Under the hot blade of the cleaver, the ingredients became a *trito*, or paste. Then she would cook the *trito* in a skillet until golden and add it to the *minestra*. In some *minestres*—like *pasta e fagioli*—she added the *trito* directly to the boiling beans and potatoes without cooking it first. During the warm months, my grandmother used olive oil to sauté the *trito*. Today, I use only olive oil to make my *trito*. I start with finely chopped garlic, onions, and fresh herbs. Sometimes I add half a carrot or half a stalk of celery and just enough additional olive oil to make a paste with the ingredients.

When I make a *trito* for *minestra*, I brown the chopped onions first, then add the rest of the *trito* ingredients to the pan and cook it lightly before adding the whole mixture to the *minestra*. In all of the *minestra* recipes that follow, you can add the *trito* or not, as you choose.

The Minestra Family Tree

Bean-and-Potato Minestre The velvety texture of these soups comes from the slow cooking of the beans and the potatoes, which are coarsely mashed and returned to the soup for the last few minutes of cooking. Soups of the bean and potato family are started by simmering presoaked beans and whole potatoes with herbs and seasonings in water. Sautéed onions and the *trito*—and sometimes other seasonings—are added along with cured, smoked, or fresh pork about halfway through the cooking. The *minestra* can be finished with any number—or combination—of ingredients, added according to how long they will take to cook. The three bean-and-potato *minestre* I offer here are finished with pasta, sauerkraut, and barley. The pasta is added about ten minutes before the soup

Types of Meat for Flavoring Minestre

All of the bean-and-potato-based *minestre* recipes in this chapter call for some kind of meat. Here are some suggestions for meats that can be used to flavor *minestre*. All of them, with the exception of the ham hocks, can be sliced and served separately, either alongside the two salads mentioned on page 57, or on their own. Before adding any of these meats, bring them to a boil in a saucepan of lightly salted water. Boil for 10 minutes to remove any impurities from the surface of the meat; you will see these impurities rise to the surface of the water. Drain and add meat to the *minestra*. Remove the meats from the soup when they are tender, even if the *minestra* is not finished.

Pork butt, smoked or fresh: A 4-ounce piece of pork butt, whether fresh or smoked, takes about half an hour to cook. Remove it when fork-tender and either chop it and return it to the soup or keep it warm to serve sliced, separate from the soup.

Sausages: Substitute an equal amount of sweet or spicy Italian sausages—without seeds—for the pork butt called for in the recipe, and add them when the recipe calls for adding the pork butt. These are especially delicious sliced and served with either of the salads referred to on page 57.

Smoked ham hocks or fresh pork hocks: Substitute two smoked or fresh ham hocks (about 12 ounces total) for the pork butt called for in the recipe. Hocks will take longer to cook than pork butt and should be added earlier in the cooking, as directed in the recipes. They have a lot of flavor but aren't very meaty. The best way to eat them is out of hand, savoring the small bits of meat and gelatin.

Pork ribs, smoked or fresh: These, like hocks, take longer to cook than pork butt. If you would like to substitute ribs for hocks, use an equal amount and add them to the *minestra* when the recipe calls for adding the hocks. These can be sliced between the bone and served separately, or the meat can be removed from the bone, diced, and returned to the soup.

is served, whereas the sauerkraut, which needs time to soften and mellow, is added about thirty minutes prior to finish. Barley, too, needs about thirty minutes of cooking to make it tender and, like pasta, must be watched and stirred carefully after it's added so it doesn't stick to the bottom of the pot and scorch. You can use these ingredients and times as a guide for your own inventions.

Potato-and-Carrot Minestre This branch of the family starts by browning diced potatoes before adding shredded carrots and, sometimes, other aromatic vegetables, like celery or squash.

Stock and seasonings are added and the soup simmered slowly until the potatoes begin to "melt" into the soup. Like the bean-and-potato soups, these can be finished with any number of ingredients, such as the rice, barley, and mushrooms I describe below, or possibly turnips, salsify, parsnips, ditalini, or spaghetti broken into short pieces.

Seafood-and-Rice Minestre Like the potato-and-carrot branch of the family, these soups start by browning diced potatoes in olive oil. Leeks and scallions or spring onions are stirred into the potatoes and wilted. Water, vegetable stock, or a simple *fumetto* made from the frame of the fish that has been filleted for the soup is added and simmered along with the potatoes and seasonings. Along the way, vegetables like tomato and broccoli may be added. Last to go into the soup are the rice and seafood. Rice is added about twelve minutes before the soup is finished, and the seafood according to its texture. Shrimp, which become rubbery if they are cooked too long, are stirred in just before the pot is removed from the stove—the heat of the soup is enough to cook them in a minute or so. Flakier fish, like red snapper, are better if cooked for about five minutes or so, and some firmer or full-flavored fish, like swordfish and skate, benefit from an even longer cooking time and can be added along with the rice. All seafood-and-rice *minestre* benefit from a generous addition of chopped fresh Italian parsley just before serving.

Rules for a Good Minestra

Remember:

- Soups that simmer slowly and for a longer time seem to have a more velvety texture than soups cooked quickly. The release of the starches from the beans, barley, or rice and the final addition of the mashed cooked potatoes also enhance this texture in the finished soup.

- *Minestra* must be watched carefully during the final simmering—when it becomes thicker—so that the soup does not scorch.

- Pasta or rice should be added in the last moments just before serving or it will swell, absorbing all the liquid, and become mushy. However, the *minestra* can be prepared without the rice or pasta up to two days in advance and refrigerated. Heat the *minestra* to a simmer before adding the rice or pasta. If you prefer, the pasta or rice can be cooked in salted water beforehand, cooled, and then added to the hot soup just before serving.

- Whenever stock or vegetable broth is called for in these soups, canned broth, reconstituted bouillon, or plain water can be substituted. Remember, however, that the end result is the sum of its parts, and if the liquid you add has no flavor, you will have to compensate accordingly with condiments to taste. But not every dish has to be a powerhouse of flavor every time. Simplicity still reigns in my kitchen.

Finishing Touches for Minestra

Here are a few simple suggestions for how to make a good thing even better:

- Drizzle the best extra virgin olive oil you can find over a bowl of *minestra* just before serving, or place a cruet of it on the table and let people help themselves.

- Pass a chunk of Parmigiano-Reggiano or Pecorino Romano cheese and a small grater at the table so people can add it to their taste.

- Place a peppermill on the table and let guests grind their own.

- Add a tablespoon or two of good red wine to each bowl of bean-and-potato-based soup when serving.

- Either the Herb Pesto on page 146 or an all-basil version is delicious stirred into a steaming bowl of vegetable or bean *minestra*.

- The addition of fresh herbs will enhance any soup; freshly chopped parsley is especially wonderful in fish-based soups.

- Croutons, like the ones prepared in step 1 of the Clam Soup on page 76, are delicious sprinkled over any of these *minestre*.

- Toasted bread in any form, like the baked sliced bread made in step 1 of Tomato and Bread Soup (page 74) or Cheese Toasts (page 70), can be floated on the *minestra* or placed in the bottom of the bowl and the soup ladled over them.

- Slices of home-baked bread brushed with oil and grilled make a great topping.

Trito for Minestra

Il Trito

This is one version of *trito,* but with olive oil and onions or garlic as a base, you can make your own *trito* according to the herbs and aromatics available to you or that you prefer. You may want to make two or three times the amount of *trito* in this recipe—covered with a thin layer of olive oil, it keeps in the refrigerator for weeks and makes a lovely finishing touch for most soups and pasta dishes.

MAKES ENOUGH TO SEASON 8 SERVINGS OF SOUP

Combine all the ingredients in a food processor or blender and process until very smooth. Stop the machine once or twice to scrape down the sides of the container. Transfer the *trito* to a small bowl and smooth the surface. To store, drizzle 1 tablespoon oil over the surface and refrigerate for up to 3 weeks.

4 garlic cloves, peeled

½ cup shredded carrots

½ cup lightly packed chopped fresh Italian parsley leaves

3 tablespoons extra virgin olive oil, plus 1 tablespoon extra if storing

Bean and Pasta Soup

🎐 Minestra di Pasta e Fagioli 🎐

Pasta-and-bean-based soups are better when the bean base has had a chance to rest. Serve them after two hours or, better yet, the next day. But remember not to add pasta or rice until the final boiling, just before serving, or they will expand and take over your soup pot.

MAKES 8 SERVINGS

1½ cups dried borlotti beans or cranberry, red kidney, pinto, or white beans

3 quarts cold water

3 large baking (Idaho) potatoes, peeled

2 sprigs fresh rosemary

2 fresh or dried bay leaves

1½ teaspoons peperoncino (crushed red pepper)

2 tablespoons extra virgin olive oil

1 medium-size onion, chopped

1 recipe *Trito* (page 55)

1 cup canned peeled Italian plum tomatoes, crushed

¼ pound ham hocks or fresh or smoked pork butt, or other meat for flavoring, parboiled (see page 52)

1 cup ditalini pasta

Salt and freshly ground black pepper

¼ cup freshly grated Parmigiano-Reggiano cheese

Pick over the beans, discarding any stones or other objects and any beans that are discolored. Place the beans in a deep bowl and pour in enough cold water to cover them by at least 4 inches. Soak the beans in a cool place for at least 8 hours, or overnight.

Drain the beans and transfer them to a deep, heavy 4- to 5-quart pot. Add the water, potatoes, rosemary, bay leaves, and peperoncino and bring to a boil over high heat. Adjust the level of heat to medium and cook, stirring occasionally, for 30 minutes.

Meanwhile, in a medium-size skillet, heat the olive oil over medium heat. Add the onion and cook, stirring often, until light golden, about 6 minutes. Stir in the *trito* and continue cooking until fragrant and very lightly browned, about 2 minutes. Add the crushed tomatoes and simmer for 10 minutes.

Scrape the *trito* mixture into the soup pot. If using ham hocks, add them now. Continue simmering until the beans are tender, about 1 hour. If using pork butt, add it 30 minutes after adding the *trito* mixture.

Meanwhile, as soon as the potatoes are cooked, transfer them to a bowl, mash them roughly, and return them to the pot. (The soup can be prepared to this point up to 2 days in advance and refrigerated. Bring the soup to a boil before continuing.)

Stir in the pasta. Cook, stirring often, until the pasta is tender, about 10 minutes.

Meanwhile, remove the meat from the pot and cut it into ¼-inch dice; return the diced meat to the *minestra*. (Alternatively, you can serve the meat separately; see page 52.)

Remove the soup from the heat and season it with salt and pepper to taste. Let it stand for 5 minutes, then serve it in warm bowls, sprinkled with the grated cheese.

Bean-and-Potato Minestra as a Multicourse Meal

Here are two wonderful, very hearty salads that can be made easily from the bean-and-potato *minestra* base. Serve them along with the meat that has simmered in the soup as a separate course.

- To make a bean-and-potato salad, add 1 extra cup of beans, 2 extra potatoes, and 1 quart water to the amount called for in any of the *minestra* recipes on pages 56–68. When the beans and potatoes are cooked, remove 2 potatoes and 1½ cups of cooked beans. Cut the potatoes into bite-size pieces and combine them with the beans. Add sliced Bermuda onion to taste. You can leave the bean-and-potato mixture at room temperature for up to 5 hours. (It won't taste the same if refrigerated.) When dinner is ready, dress the salad with extra virgin olive oil and red wine vinegar, season with salt and freshly ground black pepper, toss well, and serve.

- Another good salad is made by tossing diced warm potatoes—add 2 extra potatoes to the *minestra* base and use them for this—with the tougher outer leaves of escarole, cut into pieces, and slices of raw onion. Just before serving, dress the salad with red wine vinegar and extra virgin olive oil and season with salt and freshly ground black pepper.

Sauerkraut and Bean Soup

🔒 Yota 🔒

Yota is a soup typical of the area around Trieste. It is a hearty soup, and one that definitely is better the day after it is made. Make sure you do not lose all the acidity from the sauerkraut when you rinse it. Taste the sauerkraut after a brief first washing, keeping in mind that it will lose about half its acidity when cooking in the soup.

MAKES 8 SERVINGS

1½ cups dried borlotti beans or cranberry, red kidney, pinto, or white beans
3 quarts cold water
3 large baking (Idaho) potatoes, peeled
4 fresh or dried bay leaves
1½ teaspoons peperoncino (crushed red pepper)
1 pound sauerkraut
2 tablespoons extra virgin olive oil
1 medium-size onion, chopped
1 recipe *Trito* (page 55)
¼ pound fresh or smoked pork butt, or other meat for flavoring, parboiled (see page 52)
Salt and freshly ground black pepper
Freshly grated Parmigiano-Reggiano cheese

Pick over the beans, discarding any stones or other objects and any beans that are discolored. Place the beans in a deep bowl and pour in enough cold water to cover them by at least 4 inches. Soak the beans in a cool place for at least 8 hours, or overnight.

Drain the beans and transfer them to a tall, heavy pot. Add the water, potatoes, bay leaves, and peperoncino and bring to a boil over high heat. Adjust the level of heat to medium and cook, stirring occasionally, for 30 minutes.

Meanwhile, drain the sauerkraut and taste it. If it is mild, rinse it briefly in a colander under cold water and drain it again. If the flavor is more assertive, rinse it twice before draining.

In a medium-size skillet, heat the olive oil over medium heat. Add the onion and cook, stirring often, until light golden, about 6 minutes. Stir in the *trito* and cook until fragrant and very lightly browned, about 2 minutes. Add about 1 cup of the bean cooking liquid to the skillet and bring to a boil.

Scrape the *trito* mixture into the soup pot. If using ham hocks, add them now. Continue simmering for another 30 minutes. Add the sauerkraut to the pot. If using pork butt, add it now. Cook, stirring and skimming occasionally, until the beans are tender, about another 30 minutes.

Meanwhile, as soon as the potatoes are cooked, transfer them to a bowl and mash them roughly. Remove the meat from the pot and cut it into ¼-inch dice; return the diced meat to the *minestra*.

(Alternatively, you can serve the meat separately; see page 52.)

Return the potatoes to the pot for the last 10 minutes of cooking, then season the soup with salt and pepper to taste. (The soup is ready to serve now, but will improve if refrigerated for 1 to 2 days. Bring to a simmer before serving.)

Remove the soup from the heat and let it stand for 5 minutes. Serve in warm bowls, sprinkled with the grated cheese.

Barley and Bean Soup

⬚ Minestra di Farro ⬚

Add fresh or frozen corn kernels to this *minestra* for the last twenty minutes of cooking time and you will have *bobici,* another favorite soup from the area around Trieste.

MAKES 8 SERVINGS

1½ cups dried borlotti beans or cranberry, red kidney, pinto, or white beans

3 quarts cold water

3 large baking (Idaho) potatoes, peeled

2 sprigs fresh rosemary

4 fresh or dried bay leaves

2 tablespoons extra virgin olive oil

1 medium-size onion, chopped

1 recipe *Trito* (page 55)

1 cup canned peeled Italian plum tomatoes, crushed

¼ pound ham hocks or fresh or smoked pork butt, or other meat for flavoring, parboiled (see page 52)

1 cup barley, rinsed and drained

Salt and freshly ground black pepper

¼ cup freshly grated Parmigiano-Reggiano cheese

Pick over the beans, discarding any stones or other objects and any beans that are discolored. Place the beans in a deep bowl and pour in enough cold water to cover them by at least 4 inches. Soak the beans in a cool place for at least 8 hours, or overnight.

Drain the beans and transfer them to a tall, heavy pot. Add the water, potatoes, rosemary, and bay leaves and bring to a boil over high heat. Adjust the heat to medium and cook, stirring occasionally, for 30 minutes.

Meanwhile, in a medium-size skillet, heat the olive oil over medium heat. Add the onion and cook, stirring often, until light golden, about 6 minutes. Stir in the *trito* and cook until fragrant and very lightly browned, about 2 minutes. Add the crushed tomatoes and simmer for 10 minutes.

Scrape the *trito* mixture into the soup pot. If using ham hocks, add them now. Cook for an additional 30 minutes. (The soup can be prepared to this point up to 2 days in advance and refrigerated. Bring the soup to a simmer before continuing.)

Add the barley to the pot. If using pork butt, add it now. Cook, stirring often to prevent the barley from scorching and skimming occasionally, until the beans and barley are very tender, about another 30 minutes.

Meanwhile, once the potatoes are cooked, transfer them to a bowl and mash them roughly. Remove the meat from the pot and cut it into ¼-inch dice; return the diced meat to the *minestra*. (Alternatively, you can serve the meat separately; see the sidebar on page 52.) Return the potatoes to the pot for the last 10 minutes of cooking. Season the soup with salt and pepper to taste.

Remove the soup from the heat and let it stand for 5 minutes. Serve in warm bowls, sprinkled with the grated cheese.

Rice and Potato Soup

Minestra di Riso e Patate

This is the soup to make when you don't know how to begin a meal. It is simple, quick, tasty, and light.

MAKES 8 SERVINGS

In a deep, heavy 4- to 5-quart pot, heat the olive oil over medium heat. Add the potatoes and cook, stirring occasionally with a wooden spoon, until lightly browned, about 5 minutes. Most likely, the potatoes will stick, but that is fine; adjust the level of heat to prevent the bits of potato that stick from getting too dark. Stir in the carrots and celery and cook, stirring, until the carrots are softened, another 2 to 3 minutes. Season lightly with salt. Add the tomato paste and stir to coat the vegetables. Add the hot stock and bay leaves and bring to a boil, scraping up the bits of potato on the bottom of the pot. Adjust the level of heat to a simmer and season the soup lightly with salt and pepper. Cover the pot and simmer until the potatoes begin to fall apart, about 40 minutes. (The soup can be prepared to this point up to 2 days in advance and refrigerated. Bring the soup to a simmer before continuing.)

Stir in the rice. Cook, stirring well, until the rice is tender but still firm, about 12 minutes.

Remove the bay leaves. Stir the parsley into the soup and check the seasoning. Serve in warm soup bowls, sprinkled with the grated cheese.

3 tablespoons extra virgin olive oil

2 large baking (Idaho) potatoes, peeled and cut into ⅓-inch cubes

2 medium-size carrots, coarsely shredded

2 center celery stalks, diced

Salt

2 teaspoons tomato paste

10 cups hot Chicken Stock (page 80), Meat Stock (page 78), or canned low-sodium chicken or beef broth

2 fresh or dried bay leaves

Freshly ground black pepper

1 cup long-grain rice

½ cup lightly packed chopped fresh Italian parsley leaves

¼ cup freshly grated Pecorino Romano cheese

Mushroom and Potato Soup

Minestra di Funghi e Patate

I love mushrooms, and this is my favorite soup. You can use any mushrooms you have available. In fact, the more kinds you use, the more complex the flavor. I know you will be making this recipe often; to add a new twist, try replacing the barley with long-grain rice, but add it for just the last ten minutes of cooking.

MAKES 8 SERVINGS

10 cups hot Chicken Stock (page 80), Meat Stock (page 78), or canned low-sodium chicken or beef broth

½ ounce dried porcini mushrooms (about a generous ½ cup), chopped

¼ cup extra virgin olive oil

2 large baking (Idaho) potatoes, peeled and cut into ⅓-inch cubes

2 medium-size carrots, coarsely shredded

1 cup peeled and coarsely grated butternut squash

Salt

2 teaspoons tomato paste

2 fresh or dried bay leaves

Freshly ground black pepper

2 tablespoons chopped shallots

1 pound assorted wild mushrooms (see Note)

1 cup barley, rinsed and drained

½ cup lightly packed chopped fresh Italian parsley leaves

¼ cup freshly grated Parmigiano-Reggiano cheese

In a small bowl, pour 1 cup of the hot stock over the dried porcini mushrooms. Let stand until the porcini are softened, about 20 minutes.

Drain the porcini, straining the soaking liquid through a coffee filter or a sieve lined with a double thickness of cheesecloth. Combine the soaking liquid with the remaining stock. Rinse the soaked mushrooms thoroughly under running water to remove any sand grit. Drain them well and finely chop.

In a deep, heavy 4- to 5-quart pot, heat 3 tablespoons of the olive oil over medium heat. Add the potatoes and cook, stirring occasionally with a wooden spoon, until lightly browned, about 5 minutes. Most likely, the potatoes will stick, but that is fine; adjust the level of heat to prevent the bits that stick from getting too dark. Stir in the carrots and squash and cook, stirring, until the carrots are softened, 2 to 3 minutes. Season lightly with salt. Add the tomato paste and stir to coat the vegetables. Add the hot stock mixture, the bay leaves, and chopped porcini mushrooms and bring to a boil, scraping up the bits of potato from the bottom. Adjust the heat to a simmer and season the soup lightly with salt and pepper. Cover the pot and simmer until the potatoes begin to fall apart, about 40 minutes.

Meanwhile, in a large skillet, heat the remaining 1 tablespoon olive oil over medium-high heat. Add the shallots and cook, stirring, until lightly browned, about 2 minutes. Add the sliced fresh mushrooms, sprinkle them with salt and pepper, and cook until all the mushroom liquid has evaporated, about 6 minutes. Scrape the contents of the skillet into soup pot. (The soup can be prepared to this point up to 2 days in advance and refrigerated. Bring the soup to a simmer before continuing.)

Stir the barley into the soup. Cook, stirring often to prevent the barley from scorching, until the barley is tender, about 30 minutes.

Remove the bay leaves, then stir the parsley into the soup and check the seasoning. Serve in warm soup bowls, sprinkled with the grated cheese.

Note: Many types of wild or exotic mushrooms are available in today's market. Generally speaking, avoid washing mushrooms—they absorb water quickly. Rather, wipe firm, smooth-capped mushrooms like button, cremini, portobello, shiitake, and porcini with a clean, damp kitchen towel. Brush irregularly shaped mushrooms like oyster, chanterelle, and black trumpet with a pastry brush to remove dirt. Pull hollow-stemmed mushrooms like black trumpet and yellow-foot chanterelles into halves to expose the inner stem where grit, dirt, and other debris, like pine needles, can be lodged. In all cases, trim off and discard tough portions of the stem, or the whole stem if it is hard, as is the case with shiitakes, before slicing or cutting the rest of the mushroom. If your mushrooms are very dirty and you must wash them, plunge them into a large bowl or basin of cold water, swish them quickly to dislodge dirt, then lift them with your hands to a colander to drain. Pat them dry with paper towels before continuing.

Fava Bean and Potato Soup

Minestra di Fave e Patate

This is a wonderful spring soup. It is simple but truly exalts the flavor of fresh fava beans. If favas are not available, fresh lima beans or fresh peas make a good substitute.

MAKES 8 SERVINGS

3 tablespoons extra virgin olive oil

2 large baking (Idaho) potatoes, peeled and cut into ⅓-inch cubes

2 medium-size carrots, coarsely shredded

2 center celery stalks, diced

Salt

2 teaspoons tomato paste

10 cups Chicken Stock (page 80), Meat Stock (page 78), or canned low-sodium chicken or beef broth

2 fresh or dried bay leaves

Pinch of peperoncino (crushed red pepper)

Freshly ground black pepper

2 cups blanched and peeled fava beans (see page 233) or one 10-ounce package frozen baby lima beans, defrosted and drained

1 cup long-grain rice

½ cup lightly packed chopped fresh Italian parsley leaves

¼ cup freshly grated Pecorino Romano cheese

In a deep, heavy 4- to 5-quart pot, heat the olive oil over medium heat. Add the potatoes and cook, stirring occasionally with a wooden spoon, until lightly browned, about 5 minutes. Most likely, the potatoes will stick, but that is fine; adjust the heat to prevent the bits of potato that stick from getting too dark. Stir in the carrots and celery and cook, stirring, until the carrots are softened, 2 to 3 minutes. Season lightly with salt. Add the tomato paste and stir to coat the vegetables. Add the hot stock, bay leaves, and peperoncino and bring to a boil, scraping up the bits of potato on the bottom. Adjust the level of heat to a simmer and season the soup lightly with salt and pepper. Cover the pot and simmer until the potatoes begin to fall apart, about 40 minutes.

Add the favas or limas to the soup. Simmer, covered, for 15 minutes. (The soup can be prepared to this point up to 2 days in advance and refrigerated. Bring the soup to a simmer before continuing.)

Stir in the rice. Cook, stirring well, until the rice is tender but still firm, about 12 minutes.

Remove the bay leaves, stir the parsley into the soup, and check the seasonings. Serve the soup in warm bowls, sprinkled with the grated cheese.

Crabmeat and Skate Soup

Minestra di Granchio e Razza

Crabmeat is what makes this soup exceptional, but other seafood can be used too. Scallops are a good substitute, or for those allergic to shellfish, monkfish cut into cubes and added with the skate makes a nice dish.

MAKES 8 SERVINGS

In a deep, heavy 4- to 5-quart pot, heat the olive oil over medium heat. Add the potatoes and cook, stirring occasionally with a wooden spoon, until lightly browned, about 5 minutes. Most likely, the potatoes will stick, but that is fine; adjust the level of heat to prevent the bits of potato that stick from getting too dark. Stir in the leeks, scallions, and bay leaves. Season them lightly with salt and pepper and cook, stirring, until the leeks are wilted, 2 to 3 minutes. Add the broth and peperoncino and bring to a boil, scraping up the bits of potato from the bottom. Adjust the level of heat to a simmer and season the soup again lightly with salt and pepper if needed. Simmer, uncovered, until the potatoes begin to fall apart, about 40 minutes. (The soup can be prepared to this point up to 2 days in advance and refrigerated. Bring the soup to a simmer before continuing.)

Stir the skate and rice into the soup and cook, stirring occasionally, for 8 minutes. Add the crabmeat and cook until the rice is tender, about 5 minutes.

Remove the bay leaves, then stir the parsley into the soup and check the seasoning. Serve in warm soup bowls.

Note: One untrimmed skate "wing" that weighs about 2 pounds should yield 1 pound of skate fillets. Make sure all skin, cartilage, and membranes are removed before cutting the skate into pieces.

¼ cup extra virgin olive oil

3 large baking (Idaho) potatoes, peeled and cut into ⅓-inch cubes

2 young leeks (about 1 pound), light green and white parts, well washed and finely chopped

4 scallions or 2 spring onions, green and white parts, finely chopped

4 fresh or dried bay leaves

Salt and freshly ground black pepper

4 quarts hot Vegetable Broth (page 81) or water

½ teaspoon peperoncino (crushed red pepper)

1 pound skate fillets, cut into 1-inch pieces (see Note)

½ cup long-grain rice

10 ounces Dungeness or Alaskan King crabmeat (from about 1¼ pounds crab in the shell), picked over for cartilage and shells

½ cup lightly packed chopped fresh Italian parsley leaves

Red Snapper and Rice Soup

Minestra di Red Snapper e Riso

In Italy this soup is usually made with *branzino,* a type of bass that is not available here. I make it with red snapper, which makes the soup tasty and light. At home, this *minestra* was often prepared for someone recuperating from an illness or with stomach complaints.

MAKES 8 SERVINGS

One 3-pound cleaned red snapper, filleted, gills removed, and head and frame reserved (see Note)

For the fish broth

4 quarts water

2 celery stalks, cut into 4-inch lengths

1 medium-size carrot, sliced

2 fresh or dried bay leaves

For the soup

¼ cup extra virgin olive oil

3 large baking (Idaho) potatoes, peeled and cut into ⅓-inch cubes

2 young leeks (about 1 pound), light green and white parts, well washed and finely chopped

4 scallions or 2 spring onions, green and white parts, finely chopped

4 fresh or dried bay leaves

Salt and freshly ground black pepper

½ teaspoon peperoncino (crushed red pepper)

2 cups peeled (page 141), seeded, and diced (¼-inch) ripe tomatoes

½ cup long-grain rice

½ cup lightly packed chopped fresh Italian parsley leaves

In a large pot, combine the fish head and frame with the water, celery, carrot, and bay leaves. Bring to a boil over high heat, then adjust the level of the heat to a simmer. Simmer, uncovered, for 1 hour, skimming the surface often. While the broth is simmering, cut the fillets into ½-inch pieces and refrigerate.

Strain the broth through a fine sieve or a sieve lined with cheesecloth. You should have about 3 quarts of broth; if not, add water as necessary.

In a deep, heavy 4- to 5-quart pot, heat the olive oil over medium heat. Add the potatoes and cook, stirring occasionally with a wooden spoon, until lightly browned, about 5 minutes. Most likely, the potatoes will stick, but that is fine; adjust the level of heat to prevent the bits of potato that stick from getting too dark. Stir in the leeks, scallions, and bay leaves, season them lightly with salt and pepper, and cook, stirring, until the leeks are wilted, 2 to 3 minutes. Add the fish stock and peperoncino and bring to a boil, scraping up the bits of potato from the bottom. Adjust the level of heat to a simmer and season again lightly with salt and pepper if needed. Simmer, uncovered, until the potatoes begin to fall apart, about 40 minutes. (The soup can be prepared to this point up to 2 days in advance and refrigerated. Bring the soup to a simmer before continuing.)

Stir the diced tomatoes and rice into the soup and cook, stirring occasionally, for 7 minutes. Add the pieces of red snapper fillets and continue simmering until the rice is tender, about another 5 minutes.

Remove the bay leaves. Stir the parsley into the soup, check the final seasoning, and serve in warm soup bowls.

Note: If you cannot buy a whole red snapper, you can substitute about 1 pound red snapper fillets or other flaky firm fish fillets cut into ½-inch cubes. Skip the first step of the recipe, omitting the ingredients for the fish broth, and substitute 3 quarts Vegetable Broth (page 81) for the fish broth.

Broccoli and Shrimp Soup

Minestra di Broccoli e Gamberi

I don't usually add cheese to seafood pasta and soup dishes, but in this *minestra* the flavor of good Pecorino Romano is complementary. Do not be concerned with the broccoli losing its bright green color; it really tastes better this way.

MAKES 8 SERVINGS

¼ cup extra virgin olive oil

3 large baking (Idaho) potatoes, peeled and cut into ⅓-inch cubes

2 young leeks (about 1 pound), light green and white parts, well washed and finely chopped

4 scallions or 2 spring onions, green and white parts, finely chopped

4 fresh or dried bay leaves

Salt and freshly ground black pepper

4 quarts hot Vegetable Broth (page 81) or water

½ teaspoon peperoncino (crushed red pepper)

1 bunch broccoli

½ cup long-grain rice

1 pound small shrimp (about 40), shelled and deveined

½ cup lightly packed chopped fresh Italian parsley leaves

¼ cup freshly grated Pecorino Romano cheese

In a deep, heavy 4- to 5-quart pot, heat the olive oil over medium heat. Add the potatoes and cook, stirring occasionally with a wooden spoon, until lightly browned, about 5 minutes. Most likely, the potatoes will stick, but that is fine; adjust the level of heat to prevent the bits of potato that stick from getting too dark. Stir in the leeks, scallions, and bay leaves. Season them lightly with salt and pepper and cook, stirring, until the leeks are wilted, 2 to 3 minutes. Add the broth and peperoncino and bring to a boil, scraping up the bits of potato from the bottom. Adjust the level of heat to a simmer and season the soup lightly with salt and pepper. Simmer, uncovered, until the potatoes begin to fall apart, about 40 minutes.

Meanwhile, prepare the broccoli. Trim off and discard the ends of the stalks and any large leaves. Cut off the tops and cut them into florets no larger than ½ inch. Peel the stalks and cut them into ½-inch cubes.

Add the broccoli to the soup and simmer for another 15 minutes. (The soup can be prepared to this point up to 2 days in advance and refrigerated. Bring the soup to a simmer before continuing.)

Stir in the rice and cook for 10 minutes, stirring occasionally. Add the shrimp, bring to a boil, and remove the pot from the heat.

Remove the bay leaves. Stir the parsley into the soup and check the seasoning. Serve in warm soup bowls, sprinkled with the grated cheese.

68   *Lidia's Italian Table*

Bread Soups

(Zuppe)

Traditionally, the word *zuppa* is used to describe a dense soup that may contain squashes, root vegetables, legumes, and potatoes but not, traditionally, any pasta or rice; its thick consistency comes from bread. The word *zuppa* derives from *soppa*—bread that has been saturated with a liquid—and dates from the Middle Ages. In those times, at the table of the rich families, a slice of bread would be set in front of each guest in lieu of a plate, and the meat would rest on the bread as it was eaten. The bread would absorb the juices of the meats and, after dinner, would be cooked in the water or stock in which the dinner meats had been cooked. This simple soup became the meal for the servants. Whatever legumes, vegetables, and tubers were available to the servants would be added to the soup. (Even the vegetables had a preferential categorization: The rich ate the vegetables that grew aboveground—the farther the vegetable was from the ground, the more desirable it was—while the poor were left to eat those that grew close to or under the ground.)

Whether bread is present or not in today's *zuppe*, its texture is always dense. After that basic distinction, the possibilities for making *zuppe* are endless.

Bread and soup seem to be an inseparable duo, so it is logical that bread added to and cooked in soup would turn into a complementary combination. The family of bread-thickened *zuppe,* sometimes called *panade,* is my favorite, and all of the *zuppe* included here call for bread in one form or another.

Making *zuppa* is an ideal opportunity to use up leftover bread. To me, respect for food is an essential part of cooking, and an essential part of life. I remember that as children, every time we dropped a piece of bread to the floor, we picked it up and kissed it. No food was wasted. When it came to even the humblest leftovers, what could be used would become part of the next meal. The rest would be given to the cat, dog, chickens, and hogs—to the courtyard animals, as we called them. We would even collect the crumbs from the table and give them to the birds.

Bread especially would be set aside to be reused. In the morning, we would have *caffè latte con pane,* pieces of stale bread added to a bowl of hot milk, coffee, and sugar. To this day, it is still an option for breakfast at our house, and my brother Franco's favorite breakfast. (Recipes that call for stale bread to make *gnocchi,* stuffing, and desserts can be found in those respective chapters.)

My grandfather Giovanni had another good use for stale bread; it was one of his favorite winter meals, known as *soppa de vin*. He would warm up hearty red wine, drizzle a little virgin olive oil into it, and add freshly milled black pepper and pieces of stale bread. With a piece of Pecorino Romano cheese on the side, it was supper.

Cheese Toasts

Pane Tostato al Formaggio

MAKES 6 TOASTS

Six ½-inch-thick slices day-old Italian
  bread, each large enough to cover the
  bottom of an individual soup crock
2 tablespoons unsalted butter, at room
  temperature
½ cup freshly grated Parmigiano-Reggiano
  cheese

Heat a large, heavy cast-iron or nonstick skillet over medium heat. Meanwhile, butter both sides of the bread slices, using all the butter. Press one side of each slice firmly into the grated cheese so the cheese coats the bread in a generous, even layer. Arrange the bread cheese side down in a single layer in the skillet and toast the bread until the cheese is golden brown and crispy, about 3 minutes; move the bread around the pan as necessary to toast the slices evenly. Turn the slices and toast the other side until golden brown, about another 3 minutes.

Toasted Bread in a Savory Broth

⚜ Zuppa di Brodo ⚜

This is one of the simplest *zuppa* recipes. For the stock, I prefer capon or free-range chicken stock, like the one on page 80. However, beef and vegetable stocks can also be used. You can use canned broth or bouillon if these are not available.

MAKES 6 SERVINGS

Prepare the cheese toasts and place one in the bottom of each of six deep soup crocks.

In a medium-size saucepan, bring the stock to a boil over high heat. Season to taste with salt and pepper. Ladle the stock over the bread in the crocks. Sprinkle with the parsley and grated cheese and serve immediately.

Cheese Toasts (page 70)

6 cups Chicken Stock (page 80), Meat Stock (page 78), or Vegetable Broth (page 81) or canned low-sodium chicken, beef, or vegetable broth

Salt and freshly ground black pepper

2 tablespoons chopped fresh Italian parsley leaves

½ cup freshly grated Parmigiano-Reggiano cheese

Pavese-Style Soup

🔯 Zuppa alla Pavese 🔯

Pavia is a city in Lombardy that boasts one of the best universities in Italy. Its culinary traditions include rice, frogs, goose, and *zuppa Pavese*. In the seventh century, Pavia was the capital of what was then Italy—or the Duchy of Lombardy.

MAKES 6 SERVINGS

Cheese Toasts (page 70)

10 cups Meat Stock (page 78) or Vegetable Broth (page 81) or canned low-sodium beef or vegetable broth

Salt and freshly ground black pepper

6 large eggs

2 tablespoons chopped fresh Italian parsley leaves

½ cup freshly grated Parmigiano-Reggiano cheese

Preheat the oven to 450°F. Prepare the cheese toasts. Place one toast in the bottom of each of six deep soup crocks and place the crocks on a baking sheet.

In a medium-size saucepan, bring the stock to a boil over high heat. Season with salt and pepper to taste. Meanwhile, break an egg over the toast in each crock, trying not to break the yolk.

Gently ladle the hot stock over the bread and eggs. Sprinkle the broth with the parsley and grated cheese. Bake until the eggs are cooked as you prefer—about 3 minutes for an egg with a solid white and a runny yolk, longer for a firmer yolk. Carefully transfer each crock to a small heatproof plate and serve at once.

Toasted Bread in
Savory Spinach Broth

Zuppa di Brodo con Spinaci

This dish is also very good when made with Swiss chard. Cook the chard a minute or two longer than you would spinach.

MAKES 6 SERVINGS

Remove the thick stems from the spinach and wash the leaves in cool water to remove all sand and grit, changing the water as necessary. Drain the spinach.

Stir the spinach a handful at a time into a large pot of boiling salted water and cook just until wilted and bright green, about 1 minute. Drain the spinach and immediately cool it under cold running water. Squeeze out the excess liquid and finely chop it.

Prepare the cheese toasts and place one toast in the bottom of each of six deep soup crocks.

1½ pounds fresh spinach, preferably flat-leaf
Cheese Toasts (page 70)
2 quarts Meat Stock (page 78) or Vegetable Broth (page 81) or canned low-sodium beef or vegetable broth
Salt and freshly ground black pepper
2 tablespoons chopped fresh Italian parsley leaves
½ cup freshly grated Parmigiano-Reggiano cheese

In a medium-size saucepan, bring the stock to a boil over high heat. Add the spinach and boil for 3 minutes. Season to taste with salt and pepper. Ladle the stock and spinach over the bread in the crocks, then sprinkle with the parsley and grated cheese and serve immediately.

Tomato and Bread Soup

⚇ Pappa al Pomodoro ⚇

For this dish, ripe, flavorful tomatoes are imperative. Therefore, make the soup when tomatoes are abundant and juicy and at their best—in late summer—or else with San Marzano or other good-quality canned tomatoes. This *zuppa* is delicious warm or served at room temperature on a hot summer day.

MAKES 8 SERVINGS

Five ½-inch-thick slices Italian bread, crusts
   removed
3 tablespoons extra virgin olive oil, plus
   more for serving
½ cup finely diced onions
6 garlic cloves, crushed
2 pounds ripe plum tomatoes, peeled
   (page 141), seeded, and cut into ½-inch
   dice, juices reserved, or one 35-ounce
   can Italian plum tomatoes, preferably
   San Marzano, seeded and cut into
   ½-inch dice, juices reserved
4 cups Chicken Stock (page 80) or canned
   low-sodium chicken broth
Salt and freshly ground black pepper
10 fresh basil leaves, washed and dried

Preheat the oven to 375°F. Arrange the bread slices on a baking sheet and toast until light golden brown, about 10 minutes. Remove and set aside.

In a deep, heavy 4- to 5-quart pot, heat the olive oil over medium heat. Add the onions and cook, stirring, until wilted, about 3 minutes. Add the garlic cloves and cook, stirring, until golden, about 6 minutes.

Add the tomatoes and their juices to the pot. Bring to a boil, stirring occasionally. Add the toasted bread and stock and return to a boil. Season lightly with salt and pepper, then add the basil leaves and adjust the level of heat to a simmer. Cook, uncovered, whisking occasionally to break up the pieces of bread, until the mixture is dense and silky, about 40 minutes.

If desired, remove the garlic cloves and basil leaves. Pass the soup through a fine sieve, forcing the solids through with a ladle. (If necessary, first pass the soup through a food mill fitted with the fine disc.) Correct the seasoning. Serve in warm bowls, drizzled with extra virgin olive oil.

Bread, Potato, and Arugula Soup

Zuppa di Patate, Rucola, e Pane

The ideal arugula to use for this soup is the tougher, wilder kind; the fragile hydroponic type is too delicate for this dish.

MAKES 8 SERVINGS

In a deep, heavy 4- to 5-quart pot, combine the potatoes and water. Salt the water lightly and bring to a boil. Adjust the level of heat to medium-high and cook the potatoes, covered, until they are tender but still hold their shape, about 18 minutes.

Meanwhile, cut off the thick stems from the arugula and wash the leaves in cool water to remove all sand and grit, changing the water if necessary. Drain the arugula well and cut it into 2-inch lengths.

Stir the arugula and bread into the pot and let boil for another 10 minutes.

Meanwhile, in a small skillet, heat the olive oil over low heat. Add the garlic cloves and peperoncino and cook, stirring, until the garlic is golden, about 3 minutes.

Scrape the contents of the skillet into the soup pot and stir well. If using a dried pepper, remove it. Season the soup with salt to taste and serve in warm bowls, sprinkled with the grated cheese.

¾ pound medium-size baking (Idaho) potatoes (about 2 potatoes), peeled and cut into ½-inch-thick slices
7 cups water
Salt
1 pound arugula (2 to 3 large bunches), preferably not hydroponic or "baby"
½ cup diced (½-inch) day-old Italian bread with crusts removed (see Note)
¼ cup extra virgin olive oil
6 garlic cloves, crushed
1 whole peperoncino (dried hot red pepper) or ½ teaspoon peperoncino (crushed red pepper)
½ cup freshly grated Pecorino Romano cheese

Note: If you prefer, you may toast the bread cubes according to the directions in step 3 for Fava Bean Puree with Dandelion Greens (page 26), using 2 teaspoons olive oil.

Clam Soup

Zuppa di Vongole

One of my favorite soups, this can be served as a soup course or, along with a glass of Tocai Friulano (a white, aromatic wine, indigenous to Friuli), as a main course. Who could ask for anything more?

MAKES 8 SERVINGS

¼ cup extra virgin olive oil

2 cups diced (¼-inch) day-old bread with crusts removed

3 cups diced (½-inch) small zucchini (about 2 zucchini)

Salt

2 quarts hot Vegetable Broth (page 81) or broth made from vegetable bouillon cubes

1 teaspoon peperoncino (crushed red pepper)

6 garlic cloves, crushed

1 cup chopped clams (about 18 littlenecks or 15 top necks), drained and liquor reserved

1 cup dry white wine, such as Pinot Grigio or Chardonnay

⅓ cup lightly packed chopped fresh Italian parsley leaves

Freshly ground black pepper

In a large, heavy skillet, heat 1½ teaspoons of the oil over medium heat. Add half the bread cubes and toast, stirring constantly, until golden brown on all sides, about 4 minutes. Transfer the toasted croutons to paper towels. Add another 1½ teaspoons of the oil to the pan and repeat with the remaining bread.

In a wide, deep pot, heat 2 tablespoons of the remaining olive oil over medium-high heat. Add the zucchini, season lightly with salt, and cook until golden, stirring occasionally, about 5 minutes. Add the hot broth and peperoncino and bring to a boil. Adjust the level of heat to medium, season lightly with salt, and simmer, uncovered, for 20 minutes.

Meanwhile, in a medium-size skillet, heat the remaining 1 tablespoon olive oil over medium heat. Add the garlic cloves and cook, stirring, until golden, about 2 minutes. Carefully add the chopped clams, stir, and then immediately add the wine and reserved clam juice. Bring to a vigorous boil and cook for 1 minute. Remove the garlic cloves, if desired, and scrape the contents of the skillet into the soup pot. Bring to a boil and cook for 2 minutes.

Stir the parsley and toasted croutons into the soup. Season with pepper and salt if necessary and serve immediately.

Stock and Broth
(Brodo)

Brodo (stock or broth) is a flavorful and nutritious liquid derived from slow-cooking meat, poultry, vegetables, or fish in water. The ingredients are humble—inexpensive cuts of meat, meat bones, vegetables, herbs, or trimmings left from preparing poultry or fish. *Brodo* is an essential element in cooking—whatever you cook, the need for broth will arise: It gives raw food time to cook without scorching or burning and imparts flavor and richness to a dish. Therefore, a properly prepared stock is important to the flavor of the finished dish.

In the context of an Italian meal, *brodo* means a soup made from this stock/broth to which a small amount of pasta, rice, or vegetables has been added. Occasionally, *brodo* is served clear—without anything added—in which case it is called *brodo schietto* (literally, "straightforward broth"). In the Italian tradition, a good *brodo* is welcome at the beginning of any meal, but especially a festive meal, where it follows the antipasto. A type of poultry broth made of capon—*brodo di capone*—is often served with filled pasta such as cappelletti or any *pastina* (little pasta), such as ancini or stelline, for these special occasions. *Brodo di carne mista* can be made into a complete meal as well, by using the meat from the *brodo,* either in salads or served with salt and grated fresh horseradish.

There are many ways to prepare a *brodo,* but I will share with you three: *brodo di carne mista* (broth of mixed meats), *brodo di pollo* (poultry broth), and *brodo di verdure* (vegetable broth). Also, a simple method for preparing a *brodo* made with fish—called court bouillon or *fumetto*—can be found in the recipe for Red Snapper and Rice Soup on page 66.

As you can see from the following recipes, the technique is basically the same for preparing any *brodo:* The ingredients are combined with water and brought to a boil. After an initial boiling, the level of heat is reduced and the *brodo* simmers from 1 hour (for vegetable and fish broths) to 3 hours (for meat and poultry broths.) Throughout the cooking, but especially at the beginning, it is important to skim the foam and fat from the surface of the broth regularly to ensure that the finished broth is clear. When you become comfortable with the recipes and techniques included here, I am sure you will want to devise ones of your own, mixing and matching meats, poultry, vegetables, and seasonings.

A pot of *brodo* takes a little work to assemble, but once that's done and it is left to simmer, you will find a *brodo* that is unfussed with will yield the best results. Always remember: Add salt to the *brodo* after it has finished cooking, since the *brodo* will reduce as it cooks and any saltiness will concentrate in the process.

I prefer to use these homemade broths in cooking, but most frozen or canned broths, or broth made from bouillon cubes, are perfectly fine to use. Before cooking with these store-bought products, taste them for intensity of flavor and saltiness and take a look at their color. Always keep in mind that any dish is the sum of its parts and if you use a weaker, less flavorful broth you may want to increase some of the other seasonings. (Salt is the exception—many canned broths and bouillon cubes are very salty—and you should add additional salt carefully, if at all.) If you cook with an intensely flavored homemade stock, however, your finished dish will be richer, with more character.

Meat Stock

Brodo di Carne Mista

I recall as a child that fat in *brodo* was actually sought after, especially if it came from the marrow of the bones. I would hear my family exclaim, *"O quanti oci ga sto brodo"* in dialect, or, "Wow! Look at the eyes in this broth." The eyes were the rounds of fat floating on the surface of the *brodo*, then much appreciated, now removed.

There are two ways to go about making a meat stock: If you start cooking the bones and meat in cold water and cook them for four hours or so, you will have a rich stock and bland meat because the liquid has extracted most of the flavor from the meat. If you would like to serve the meat used to make the stock as a meal, then start the stock by adding the meat to the hot water and cook it a little less, which will seal more of the flavor in the meat. Broth made this way will be a little less rich, but still delicious enough to use in any of the recipes in this chapter.

Charring the onion before adding it to the stock softens its flavor and cuts the acidity it will add to the stock. It also adds complexity of flavor to the finished product.

MAKES 4 QUARTS

1 pound beef short ribs

1 pound meaty veal shank

1 pound chicken necks, wings, and backs

5 quarts water

1 large onion, loose outer layers removed and cut in half

3 cups 1-inch-thick carrot slices

3 celery stalks, each cut into 4 pieces

6 garlic cloves, peeled

6 sprigs fresh Italian parsley

6 black peppercorns

Salt

Wash the beef, veal, and chicken under cold running water and drain them well. If you plan to serve the cooked veal and beef, bring the water to a boil in a large (at least 10-quart) stockpot over high heat before adding the meat. If you plan to make a richer stock and discard the meat after making the stock, add the meat to the cold water in the pot and bring to a boil over high heat. Adjust the level of heat to medium-low and continue simmering for 1 hour, occasionally skimming any foam and fat off the surface.

Meanwhile, place the onion halves cut side down directly over an open flame or cut side up under a preheated broiler and cook until the cut surfaces are well browned, about 3 minutes. Move the onion halves with a pair of tongs as necessary to brown the onion evenly. (Alternatively, the onion can be browned cut side down in a heavy nonstick or seasoned skillet over medium heat.)

Add the onion and the remaining ingredients except the salt to the stockpot and continue cooking, skimming occasionally, until the liquid returns to a boil. Lower the heat until the liquid is "perking"—one or two large bubbles rising to the surface at a time. Cook, partially covered, for 2 hours if you plan to serve the meat, 3 hours if you plan to discard the meat. Add salt to taste.

Strain the broth through a colander lined with a dampened kitchen towel or cheesecloth. If you want to use the stock immediately, you can remove much of the liquid fat floating on the surface by lightly dragging a folded paper towel over the surface. However, it will be easier to degrease the stock if you have time to chill it completely in the refrigerator. The fat will rise to the surface and solidify and can be easily lifted off. The stock can be refrigerated for up to 4 days or frozen for up to 3 months. The stock will be easier to use if frozen in small (1- to 2-cup) containers. Once frozen, the stock can be removed from the containers and stored in resealable freezer bags, to be taken from the freezer as needed.

Chicken Stock

Brodo di Pollo

Free-range chickens, if you can find them, will make a superior stock. I also like the richness that turkey wings add to a chicken stock, so I use them all the time. You can accumulate the chicken parts you need for stock in a resealable bag or container in the freezer, or perhaps your butcher can sell you what you need. Be sure to remove the livers from the giblet bag before making stock—livers will add a bitter flavor.

MAKES 4 QUARTS

3 pounds chicken and/or capon wings, backs, necks, and giblets (not including the liver), preferably from free-range or organically raised birds

1 pound turkey wings

5 quarts water

1 large onion, loose outer layers removed and cut in half

3 cups 1-inch-thick carrot slices

3 celery stalks, each cut into 4 pieces

6 garlic cloves, peeled

6 sprigs fresh Italian parsley

6 black peppercorns

Salt

Wash the chicken parts and turkey wings thoroughly under cold running water and drain them well. Combine them with the water in a large (at least 10-quart) stockpot and bring to a boil over high heat. Adjust the level of heat to medium and continue boiling for 1 hour. Skim any foam and fat off the surface occasionally.

Meanwhile, place the onion halves cut side down directly over an open flame or cut side up under a preheated broiler and cook until the cut surfaces are well browned, about 3 minutes. Move the onion halves with a pair of tongs as necessary to brown the onion evenly. (Alternatively, the onion can be browned cut side down in a heavy nonstick or seasoned skillet over medium heat.)

Add the onion and the remaining ingredients except the salt to the stockpot and bring to a boil again, skimming occasionally. Lower the heat until the liquid is "perking"—one or two large bubbles rising to the surface at a time. Cook, partially covered, for 3 hours. Add salt to taste.

Strain the broth through a colander lined with a dampened kitchen towel or cheesecloth. If you want to use the stock immediately, you can remove much of the liquid fat floating on the surface by lightly dragging a folded paper towel over the surface. However, it will be easier to degrease the stock if you have time to chill it completely in the refrigerator. The fat will rise to the surface and solidify and can be easily lifted off. The stock can be refrigerated for up to 4 days or frozen for up to 3 months. The stock will be easier to use if frozen in small (1- to 2-cup) containers. Once frozen, the stock can be removed from the containers and stored in resealable freezer bags, to be taken from the freezer as needed.

Vegetable Broth

 Brodo di Verdure

Avoid red and dark green vegetables like beets, ruby chard, and kale in vegetable broth. Their color is too pronounced—you want a golden-green broth. Also stay away from strong-tasting vegetables like turnips. Fresh-tasting herbs like dill and fennel tops would make a welcome addition.

MAKES 1½ QUARTS

Combine all the ingredients except the salt in a large (at least 8-quart) stockpot. Bring slowly to a boil over medium heat, skimming off any foam that rises to the surface. Adjust the level of heat to a simmer and cook, partially covered, for 1 hour, skimming occasionally. Add salt to taste.

Strain the broth through a colander lined with a dampened kitchen towel or cheesecloth. The stock can be refrigerated for up to 4 days, or frozen for up to 3 months. The stock will be easier to use if frozen in small (1- to 2-cup) containers. Once frozen, the stock can be removed from the containers and stored in resealable freezer bags, to be taken from the freezer as needed.

4 quarts cold water

4 celery stalks with leaves, cut into large dice

6 medium-size carrots, coarsely chopped

2 medium-size onions, cut into quarters

6 sprigs fresh Italian parsley

2 medium-size leeks, white and green parts, well washed and sliced

2 fresh or dried bay leaves

6 black peppercorns

2 sprigs fresh thyme

Salt

Semolina Gnocchi in Mixed Meat Broth

Gnocchetti di Gries in Brodo

I loved these golden dumplings as a child, and I enjoy them no less now. Try them not only in soup, but also baked with cream and grated Parmigiano-Reggiano cheese or tossed with a light tomato sauce and fresh basil.

MAKES 6 SERVINGS (ABOUT 50 DUMPLINGS)

6 tablespoons (¾ stick) unsalted butter, at room temperature

2 large eggs, separated

1 cup semolina flour (available at Italian groceries or health food stores)

8 cups Meat Stock (page 78) or canned low-sodium beef broth

2 tablespoons chopped fresh Italian parsley leaves

Salt and freshly ground black pepper

½ cup freshly grated Parmigiano-Reggiano cheese

In a medium-size bowl, with an electric mixer at medium-high speed, beat the butter and egg yolks together until smooth. Continue beating while adding the semolina slowly. If the mixture becomes too thick to beat with the mixer, fold in the remaining semolina with a rubber spatula.

In a small bowl, beat the egg whites with a wire whisk or electric mixer at high speed until they hold stiff peaks when you lift up the whisk or beaters. With a rubber spatula, fold one third of the beaten whites into the semolina mixture to loosen the mixture slightly, then fold in the remaining whites thoroughly.

In a small saucepan, bring 2 cups of the stock to a boil over high heat. Adjust the level of heat to maintain the broth at a gentle boil. Dip two espresso spoons into cold water and use them to shape the semolina mixture into small oval dumplings. Scrape the gnocchi onto a small plate as you form them, and dip the spoons in water before making each dumpling. When you have made about six gnocchi, slide them into the boiling broth and cook until they rise to the surface, about 3 minutes. Continue boiling until they are cooked through—pale yellow throughout, with no trace of darker yellow in the center—about another 3 minutes. Remove with a slotted spoon and set on a plate. Continue forming gnocchi and poaching them until all are finished.

To serve, bring the remaining stock to a boil. (You can strain the gnocchi cooking broth into the remaining broth if you like.) Slip the cooked gnocchi into the broth and add the parsley. Season the broth with salt and pepper to taste. Ladle the broth and gnocchi into soup bowls or a tureen, sprinkle with the grated cheese, and serve.

Note: The gnocchi can be frozen before cooking. Shape them as described above, scraping them onto a plastic wrap–lined baking sheet as you form them. Place the baking sheet in the freezer and when the gnocchi are frozen solid, transfer them to a resealable plastic bag. They can be stored in the freezer for up to 4 weeks. Cook them as needed, directly from the freezer. Frozen gnocchi will take a little longer to cook than freshly made ones; they will rise to the surface of the boiling broth in about 2 minutes and will be cooked through after about 8 minutes more.

Tagliolini in Vegetable Broth
Tagliolini in Brodo di Verdure

Whenever I make fresh pasta, I always make a little bit of tagliolini, cut even finer than usual, for *brodo*. I put it in the freezer and have it on hand, ready to go.

MAKES 6 SERVINGS

6 cups Vegetable Broth (page 81)
¼ recipe Basic Egg Pasta Dough (page 89), cut into very thin tagliolini as described on page 92
2 cups shredded spinach leaves
½ cup freshly grated Parmigiano-Reggiano cheese
Salt and freshly ground black pepper

In a large saucepan, bring the broth to a boil over high heat. Shake any flour from the tagliolini and add the pasta to the boiling broth. Stir well to separate the strands of pasta and stir in the spinach. Boil until the pasta is al dente—tender but firm—3 to 4 minutes, or slightly longer for pasta taken directly from the freezer.

Remove from the heat and stir in the grated cheese. Add salt, if necessary, and pepper to taste. Serve immediately in warm bowls.

Fresh Pasta

Pasta Fresca

Not one Sunday would pass without my making fresh pasta during '*i miei spensierati giorni di giventu*' (my carefree days of childhood). Helping to make pasta was one commitment that I had to keep, but I didn't mind—getting my hands in the warm dough felt so special.

For pasta making, the flour had to be milled fresh, and by March the seedlings of wheat for that flour were already sprouting. By May or early June, the cherries were ripe and the wheat almost as high as I was at eight years of age. I remember a wonderful cherry tree that we had on the border of the wheat field, and my friend Silva and I would climb the tree—

unintentionally trampling the wheat around it—to reach the cherries. First we ate our fill, and then we sang and swayed on the branches like birds. I still recall the flavor of those big cherries—as I opened my mouth, the fresh air would fill it, and the flavors would intensify, filling my every sense. We collected clusters of cherries with stems and decorated ourselves, hanging them over our ears like big earrings. We felt beautiful.

From the cherry tree, I could see the whole wheat field, silvery green with polka dots of vibrant red poppies that swayed in the wind. I could usually also see my grandfather coming down the road to shoo us away and determine how much damage we had done to his field. By the end of June, the fields were golden and the wheat was ready to harvest. When my grandmother needed another batch of flour for the pasta, she would carry the golden kernels of wheat in burlap bags to be ground in the communal mill.

Pasta fresca—fresh pasta—has been a kitchen staple since the time of the Greeks and Romans. *Laganon* (strips of dough), a Greek word, is the source of *lagnum,* the Latin name for lasagne, which was a mainstay of the Romans. Milled grains mixed with water and called *pultes* (mush) would be cooked until thick, spread out to dry, then cut into lozenges. These *lagnum* were used in soups, or boiled and seasoned with oil, honey, and pepper. By the Middle Ages, the preparation technique evolved from cooking the mush to today's familiar kneading, shaping, and cutting of the dough.

Fresh pasta may vary in color from deep yellow to pale golden, depending on the amount of eggs and the flour used. Uncooked, it should be dry enough to be rolled, cut, and shaped easily; cooked, it should be silken, soft, and tender but resilient to the bite, what's called *al dente,* literally, "to the tooth."

The four basic types of fresh pasta are: *pasta fresca all'uovo* (egg pasta), *pasta di semolina* (semolina pasta), *pasta ai sapori* (flavored pasta), and *pasta ripiena* (stuffed pasta).

Although basic egg pasta is made only of unbleached flour, egg, salt, and oil, there is a saying in Reggio Emilia—the home of egg pasta—that the ingredients constitute only a small portion of the pasta's quality: The rest is the soul, the energy, and the transmission of flavor from the hands of the cook.

The following are but a few of the many different forms that egg pasta may take:

- Tagliatelle, fettuccine, taglieri, and pappardelle are all ribbon-like strips of pasta, each of a different width.

- *Maccheroni alla chitarra* is a traditional fresh pasta from Abruzzo that is cut on a stringed wood utensil called a *chitarra* (guitar) and looks like square spaghetti.

- *Pinci,* from Montalcino, are strands of fresh pasta worked by rolling the dough between the palms of the hands until it is about ⅛ inch thick and long like spaghetti.

- All the sheet pastas for lasagne, cannelloni, ravioli, and other filled pasta are also made from egg pasta.

For flavored pastas, pureed vegetables and/or herbs are added to egg pasta dough while the dough is kneaded. The flavorings can range from spinach, beets, artichokes, olives, asparagus, and cuttlefish ink to chocolate and wine—the list is endless—and the pasta can be made in many shapes.

Pasta ripiena, stuffed pasta, is widely made throughout Northern Italy, but it is certain that cappelletti and tortellini (both hat-shaped stuffed pastas) were invented in Emilia-Romagna, and agnolotti, a similarly shaped pasta, is indisputably Piedmontese. The basic dough for *pasta ripiena* is egg pasta, but in some cases a flavored dough is used. The fillings can contain meat, as in tortellini, cappelletti, and agnolotti, or meat and vegetables, as in *ofelle triestine,* a potato dough stuffed with meat, spinach or Swiss chard, and cheese. A vegetable filling, or *ripieno di magro* (literally, "lean stuffing"), can include all kinds of leafy green vegetables or perhaps garden herbs with eggs and ricotta and grated Parmigiano-Reggiano cheese. Around Mantova, there is a pumpkin-filled *raviolo*, and a few kilometers away in Cremona a version of the same, made with the addition of crushed macaroons, raisins, and candied citron—but still eaten as a pasta course. Then there is the coastal region, which uses seafood to fill pasta, as in the *ravioli di magro* made in Liguria which contains local fish plus wild and garden herbs, including nettle and fennel.

There is also a type of fresh pasta made from semolina (durum wheat) flour mixed with unbleached flour, water, and salt. It is the pasta dough commonly used in the southern part of Italy to make pasta shapes like orecchiette (earlobe-like shapes), which are a specialty of Puglia, and *malloreddus,* little gnocchi-like shapes made by pressing a thumbnail-size piece of semolina pasta dough against a *ciulirri,* a utensil that looks like the bottom of a Chinese steamer basket. *Cavatieddi*, also from Puglia, are pieces of semolina dough, also the size of a thumbnail, pressed out with the tip of a butter knife so that the dough rolls around the knife to make a seashell shape.

Flours for Making Fresh Pasta

All flour is composed mostly of starch (65 to 70 percent) and gluten-forming proteins (9 to 14 percent); gluten is formed once a liquid is added to the flour and the mixture is agitated. It is the amount of each of these two components in different flours that dictates the best use of that flour. Generally speaking, the higher a flour's gluten-forming protein content—and therefore the lower its starch content—the greater durability and structure the finished product will have. Pastry flours are low in protein and will produce tender and flaky results, while bread flour, with around 12.5 percent protein, will produce chewy, crusty loaves of bread.

I use two types of flour to make pasta at home: semolina flour and unbleached all-purpose flour. Semolina flour is a coarse-milled flour made from durum wheat, the hardest wheat grown. ("Hard" is another way to say the flour has a higher ratio of protein to starch.) Unbleached all-purpose flour is softer, with a higher starch content, and usually is produced by blending flours milled from different types of wheat.

All-purpose flour is mixed with eggs and oil to make *pasta all'uovo* (egg pasta)—the tender but resilient pasta that is rolled very thin and cut into noodles or shapes. It is usually cooked while freshly made and still soft, as it tends to become brittle and crack easily when dried.

Semolina flour is rarely, if ever, used alone to make pasta in the home. But it is used commercially—the best dried pastas are made from 100 percent semolina flour. I use a combination of semolina and all-purpose flours to make fresh semolina pasta. When kneaded well, the dough is elastic, silky, and durable, and it dries well—any of the sturdy pasta shapes made from semolina pasta dough in this chapter can be cooked when freshly made or completely dried.

The best way to learn the difference between these flours is to prepare both *pasta all'uovo* and semolina pasta. You will feel the difference between the doughs when you knead and shape them, and when you bite into them, you will experience the difference in texture and flavor. After making each once or twice, feel free to experiment with the proportion of flour given in the recipes. It is the understanding of these basic products that promotes success and versatility in the kitchen.

How to Cook Fresh Pasta

To cook fresh pasta for six, bring 6 quarts of salted water (about 2 tablespoons salt) to a rapid boil in a large pot—pasta should have enough space to turn comfortably in the pot when you stir it. Shake the pasta lightly in a colander to remove any excess flour. Drop the pasta into the boiling water a handful at a time. Immediately stir with a fork or wooden spoon after the addition of each handful, separating any pieces that stick together. When the pasta rises to the top of the water after it has returned to a full boil, it is done. (Semolina pasta that has been fully dried at room temperature, however, may require additional cooking time—up to 10 minutes after the water returns to a boil.) Watch carefully to avoid overcooking.

Drain the pasta gently, lowering the pot as close as possible to the colander. Shake the colander gently to remove excess water and return the pasta to the pot before adding sauce and cheese.

Stuffed pasta should not be drained in a colander, but rather lifted from the boiling water with a slotted spoon or a skimmer. Shake the spoon gently to remove water before transferring the pasta to serving bowls or a skillet containing the sauce.

Approximate Cooking Times for Fresh Pasta

- *Basic egg pasta:* 3 to 5 minutes, depending on whether or how long the pasta was dried before cooking

- *Stuffed pasta:* 6 to 8 minutes for freshly made pasta; slightly longer for pasta that has been refrigerated; up to 12 minutes for pasta cooked directly from the freezer

- *Semolina pasta:* 8 to 10 minutes for freshly made pasta; up to 16 minutes for fully dried pasta

Basic Egg Pasta Dough

Pasta all'Uovo

The ingredients for fresh egg pasta are simple. Figure one egg per person, and about half to two thirds of a cup of flour per egg. A little salt, olive oil, and possibly water are the only other things needed.

The kneading of the dough is what ultimately determines the texture of the pasta. Food processors and dough mixers do a great job of forming a dough from the raw ingredients, but I always like to finish kneading it by hand. I like the feel of the dough in my hands, and I can tell by touch when it feels right. You, too, can develop this touch—when the dough feels silky, rolls smoothly, and has a subtle sheen, it is ready. It will take some practice to develop this feel, but once you have it, it is yours to keep.

The way I knead pasta dough is probably different from other methods you may have read about or tried. My grandmother always did it this way, and I continue the tradition. By using different parts of my hands to knead the dough, and different ways to work the dough, I distribute the task of kneading evenly. It also helps me to tell when the dough is ready.

MAKES 6 SERVINGS

To mix the dough by hand: On a marble or wooden work surface, pile the flour into a mound. Make a well in the center of the mound that goes all the way down to the work surface. In a small bowl, beat the eggs, salt, and olive oil together with a fork until blended, then add them to the well. Continue beating the egg mixture with the fork, gradually working the flour from the sides of the well into the egg mixture. As you work, the egg mixture will become thicker and the size of the well will expand. Continue beating until there is just a thin ring of flour around the egg mixture and the dough becomes too stiff to mix with a fork. If the dough becomes too thick to mix with a fork before almost all of the flour is incorporated, drizzle a tiny amount of the warm water over the egg mixture and continue mixing. It is possible you will not need any water at all.

4 cups unbleached all-purpose flour
6 large eggs
½ teaspoon salt
½ teaspoon extra virgin olive oil
Warm water as needed

Work the remaining flour into the dough with your hands just until a rough, firm dough is formed. Rub your hands together to remove as much dough as possible and add that to the rest of the dough. Shape the dough into a rough ball and set it aside.

Sprinkle your hands liberally with flour, rubbing them together to remove any remaining scraps of dough from your skin. With a knife, loosen any dough and flour from the work surface. Pass these scrapings through a sieve so you can reuse the flour and discard the scraps in the sieve. Make sure your hands are clean and flour them lightly.

To mix the dough in an electric mixer: Place all but ⅓ cup of the flour in the mixing bowl of a heavy-duty electric mixer fitted with the dough hook. In a small bowl, beat the eggs, salt, and olive oil together until blended. With the mixer on low speed, pour the egg mixture into the mixing bowl. Knead just until the mixture comes together to form a rough dough. If necessary, drizzle a very small amount of warm water into the bowl. Remove the dough from the bowl and knead, using the remaining flour, and more if necessary, as described below.

To mix the dough in a food processor: Place all but ⅓ cup of the flour in the work bowl of a large-capacity food processor fitted with the metal blade. In a small bowl, beat the eggs, salt, and olive oil together until blended. With the motor running, pour the egg mixture into the feed tube and mix until the mixture forms a stiff dough. If necessary, drizzle a very small amount of warm water into the feed tube. Remove the dough from the machine and knead, using the remaining flour, and more if necessary, as described below.

To knead the dough: Once you have formed a rough dough, it is ready to knead. Flour a marble or wooden work surface. (For effective kneading by hand, the surface should be hip-high; this will allow you to put your body weight into the kneading motion.) Press the heel of one hand deep into the dough, keeping your fingers high. Then press down on the dough while pushing it firmly away from you—the dough will stretch and roll under your hand like a large shell. Turn the dough over, then press into the dough, first with the knuckles of one hand, then with the other; do this about ten times with the knuckles of each hand. Use the knuckles of your forefingers especially during this process. Then repeat the stretching and "knuckling" process, using more flour if needed to prevent sticking, until the dough is smooth and silky, 10 to 20 minutes. Roll the dough into a smooth ball.

Place the dough in a small bowl and cover with plastic wrap. Let the dough rest for at least 1 hour at room temperature, or up to 1 day in the refrigerator, before rolling and shaping the pasta. If the dough has been refrigerated, let it stand at room temperature for at least 1 hour before rolling and shaping.

Rolling Egg Pasta Dough

"Nervous" dough: Sometimes the dough will feel tight and actually fight back and shrink when you roll it. I call this "nervous" dough, and it can be caused by a number of things: inadequate kneading of the dough, stale flour, or using water that is too hot. Try kneading the dough for an additional 5 minutes and letting it rest for an extra 30 minutes wrapped in plastic wrap before trying again.

To roll the dough out by hand: Cut the rested dough into four equal pieces. Work with one piece of dough at a time and keep the others covered with a kitchen towel. Roll the pasta out on a lightly floured work surface until it is very thin (about 1/16 inch) and forms a rectangle approximately 10 × 20 inches. Use just enough flour to prevent the dough from sticking; too much flour will make the dough dry and difficult to roll. If you find that the dough is very elastic and difficult to roll, let it rest under a kitchen towel for 10 to 15 minutes. Start rolling another piece of dough and come back to the first one once it has had a chance to rest. Let the pasta sheets rest, separated by kitchen towels, for at least 15 minutes before cutting them.

To roll the dough out with a manual pasta machine: Cut the dough into six equal pieces. Shape each into a rectangle about 5 × 3 inches. Lightly flour the pasta rectangles and cover them with a kitchen towel. Set the rollers of the pasta machine to the widest setting. Pass one of the pasta rectangles through the rollers long side first, then pass it through the rollers a second time. Repeat with the remaining pieces of dough. Keep the dough lightly floured—just enough to prevent it from sticking to the rollers. Reduce the width by one setting and pass each piece of dough through the rollers two times. Support the dough with your hand as it comes through the rollers—don't pull it through, or the dough will shrink so it is narrower than the width of the rollers. Continue working with the pieces of dough in the same order and reducing the width by one setting each time until all the pieces of dough have been passed through the next-to-thinnest setting on the pasta machine; the pasta sheets should be about 5½ × 30 inches. Always keep the pieces of dough that aren't being rolled covered with a towel. If you find that the dough is very elastic, let all the pieces rest for 5 to 10 minutes before continuing. Once all the pasta has been rolled into sheets, let them rest, completely covered with towels, for about 15 minutes before cutting them.

Cutting Egg Pasta Dough

For papardelle: Cut the pasta sheets lengthwise into 1½-inch-wide strips. (The machine-rolled pasta sheets will be easier to work with if you first cut them in half crosswise to make two pieces, each about 15 × 5 inches.) Flour them lightly and stack four of the 1½-inch-wide strips. Cut the stack crosswise into 5-inch lengths. You will have wide ribbons of pasta, each about 5 × 1½ inches. Set the ribbons on a clean kitchen towel dusted with flour until ready to cook.

For malfatti: Proceed as above but cut the stacks of ribbon pasta diagonally at 1½-inch intervals to form rhomboid shapes. Toss the malfatti lightly with flour and set them apart on a clean kitchen towel dusted with flour.

For garganelli: Cut malfatti as described above and keep them covered with a towel. Lightly flour a chopstick or a similarly shaped short and narrow wooden dowel. Place one of the malfatti on the work surface in front of you with one of the shorter points facing you. Place the chopstick over the point nearest you and roll the dough around the chopstick to form a pointed cylinder. Press the seam to seal it and slide the cylinder off the chopstick. Set on a floured kitchen towel and continue until all are finished, spacing the cylinders on the towel so they aren't touching.

Both malfatti and garganelli can be frozen. Arrange them in a single layer on floured baking sheets and set the sheets in the freezer until the pasta is completely frozen. When frozen, transfer them to resealable freezer bags, dividing them into portions, if you like. They will keep for 4 to 6 weeks. To cook frozen malfatti and garganelli, take them directly from the freezer to boiling water; defrosting them first will make them stick to one another.

For tagliatelle: Cut the sheets of pasta into 10-inch lengths. Flour the sheets lightly and roll them up from a short end, as you would a jelly roll. With a knife, cut the rolls into ½-inch-wide strips. Unroll the strips and toss them lightly to separate them. Set on a clean kitchen towel dusted with flour.

For tagliolini: Proceed as for tagliatelle, cutting the pasta rolls into ¼-inch-wide strips.

To freeze tagliatelle, tagliolini, and other "ribbon" shapes made from egg pasta, toss a handful of the pasta with flour or coarse cornmeal, then form the strands into a *nido* (nest). Arrange the nests on a baking sheet and place in the freezer until solid. Transfer the pasta to resealable freezer bags and store in the freezer for up to 6 weeks.

There is plenty of room for flexibility between the time fresh pasta dough is made and when the final product is cooked. The dough can be refrigerated, wrapped in plastic wrap, for up to 3 days before rolling and cutting it. (With the exception of stuffed pasta shapes, which can be refrigerated briefly, I don't recommend refrigerating fresh pasta once it has been cut into shapes—the dough will become soft and stick together.)

Once the dough is cut and rolled, it can be cooked immediately or dried completely in a well-ventilated area (preferably on a low-humidity day) before cooking. It can also be cooked at any point in between. The longer fresh pasta is dried before cooking, the more time it will take to cook (see How to Cook Fresh Pasta, page 88). It is up to the cook to decide how long fresh pasta should dry—it is a matter of convenience and taste.

Tagliolini with Herb Pesto

Tagliolini con Pesto d'Erbe

MAKES 6 SERVINGS

Prepare the tagliolini.

Bring the salted water to a boil in a large pot.

Meanwhile, in a large skillet, bring the chicken stock and butter to a boil. Add the herb pesto and salt and pepper to taste and remove from the heat.

Cook the tagliolini according to the directions on page 88. Drain the pasta and return it to the pot over low heat. Add the sauce and toss well until the pasta is evenly coated. Remove the pot from the heat and sprinkle with the grated cheese. Toss well, transfer to a warm platter or individual bowls, and serve immediately.

Tagliolini made from 1 recipe Basic Egg
   Pasta Dough (page 89)
6 quarts salted water
1½ cups Chicken Stock (page 80), canned
   low-sodium chicken broth, or pasta
   cooking water
2 tablespoons unsalted butter
6 tablespoons Herb Pesto (page 146)
Salt and freshly ground black pepper
1 cup freshly grated Pecorino Romano
   cheese

Tagliatelle with Porcini Mushroom Sauce

▣ Tagliatelle con Salsa di Funghi ▣

At our restaurant Felidia, this is one of our customers' favorite pasta dishes. People love mushrooms, especially in a rich-tasting sauce over fresh pasta. Mushrooms give pasta sauce a tremendous complexity of flavor, yet the dish remains light.

MAKES 6 SERVINGS

Tagliatelle made from 1 recipe Basic Egg
   Pasta Dough (page 89)
6 quarts salted water
3 tablespoons extra virgin olive oil
4 garlic cloves, lightly crushed
1½ pounds fresh porcini mushrooms, wiped
   clean, trimmed, and sliced (see Note)
1 cup Chicken Stock (page 80) or canned
   low-sodium chicken broth
3 tablespoons unsalted butter
Salt and freshly ground black pepper
3 tablespoons chopped fresh Italian parsley
   leaves
½ cup freshly grated Parmigiano-Reggiano
   cheese

Prepare the tagliatelle.

Bring the salted water to a boil in a large pot.

In a large skillet, heat the oil over medium heat. Add the garlic and cook, stirring, until golden brown, about 2 minutes. Add about half the mushrooms and toss them in the hot oil. Add the remaining mushrooms in batches as the mushrooms in the pan wilt. Cook, stirring occasionally, until the mushroom liquid has evaporated, about 10 minutes. Add the chicken stock and butter and bring to a simmer. Simmer until the butter is incorporated into the sauce, about 3 minutes. Add salt and pepper to taste.

Meanwhile, cook the tagliatelle according to the directions on page 88. Drain well and return to the pot over low heat.

Add the sauce and parsley to the pasta and toss gently until the pasta is evenly coated. Remove from the heat, add half of the grated cheese, and toss well. Transfer the pasta to a serving platter or individual bowls and serve immediately, passing the remaining cheese at the table.

Note: Other wild or exotic mushrooms such as morels, shiitakes, chanterelles, or any mix of mushrooms can be substituted for all or part of the porcini. (See Note on page 63 for cleaning and preparation instructions.) Frozen porcini are sometimes available and can be substituted for the fresh; they will be easier to slice if still partially frozen.

Malfatti with Shellfish

▣ Malfatti con Frutti di Mare ▣

Malfatti translates as "ill-made" or "ill-cut," meaning there are no rigid guidelines for cutting the pasta. Most of the regions of Italy have some form of malfatti. They are used for pasta recipes as well as in soups.

MAKES 6 SERVINGS

Prepare the malfatti.

Scrub the clam shells under cold running water to remove sand, especially from the crevices. Rinse the clams well and drain them. Discard any with open or broken shells. Refrigerate until ready to cook.

In a medium-size nonreactive skillet, heat 2 tablespoons of the oil over medium heat. Add the garlic cloves and cook, stirring, until lightly browned, about 2 minutes. Add the marinara sauce and peperoncino and bring to a boil, then reduce the level of heat to a simmer and cook until the sauce has thickened, stirring occasionally, about 20 minutes. Remove from the heat and discard the garlic.

Bring the salted water to a boil in a large pot. Meanwhile, place the clams in a medium-size saucepan with ½ inch of water. Cover and steam over medium-high heat, shaking the pan occasionally, until the clams open, 4 to 6 minutes. Discard any that do not open. Remove the clams from the shells and chop them. Strain the clam cooking liquid through a coffee filter or cheesecloth-lined sieve, add the chopped clams to it, and set aside.

> Malfatti made from 1 recipe Basic Egg Pasta Dough (page 89)
> 18 littleneck or other small hard-shell clams
> ¼ cup extra virgin olive oil
> 6 garlic cloves, crushed
> 2 cups Marinara Sauce (page 143)
> 1 teaspoon peperoncino (crushed red pepper)
> 6 quarts salted water
> 1 pound medium-size shrimp (about 30), peeled and deveined
> ½ pound sea scallops, quartered
> 1 tablespoon chopped fresh Italian parsley leaves

In a large nonreactive skillet, heat the remaining 2 tablespoons oil over high heat. Add the shrimp and scallops and sauté until the shrimp are bright pink, about 2 minutes. Add the chopped clams with their liquid and the marinara sauce. Bring to a boil, reduce the level of heat to a simmer, and cook until the sauce is slightly reduced, about 3 minutes. Stir in the parsley.

While the sauce is cooking, cook the malfatti according to the directions on page 88. Drain the pasta well and return it to the pot over low heat.

Add half the sauce to the pasta and toss until the pasta is evenly coated. Transfer the pasta to a warm platter or individual bowls, top with the remaining sauce, and serve immediately.

Guazzetto

The sauces for the next three pasta recipes are all prepared using the same cooking technique—*guazzetto*. *Guazzetto* is a slow simmering of meats with stock, tomato, and lots of seasoning. Whatever is prepared *in guazzetto*, the result is always tender, flavorful meat in a velvety sauce that coats pasta wonderfully. Once you have mastered the technique by cooking these recipes, try substituting different meats, game, and birds of your choice for the ones called for here. It would make me very happy to know that you have made this technique your own.

Garganelli with Pheasant in Guazzetto
Garganelli con Fagiano in Guazzetto

MAKES 6 SERVINGS

Garganelli made from 1 recipe Basic Egg
    Pasta Dough (page 89)
½ cup dried porcini mushrooms
    (about ½ ounce)
2 cups warm water
4 cloves
2 fresh or dried bay leaves
1 sprig fresh rosemary or 1 teaspoon dried
    rosemary
¼ cup extra virgin olive oil
One 2½-pound pheasant, cut into 6 pieces
    (see Note)
Salt and freshly ground black pepper
3 medium-size onions, chopped
⅓ cup finely chopped pancetta or bacon
    (about 1½ ounces)
½ cup chicken livers (about 4 ounces),
    trimmed of membranes and finely
    chopped

Prepare the garganelli.

Soak the porcini in the warm water until softened, about 30 minutes. Drain them, reserving the liquid. Rinse the mushrooms and coarsely chop them, discarding any tough bits. Strain the soaking liquid through a coffee filter or sieve lined with paper towels. Set the liquid and chopped mushrooms aside.

Tie the cloves, bay leaves, and rosemary securely in a small square of cheesecloth.

In a large nonreactive casserole, heat the oil over high heat. Add the pheasant pieces and sprinkle lightly with salt and pepper. Reduce the level of heat to medium-high and cook, turning often to prevent sticking, until lightly browned, about 10 minutes. Remove the pheasant pieces.

Pour off all but 2 tablespoons of the fat from the pot. Add the onions and pancetta to the casserole, season them lightly with salt and pepper, and cook until golden, about 5 minutes. Add the chicken livers and cook, stirring as necessary, until browned, about 4 minutes; adjust the level of heat if necessary so the livers brown without the drippings/browned bits in the pot burning. Add the chopped porcini and cook, stirring, until they are dry, about 5 minutes.

Add the wine and cook, stirring, until nearly evaporated, about 4 minutes. Stir in the tomato paste until the vegetables are coated. Add the reserved porcini liquid and about ½ cup of the chicken stock and bring to a boil.

1 cup dry white wine

3 tablespoons plus 2 teaspoons tomato paste

3 cups Chicken Stock (page 80) or canned low-sodium chicken broth

6 quarts salted water

½ cup freshly grated Parmigiano-Reggiano cheese, plus more for serving

Return the pheasant pieces to the pot and tuck the cheesecloth packet into the liquid. Adjust the level of heat to a simmer. Partially cover the casserole and simmer gently until the liquid is reduced by about half, about 15 minutes. Add another ½ cup stock and continue simmering, adding chicken stock ½ cup at a time and waiting until the liquid is reduced by half before adding more, until the pheasant is tender and the liquid is velvety, about 1 hour longer. Remove and discard the cheesecloth packet. (The pheasant sauce can be made up to 2 days ahead and refrigerated, covered.)

Remove the pheasant pieces from the liquid and skim the fat from the surface of the sauce. (It will be easier to remove the fat if the sauce has been refrigerated.) Pull all the meat from the bones. Discard the skin and bones. Coarsely shred the meat and return it to the sauce. Reheat the sauce to a simmer. Taste the sauce, adding salt and pepper if necessary.

Meanwhile, bring the salted water to a boil in a large pot.

Cook the garganelli according to the directions on page 88. Drain the garganelli and return them to the pot over low heat.

Add half of the liquid from the pheasant sauce to the garganelli and toss until the pasta is coated. Remove from the heat and stir in the grated cheese. Transfer the pasta to a serving platter or individual plates, spoon the remaining sauce over the pasta, and sprinkle with a little more grated cheese before serving.

Note: Have the butcher cut up your pheasant, if possible. To do it yourself, you will need a heavy cleaver and, preferably, a pair of kitchen shears: Open up the bird by cutting through the length of the backbone. Then cut the pheasant in half through the breastbone. Cut each of the halves into 3 pieces: Cut each half into leg and breast pieces by cutting through the backbone, then cut off the wings.

Pappardelle with Quail in Guazzetto

Pappardelle con Quaglie in Guazzetto

MAKES 6 SERVINGS

Pappardelle made from 1 recipe Basic Egg
  Pasta Dough (page 89)
½ cup dried porcini mushrooms
  (about ½ ounce)
2 cups warm water
4 cloves
2 fresh or dried bay leaves
1 sprig fresh rosemary or 1 teaspoon dried
  rosemary
¼ cup extra virgin olive oil
Six 4-ounce quail, giblets removed if
  necessary, patted dry
Salt
3 medium-size onions, chopped
⅓ cup finely chopped pancetta or bacon
  (about 1½ ounces)
Freshly ground black pepper
½ cup chicken livers (about ¼ pound),
  trimmed of membranes and finely
  chopped
½ cup shredded carrots
1 cup dry white wine
3 tablespoons tomato paste
3 cups Chicken Stock (page 80) or canned
  low-sodium chicken broth
6 quarts salted water
Freshly grated Parmigiano-Reggiano cheese
  for serving

Prepare the pappardelle.

Soak the porcini in the warm water until softened, about 30 minutes. Remove the porcini from the soaking liquid and rinse them well. Coarsely chop the porcini, discarding any tough bits. Strain the soaking liquid through a coffee filter or sieve lined with paper towels. Set the chopped porcini and soaking liquid aside.

Tie the cloves, bay leaves, and rosemary securely in a small square of cheesecloth.

In a large, heavy casserole, heat the olive oil over high heat. Add the quail and sprinkle lightly with salt. Reduce the level of heat to medium-high and cook, turning often, until lightly golden on all sides, about 10 minutes. Remove the quail to a plate.

Pour off all but 2 tablespoons of the fat from the pot. Add the onions and pancetta to the casserole and sprinkle them lightly with salt and pepper. Cook, stirring, until golden, about 5 minutes. Add the chicken livers and cook, stirring as necessary, until browned, about 4 minutes. Adjust the level of heat if necessary so the livers brown without the drippings/brown bits in the pot burning. Add the porcini and carrots and cook, stirring, until the porcini are dry, about 5 minutes.

Add the wine and cook, stirring, until the wine has nearly evaporated, about 5 minutes. Stir in the tomato paste until all the ingredients are evenly coated. Add the reserved mushroom liquid and about ½ cup of the chicken stock and bring to a boil. Reduce the level of heat to a simmer.

Return the quail to the pan and tuck the cheesecloth packet into the liquid. Cover the casserole partially and cook until the liquid is reduced by half, about 15 minutes. Add another ½ cup stock and continue to simmer, adding chicken stock ½ cup at a time and waiting until the liquid is reduced by half before adding more, until the quail are tender and the sauce velvety, about 1 hour longer. Remove and discard the cheesecloth bundle. (The quail sauce can be made up to 2 days ahead and refrigerated, covered.)

Remove the quail from the sauce. Skim off the surface fat. (It will be easier to skim the fat if the sauce has been refrigerated.) Pull the meat from the bones, discarding the skin and bones. Coarsely shred the meat and return it to the sauce. Heat the sauce to a simmer. Taste the sauce and adjust the seasoning if necessary.

Meanwhile, bring the salted water to a boil in a large pot.

Cook the pappardelle according to the directions on page 88. Drain well and return to the pot over low heat.

Add half of the liquid from the quail sauce to the pappardelle and toss until the pasta is evenly coated. Remove from the heat, add grated cheese to taste, and toss well. Transfer the pasta to a serving platter or individual bowls, top with the remaining sauce, and serve immediately.

Garganelli with Rabbit in Guazzetto

Garganelli con Coniglio in Guazzetto

Garganelli made from 1 recipe Basic Egg
  Pasta Dough (page 89)

½ cup dried porcini mushrooms
  (about ½ ounce)

3 cups hot Chicken Stock (page 80) or
  canned low-sodium chicken broth

4 fresh or dried bay leaves

4 cloves

1 sprig fresh rosemary or 1 teaspoon dried
  rosemary

¼ cup extra virgin olive oil

One 2½-pound dressed rabbit, cut into
  quarters

Salt

1 medium-size onion, chopped

Freshly ground black pepper

1 medium-size carrot, shredded

1 celery stalk, finely chopped

1 cup dry white wine

1 tablespoon tomato paste

1 cup drained canned peeled Italian
  tomatoes, chopped

2 tablespoons finely chopped fresh Italian
  parsley leaves

6 quarts salted water

½ cup freshly grated Parmigiano-Reggiano
  cheese

Prepare the garganelli.

Soak the porcini in 1 cup of the hot stock until softened, about 30 minutes. Drain the mushrooms, reserving the liquid. Rinse and chop the mushrooms, discarding any tough bits. Strain the liquid through a coffee filter or a sieve lined with paper towels. Set the strained soaking liquid and chopped mushrooms aside.

Tie the bay leaves, cloves, and rosemary together securely in a small square of cheesecloth.

In a large casserole, heat the oil over medium-high heat. Add the rabbit pieces in a single layer, sprinkle lightly with salt, and cook, turning as necessary, until browned on all sides, about 8 minutes. Remove the rabbit pieces to a plate.

Pour off all but 2 tablespoons of the fat from the pot. Add the onion and sprinkle it with salt and pepper. Cook, stirring often, until golden, about 5 minutes. Add the carrot and celery and cook, stirring occasionally, until wilted, about 5 minutes. Add the wine and cook, stirring, until almost completely evaporated, about 5 minutes. Reduce the level of heat to medium, add the tomato paste, and stir until the vegetables are coated. Stir in the tomatoes, the chopped porcini with their liquid, and about ½ cup of the remaining chicken stock. Bring to a boil.

Return the rabbit pieces to the pot and tuck the cheesecloth packet into the liquid. Adjust the level of heat to a simmer, cover the casserole partially, and simmer gently until the liquid is reduced by about half, about 20 minutes. Add another ½ cup stock and continue simmering, adding chicken stock ½ cup at a time and waiting until the liquid is reduced by half before adding more, until the rabbit is tender and the liquid velvety, about 1 hour and 15 minutes. Remove and discard the cheesecloth packet. (The rabbit sauce can be made up to 2 days ahead and refrigerated, covered.)

Remove the rabbit from the sauce and skim the fat from the surface. (This will be easier if the sauce has been refrigerated.) Pull the meat from the bones and discard the bones. Coarsely shred the meat and return it to the sauce. Add the parsley and reheat the sauce to a simmer. Taste the sauce, adding salt and pepper if necessary.

Meanwhile, bring the salted water to a boil in a large pot.

Cook the garganelli according to the directions on page 88. Drain well and return to the pot over low heat.

Add half of the liquid from the sauce to the pasta and toss until the pasta is evenly coated. Remove from the heat, add the grated cheese, and toss well. Transfer to a serving platter or individual plates, spoon the rabbit and remaining sauce over the pasta, and serve immediately.

Stuffed Pasta
(Pasta Ripiena)

Pasta ripiena—stuffed pasta like ravioli—requires more preparation than shapes made from basic egg pasta. But once you have the pasta filled and cut, most of the work is done; because of the complexity of flavor in the fillings, the sauces are usually very simple.

Making Stuffed Pasta Shapes

With hand-rolled dough: Divide the pasta dough into three equal pieces. Roll one of the pieces out as described on page 90 to a rectangle that measures about 30 × 11 inches. Keep the remaining pieces of dough covered with a kitchen towel. Place the dough rectangle on your floured work surface, with one of the long sides facing you. Imagine a line that divides the dough into upper and lower halves. Arrange the mounds of filling in two rows of ten each on the upper half of the dough. The rows should start about 1½ inches from the sides and top of the dough rectangle and the mounds of filling should be spaced about 2½ inches apart.

With a pastry brush or the tip of your finger, moisten the edges of the top half of the dough and the dough all around the mounds of filling. Fold the bottom of the dough over the filling, lining up the edges. Press the two layers of dough together firmly, pressing out any air trapped between them as you go. Cut and seal the pasta shapes as described in the particular recipe. Discard any scraps and repeat with the remaining two pieces of dough.

With machine-rolled dough: Divide the pasta dough into six equal pieces and roll each out as described on page 90 to a 5½ × 30-inch rectangle. Place the rectangle on your floured work surface with a long edge facing you. Make a row of twelve mounds of the filling along the length of the top half of the pasta sheet. The row should start about 1¼ inches from the sides and top edge of the pasta sheet and the mounds should be spaced about 2½ inches apart.

With a pastry brush or the tip of your finger, moisten the edges of the top half of the dough and the dough all around the filling. Fold the bottom of the dough over the filling, lining up the edges. Press the two layers of dough together firmly, pressing out any air trapped between them as you go. Cut and seal the pasta shapes as instructed in the particular recipe. Discard any scraps and repeat with the remaining five pieces of dough.

Storing Uncooked Stuffed Pasta

All of the following stuffed pastas can be made hours in advance and refrigerated or weeks in advance and frozen.

To prepare stuffed pasta on the same day you plan to serve it: Any of the following stuffed pastas can be prepared up to six hours in advance. (If you'd like to prepare them any farther ahead, they should be frozen.) Prepare the stuffed pasta as described in the recipe. Sprinkle the towels used to line the baking sheets with coarse cornmeal before you arrange the stuffed pasta on them. (The cornmeal will absorb moisture and prevent the centers of the pasta shapes from becoming soggy while the edges dry out.)

To prepare stuffed pasta up to several weeks in advance: Prepare the stuffed pasta shapes and arrange them on a baking sheet as described in the recipe. Place the trays in the freezer until the shapes are solid. Transfer them to resealable freezer bags—in portion sizes, if you like. To cook frozen stuffed pasta: Increase the amount of water called for in the directions on page 88 to 7 quarts. Add the frozen pasta directly from the freezer to the boiling water a few at a time, stirring well after each addition.

Squash-Filled Ravioli with Marjoram Sauce

Ravioli di Zucca con Salsa di Maggiorana

MAKES 6 SERVINGS (ABOUT 60 RAVIOLI)

For the stuffing

1 small butternut squash (about 2 pounds)

1 cup freshly grated Parmigiano-Reggiano
  cheese

½ cup finely diced mostarda di Cremona
  (see Note on page 302)

8 amaretti cookies, crushed to fine crumbs
  (about ⅔ cup)

Freshly grated nutmeg

Freshly ground black pepper

2 large egg yolks

1 recipe Basic Egg Pasta Dough (page 89)

6 quarts salted water

For the sauce

5 to 7 tablespoons unsalted butter
  (to your taste)

Leaves from 5 sprigs fresh marjoram

¼ cup reserved pasta cooking water

Salt and freshly ground black pepper

⅔ to 1 cup freshly grated Parmigiano-
  Reggiano cheese (to your taste)

Preheat the oven to 375°F. With a sturdy serrated knife, carefully cut the squash into quarters and scrape out the seeds. Arrange the squash pieces cut side up in a baking dish and bake until it feels soft and is easily pierced with a knife, about 1 hour. Allow to cool.

Peel off the skin from the squash. Place the flesh in a food processor and process just until no longer chunky, a few seconds. Transfer the squash to a sieve lined with cheesecloth and set it over a bowl; allow to drain in a cool place overnight.

Transfer the squash to a large mixing bowl. Beat in the grated cheese, mostarda, and crushed amaretti and season with nutmeg and pepper to taste. Beat in the egg yolks until smooth and well blended. Set the mixture in the refrigerator for at least 30 minutes.

Meanwhile, prepare the pasta dough.

Roll out and fill the dough as described on pages 90 and 102, using a scant tablespoon of the squash filling for each *raviolo*. Cut out the ravioli using a 2½-inch round cutter. Press the edges of the ravioli firmly to seal them tightly. Arrange them in a single layer on baking sheets lined with lightly floured kitchen towels and cover with additional towels. The ravioli can be cooked immediately or refrigerated or frozen according to the directions on page 103.

When ready to cook, bring the salted water to a boil in a large pot (see Note). Add the ravioli to the boiling water one at a time, stirring gently as you do. Cook until they rise to the surface and the edges are tender but still firm to the bite, about 6 minutes after the water returns to a boil.

Meanwhile, make the sauce. In a small saucepan, melt the butter with the marjoram. Add the ¼ cup pasta cooking water and season with salt and pepper to taste. Let simmer for 3 to 5 minutes.

Use a big skimmer or large flat slotted spoon to gently scoop out the ravioli, draining them well. Set them on a warmed serving platter or in individual bowls. Pour the butter sauce over the ravioli and sprinkle with the grated cheese. Serve immediately.

Note: If you do not have a pan that fits all the pasta shapes comfortably, you can cook them in two large pots or in two batches. Drain the first batch and keep it warm on a warm platter covered with aluminum foil while cooking the remaining batch.

Istrian Wedding Pillows

🔒 K r a f i 🔒

The peninsula of Istria was part of the Serenissima, or Venetian Republic, from 1420 to the early eighteenth century. During that time, most of Europe's spice trade was dominated by the Venetians. Spices were much more than a seasoning; they served as the economic barometer of the time. In fact, the value of the currency was determined by the price of black pepper as it was traded on a daily basis. The spices in this recipe were frequently used in the noble houses, but for most families their exorbitant cost put them out of reach. Therefore, they were reserved for special occasions, like weddings and celebratory dishes, such as these soft little "pillows" filled with raisins, cheese, and rum.

MAKES 6 SERVINGS (ABOUT 60 PILLOWS)

1 recipe Basic Egg Pasta Dough (page 89)

For the stuffing

½ cup golden raisins

2 tablespoons dark rum

1 large egg

1½ teaspoons sugar

2¾ cups shredded Montasio cheese
(about 10 ounces; see page 42)

2½ cups shredded Fontina cheese
(about 9 ounces)

1¼ cups grated Parmigiano-Reggiano
cheese (about ¼ pound)

¼ cup fresh bread crumbs

¾ teaspoon grated lemon zest (yellow part
only, not the underlying white part)

½ teaspoon grated orange zest (orange part
only, not the white part)

½ teaspoon chopped fresh thyme leaves

Prepare the pasta dough.

Toss the raisins with the rum. Let them stand, tossing once or twice, until the raisins absorb most of the rum, 20 to 30 minutes.

In a large bowl, beat together the egg and sugar. Add the remaining filling ingredients and mix well with your hands until thoroughly blended. Cover and set aside, or refrigerate for up to 1 day.

Roll out and fill the pasta dough as described on pages 90 and 102, using a full tablespoon of the cheese filling for each *krafi*. Cut out the *krafi* using a 2½-inch round cutter. Press the edges of the *krafi* firmly again to seal them tightly.

Arrange the *krafi* in a single layer on baking sheets lined with lightly floured kitchen towels and cover them with additional towels. The *krafi* can be cooked immediately or refrigerated or frozen according to the directions on page 103.

When ready to cook, bring the salted water to a boil in a large pot. Add the *krafi* to the water one at a time, stirring gently as you do (see Note, page 105). Cook until they rise to the surface and the edges are tender but still firm to the bite, about 6 minutes after the water returns to a boil.

Use a big skimmer or large flat slotted spoon to gently scoop out the *krafi,* draining them well. Place them on a serving platter or in individual bowls. Drizzle the melted butter over the *krafi,* sprinkle them with the grated cheese and freshly ground black pepper, and serve immediately.

2 cloves, ground or very finely chopped, or
    ¼ teaspoon ground cloves

6 quarts salted water

T o   s e r v e

5 to 6 tablespoons unsalted butter (to your
    taste), melted and kept warm
½ cup grated Parmigiano-Reggiano cheese,
    or more to your taste
Freshly ground black pepper

Raviolacci Stuffed with Spring Herbs and Cheese

🔑 Raviolacci alle Erbe con Burro e Salvia 🔑

There are many versions of pasta stuffed with herbs and cheese, but this was shared with me by Dante Laurenti, a longtime friend and employee at Felidia restaurant. Dante hails from Parma in the region of Emilia-Romagna, the source of unquestionably some of the best stuffed pasta in Italy.

MAKES 6 SERVINGS (ABOUT 60 RAVIOLACCI)

1 recipe Basic Egg Pasta Dough (page 89)

For the stuffing

1½ teaspoons extra virgin olive oil

1 cup minced leek whites (from about 2 medium-size leeks), well washed

½ cup minced scallions, including green part (about 6 scallions)

4 cups thoroughly washed, stemmed, and chopped Swiss chard or spinach leaves

2 tablespoons chopped fresh basil leaves

Salt and freshly ground black pepper

1 pound fresh ricotta or one 15-ounce container whole-milk ricotta

⅔ cup coarsely grated ricotta salata cheese (see Note on page 179)

½ cup mascarpone cheese

¼ cup freshly grated Parmigiano-Reggiano cheese

2 tablespoons chopped fresh Italian parsley leaves

1 large egg, beaten

6 quarts salted water

Prepare the pasta dough.

In a small casserole, heat the oil over medium-low heat. Add the leeks and scallions and cook, stirring, until softened, about 3 minutes. Stir in the Swiss chard and basil, then increase the level of heat to medium. Season lightly with salt and pepper and cook, stirring, until the vegetables are tender and the liquid has evaporated, about 15 minutes. Let cool completely.

In a large bowl, combine the fresh ricotta, ricotta salata, mascarpone, Parmigiano, and parsley. Add the cooked greens and season with salt and pepper. Stir in the beaten egg and mix well.

Roll out and fill the pasta dough as described on pages 90 and 102, using a full tablespoon of the vegetable-cheese filling for each *raviolaccio*. Using a ridged pastry wheel, cut the *raviolacci* into rectangles about 3 × 2½ inches. Press the edges of the *raviolacci* firmly to seal them tightly. Arrange them in a single layer on baking sheets lined with lightly floured kitchen towels and cover them with additional towels. The *raviolacci* can be cooked immediately or refrigerated or frozen according to the directions on page 103.

When ready to cook, bring the salted water to a boil in a large pot. Add the *raviolacci* to the water one at a time, stirring gently as you do (see Note, page 105). Cook until they rise to the surface and the edges are tender but still firm to the bite, about 6 minutes after the water returns to a boil.

Meanwhile, in a large skillet, melt the butter over medium-high heat. Stir in the milk, cream, sage leaves, and ¼ cup of the pasta cooking water, bring to a gentle boil, and allow to boil for 3 minutes.

For the sauce
½ cup (1 stick) unsalted butter
¼ cup milk
¼ cup heavy cream
8 fresh sage leaves
¼ cup reserved pasta cooking water
¼ cup grated Parmigiano-Reggiano cheese
Salt and freshly ground black pepper

Pour half of the butter sauce into a second large skillet. Use a big skimmer or large flat slotted spoon to gently scoop out the *raviolacci,* draining them well. Divide the cooked *raviolacci* between the skillets and stir them gently with a wooden spoon to coat them evenly with the sauce. Sprinkle 2 tablespoons of the grated cheese over the *raviolacci* in each skillet, then shake the pans until the sauce is lightly reduced and coats the *raviolacci*. Season with salt and pepper. Transfer to a warm serving platter or individual plates and serve immediately.

Semolina Pasta Dough

🏺 Pasta di Grano Duro 🏺

Typically, pasta dough in the north of Italy is made with flour called "*doppio zero*" (double zero), which is close to American all-purpose flour, with a relatively low protein content. In the south, where durum wheat is prevalent, the flour of choice for fresh pasta is semolina flour—a coarser grind of flour milled from durum, or hard, wheat. The textures of the two pastas are completely different, whether you cook them fresh or after you have dried them at room temperature. Egg pasta is softer and more tender with a delicate bite, while semolina pasta is firmer, with a more pronounced bite. Although some fresh pasta is made entirely with semolina flour, I prefer to use a blend of semolina and all-purpose flour, which makes a firm but tender pasta.

MAKES 6 SERVINGS

2½ cups unbleached all-purpose flour

1½ cups semolina flour (available at Italian groceries and some health food stores)

1 large egg, beaten

1 teaspoon salt

1¼ cups tepid water, or as needed

To mix the dough by hand: In a medium-size bowl, stir the two flours together until blended. Pile the flour mixture into a mound on a marble or wooden work surface. Form a well in the center of the mound that goes all the way down to the work surface. Place the beaten egg and salt in the well. Gradually pour in 1 cup of the water, beating constantly with a fork until well blended. Continue beating the egg mixture, gradually working the flour from the sides of the well into it. As you work, the egg mixture will become thick and the size of the well will expand. Continue beating until there is just a thin ring of flour around the egg mixture and the dough becomes too stiff to mix with a fork. If the dough becomes too thick to mix with a fork before almost all of the flour is incorporated, drizzle a tiny amount of the remaining tepid water over the egg mixture and continue mixing. It is possible you will not need any additional water.

Work the remaining flour into the dough with your hands just until a rough, firm dough is formed. Rub your hands together to remove as much dough as possible and add that to the rest of the dough. Shape the dough into a rough ball and set it aside.

Sprinkle your hands liberally with flour, rubbing them together to remove any remaining scraps of dough from your skin. With a knife, loosen any dough and flour from the work surface. Pass these scrapings through a sieve onto the clean work surface and discard the scraps in the sieve. Make sure your hands are clean and flour them lightly.

Knead the dough, using the sieved flour—and more all-purpose flour if necessary—to prevent the dough from sticking to your hands and the surface, as described on page 90.

Place the dough in a small bowl and cover with plastic wrap. Let the dough rest for at least 1 hour at room temperature, or for up to 1 day in the refrigerator, before rolling and shaping the pasta. If the dough has been refrigerated, let it stand at room temperature for at least 1 hour before rolling and shaping.

To mix the dough in an electric mixer or food processor: This dough, like the Basic Egg Pasta Dough, can be prepared in an electric mixer or food processor. Follow the instructions for making Basic Egg Pasta Dough on page 89, replacing the egg/olive oil mixture in that recipe with the egg beaten with 1 cup of the tepid water.

To Cut and Shape Semolina Pasta Dough

For orecchiette: Cut the semolina pasta dough into six pieces. Work with one piece at a time and keep the others covered with a kitchen towel. By applying light pressure and a gentle back-and-forth motion with the palms of your hands, roll each piece of semolina dough on an unfloured surface until it is stretched into a cylinder ¾ inch thick (about twice the diameter of a pencil). Let the rolled-out pieces rest, covered, for at least 5 minutes before continuing.

If this is your first time working with semolina dough, cut the cylinder into ¼-inch-thick slices. As you become more familiar with the dough, you may want to cut them slightly thinner, making more delicate and tender orecchiette. Dust the work surface lightly with semolina flour. Lay the slices on one of their cut sides and pat them into more or less round shapes. Flour the tops of the rounds. Choose a butter knife—not a dinner knife—that has a wide, well-rounded tip. Place the tip of the butter knife over a round of dough with the handle more or less parallel to the work surface. Drag the dough toward you, pressing lightly and lifting the handle of the knife as you do. The dough will stretch and curl up into a cup shape with a roughly textured surface around the tip of the knife. Invert the cup and press down on the center of the dome to make orecchiette—little ears. Alternatively, you can use your thumb to shape the orecchiette. Lightly flour the tip of your thumb and drag the dough round away from you, while pressing down lightly. The dough will form the cup shape around your thumb. Press down on the dome as described above.

Set the orecchiette on a lightly floured kitchen towel without touching one another and let them rest, covered, for 2 to 3 hours before cooking.

For maccheroni inferrattati (skewer maccheroni, or fusilli): To shape these *maccheroni*, you will need square-shaped stainless steel skewers, preferably without handles. Cut the dough into ten pieces. Work with one piece of dough at a time and keep the others covered with a kitchen towel. By applying light pressure and a gentle back-and-forth motion with the palms of your hands, roll each piece of dough into a long cylinder about ⅜ inch thick (about the diameter of a pencil). Let the rolled-out dough rest for at least 5 minutes before continuing. (Alternatively, you can divide the dough into six pieces and pass each two times through a pasta machine set to its widest setting. Let the dough rest for at least 5 minutes, them cut lengthwise into ⅜-inch strips. Cut the strips crosswise into 1- to 1½-inch lengths.)

Cut each cylinder into 1- to 1½-inch lengths and place three or four of these pieces equidistant—at least two finger widths apart—from each other in a line, with their long sides facing you, on a lightly floured wooden or marble work surface. (You may find it easier to start with one length of the dough at first, working up to more as you get the knack.)

Lay the lightly floured skewer over the dough pieces and, with both hands, rock the skewer back and forth while applying light pressure. The dough pieces will wrap around the skewer and stretch out at the same time. (If your skewer has a looped handle, make sure that the handle extends over the side of the work surface so it doesn't interfere with a smooth rocking motion.) When the *maccheroni* are about 1½ to 2 inches long and wrapped around the skewer, pick up one end of the skewer, tap lightly on the surface, and gently slide the *maccheroni* off. Place the finished *maccheroni* on a lightly floured kitchen towel without touching one another. Repeat with the remaining dough.

For malloreddus: *Malloreddus* is the name given a small Sardinian gnocchi-shaped pasta made with a semolina flour dough flavored with saffron. The dough is prepared exactly as the semolina pasta dough on page 110, with one exception: About half an hour before preparing the dough, add ½ teaspoon saffron threads to 1¼ cups of the warm water. Let it steep until the liquid is bright gold. Mix the dough as instructed in the recipe, using the saffron liquid, unstrained. Knead the dough and let rest as instructed before shaping the *malloreddus*.

Cut the saffron pasta dough into ten pieces. Work with one piece at a time and keep the others covered with a kitchen towel. By applying light pressure and a gentle back-and-forth motion with the palms of your hands, roll each piece of semolina dough on an unfloured surface until it is stretched into a cylinder ½ inch thick. Let the rolled-out pieces rest for at least 5 minutes before continuing.

Cut each cylinder into ⅛-inch-thick slices. If this is your first time working with semolina dough, you may want to cut them slightly thicker—they will be a little easier to shape. With practice, you can reduce the thickness of the rounds, making more delicate and tender *malloreddus*. Dust your work surface lightly with semolina flour. Lay the slices on one of their cut sides and sprinkle the tops with semolina flour. Flour the tip of your thumb and the inside (not the grating part) of a half-moon cheese grater. Roll each piece of the dough along the inside of the grater with the tip of your thumb, applying pressure, until the dough has rolled over your thumb into a little shell shape with a distinctive textured surface. Continue, periodically flouring your thumb and the grater, until all the pieces are shaped. Set them on a lightly floured kitchen towel without touching one another and let them rest, covered, for 2 to 3 hours before cooking.

Storing Uncooked Pasta Shapes

Orecchiette, *maccheroni inferrattati*, and *malloreddus* can be made a day in advance and dried completely at room temperature. Turn them once or twice as they dry. To freeze any of these pasta shapes, arrange them in a single layer on floured baking sheets and place in the freezer until the pasta is completely frozen. When frozen, put them in resealable freezer bags and freeze for up to 6 weeks. Like all fresh pasta that has been frozen, they should be taken directly from the freezer to boiling water without defrosting them (see How to Cook Fresh Pasta, page 88).

Orecchiette with Broccoli di Rape

Orecchiette con Broccoletti

This dish can be made with or without the sausages. The broccoli di rape has such an intense and wonderful flavor that the orecchiette will be delicious either way.

MAKES 6 SERVINGS

Orecchiette made from 1 recipe Semolina
Pasta Dough (page 110)
2 pounds broccoli di rape
½ pound sweet Italian sausage (about 2
links)
5 tablespoons extra virgin olive oil
3 large garlic cloves, crushed
6 quarts salted water
Salt
¼ teaspoon peperoncino (crushed red
pepper)
1 to 3 tablespoons unsalted butter (to your
taste)
1 cup Chicken Stock (page 80) or canned
low-sodium chicken broth, or as needed
⅓ cup freshly grated Pecorino Romano
cheese

Prepare the orecchiette.

Cut off and discard the ends of the broccoli di rape stems, leaving the stalks about 8 inches long. Remove the large tough leaves, leaving just tender leaves and flower buds. Peel the thick lower part of the stems by lifting strips from the stem end with a paring knife or vegetable peeler and drawing them up toward the bud area. A perfect peel is not necessary, but removing the peel does remove bitterness. Cut the stems into 1½- to 2-inch lengths. Wash the broccoli thoroughly and dry it well, preferably in a salad spinner.

Remove the casings from the sausage and crumble it. In a large skillet, heat 1 tablespoon of the olive oil over medium-high heat. Add the sausage meat and cook until it is no longer pink, about 3 minutes. Add the crushed garlic and continue cooking until the sausage is lightly browned, 2 to 3 minutes.

Meanwhile, bring the salted water to a boil in a large pot.

Drain the fat from the skillet and add the remaining ¼ cup olive oil. Add about half the broccoli di rape to the pan and toss until it begins to wilt. Add the remainder of the broccoli, cover the pan, and cook until wilted and bright green, about 4 minutes. Taste, and season lightly with salt and with the peperoncino. Stir in the butter until melted, then add 1 cup of the stock and bring to a boil. Boil gently, uncovered, until the broccoli rape is tender, about 8 minutes. Add more stock if necessary to keep the broccoli from drying out. Taste again and correct the seasoning. Set the sauce aside until the pasta is ready.

Cook the orecchiette according to the directions on page 88. Drain well and return to the pot over low heat.

Add the broccoli di rape sauce and toss gently to blend. Taste carefully for seasoning, and remove from the heat. Add half of the grated cheese and toss to blend. Transfer to a serving platter or individual bowls and sprinkle with the rest of the grated cheese. Serve immediately.

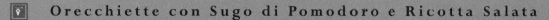

Orecchiette with Tomato Sauce and Dry Ricotta

 Orecchiette con Sugo di Pomodoro e Ricotta Salata

The beauty of the next four recipes is the flavor of a good tomato sauce coupled with a pasta full of texture accented in each case by one other intensely flavored ingredient—ricotta salata, oregano, green olives, or sausages.

MAKES 6 SERVINGS

Prepare the orecchiette.

Bring the salted water to a boil in a large pot. Cook the orecchiette according to the directions on page 88.

Meanwhile, in a small saucepan, bring the tomato sauce to a simmer over low heat.

Drain the orecchiette well and return to the pot over low heat. Add the tomato sauce and toss until the pasta is evenly coated. Remove from the heat, add the ricotta salata, basil, and parsley, and toss well. Transfer the pasta to a serving platter or individual bowls, sprinkle with the Pecorino, and serve immediately.

Orecchiette made from 1 recipe Semolina
    Pasta Dough (page 110)
6 quarts salted water
3 cups Tomato Sauce (page 144)
2 cups grated ricotta salata cheese
    (about 6 ounces)
10 fresh basil leaves, washed, dried, and cut
    into strips
2 tablespoons chopped fresh Italian parsley
    leaves
1 cup freshly grated Pecorino Romano
    cheese

Skewer Maccheroni in Tomato Sauce and Oregano

 Maccheroni Inferrattati al Pomodoro ed Oregano

MAKES 6 SERVINGS

Skewer *maccheroni* made from 1 recipe
 Semolina Pasta Dough (page 110)
6 quarts salted water
3 cups Tomato Sauce (page 144)
2 tablespoons chopped fresh oregano leaves
 or 1 teaspoon dried oregano
2 teaspoons extra virgin olive oil
1 cup freshly grated Pecorino Romano
 cheese

Prepare the skewer *maccheroni*.

Bring the salted water to a boil in a large pot. Cook the *maccheroni* according to the directions on page 88.

Meanwhile, in a small saucepan, bring the tomato sauce to a simmer over low heat. Add the oregano and simmer for 3 minutes.

Drain the *maccheroni* well and return to the pot over low heat. Add the tomato sauce and toss until the pasta is evenly coated. Stir in the olive oil and remove from the heat. Add the grated cheese and toss well. Transfer the pasta to a serving platter or individual bowls and serve immediately.

Skewer Maccheroni
with Green Olives and Capers

 Maccheroni Inferrattati con Olive Verde e Capperi

MAKES 6 SERVINGS

Prepare the skewer *maccheroni*.

Bring the salted water to a boil in a large pot.

Meanwhile, in a medium-size skillet, heat the oil over medium heat. Add the garlic and cook, stirring, until golden, about 2 minutes. Add the olives and capers and cook, stirring, for 2 minutes. Add the marinara sauce and peperoncino and bring to a boil. Set aside.

Cook the *maccheroni* according to the directions on page 88. Drain well and return to the pot over low heat. Add the sauce and toss until the pasta is evenly coated and the sauce heated through, about 1 minute. Stir in the parsley. Transfer to a serving platter or individual bowls and serve immediately.

Skewer *maccheroni* made from 1 recipe
  Semolina Pasta Dough (page 110)
6 quarts salted water
2 tablespoons extra virgin olive oil
4 garlic cloves, sliced
1 cup pitted and halved green olives
¼ cup small capers, drained and rinsed
3 cups Marinara Sauce (page 143)
½ teaspoon peperoncino (crushed red
  pepper)
¼ cup chopped fresh Italian parsley leaves

Malloreddus with Sausage and Tomato Sauce

Malloreddus con Salsiccia e Pomodoro

The first time I had this dish was on a family vacation in Sardegna when my children, Tanya and Joseph, were still small. We were in the restaurant of the Hotel Porto Cervo overlooking the port; the spot was magical. We had an antipasto of local salami with *carta di musica* (bread as thin as sheet music) and marinated vegetables. The *malloreddus* followed, and I knew after tasting it that I would make that experience mine.

MAKES 6 SERVINGS

Malloreddus made from 1 recipe Semolina
  Pasta Dough (page 110)
2 tablespoons extra virgin olive oil
1 cup sliced onions
1 pound sweet Italian sausages (about
  5 links), casings removed
3 cups Tomato Sauce (page 144)
½ teaspoon peperoncino (crushed red
  pepper)
6 quarts salted water
6 fresh basil leaves, washed, dried, and
  shredded
½ cup freshly grated Pecorino Romano
  cheese

Prepare the *malloreddus*.

In a large skillet, heat the olive oil over medium heat. Add the onions and cook, stirring, until wilted, about 3 minutes. Crumble the sausage into the skillet and stir until it is golden and has rendered most of its fat, about 5 minutes. Drain the excess fat from the skillet. Add the tomato sauce and peperoncino, return the skillet to the heat, and bring to a simmer. Let simmer, stirring occasionally, until thickened, about 20 minutes.

Meanwhile, bring the salted water to a boil in a large pot.

Cook the *malloreddus* according to the directions on page 88. Drain well, reserving about ½ cup of the pasta cooking water.

Return the *malloreddus* to the pot over low heat. Add three quarters of the tomato sauce and the basil leaves and stir until the pasta is evenly coated. The sauce should be just dense enough to lightly coat the pasta; if necessary, add a little of the reserved pasta cooking water. Remove from the heat and add half of the Pecorino. Toss well, then transfer to a serving platter or individual bowls, top with the remaining sauce and cheese, and serve immediately.

Malloreddus in Butter Sauce

Malloreddus Conditi in Bianco

MAKES 6 SERVINGS

Prepare the *malloreddus*.

Bring the salted water to a boil in a large pot. Cook the *malloreddus* as described on page 88.

Meanwhile, in a medium-size skillet, melt the butter over very low heat, swirling the pan to prevent the butter from separating; it should look milky.

Drain the *malloreddus* and return to the pot over low heat. Add the melted butter and toss to coat the pasta evenly. Add the nutmeg and coarsely ground pepper to taste. Toss and remove from the heat. Add the Pecorino, toss once more, transfer to a serving platter or individual bowls, and serve immediately.

Malloreddus made from 1 recipe Semolina
  Pasta Dough (page 110)
6 quarts salted water
1 cup (2 sticks) unsalted butter
½ teaspoon freshly grated nutmeg
Coarsely ground black pepper
1 cup freshly grated Pecorino Romano
  cheese

Dry Pasta

Pasta Asciutta

Today dry pasta comes in many different shapes, packaged in bags, cellophane, and colorful cardboard boxes, but I vividly remember my mother and grandmother buying spaghetti loose, by the *etto* (100 grams) or kilogram. It came in long wooden boxes marked "Fragile." My mother, Erminia, still sadly reminisces about wartime and spaghetti boxes to my brother and me and our children.

One story she tells is about my older brother, Franco, who was born in 1944. Although the war was ending, there were still periodic siren warnings that caused everyone to run to the subterranean shelters for safety. My mother was a teacher at the elementary school near our house, which had a shelter. When the sirens blew, my mother had a spaghetti box ready to go—she wrapped my infant brother, set him in the box, and ran to the shelter with the box and baby. We smile at the story now, but it surely was not a laughing matter then.

Pasta has given me happier memories—it was and is one of my favorite foods to eat and prepare. Versatile, delicious, nutritious, simple to make, and satisfying to eat, pasta has become a universally favorite food. But as universal as pasta can be, its nuances and combinations are infinite.

It is sometimes falsely claimed that pasta was brought to Italy by Marco Polo from his travels to the Orient, perhaps because the Chinese had long been using noodles. However, *pasta asciutta,* or dry pasta, likely reached the shores of Italy during the seventh century, a traveler from the Arab world. The Arabic word *itriya* is used to this day in Sicily to refer to strands of air-dried noodles that have a hole running through them. The nomadic Arab tribes carried different foods with them in their travels along the spice routes, among them flour, which would be made into a dough and then dried on rocks in the sun. This drying helped preserve the pasta and made it easy to carry. The hole in the pasta resulted in a drier product with a longer lifespan and better texture.

Dry pasta was thus introduced to the southern shores of Italy, Sicily, and Puglia, but its use truly began to flourish in and around Naples in Campania during the fourteenth and fifteenth centuries. In the streets of Naples, *maccheroni* was sold from stands and eaten by holding the bowl close to the mouth, picking up the strands with the fingers, and slurping them into the mouth. As the Tuscans were known as *mangiafagioli* (bean eaters), the Neapolitans were *mangiamaccheroni*. Indeed, development of the four-tine fork is credited to King Ferdinando II of Naples (1467–1496), who, frustrated by not being able to serve *maccheroni*, the delectable plebeian food eaten with the fingers, to his guests of honor, complained to his loyal *ciambellano* (chamberlain), Gennaro Spadacchi. To please his lord, Spadacchi invented the fork specifically to allow the *maccheroni* to be eaten in polite society.

The best dry pasta is made from 100 percent durum wheat, salt, and water. The quality of these ingredients, including the water, is extremely important, and fresh spring water yields the best results. Durum is the hardest wheat grain, with a high ratio of protein to carbohydrates in comparison to other wheats. When it is mixed with water, the large amount of protein and the relatively small amount of starch work to form a tight, elastic dough.

The mixing, shaping, and drying techniques used to make dry pasta are also very important. The flour and water have to be worked intensively by a machine to transform the high percentage of proteins in the durum wheat into a tightly knit fabric: pasta. This dough is passed through an extruding machine, the shape of the pasta being determined by the die with which the extruder is fit. The pasta shapes are then dried under carefully controlled conditions, giving the pasta a chance to dry thoroughly and from the inside out to provide an even texture and to discourage breakage. This carefully controlled process of making dry pasta can't be duplicated successfully at home. The finished product is different from, but just as wonderful as, fresh pasta made by hand.

When you buy *pasta asciutta,* look for these qualities: It should have a sheen; it should be translucent, not blotchy or dull; it should not be cracked or broken. Imported Italian pasta is more likely to possess these characteristics than any other, although there are some very good pastas now being produced in the United States.

There are three main types of dry pasta: short pasta, long pasta, and the various *pastine,* or little pastas. Short pasta has the widest range of selection—there are more than one hundred different shapes. Short pastas can be smooth or have a ridged finish and the shapes can be straight-forward or fanciful. They can be tubular (rigatoni, ziti, penne, *mezzani*) or tubular-with-a-twist— *gomiti rigati* (ridged elbows), *lumache* (snails), and *creste di gallo* (cock's comb). Furthermore, the tubular pastas can be cut straight or on a slant. For example, penne and *genovesine* are cut on a slant, whereas rigatoni, ziti, and *cannolicchi* are cut straight across. Other distinctive shapes include *rotelle* (wheels), *radiatori* (radiators), *dischi volanti* (flying saucers), *farfalle* (bow ties), *fusilli* (spirals), *tofe* (shell-like), *margherite* (daisies), and *perline* (pearls).

Among the long pastas, the main difference is the diameter. Some are long and round, such as spaghetti, vermicelli, and capellini; some are long and flat (linguine, *fresine,* and *malfatti*); and some round with a hole in the middle, such as perciatelli, bucatini, and *mezzanelli.* Of the "ribbon" pastas, those that are flat and wide, only fettuccine is commonly found dry. Some long pastas can be shaped and dried in nest-like formations, called *nidi.* Fettuccine, capellini, and fidelini are a few of the pastas that can be found in *nido* forms.

The *pastina* category consists mainly of pastas used in soups and *minestre.* The pasta is cut into small bits that usually cook right in the soup, like *pepe* (peppercorn-like kernels), *stelle* (stars), *semi di melone* (melon seeds), *anellini* (small rings), *rosmarino* (rosemary leaves), orzo (grains), and others.

How to Cook Dry Pasta

To cook a pound of pasta, bring 6 quarts of water to a rapid boil in a large pot—pasta should have enough space to turn comfortably in the pot when you stir it. Stir in 2 tablespoons coarse salt. (If the sauce for the pasta will be salty, then adjust by using less salt in the cooking water—but remember that the taste of the pasta will be flat if cooked in water with no salt at all.) Add the pasta to the boiling water and immediately stir it well. Cover the pot to bring the water back to a boil as quickly as possible. Pasta cooked with the lid on uses only one third the amount of energy, but reduce the heat if you cook pasta this way to prevent the water from boiling over. Once the water comes back to a boil, remove the lid and stir the pasta once or twice during cooking to prevent sticking.

It is always a good idea to reserve a little of the pasta cooking water before you drain the pasta so it can be used to thin the sauce if it has become a little too thick.

General Guide for Cooking Times

*Long, thin dry pasta shapes like linguine and spaghetti will take 6 to 10 minutes; very thin shapes like capellini or vermicelli, even less time.
*Short, tubular shapes like ziti or penne and other small shapes like rotelle and shells will take 10 to 15 minutes.

Pasta Cooking Tips

- Oil should not be added to cooking water except when cooking wide fresh pasta such as lasagne, or the sauce won't adhere properly to the pasta.

- To test for doneness, bite into a strand to determine whether or not the pasta has the appropriate al dente texture.

- As soon as the pasta is done, immediately drain it well, shaking off the excess water— do not let it sit in hot water or stop the boiling with cold water. Pasta should never be rinsed, except when making cold pasta dishes.

- Pasta should be sauced immediately, while still hot. After you have drained the pasta, return it to the cooking pot or transfer it to a warmed bowl; immediately add at least a few tablespoons of sauce. (Depending on the sauce and the pasta, you may add up to the full amount of the sauce to the pasta before plating it.) Add cheese if you like and toss well, then plate the dish and top with the rest of the sauce if necessary.

- Cheese, when called for, should always be added during the final tossing, off the heat, as a finishing touch.

Pasta and Sauces

Whether it is the simplest sauce made from summer's best uncooked, vine-ripened tomatoes, a luxurious mixture of butter and Parmigiano-Reggiano cheese, or a thrifty but rich and robust ragù of meat and vegetables, the right sauce in combination with the right pasta creates gustatory magic.

Different shapes of pasta work best when paired with specific types of sauces. The smoothness or ridges, the nooks and crannies, the thickness or thinness of the selected pasta capture and absorb sauce in different ways and provide a pleasing play of texture with the components of the sauce. Whatever the sauce, the pasta should be lubricated but not suffocated by it. Pasta should be thoroughly coated without lying in pools of sauce; it should glide on the plate when touched with a fork without becoming glued together.

The possible combinations of both fresh and dry pasta and sauce are limitless, but there are some classic pairings arrived at over centuries that seem to harmonize best time after time.

Long dry pasta such as capellini, spaghetti, and linguine marry best with olive oil–based sauces because the oil coats the pasta completely without drowning it. Flavors that go well with oil-based sauces are fish, vegetables, and chopped and pureed herbs. It is important to bear in mind the shape of the pasta when cutting up the ingredients for the sauce. For long pasta, the vegetables should be cut into long thin strips rather than cubed so they will blend better with the pasta and sauce when eaten.

Short tubular pasta goes especially well with sauces that are chunky. The pieces of meat, vegetable, or beans in the sauce are captured in the crevices of the pasta. Ricotta cheese, olives, or mozzarella sauces also go very well with the short dry pastas. Short pasta is also better for oven-baked preparations.

Tomato and simple cream and butter sauces will go well with almost any pasta shape, fresh or dry.

Serving Pasta

What's of utmost important in serving pasta is that the pasta be served hot and as soon as it's ready. The vessel of service should always be hot, whether it is a platter or individual dishes. If you are having up to eight people at the table, I recommend individual plating. Remember that everyone should be served within three to four minutes so that the pasta does not suffer. The individual presentations can be adorned with sprigs of herbs, topped with additional sauce, and sprinkled with cheese. I like to serve my pasta in soup bowls with a rim—European style—and I pile my pasta into a heap in the center. This way the pasta is more contained, it stays hot for longer periods, and you don't lose your sauce to the sides of the plate.

On the other hand, if you have a large group, serve the pasta in a large warm pasta bowl with the pasta mounded in the middle. If the group is large—twenty or more—split the pasta and serve it in two bowls to make serving easier and allow everyone to eat the pasta as soon as possible. Family-style service, which this is, is quite typical of the traditional Italian table. It is an effortless way to create interaction between diners, especially if you are having a dinner party where the guests are not very familiar with one another. Don't stop with the pasta course; carry this idea through the whole meal, serving the appetizer on platters, the soup in a terrine, and the main course on platters. Just make sure that each item has the appropriate serving utensils.

Pasta and Cheese

There is a natural affinity between pasta and cheese, but it is not as indiscriminate as one might think. In Italy, cheese is used with pasta very selectively and judiciously, with careful attention paid to timing.

Cheese is never served with seafood pasta. When preparing pasta with game or pasta with hot pepper, cheese is optional, since the flavors are very intense. The addition of cheese for some might not be necessary. I enjoy cheese with both.

For optimal results, grate the cheese as close as possible to serving time. (Otherwise, keep it in an airtight container in the refrigerator or freezer.) The cheese should be added to pasta at the last minute, after removing the pot from the heat. Otherwise, the heat will cause the proteins of the cheese to separate from the fat and you may end up with a mixing spoon full of stringy cheese and oily pasta. To add a classical final touch, grate or shave cheese over plated pasta. The steam of the pasta will lift and intensify the aroma of the cheese.

Shells with Young Peas and Mushrooms

Conchiglie con Piselli e Funghi

MAKES 6 SERVINGS

Bring the salted water to a boil.

Meanwhile, if using fresh peas, blanch them in a medium-size saucepan of boiling water for 2 minutes. Drain, rinse them under cold water until cool, and then drain again thoroughly.

In a large skillet, heat the olive oil over medium heat. Add the bacon and onions and cook, stirring, until the onions are wilted, about 4 minutes. Add the mushrooms and sprinkle them with salt. Continue to cook, stirring occasionally, until all the mushrooms have lost their moisture, about 5 minutes. Add the chicken stock, peas, and butter and season lightly with salt and pepper. Simmer until the liquid is reduced by half, about 10 minutes. Check the seasoning and add more salt and pepper if necessary.

Meanwhile, stir the shells into the boiling water. Cover the pot and reheat to boiling, stirring once or twice. When the water returns to a boil, uncover the pot. Cook the pasta, stirring occasionally, until al dente—tender but firm—about 12 minutes. Drain the pasta and return it to the pot over low heat.

Add the sauce to the pasta and stir until the pasta is coated. Remove from the heat and add the grated cheese. Toss well and transfer to a warmed serving platter or individual bowls. Serve immediately.

6 quarts salted water

1½ cups shelled young peas or defrosted and drained frozen baby peas

2 tablespoons extra virgin olive oil

2 slices bacon, finely chopped

½ cup chopped spring onions or scallions

2 cups cleaned (see Note on page 63) and sliced mixed mushrooms, such as shiitake, oyster, and cremini

Salt

2 cups Chicken Stock (page 80) or canned low-sodium chicken broth

1 tablespoon unsalted butter

Freshly ground black pepper

1 pound pasta shells (*conchiglie*)

½ cup freshly grated Parmigiano-Reggiano cheese

Orecchiette with Artichokes

Orecchiette con Carciofi

MAKES 6 SERVINGS

Juice of 1 lemon

3 cups water

8 small spring artichokes (about ¾ pound)

6 quarts salted water

3 tablespoons extra virgin olive oil

½ cup chopped spring onions (see Note)

4 scallions, including three quarters of the green part, chopped

Salt

1 teaspoon peperoncino (crushed red pepper)

1 cup diced (½-inch) young zucchini

2 cups shelled young fava beans (about 1½ pounds in the shell), blanched and peeled (see page 233), or one 10-ounce box frozen baby lima beans, cooked according to the package directions

1 cup young peas, blanched in boiling water for 2 minutes, or defrosted and drained frozen baby peas

2 cups hot Chicken Stock (page 80) or canned low-sodium chicken broth

1 pound orecchiette

2 tablespoons unsalted butter

½ cup freshly grated Pecorino Romano cheese

In a small bowl, stir the lemon juice into the water. Pluck the tough outer leaves from the artichokes, stopping when the remaining leaves are all yellow. Cut the tough tips off the leaves. With a vegetable peeler or paring knife, peel the artichoke stems and the bases of the leaves down to the pale green flesh, then cut the artichokes in half through the stems. With a teaspoon, scrape out the furry chokes and the purple-tipped leaves, leaving only the yellow leaves attached to the hearts. Slice the artichokes lengthwise into very thin slices and quickly immerse in the lemon water to prevent them from turning brown.

Bring the salted water to a boil.

Meanwhile, in a large, deep skillet, heat the olive oil over medium-high heat. Add the onions and scallions and cook, stirring, until wilted, about 2 minutes. Drain the artichokes well and add to the skillet. Season the artichokes lightly with salt and stir in the peperoncino. Cook the artichokes, stirring constantly, until they are softened and beginning to brown around the edges, about 10 minutes.

Add the zucchini, fava beans, and peas to the skillet, reduce the heat to medium, and continue stirring until the zucchini is softened, about 5 minutes. Add a small amount (about ¼ cup) of the hot stock. Cook, stirring frequently, until the liquid is almost evaporated. Continue adding stock and stirring until all the stock has been added and the vegetables are very tender, about 15 minutes. Enough of the liquid should remain to make a sauce that lightly coats the vegetables. Season with salt.

While the sauce cooks, stir the orecchiette into the boiling water. Cover the pot and reheat to boiling, stirring once or twice. When the water returns to a boil, uncover the pot. Cook the pasta, stirring occasionally, until al dente—tender but firm—about 12 minutes. Reserve about ½ cup of the pasta cooking water. Drain the pasta well and return it to the pot over low heat.

Add the artichoke sauce and the butter to the pasta, tossing until the butter is melted. If necessary, add enough of the reserved pasta water to make a creamy sauce that coats the pasta. Remove the pot from the heat and stir in the grated cheese. Toss well and transfer to a warmed serving platter or individual bowls. Serve immediately.

Note: If spring onions are unavailable, omit them and double the amount of scallions.

Fusilli with Fresh Spinach and Ricotta

Fusilli con Spinaci e Ricotta

MAKES 6 SERVINGS

6 quarts salted water

1½ pounds young spinach

1 pound fusilli

2 tablespoons extra virgin olive oil

¼ cup chopped spring onions or scallions

Salt and freshly ground black pepper

1 cup ricotta, preferably fresh

1 cup half-and-half or light cream

1 tablespoon unsalted butter

½ cup freshly grated Parmigiano-Reggiano cheese

Bring the salted water to a boil.

Meanwhile, remove the stems from the spinach. Swish the spinach leaves in a large bowl or sinkful of cool water to clean. If there is a lot of sand and grit in the bottom of the bowl, change the water and wash the leaves again. Drain the spinach leaves and dry them well, preferably in a salad spinner. Stack several of the leaves at a time and cut them crosswise into ¼-inch-wide strips. You should have about 8 packed cups of shredded spinach.

Stir the fusilli into the boiling water. Cover the pot and reheat to boiling, stirring once or twice. When the water returns to a boil, uncover the pot. Cook the pasta, stirring occasionally, until al dente—tender but firm—about 12 minutes.

Meanwhile, in a large skillet, heat the olive oil over medium heat. Add the onions and cook, stirring, until wilted, about 3 minutes. Stir in the spinach and a pinch each of salt and pepper. Cover the skillet and steam the spinach until wilted but still bright green, about 3 minutes.

In a small bowl, stir together the ricotta and half-and-half until smooth. Stir the ricotta mixture and the butter into the skillet, then season with salt and pepper. Reduce the heat to medium-low and simmer for 5 minutes.

Reserve ½ cup of the pasta cooking liquid. Drain the pasta well and return it to the pot over low heat. Add the spinach mixture and enough of the reserved cooking liquid to make a sauce that lightly coats the pasta. Toss thoroughly. Remove the pot from the heat and stir in the grated cheese. Transfer the pasta to a warm serving platter or individual bowls and serve immediately.

Spaghetti with Shrimp and Basil Sauce

Spaghetti con Salsa di Gamberi e Basilico

This sauce is so quick to prepare that it can be put together by the time the pasta is cooked. Although it's quick, it is intensely flavored. Hot cherry peppers can be found in the Italian section of supermarkets or in specialty food stores.

MAKES 6 SERVINGS

Bring the salted water to a boil.

Meanwhile, peel the shrimp. With a small knife, make a shallow cut down the back of each shrimp to remove the dark vein. Cut the shrimp crosswise in half.

In a large skillet, heat ¼ cup of the olive oil over medium heat. Stir in the garlic and shallots and cook, stirring, until the shallots are translucent, about 4 minutes. Add the cherry pepper and shrimp, taking care not to crowd the shrimp, or they will steam in their own juices. (If necessary, cook the shrimp in two batches.) Cook, stirring, until the shrimp are bright pink, about 2 minutes. Add the wine and season with salt and pepper. Bring to a boil and boil for 1 minute. Remove the shrimp with a slotted spoon and set aside.

Stir the spaghetti into the boiling water. Cover the pot and reheat to boiling, stirring once or twice. When the water returns to a boil, uncover the pot. Cook the pasta, stirring occasionally, until al dente—tender but firm—about 8 minutes.

Meanwhile, add the remaining 2 tablespoons olive oil, the basil, parsley, mint, and ½ cup of the pasta cooking liquid to the sauce. Bring to a vigorous boil and continue to boil until the sauce is slightly thickened, about 5 minutes. Reduce the heat to a simmer. Return the shrimp to the pan until heated through, just a few seconds.

Drain the spaghetti and return it to the pot over low heat. Pour three quarters of the sauce over the spaghetti and toss over low heat, mixing well. Transfer the pasta to a warm serving platter or individual bowls. Spoon the remaining sauce over the pasta and serve immediately.

6 quarts salted water

1 pound medium-size shrimp (about 30)

6 tablespoons extra virgin olive oil

4 garlic cloves, crushed

1 tablespoon minced shallots

1 bottled hot cherry pepper, seeded and chopped

1 cup dry white wine

Salt and freshly ground black pepper

1 pound spaghetti

18 fresh basil leaves, washed, dried, and quartered

2 tablespoons minced fresh Italian parsley leaves

4 fresh mint leaves, washed, dried, and minced

Vermicelli with Green Beans and Shellfish

Vermicelli con Fagiolini e Crostacei

18 littleneck clams

¼ pound haricots verts (see Note), cut into 1-inch lengths (about 1 cup)

6 quarts salted water

¼ cup extra virgin olive oil

6 garlic cloves, crushed

2 cups cored, peeled (see page 141), and crushed fresh tomatoes or one 28-ounce can peeled Italian plum tomatoes, drained, seeded, and crushed

1 teaspoon peperoncino (crushed red pepper)

1 pound vermicelli or thin spaghetti

½ pound large sea scallops (about 8), quartered and patted dry

1 tablespoon chopped fresh Italian parsley leaves

Scrub the clamshells under cold running water to remove sand, especially from the crevices. Discard any clams with broken shells or that remain open. Rinse the clams well, drain them, and set aside.

Cook the beans in a small saucepan of boiling salted water just until softened, about 2 minutes.

Bring the salted water to a boil.

Meanwhile, place the clams in a medium-size saucepan with ½ inch of water. Cover, bring to a boil, and steam over medium-high heat, shaking the pan occasionally, until the clams open, 4 to 6 minutes. Discard any that do not open. Remove the clams from the shells and chop them. Strain the clam cooking liquid through a coffee filter or sieve lined with paper towels, add the chopped clams to it, and set aside.

In a medium-size skillet, heat 2 tablespoons of the oil over medium heat. Add the garlic and cook, stirring, until lightly browned, about 2 minutes. Add the tomatoes and peperoncino and bring to a boil. Reduce the heat to medium-low and simmer for 15 minutes. Remove from the heat and discard the garlic.

Stir the vermicelli into the boiling water. Cover the pot and reheat to boiling, stirring once or twice. When the water returns to a boil, uncover the pot. Cook the pasta, stirring occasionally, until al dente—tender but firm—about 7 minutes.

Meanwhile, in a large nonreactive skillet, heat the remaining 2 tablespoons oil over medium-high heat. Add the scallops and cook until they begin to brown, about 2 minutes, turning them once.

Carefully add the chopped clams with their liquid, the tomato sauce, and green beans. Heat to a simmer and cook over medium heat until the sauce is slightly reduced, about 3 minutes. Stir in the parsley.

Drain the vermicelli and return it to the pot over low heat. Pour half the sauce over the pasta and toss until coated. Transfer the pasta to a warm serving platter or individual bowls, top with the remaining sauce, and serve immediately.

Note: Haricots verts are slender young French green beans, about 3 inches in length. If you cannot find them, substitute the thinnest, freshest green beans available. In either case, trim both ends before cutting into 1-inch lengths. Regular green beans will take a little bit longer than the haricots verts to cook.

Linguine with Mussels and Zucchini with Its Flowers

MAKES 6 SERVINGS

2 pounds mussels, preferably cultivated

6 quarts salted water

¼ cup extra virgin olive oil

4 garlic cloves, crushed, plus 6 garlic cloves, sliced

¼ cup dry white wine

1 teaspoon fresh thyme leaves

1 cup zucchini cut into 2 × ⅛ × ⅛-inch strips

1 teaspoon peperoncino (crushed red pepper)

1 cup zucchini flowers, cut into strips (see Note)

2 tablespoons chopped fresh Italian parsley leaves

1 pound linguine

Pull off the beards that stick out of the flat side of the mussel shells if necessary. Scrub the mussels well under cold water and drain them completely. Discard any with broken shells or that do not close.

Bring the salted water to a boil.

Meanwhile, in a large skillet, heat 2 tablespoons of the olive oil over medium heat. Add the crushed garlic and cook until golden, about 2 minutes. Add the mussels, wine, and thyme, cover the skillet, and steam, shaking the skillet once or twice, until the mussels open, 2 to 3 minutes. Discard any mussels that do not open.

With a slotted spoon, transfer the mussels to a bowl and let them stand until cool enough to handle. Strain the mussel broth through a sieve lined with cheesecloth. If necessary, return the broth to the skillet and boil the liquid until reduced to 1½ cups. Pick most of the mussels out of the shells, leaving 18 in the shell for garnish.

Meanwhile, in a large skillet, heat the remaining 2 tablespoons olive oil over medium heat. Add the sliced garlic and cook, stirring, until lightly browned, about 1 minute. Immediately add the zucchini strips and peperoncino and stir until the zucchini is wilted, about 2 minutes. Add the zucchini flowers and stir until wilted, about 2 minutes. (If using zucchini strips in place of the flowers, cook about 4 minutes total, until the zucchini begins to give off liquid.) Add the shelled mussels and stir for 1 minute. Finally, add the mussel broth and bring to a boil. Boil until the sauce is slightly reduced, about 3 minutes. Stir in the parsley and remove from the heat.

While the sauce is cooking, stir the linguine into the boiling water and cover the pot. When the water returns to a boil, uncover the pot. Cook the pasta, stirring occasionally, until al dente—tender but firm—about 8 minutes.

Drain the linguine and return it to the pot over low heat. Pour half of the mussel sauce over the pasta and toss well to coat. Serve on individual plates, spooning on the remaining sauce and garnishing with the reserved whole mussels.

Note: Zucchini flowers appear in early spring in greenmarkets, specialty food stores, and some supermarkets. If they are unavailable, substitute an additional cup of zucchini strips.

Bow Ties with Sausage and Leek Sauce

Farfalle ai Porri e Salsicce

MAKES 6 SERVINGS

6 quarts salted water

2 large leeks (about 1 pound)

2 tablespoons extra virgin olive oil

2 sweet Italian sausages (about 6 ounces), casings removed

1 tablespoon minced shallots

2 tablespoons unsalted butter

1 cup young peas, blanched in boiling water for 2 minutes, or defrosted and drained frozen baby peas

1 cup Chicken Stock (page 80) or canned low-sodium chicken broth

Salt and freshly ground black pepper

1 pound bow-tie pasta (*farfalle*)

½ cup freshly grated Parmigiano-Reggiano cheese, plus more for serving, if you like

Bring the salted water to a boil.

Meanwhile, prepare the leeks: Cut off and discard the top third of the rough green portion and the root ends. Remove any brown or wilted outer layers. Slice the remaining green and white parts into ½-inch-thick rounds. Rinse the leek slices in several changes of cold water, swishing them around to remove all soil and grit.

In a large skillet, heat the olive oil over medium heat. Crumble the sausage meat into the skillet and cook, breaking up the lumps, until golden, about 5 minutes. Add the leeks to the skillet and cook, stirring, until wilted, about 5 minutes. Stir in the shallots and cook for 1 minute. Add 1 tablespoon of the butter, the peas, and stock. Heat to a boil, reduce the heat to medium-low, and simmer gently for 5 minutes. Season with salt and pepper, cover the skillet, and set aside.

Meanwhile, stir the bow ties into the boiling water. When the water returns to a boil, uncover the pot. Cook the pasta, stirring occasionally, until al dente—tender but firm—about 12 minutes. Drain the bow ties well and return them to the pot over low heat.

Add the sausage and leek sauce to the pasta and toss well until the pasta is coated. Remove the pot from the heat, add the remaining 1 tablespoon butter and the grated cheese, and toss well. Transfer to a warmed serving platter or individual bowls. Serve immediately, passing additional grated cheese on the side, if you like.

Summer Ziti in Parchment

☙ Ziti Estive al Cartoccio ☙

This dish is wonderful in its simplicity, but you can be creative and add other summer vegetables. Zucchini and/or eggplant, lightly grilled or roasted, will add complexity of flavor.

MAKES 6 SERVINGS

Bring the salted water to a boil.

Meanwhile, preheat the oven to 475°F and place a rack in the center position. Fold six 26 × 18-inch sheets of parchment paper in half to form 18 × 13-inch rectangles. (Alternatively, tear off six 30-inch lengths from a 12-inch-wide roll of parchment paper and fold them in half crosswise to form 15 × 12-inch rectangles.) Grease the center of each rectangle with some of the butter. Use the remaining butter to grease six individual ovenproof dishes, each about 10 × 4 inches, or one ovenproof dish large enough (at least 18 × 12 inches) to hold the parchment packages side by side without touching.

Stir the ziti into the boiling water. Cover the pot and reheat to boiling, stirring once or twice. When the water returns to a boil, uncover the pot. Cook the pasta, stirring occasionally, until quite al dente—with a visible ring of white in the center—about 10 minutes.

> 6 quarts salted water
>
> 3 tablespoons unsalted butter, at room temperature
>
> 1 pound ziti
>
> 2 cups Marinara Sauce (page 143)
>
> 1 tablespoon chopped fresh Italian parsley leaves
>
> 1 tablespoon chopped fresh basil leaves
>
> 1 tablespoon chopped fresh marjoram leaves
>
> 12 fresh bocconcini (small balls of fresh mozzarella, about 1 ounce each; see Note, page 37)
>
> 2 tablespoons extra virgin olive oil

Meanwhile, in a small saucepan, heat the marinara sauce over medium-low heat to a boil. Transfer the sauce to a large bowl and stir in the parsley, basil, and marjoram.

Drain the ziti well and add it to the seasoned sauce. Toss well.

Place one of the parchment rectangles on a work surface with one of the long sides toward you. (If you have enough space, you can fill and roll all the packages at the same time.) Place one sixth of the ziti mixture in a mound over the lower right-hand quarter of the rectangle, about 2 inches from the edges of the parchment. Place 2 bocconcini over the mound of pasta and drizzle with the olive oil.

continued

To make the package, fold the long side of the parchment nearest you over the ziti and continue rolling the parchment so it forms a loose cone that encloses the ziti. Tuck the large open end of the cone underneath the package and place the *cartoccio* seam side down in a prepared baking dish. Repeat with the remaining parchment and filling. If using one large baking dish, transfer the packages to the dish, leaving some space between each.

Place the individual dishes or the large dish on the oven rack. Bake until the tops of the paper packages are well browned and the cheese is melted, about 8 minutes, if using individual dishes, slightly longer for packages baked in one large dish. Serve immediately and let each guest open a parchment package and spoon the pasta and sauce out onto a hot plate.

Dry Pasta Cooked in Parchment Paper
(Pasta al Cartoccio)

This approach to cooking pasta—wrapping it in parchment paper, then baking it—is unusual, but not difficult and quite effective. For this technique, the pasta is undercooked by two minutes, then dressed with the sauce, and cheese where appropriate, and placed in portions on parchment paper. The parchment is folded into cone-shaped *cartocci* (cornets) and baked. The aroma and flavors are all contained in the parchment. Each guest opens a package and, in a cloud of fragrant steam, discovers the tasty contents.

Serving *pasta al cartoccio* takes the pressure off the cook. The pasta can be prepared and wrapped in parchment paper half an hour before the guests arrive and set in the oven while they enjoy an aperitif.

For best results, you will need individual ovenproof casseroles and, ideally, parchment sheet pan liners (approximately 28 × 16 inches), which are available in restaurant supply houses. The store-bought rolls of parchment paper are fine, but they will give you a little less room to work with. Do not use unbleached (tan) parchment; it is very brittle.

Rigatoni in Parchment with Five Cheeses

Rigatoni ai Cinque Formaggi in Cartoccio

Bring the salted water to a boil.

Meanwhile, preheat the oven to 475°F and place a rack in the center position. Fold six 26 × 18-inch sheets of parchment paper in half to form 18 × 13-inch rectangles. (Alternatively, tear off six 30-inch lengths from a 12-inch-wide roll of parchment paper and fold them in half crosswise to form 15 × 12-inch rectangles.) Using 2 tablespoons of the butter, grease the center of each rectangle and six individual ovenproof dishes, each about 10 × 4 inches, or one ovenproof dish large enough (at least 18 × 12 inches) to hold the parchment packages side by side without touching.

Stir the rigatoni into the boiling water. Cover the pot and reheat to boiling, stirring once or twice. When the water returns to a boil, uncover the pot. Cook the pasta, stirring occasionally, until quite al dente—with a visible ring of white in the center—about 10 minutes.

Meanwhile, in a large bowl, stir together the ricotta and cream. Stir in the thyme.

> 6 quarts salted water
> ½ cup (1 stick) unsalted butter, at room temperature
> 1 pound rigatoni
> 2 cups fresh ricotta or one 15-ounce container ricotta
> ½ cup heavy cream
> 1 teaspoon fresh thyme leaves
> 6 fresh sage leaves
> 1½ cups shredded Swiss cheese (about 5 ounces)
> 1½ cups shredded Fontina cheese (about 5 ounces)
> ½ cup freshly grated Pecorino Romano cheese
> ½ cup freshly grated Parmigiano-Reggiano cheese

In a small skillet over very low heat, combine the remaining 6 tablespoons butter with the sage leaves. Heat the butter slowly, stirring it once or twice, until melted and creamy but not separated. Remove from the heat.

Drain the rigatoni well and add it to the ricotta mixture. Toss well to coat.

Place one of the parchment rectangles on a work surface with one of the long sides toward you. (If you have enough space, you can fill and roll all the packages at the same time.) Place one sixth of the rigatoni mixture in a mound over the lower right-hand quarter of the rectangle, about 2 inches from the edges of the parchment. Sprinkle the mound of pasta with one sixth each of the Swiss cheese, the Fontina, and, finally, the two grated cheeses. Discard the sage leaves and drizzle some of the butter over the pasta.

To make the packages, fold the long side of the parchment nearest you over the rigatoni and continue rolling the parchment into a loose cone that encloses the rigatoni. Tuck the large open end of the cone underneath the package and place the *cartoccio* seam side down into a prepared baking dish. Repeat with the remaining parchment and filling. If using one large baking dish, transfer the packages to the dish, leaving some space between each.

Place the individual dishes or the large dish on the oven rack. Bake until the tops of the paper packages are well browned and the cheese is melted, about 8 minutes, if using individual dishes, slightly longer for packages baked in one large dish. Serve immediately and let each guest open a package and spoon the pasta onto a hot plate.

The Tomato

(Il Pomodoro)

The tomato (originally from Peru) reached Italy in the sixteenth century, but it wasn't until the eighteenth century that it took a prominent place on the Italian table. The uses of tomatoes in Italian cooking are endless, but an often-asked question is, "Which one do I use to make sauce for pasta?"

Fresh Tomatoes

The fresh plum tomato is the ideal sauce tomato—it is rich in pulp and low on seeds and juice. In Italy, the best plum tomatoes come from San Marzano, near Naples. Vine-ripened on the volcanic hills, the tomatoes capture the intense Italian sun. The volcanic earth is porous and full of minerals, giving ample nourishment and reflecting the sun back up to the maturing tomatoes.

When buying plum tomatoes, look for sound, plump specimens—vine-ripened if possible—with the peppery scent of their leaves still lingering. They should be firm with a healthy, deep red color. If they are not at their peak of maturity, keep them on the windowsill or in a brown paper bag in the kitchen for a few days. The Roman, or Roma, tomato is also available in the United States and is a good substitute for the San Marzano tomato.

To peel fresh plum tomatoes, cut a small X in the bottom of each with a paring knife and remove the core. Plunge the tomatoes into boiling water for about 15 seconds, fish them out with a slotted spoon, and place in ice water. Drain, and the skin should peel right off. Cut the tomato in half, squeeze out the seeds over a strainer, and save the juice for making the sauce.

A wonderful recent addition to the market is the vine-ripened tomato sold in small clusters still clinging to the vine. These are a little larger than the cherry tomatoes and usually come from Israel, Holland, Mexico, or Spain. When ripened, they are exceptionally sweet and aromatic and are excellent in raw tomato sauces for pasta (see page 145) or in any recipe calling for fresh tomatoes. The skin and seeds are fine enough that you can use these tomatoes without peeling or seeding.

Canned Tomatoes

The choices of canned tomatoes include: peeled tomatoes in their own juice, tomato puree, tomato paste (*concentrato*), crushed tomatoes, and peeled tomatoes in tomato puree. Each will give you a different intensity and density in the finished sauce. Look for the label that says "Grown and packed in Italy" to ensure that you have an authentic product. A label that reads "Italian-style" does not indicate authenticity or country of origin but rather a style of preparation. I recommend looking for a product that reads *Pomodori Pelati di San Marzano* (peeled tomatoes from San Marzano).

Peeled plum tomatoes in their own juice: For basic light tomato and marinara sauces, I use peeled tomatoes in their juice when fresh tomatoes are not available. I crush them lightly with my hands before using them for marinara; for the tomato sauce, I pass them through a food mill. If you don't own a food mill, crush them as fine as possible with a wire whisk, but don't puree them in a food processor or blender—that will change the color and texture. I also use peeled tomatoes in their juice when making fresh quick dishes with fish, chicken, and vegetables.

Tomato puree and paste: When I am preparing a sauce with meat, such as a bolognese or game sauce, I use tomato puree and/or paste. In this case, the puree or paste is simmered for a long time, giving a velvety density and complexity to the sauce.

Crushed tomatoes and peeled tomatoes in puree: Crushed tomatoes and peeled tomatoes in puree are good when making sauces for lasagne, baked pasta dishes, or vegetables and meats *parmigiana*. For these dishes, the sauce should be on the tight side, not thin and runny, and the use of crushed or peeled tomatoes in puree will give you density and a fresh taste as well.

All canned tomato products are best used as soon as possible after opening. To store once opened, transfer them from the cans to tightly covered plastic containers or glass jars and keep refrigerated. Cover tomato paste with a thin layer of olive oil to keep it from drying and forming mold.

Basic Sauces

Marinara sauce and tomato sauce are two seemingly similar sauces, but they are quite different in flavor and in the role they play in Italian cuisine. Longer cooking time and the addition of vegetables makes tomato sauce sweeter, whereas the shorter cooking time of the marinara leaves more of the tomatoes' natural acidity, hence a feeling of freshness.

For a good marinara, the aroma of garlic should gently linger with the freshness of tomato pulp and basil—like biting into a fresh ripe tomato. Marinara sauce is used in most quick pasta preparations and in most fish dishes that call for tomatoes. The flavor of tomato sauce is more complex—more like a harmony of tomatoes, onions, celery, carrots, and bay leaves. This more intense flavor is used in pasta sauces that require a longer cooking time, like those made with meat or mushrooms. It is also used in all kinds of meat preparations that call for tomatoes.

I have also included a recipe for Herb Pesto, which I love more than pesto made with all basil. Like tomato and marinara sauces, this pesto is at home in dishes other than pasta. Stir some into soup or spoon some over pan-fried lamb chops.

Marinara Sauce

Salsa Marinara

In a medium-size nonreactive saucepan, heat the olive oil over medium heat. Add the garlic and cook, stirring, until lightly browned, about 2 minutes. Carefully add the tomatoes and their liquid. Bring to a boil and season lightly with salt and peperoncino. Reduce the heat to medium-low and simmer, breaking up the tomatoes with a whisk as they cook, until the sauce is chunky and thick, about 20 minutes. Remove the garlic cloves, if desired. About 5 minutes before the sauce is finished, stir in the basil. Taste the sauce and add more salt and peperoncino if necessary.

Note: If using fresh plum tomatoes, the extra virgin olive oil can be increased to ½ cup for optimal results.

¼ cup extra virgin olive oil

8 garlic cloves, crushed

3 pounds ripe plum tomatoes, cored, peeled (see page 141), and seeded, or one 35-ounce can peeled Italian plum tomatoes, seeded and lightly crushed, with their liquid

Salt

Peperoncino (crushed red pepper)

10 fresh basil leaves, washed, dried, and roughly torn

Tomato Sauce

Salsa di Pomodoro

MAKES ABOUT 3 CUPS;
ENOUGH TO SAUCE 6 SERVINGS OF PASTA

3 pounds ripe plum tomatoes, cored, peeled
(see page 141), and seeded, or one
35-ounce can peeled Italian plum
tomatoes, seeded and lightly crushed,
with their liquid
¼ cup extra virgin olive oil
1 small onion, finely chopped
¼ cup finely chopped carrots
¼ cup finely chopped celery
4 fresh bay leaves or 2 dried bay leaves
Salt
Peperoncino (crushed red pepper)

Pass the tomatoes through a food mill fitted with the fine disc or crush them as fine as possible in a bowl with a wire whisk.

In a medium-size nonreactive saucepan, heat the olive oil over medium heat. Add the onion and simmer until wilted. Add the carrots and celery and cook, stirring occasionally, until golden, about 10 minutes. Add the tomatoes and bay leaves, season lightly with salt and peperoncino, and heat to a simmer. Simmer the sauce over medium-low heat, stirring occasionally, until thickened, about 45 minutes. Remove the bay leaves. Check the seasoning and add more salt and peperoncino if necessary.

Uncooked Tomato Sauce

❡ Salsa Cruda ❡

I had this dish for the first time in the only trattoria overlooking the port of Salina, one of the small islands that form the archipelago of the Lipari Islands north of Sicily. Everything is so intense on these islands—the sun, the people, the capers, the basil, the oregano, the Malvasia (an intensely flavored sweet wine made from a grape of the same name), the eggplants, and the tomatoes. In this dish, the sun seemed to explode in my very mouth with each bite of pasta that I took.

MAKES 6 SERVINGS

In a large serving bowl, toss the tomatoes with the oil, peperoncino, and salt. Let the tomatoes marinate at room temperature for 20 minutes, tossing occasionally.

Bring the salted water to a boil.

Stir the pasta into the boiling water. When the water returns to a boil, uncover the pot. Cook the pasta, stirring occasionally, until al dente—tender but firm—about 12 minutes. Reserve ½ cup of the pasta cooking water. Drain the pasta well.

Stir the reserved water and the basil into the tomatoes. Add the pasta and toss to coat. Add the Pecorino, toss again, and serve.

4 cups halved vine-ripened cherry tomatoes

⅓ cup extra virgin olive oil

½ teaspoon peperoncino (crushed red pepper)

¼ teaspoon salt

6 quarts salted water

1 pound large pasta shapes, such as rigatoni, ziti, or fusilli

10 fresh basil leaves, washed, dried, and finely shredded

1 cup freshly grated Pecorino Romano cheese

Herb Pesto

Pesto d'Erbe Miste

Spring heralds the awakening of the herb garden, and herbs are the *anima,* or soul, of a dish. Herbs can be used individually or in harmony with one other, but using more does not necessarily mean better. Moderation is the key.

I usually have a jar of mixed herb pesto that can be used as a sauce on pasta or as an added condiment to a pasta recipe or soup. Adding a teaspoon of pesto to a dish can give it life and, yes, soul.

MAKES 1½ CUPS

1 cup packed fresh Italian parsley leaves
½ cup packed fresh basil leaves
½ cup packed mixed fresh sage, thyme, and
    marjoram leaves
4 garlic cloves, peeled
1 cup extra virgin olive oil
Salt

Wash the herb leaves in cool water and dry them thoroughly, preferably in a salad spinner. Combine the herbs and garlic in a blender and blend on low speed, slowly adding the oil while the machine is running, until the pesto is smooth and all the oil is incorporated. Add salt to taste.

Keep in a sealed jar in the refrigerator and use as needed. Pesto will keep refrigerated for up to 4 weeks or it may be frozen for up to 3 months. Make sure there is a thin film of oil over the pesto to keep its flavor and color bright.

Leftover Pasta

Leftover pasta is delicious reheated the next day. The texture becomes different; it is not as resilient as it was when first cooked, but it takes on a new dimension since it has absorbed some of the sauce. To heat leftover pasta, you can add any remaining sauce, chicken stock, or just plain water. Heat the pasta over a low flame in a nonstick pan, stirring regularly. I love it when the reheated pasta begins to form a crust.

Leftover pasta can be used to make a frittata by adding it to whole eggs beaten with a little salt. Try adding small pieces of blanched vegetables, or some olives, capers, or crumbled and cooked sausages. Heat a few teaspoons of olive oil in a nonstick pan and pour in the frittata mixture. When the frittata is set and lightly browned underneath, flip it over and cook for a few additional minutes, or finish it in a hot oven as in the following recipe. Serve the frittata hot, cut into wedges like a pizza.

Leftover pasta, especially the short tubular kinds, can also be baked. Heat the pasta in a pan with leftover sauce, stock, or water. Add leftover or freshly braised vegetables such as zucchini, eggplant, or peppers. Ricotta cheese can also be added. Always remember when baking leftover pasta that it should be slightly saucier than it was when first served. Put the pasta in a buttered casserole. Sprinkle the top with grated Parmigiano-Reggiano or Fontina cheese, shaved mozzarella, or a combination. Bake in a preheated 475°F oven until a crispy golden top has formed and serve hot.

Capellini and Asparagus Frittata

Frittata di Capellini ed Asparagi

MAKES 6 SERVINGS

2 cups leftover cooked capellini or about
   3 ounces uncooked capellini
6 quarts salted water
1 pound thin asparagus
6 large eggs or 4 goose eggs
Freshly ground black pepper
2 tablespoons olive oil
1 tablespoon unsalted butter
8 scallions, including two thirds of the
   green part, thinly sliced
¼ cup packed chopped fresh Italian parsley
   leaves
½ cup freshly grated Parmigiano-Reggiano
   cheese

If starting with uncooked capellini, stir the pasta into a large pot of boiling salted water. Cover the pot and reheat to boiling, stirring once or twice. When the water returns to a boil, uncover the pot. Cook the pasta, stirring occasionally, until al dente—tender but firm—about 2 minutes. Drain the pasta well and run it under cold water until completely cool. Drain the pasta thoroughly.

Snap off and discard the tough ends of the asparagus. Cut the stalks into ½-inch pieces. In a medium-size saucepan of boiling salted water, blanch the asparagus just until it turns bright green, about 2 minutes. Drain the asparagus and refresh under cold water. Drain thoroughly.

Preheat the oven to 475°F.

With a fork, beat the eggs well and season with salt and pepper. In a large, ovenproof nonstick or well-seasoned cast-iron skillet, heat the oil and butter together over medium heat. Add the scallions and cook, stirring, until wilted, about 2 minutes. Reduce the heat to low and add the asparagus. Cover the skillet and cook until the asparagus is tender, about 10 minutes. Season with salt and pepper.

Add the capellini and chopped parsley to the skillet and toss well with the asparagus. Spread the pasta evenly in the skillet and slowly pour the egg mixture over it. The eggs should completely cover the pasta. Increase the heat to medium, cover the skillet, and let the frittata cook, without stirring, until it begins to form a crust underneath, 2 to 3 minutes. Sprinkle the grated cheese over the frittata, transfer the skillet to the oven, and bake, uncovered, until firm and the eggs are completely cooked in the center, 5 to 7 minutes.

Remove from the oven and let stand for about 5 minutes. Cut into 6 wedges and serve.

Rice

Riso

When I was a child, rice was bought by the kilo or half kilo. It came in large burlap bags with their tops rolled down like sleeves, with large scoops to pick up the rice. It was all short-grain rice but divided into three grades: The least expensive contained broken kernels, bran, and little pebbles; the middle grade was a bit better, with less debris; and the best was ready-to-use, shiny kernels. My mother would run all three of them through her fingers and usually chose the middle one, which meant that I had to help clean it before cooking. I would sit at the marble kitchen table, slowly spread the rice out of its paper cone onto the smooth surface, and, with my middle finger, press on the brown, alien seeds or pebbles. They would stick to my fingers, and I would pull them out one by one, making a little pile of debris to show my effort. There was nothing worse than biting into a risotto and finding a pebble between your teeth. Therefore, I had to be very meticulous.

I enjoyed risotto, but I have especially fond memories of rice cooked in goat's milk and dressed with honey. And on those days when I felt queasy, a bowl of rice cooked with olive oil and dressed with Parmigiano-Reggiano and love comforted me and soothed my stomach.

Rice, along with pasta and polenta, is a staple of the Italian table. It is one of those comfort foods that serves as a carrier for a wide variety of the flavors in Italian cuisine, but in its modesty and simplicity, it gives extraordinary results in added taste and texture.

There are about 120 different species of rice, a basic food for approximately three fourths of the world's population and most likely one of the oldest foods on this planet. Rice probably came to Italy between the ninth and tenth centuries. It traveled through northern Africa, reached Spain around the sixth and seventh centuries, and then moved through Sicily into mainland Italy. The cultivation of rice in Italy took hold around the fourteenth century—basically in the north.

Italy is Europe's largest producer of rice, and Vercelli in Piemonte is the capital of Italian rice production. The Italian production areas extend along the Valle Padana from the Veneto westward into Piemonte and reach down into Emilia-Romagna.

Rice is 100 percent natural, and since it is extremely versatile, it can be, and is, used in every course from salads and appetizer *frittelle* (pancakes) to soups, second-course *risotti*, and desserts—such as *budino di riso* (pudding), *torta di riso* (rice tart), or *gelato di riso* (rice ice cream).

Short-grain rice is the type of rice primarily used in Italian cuisine and it is essential for the making of risotto. It is notably shorter and plumper than long-grain rice and has a starchier character. It is translucent, with a visible center called *la perla* (the pearl). The special culinary quality of short-grain rice is that it readily releases its starches during the cooking process to create the creamy texture of a perfect risotto while the kernel remains al dente.

Vialone Nano, Carnaroli, Originario, and Arborio are the varieties of short-grain rice used most in Italy, and one or more of them can be found nearly everywhere in the United States. Vialone Nano is large and round and is used in soups and *risotti* preparations; Carnaroli is round and meaty and excellent for *risotti*; Originario is round and small and is used for soups and desserts or fried; and Arborio is large and meaty, wonderful for *risotti* and as an accompaniment to meat sauces and in desserts.

The nuances of these varieties are very important to Italian cuisine. The affecting element is texture—how does each variety respond to cooking, how does each hold its *cottura* (cooking texture) when prepared in soups, *risotti*, and desserts? *Al dente* is a common adjective used in Italian cuisine; it gauges the resistance of the pasta or rice to the bite after it has been cooked. A properly cooked risotto is both al dente and creamy.

When I was a child, we had risotto at least once a week. It is one of those dishes that can be frugal and simple or a feast in itself. It can be made with a base of onions and beans or with shrimp, lobster, and saffron—depending on the market, depending on the budget, and depending on who is coming to dinner. But there is one demand of the diner from this simple food: that you be at the table when risotto is served—even one minute of overcooking will yield a less-than-perfect risotto.

On risotto days, my mother would remind me as I left to go play after school, "*Vieni in tempo che il riso non t'aspetti alla porta*" ("Come back on time, otherwise the rice will be waiting for you at the door").

What is risotto? Risotto is Italian-grown, short-grain rice cooked using a technique that slowly coaxes the starches out of the rice to blend with the flavors of choice into a unique dish in which each kernel retains its al dente texture in a creamy suspension.

When buying rice for risotto dishes, look for shiny kernels of uniform pearly color, with no blotchiness, and a smooth surface that doesn't feel floury to the touch. Rice should be stored in an airy, cool, dark place; it has a storage life of approximately three months. Don't wash rice before cooking; water will initiate a premature release of starches.

The best cooking vessel for risotto is a wide, heavy, 3- to 4-quart casserole or pot that is wider than it is high and evenly disperses heat and allows evaporation to occur uniformly. The proper ratio of rice to liquid is 1 to 3½, and the yield of cooked risotto will be double the bulk of the raw rice, plus the quantity of ingredients that are added to the rice.

The distinguishing texture of a well-made risotto, *ben mantecato* (well amalgamated and creamy) and al dente, is the result of several procedures: First is the even and gradual release of the starch, which initially is controlled by toasting the unwashed rice in olive oil or butter, a process that simultaneously tempers each kernel's outer layer of starch and coats the grain with liquid-resistant fats, and prevents the overly rapid absorption of the cooking liquid. Then, release of starch is further controlled by the gradual addition of simmering broth—simmering because the cooking temperature of the rice must be kept constant to prevent hardening of the starches and loss of creaminess. Finally, the rice must be stirred regularly, to prevent the released starch from scorching and to amalgamate fat and starch. Choose a narrow wooden spoon or flat wooden paddle that can get into corners. Stir the risotto constantly, moving the rice away from the bottom and edges of the pan to prevent scorching.

It's imperative that risotto be served and eaten immediately—thus my mother's admonition. Otherwise, the rice will continue to absorb moisture, release too much starch, and become *pappa*, or as soft and gummy as baby food.

Once the basic technique is understood, risotto can be flavored any way you wish; it's just a matter of orchestrating the cooking times of the rice and its accompaniments. Seafood, meats, vegetables, mushrooms, truffles—everything's good in risotto.

And finally, while it is true that risotto will not wait for the diner, leftover risotto can be used in another dish for another meal that is so good, it makes sense to deliberately make too much.

Risotto Rules

1. For proper results, use only the traditional short-grain rice varieties for making risotto.

2. The ratio of rice to cooking liquid is approximately 1 to 3½. Although a recipe calls for a specific amount of stock, the actual amount used may vary. Let proper consistency near the end of the cooking time be your guide.

3. The rice will double in volume when it is cooked.

4. Always use a wide, heavy, 3- to 4-quart casserole or pot.

5. Control the heat during the browning of the onion, shallot, or leek. Cook slowly, just until evenly golden brown.

6. The stock or cooking liquid must be kept hot over low heat so that its addition does not interrupt the cooking process. It should be added about ½ cup at a time.

7. Stir risotto until each addition of stock is completely absorbed and you can see the bottom of the pot as you stir the contents.

8. Average cooking time for risotto is 16 to 20 minutes after the first liquid has been added, depending on the amount of ingredients, the level of heat, and the cooking vessel.

9. Risotto can be tight and dense or soft and runny (*all'onda*), depending on personal taste. It is a matter of adding more stock at the end of the cooking process and not cooking that last addition of stock until the rice has absorbed it. There is a general rule that risotto with seafood is looser and that, as risotto moves inland and is prepared with meats, game, and mushrooms, it becomes denser.

10. When in doubt, undercook; risotto continues to cook before it is served.

11. Always serve risotto immediately after cooking.

12. By tradition, cheese is never added to fish or seafood *risotti*.

13. Leftover risotto should always be saved. It will safely stay refrigerated for 4 to 5 days and can be used to make *Risotto Pancake* (page 167) or *Risotto Fritters* (page 168).

Basic Risotto

 Risotto

This is the basic recipe for risotto—through this recipe you can truly appreciate and understand how short-grain rice, when cooked using the right technique, truly becomes a marvel of texture and viscosity. Any flavoring can be added to this base, giving the basic risotto a new personality each time.

MAKES 6 SERVINGS

In a heavy, wide, 3- to 4-quart casserole or pot, heat the olive oil over medium heat. Cook the onions and shallots together until golden, stirring often, about 8 minutes. Add the rice and stir to coat with the oil. Toast the rice until the edges become translucent, 1 to 2 minutes.

Pour in the wine and stir well until evaporated. Add ½ cup of the hot stock and ½ teaspoon of the salt. Cook, stirring constantly, until all the stock has been absorbed. Continue to add hot stock in small batches—just enough to completely moisten the rice—and cook until each successive batch has been absorbed. Stir constantly and adjust the level of heat so the rice is simmering very gently until the rice is creamy but al dente. This will take 16 to 20 minutes from the time the wine was added.

3 tablespoons extra virgin olive oil
1 cup minced onions
2 tablespoons minced shallots
2½ cups Arborio or Carnaroli rice
½ cup dry white wine
6½ cups hot Chicken Stock (page 80) or
    canned low-sodium chicken broth
½ teaspoon salt, or as needed
2 teaspoons unsalted butter, cut into bits
½ cup freshly grated Parmigiano-Reggiano
    cheese, plus more for serving
Freshly ground black pepper

Remove the casserole from the heat and beat in the butter until completely melted and then the cheese. Adjust the seasoning with salt, if necessary, and pepper.

Serve immediately, ladled into warm shallow bowls. Top each serving with additional grated cheese to taste.

Simple Additions to Basic Risotto

Basic risotto is easy to master and lends itself to a wide range of variations. But it is important that whatever is added to risotto has a flavor of its own. For example:

- *Vegetables:* Asparagus, zucchini and zucchini flowers, radicchio di Treviso, fresh peas, or spring onions. Stir-fry the vegetables a few minutes and season them with salt and pepper before adding.

- *Mushrooms:* Porcini, portobello, or a mélange of wild and cultivated mushroom types. Sauté the mushrooms, all cut into roughly the same size pieces, in olive oil with onions, garlic, and/or shallots until all the mushrooms' moisture is evaporated. Season them before adding to the risotto.

- *Fish or shellfish:* Shrimp, scallops, clams, mussels, lobster, or crab. Shrimp or scallops can be quickly seared as in the recipe for *Shrimp Risotto* (page 158) before adding them to the risotto. Cook clams, mussels, lobster, or crab and remove them from the shell before adding to the risotto. Large pieces of lobster or other shellfish should be cut into manageable pieces before adding them.

- *Meats and birds:* Veal, quail, pheasant, or squab. Simmer meat or birds on the bone until tender enough to fall off the bone (see Risotto with Squab, page 156, or Garganelli with Pheasant in Guazzetto, page 96, as examples). Remove the meat from the bones and use the cooking liquid and meat to flavor the risotto.

Add whatever ingredients you choose toward the end of the cooking time—just to heat them through and allow the flavors to blend with the rice. Especially watch the timing of fish and shellfish; add them very near the end of cooking so that they are not tough and overdone.

Creamy Risotto Milanese Style

Risotto alla Milanese

This is the classic yellow risotto with saffron that is associated with the city of Milano. There is a legend surrounding the origin of this dish concerning the wedding banquet in 1574 of the daughter of Valerio da Profondavalle, a Flemish artisan responsible for the fabrication of the glass windows of the Duomo, the renowned Gothic cathedral. In those days, saffron was used to give the yellow color to glass, and since the banquet was held in one of the building annexes of the Duomo, supposedly a sachet of saffron accidentally fell into the risotto while it was cooking.

A beautiful story—and possibly true. Saffron was already being used in cooking at the time, but maybe for *risotto* it did happen that way.

MAKES 6 SERVINGS

Pour ½ cup of the hot stock over the saffron in a small heatproof bowl. Let it stand.

In a heavy, wide, 3- to 4-quart casserole or pot, heat the olive oil over medium heat. Cook the onions and shallots together until golden, stirring often, about 8 minutes. Add the rice and stir to coat with the oil. Toast the rice until the edges become translucent, 1 to 2 minutes.

Pour in the wine and stir well until evaporated. Add ½ cup of the remaining hot stock and ½ teaspoon of the salt. Cook, stirring constantly, until all the stock has been absorbed. Stir in the beef marrow, if using. Continue to add hot stock in small batches—just enough to completely moisten the rice—and cook until each successive batch has been absorbed. About 10 minutes after adding the first addition of stock, stir in the saffron mixture. Stir constantly and adjust the level of heat so the rice is simmering very gently until the rice mixture is creamy but al dente. This will take 16 to 20 minutes from the time the wine was added.

Remove the casserole from the heat. Beat in the butter until completely melted and then beat in the cheese. Adjust the seasoning with salt, if necessary, and pepper. Serve immediately, ladled into warm shallow bowls.

7 cups hot Meat Stock (page 78) or canned low-sodium beef broth
½ teaspoon saffron threads
3 tablespoons extra virgin olive oil
1 cup minced onions
2 tablespoons minced shallots
2½ cups Arborio or Carnaroli rice
½ cup dry white wine
½ teaspoon salt, or as needed
2 ounces beef marrow (optional), cut into ¼-inch pieces (see Note)
2 tablespoons unsalted butter, cut into bits
½ cup freshly grated Parmigiano-Reggiano cheese
Freshly ground black pepper to taste

continued

Note: Few butchers sell beef marrow separately anymore, but it is easy to come up with your own. For about 2 ounces of marrow, start with five to six 1- to 1½-inch beef marrow bones. (Your butcher can supply them and cut them to the correct size.) Heat the stock for the risotto and warm the bones in the stock two at a time for 3 minutes. Remove the bones with a slotted spoon and let them stand just until cool enough to handle. Try to push the marrow through the bone with your finger; it should come right out. If not, use a small spoon to scoop it out. The marrow may be soft around the edges, but the center should still be firm enough to chop.

Risotto with Squab

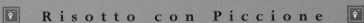 ## Risotto con Piccione

Squab was one of the *animali di cortile* (courtyard animals) that we kept in the town of Busoler. My cousin Renato built little wooden boxes with vaulted openings on the roof of the *cantina* (wine cellar) that served as home to our family's flock of squabs. The loyal squabs would follow Renato in flight for kilometers and with a single call of "Tubi-Tubi," they would affectionately land on him, covering all of his head, arms, and shoulders.

The family gathering together for a dinner of *Risotto con Piccione* on Sundays sometimes made me sensitive but it was so delicious, somehow all of life's elements seemed to be in harmony. The food chain took its natural course.

MAKES 6 SERVINGS

For the squab sauce

2½ cups Chicken Stock (page 80) or canned
    low-sodium chicken broth
¼ cup dried porcini mushrooms
4 medium-size squab (about 3½ pounds
    total)
3 fresh or dried bay leaves
1 teaspoon fresh rosemary leaves
4 cloves

Make the squab sauce. In a small saucepan, heat ½ cup of the chicken stock to a boil. Remove the pan from the heat and stir in the porcini. Let stand until the porcini are softened, about 20 minutes.

Drain the mushrooms and reserve the liquid. Rinse the porcini briefly under cold water. Drain them well and finely chop them. Strain the soaking liquid through a coffee filter or a sieve lined with cheesecloth. Set the soaking liquid and chopped porcini aside.

Remove the backbones from the squab—kitchen shears work well for this. Cut each bird into quarters: two leg and two half-breast pieces each. Wash the squab pieces, removing any traces of viscera, and pat dry with paper towels. Tie the bay leaves, rosemary, and cloves together in a small square of cheesecloth and set aside.

In a large skillet, heat the oil over medium heat. Add the onion and bacon and cook, stirring, until the onion is wilted, about 3 minutes. Add the squab pieces and brown on both sides, turning as necessary, about 5 minutes. Reduce the heat if necessary to avoid burning the onion. If the squab pieces don't all fit in the skillet in one layer, brown them in batches, removing the onions as they brown. Add the carrots and chopped porcini. Add the wine and stir until evaporated. Stir in the tomato paste and cook until the carrots are browned, stirring and turning the squab pieces frequently, about 10 minutes.

Add the reserved porcini soaking liquid, the remaining 2 cups chicken stock, and the cheesecloth bundle. Heat to boiling, then reduce the heat to medium-low. Cook, uncovered, at a gentle simmer until the squab is tender when pierced with a fork or skewer, 30 to 45 minutes, depending on the quality of the birds. The legs may be tender before the breasts. If so, remove them and let the breasts continue to cook.

Remove the spice packet and discard. Remove the squab to a platter and cover with a sheet of aluminum foil. When cool, peel off the skin and remove the meat from the bones. Shred the meat into small pieces. Skim off as much fat as possible from the sauce. Return the squab meat to the sauce and simmer over low heat until reduced slightly, about 15 minutes. Skim the fat from the surface as it simmers. Season to taste with salt and pepper and set aside.

Make the risotto. In a heavy, wide, 3- to 4-quart casserole or pot, heat the olive oil over medium heat. Cook the onions and shallots together until golden, stirring often, about 8 minutes. Add the rice and stir to coat with the oil. Toast the rice until the edges become translucent, 1 to 2 minutes.

Pour in the wine and stir well until evaporated. Add ½ cup of the hot stock and ½ teaspoon of the salt. Cook, stirring constantly, until all the stock has been absorbed. Add the squab and its sauce. Stir constantly until all the liquid is almost entirely absorbed. Continue to add the hot stock in

½ cup extra virgin olive oil

1 large onion, chopped

2 slices lean bacon, finely diced

½ cup shredded carrots

1 cup dry white wine

1½ tablespoons tomato paste

Salt and freshly ground black pepper

For the risotto

3 tablespoons extra virgin olive oil

½ cup minced onions

2 tablespoons minced shallots

2½ cups Arborio or Carnaroli rice

½ cup dry white wine

6½ cups hot Chicken Stock (page 80) or canned low-sodium chicken broth

½ teaspoon salt, or as needed

2 tablespoons unsalted butter, cut into bits

½ cup freshly grated Parmigiano-Reggiano cheese, plus additional for serving

Freshly ground black pepper

small batches—just enough to completely moisten the rice—and cook until each successive batch has been absorbed. Stir constantly and adjust the level of heat so the rice is simmering very gently until the rice mixture is creamy but al dente. This will take 16 to 20 minutes from the addition of the wine.

Remove the casserole from the heat. Beat in the butter first until melted, then the grated cheese. Adjust the seasoning with salt, if necessary, and pepper.

Serve immediately, ladled into warm shallow bowls. Top each serving with additional grated cheese to taste.

Shrimp Risotto
Risotto ai Gamberi

It is important to synchronize the timing of the risotto with the cooking time of the added ingredients—in this case, the shrimp need a very short cooking time, five to six minutes or, depending on their size, two minutes more or less. Begin cooking the shrimp in the last six minutes of cooking the risotto so they remain crunchy and juicy. Sear them first to intensify their flavor and to prevent them from losing all their flavor to the rice.

MAKES 6 SERVINGS

1 pound medium-size shrimp (about 25)

One 28-ounce can Italian plum tomatoes

6 tablespoons extra virgin olive oil

½ cup minced onions

½ cup minced shallots

1½ cups Carnaroli or Arborio rice

½ cup dry white wine

5 to 6 cups hot lightly salted water

2 garlic cloves, crushed

2 tablespoons minced fresh Italian parsley leaves

Salt and freshly ground black pepper

Peel the shrimp. (You can leave the tails on 6 shrimp if you like, and leave these shrimp whole to place as a decoration on top of each bowl of risotto. Sear the whole shrimp along with the cut-up shrimp as described later in the recipe.) With a small knife, make a shallow cut down the back of the shrimp to remove the dark vein. Cut the shrimp crosswise into thirds.

Drain the plum tomatoes and remove their seeds. Puree the tomatoes in a blender until smooth. Pass the puree through a sieve. Set the puree aside.

In a heavy, wide, 3- to 4-quart casserole or pot, heat 3 tablespoons of the olive oil over medium heat. Cook the onions and shallots together until golden, stirring often, about 8 minutes. Add the rice and stir to coat with the oil. Toast the rice until the edges become translucent, 1 to 2 minutes.

Pour in the wine and stir well until evaporated. Add the tomato puree and cook, stirring, for 3 minutes. The tomatoes should be simmering at this point. Add 1 cup of the hot water. Cook, stirring constantly, until all the liquid has been absorbed. Continue to add the hot water in small batches—just enough to completely moisten the rice—and cook until each successive batch has been absorbed. Stir constantly and adjust the level of heat so the rice is simmering very gently.

Meanwhile, about 10 minutes after adding the tomato puree, heat the remaining 3 tablespoons olive oil in a deep skillet over medium heat. Add the garlic and cook, stirring, until lightly browned, about 2 minutes. Remove and discard the garlic, then add the shrimp pieces and whole shrimp, if using, to the skillet and cook until they are bright pink on both sides and firm, about 2 minutes. Remove the whole shrimp and set aside.

Add the contents of the skillet to the rice. Mix well and cook, adding more water as described above, until the rice is creamy and al dente, 3 to 4 minutes longer. (The total cooking time for the rice after adding the tomato puree is about 18 minutes.)

Remove the casserole from the heat and stir in the chopped parsley. Adjust the seasoning with salt, if necessary, and pepper. Serve immediately, ladled into warm shallow bowls. Place one of the whole shrimp on top of each serving, if using.

Risotto with Barolo on a Bed of Carrot Puree

◧ Risotto al Barolo su Purè di Carrote ◧

This risotto is typical of the cooking of *Piemonte*—a region where good red wine abounds and rice is king; their marriage is a natural. The addition of a bed of seasoned carrot puree, which is sweet, creates a nice balance and adds complexity to the taste. Any good wine can be used to make the risotto, but I prefer Barolo—in the *tradizione Piemontese*.

MAKES 6 SERVINGS

For the carrot puree
3 cups chopped carrots (about 1¼ pounds)
3 tablespoons unsalted butter
Pinch of freshly grated nutmeg
Salt

For the risotto
3 tablespoons extra virgin olive oil
1 cup minced onions
2 tablespoons minced shallots
2 cups Arborio or Carnaroli rice
1½ to 2 cups good Barolo wine
5 cups hot Chicken Stock (page 80) or
    Meat Stock (page 78) or canned low-
    sodium chicken or beef broth
½ teaspoon salt, or as needed
2 tablespoons unsalted butter, cut into bits
½ cup freshly grated Parmigiano-Reggiano
    cheese, plus additional for serving
Freshly ground black pepper

Cook the carrots in a medium-size saucepan of boiling salted water to cover until very tender, about 12 minutes. Drain well and pass through a sieve or food mill. Beat in the butter, nutmeg, and salt to taste. Cover and keep warm.

In a heavy, wide, 3- to 4-quart casserole or pot, heat the olive oil over medium heat. Cook the onions and shallots together until golden, stirring often, about 8 minutes. Add the rice and stir to coat with the oil. Toast the rice until the edges become translucent, 1 to 2 minutes.

Pour in the wine and stir well until all the wine is evaporated, about 4 minutes. Add ½ cup of the hot stock and ½ teaspoon of the salt. Cook, stirring constantly, until all the stock has been absorbed. Continue to add hot stock in small batches—just enough to completely moisten the rice—and cook until each successive batch has been absorbed. Stir constantly and adjust the level of heat so the rice is simmering very gently until the rice mixture is creamy but al dente. This will take 16 to 20 minutes from the time the wine was added.

Remove the casserole from the heat. Beat in the butter first until completely melted, then the cheese. Adjust the seasoning with salt, if necessary, and pepper.

To serve, spread the warm carrot puree over the bottom of six warm shallow bowls. Top with the hot risotto. Top each serving with additional grated cheese to taste. Serve immediately.

Beet Risotto

Risotto alla Barbabietola

The vibrant color of this dish will add pizzazz to any table. But the real surprise is the flavor—a mellow and rich blend of rice and beets.

MAKES 6 SERVINGS

Cut off the beet tops if any, then scrub the beets well under cold running water. In a medium-size saucepan, simmer the beets until they are tender when pierced with a small knife. This can take anywhere from 40 minutes to an hour, depending on the beets. Drain, reserving 1 cup of the cooking liquid, and cool the beets.

Peel the beets and cut them into ¼-inch dice. Strain the reserved cooking liquid through a coffee filter or sieve lined with cheesecloth or paper towel. Set the beets and their liquid aside.

In a heavy, wide 3- to 4-quart casserole or pot, heat the olive oil over medium heat. Cook the onions and shallots together until golden, stirring often, about 8 minutes. Add the rice and stir to coat with the oil. Toast the rice until the edges become translucent, 1 to 2 minutes.

2 beets (about 1¼ pounds without the tops)

3 tablespoons extra virgin olive oil

½ cup minced onions

2 tablespoons minced shallots

2½ cups Arborio or Carnaroli rice

½ cup dry white wine

6½ cups hot Chicken Stock (page 80) or canned low-sodium chicken broth

½ teaspoon salt, or as needed

2 tablespoons unsalted butter

3 tablespoons freshly grated Parmigiano-Reggiano cheese

Freshly ground black pepper

Pour in the wine and stir well until evaporated. Add ½ cup of the hot stock and ½ teaspoon of the salt. Cook, stirring constantly, until all the stock has been absorbed. Continue to add hot stock in small batches—just enough to completely moisten the rice—and cook until each successive batch has been absorbed. After about 10 minutes, stir in the beets and beet liquid. Stir until the beet liquid is absorbed, then continue adding the stock as above. Stir constantly and adjust the level of heat so the rice is simmering very gently until the rice mixture is creamy and al dente. This will take 16 to 20 minutes after adding the wine.

Remove the casserole from the heat. Beat in the butter first until completely melted, then the cheese. Season with salt, if necessary, and pepper. Serve immediately, ladled into warm shallow bowls.

Risotto with Shavings of White Truffle

Risotto al Tartufo

MAKES 6 SERVINGS

2 ounces fresh white Alba truffles (see page 5)

3 tablespoons extra virgin olive oil

1 cup minced onions

2 tablespoons minced shallots

2½ cups Arborio or Carnaroli rice

½ cup dry white wine

6½ cups hot Chicken Stock (page 80) or Meat Stock (page 78) or canned low-sodium chicken or beef broth

½ teaspoon salt, or as needed

2 tablespoons unsalted butter, cut into bits

1 teaspoon truffle oil

¼ cup freshly grated Parmigiano-Reggiano cheese

Freshly ground black pepper

Brush the truffles thoroughly with a vegetable brush to remove as much loose dirt as possible. With a damp paper towel, clean them thoroughly. You may store the truffles surrounded with the rice to be used in the risotto in the refrigerator for up to two days.

In a heavy, wide, 3- to 4-quart casserole or pot, heat the olive oil over medium heat. Add the onions and shallots and cook them until golden, stirring often, about 8 minutes. Add the rice and stir to coat with the oil. Toast the rice until the edges become translucent, 1 to 2 minutes.

Pour in the wine and stir well until evaporated. Add ½ cup of the hot stock and ½ teaspoon of the salt. Cook, stirring constantly, until all the stock has been absorbed. Continue to add hot stock in small batches—just enough to completely moisten the rice—and cook until each successive batch has been absorbed. Stir constantly and adjust the level of heat so the rice is simmering very gently while adding the stock until the rice mixture is creamy but al dente. This will take 16 to 20 minutes from the time the wine was added.

Remove the casserole from the heat. Beat in the butter and truffle oil until the butter is melted, then beat in the grated cheese. Adjust the seasoning with salt, if necessary, and pepper. Serve immediately, ladled into warm shallow bowls. Use a truffle slicer or the coarse side of a box grater to shave the truffles over the risotto at the table and let the sublime aroma rise to delight each guest.

Risotto with Orange Juice

⬛ Risotto all'Arancia ⬛

Anna Tasca Lanza first prepared this dish for me at her family's Regaleali estate in Sicily. Anna is a gifted chef and cookbook author who is in love with the foods of her native land. The family estate also produces some of the best wines of the region. The risotto was so wonderful and refreshing that I began making it here, changing it slightly each time, as I do with most recipes that please me.

MAKES 6 SERVINGS

With a vegetable peeler, remove the zest from two of the oranges, being careful not to include the white part—it is very bitter. Cut the zest crosswise into thin strips. (There should be about ½ cup lightly packed.) Juice the oranges. (There should be about 1 cup juice.)

In a heavy, wide, 3- to 4-quart casserole or pot, heat the olive oil over medium heat. Cook the onions and shallots together until golden, stirring often, about 8 minutes. Add the rice and stir to coat with the oil. Toast the rice until the edges become translucent, 1 to 2 minutes.

Add the wine and orange zest. Stir well until the wine has evaporated. Add ½ cup of the hot stock and ½ teaspoon of the salt. Cook, stirring constantly, until all the stock has been absorbed. Continue to add hot stock in small batches—just enough to completely moisten the rice—and cook until each successive batch has been absorbed. When all the stock has been added, begin adding the orange juice in the same manner. Stir constantly and adjust the level of heat so the rice is simmering very gently until the rice mixture is creamy but al dente. This will take 16 to 20 minutes from the time the wine was added.

Remove from the heat. Beat in the butter first until completely melted, then the cheese. Adjust the seasoning with salt, if necessary, and pepper. Serve immediately, ladled into warm shallow bowls.

---

3 juicy oranges, with bright, unblemished skins

3 tablespoons extra virgin olive oil

½ cup minced onions

2 tablespoons minced shallots

2½ cups Arborio or Carnaroli rice

½ cup dry white wine

5½ cups hot Chicken Stock (page 80) or canned low-sodium chicken broth

½ teaspoon salt, or as needed

½ cup freshly grated Parmigiano-Reggiano cheese

2 tablespoons unsalted butter, cut into bits

Freshly ground black pepper

Risotto with Vegetables

Risotto con Verdure

When making this risotto, choose any vegetable or combination of vegetables that is available. It is a wonderful way of cooking with what's in season, and, by using some of your favorite vegetables, you can create an exciting and new combination of flavors that will be yours to pass on.

MAKES 6 SERVINGS

½ pound broccoli (about 1 medium-size stalk)

1 cup blanched and peeled shelled fava beans (see page 233) or frozen baby lima beans

3 tablespoons extra virgin olive oil

½ cup minced scallions (about 6)

1 tablespoon minced shallots

2½ cups Arborio or Carnaroli rice

½ cup dry white wine

6½ cups hot Chicken Stock (page 80) or canned low-sodium chicken broth

½ teaspoon salt, or as needed

2 tablespoons unsalted butter, cut into bits

½ cup freshly grated Pecorino Romano cheese

Freshly ground black pepper

Cut the florets from the broccoli stems. Keep the florets small—they have to fit on a spoon. Peel the broccoli stems with a small knife or vegetable peeler, then cut them into 2-inch pieces. Steam the florets just until bright green, about 1 minute. Steam the stems until very tender, about 4 minutes. Reserve the steaming liquid.

Transfer the stems to a blender or food processor and process until smooth; you will probably have to add some of the steaming liquid to make a smooth mixture. Scrape the puree into a small bowl and set the florets and puree aside.

If using baby lima beans, cook them in a small saucepan of boiling salted water for 2 minutes. Drain them thoroughly and set aside.

In a heavy, wide, 3- to 4-quart casserole or pot, heat the olive oil over medium heat. Cook the scallions and shallots together until translucent, stirring often, about 4 minutes. Add the rice and stir to coat with the oil. Toast the rice until the edges become translucent, 1 to 2 minutes.

Pour in the wine and stir well until evaporated. Add ½ cup of the hot stock and ½ teaspoon of the salt. Cook, stirring constantly, until all the stock has been absorbed. Continue to add hot stock in small batches—just enough to completely moisten the rice—and cook until each successive batch has been absorbed. About 12 minutes after the first addition of stock, stir in the broccoli puree and the favas or limas. About 3 minutes after that, stir in the broccoli florets. Stir constantly and adjust the level of heat so the rice is simmering very gently until the rice mixture is creamy but al dente. This will take about 18 minutes from the first addition of stock.

Remove the casserole from the heat and beat in the butter first until melted, then the grated cheese. Adjust the seasoning with salt, if necessary, and pepper. Serve immediately, ladled into warm shallow bowls.

Risotto with Squash

Risotto con Zucca

Rissotto with squash is excellent since it truly reflects the fall season. To give this risotto more complexity, try adding diced apples and a touch of cinnamon.

MAKES 6 SERVINGS

1 pound butternut squash, peeled, seeded, and cut into ¼-inch cubes

3 tablespoons extra virgin olive oil

1 cup minced onions

2 tablespoons minced shallots

2 cups Arborio or Carnaroli rice

½ cup dry white wine

6½ cups hot Chicken Stock (page 80) or canned low-sodium chicken broth

½ teaspoon salt, or as needed

½ cup chopped scallions (about 6)

Pinch of freshly grated nutmeg

2 tablespoons unsalted butter, cut into bits

½ cup freshly grated Parmigiano-Reggiano cheese

Freshly ground black pepper

Steam the squash until tender but still firm, about 10 minutes. Transfer half of it to a food processor or blender and process until smooth. Scrape out the squash puree into a small bowl. Set the puree and diced squash aside.

In a heavy, wide, 3- to 4-quart casserole or pot, heat the olive oil over medium heat. Cook the onions and shallots together until golden, stirring often, about 8 minutes. Add the rice and stir to coat with the oil. Toast the rice until the edges become translucent, 1 to 2 minutes.

Pour in the wine and stir well until evaporated. Add ½ cup of the hot stock and ½ teaspoon of the salt. Cook, stirring constantly, until all the stock has been absorbed. Add the squash puree, diced squash, and scallions. Continue to add hot stock in small batches—just enough to completely moisten the rice—and cook until each successive batch has been absorbed. Stir constantly and adjust the level of heat so the rice is simmering very gently until the rice mixture is creamy but al dente. This will take 16 to 20 minutes from the first addition of stock.

Remove the casserole from the heat. Beat in the butter first until melted, then the cheese. Adjust the seasoning with salt, if necessary, and pepper. Serve immediately, ladled into warm shallow bowls.

Risotto Pancake

Risotto al Salto

No food should be wasted, but when you cook risotto, you might intentionally make a little more so that the next day you can have it *al salto*. *Al salto* means "to flip," because that's what you do to it when this pancake is crisp and crunchy on the bottom. It is delicious by itself or as an accompaniment to meats. You can serve vegetables or a poached egg on top, or make it into a pizza by adding sauce and cheese and setting it under the broiler.

MAKES 2 TO 4 SERVINGS

In a small bowl, stir the risotto and the grated cheese together. In a heavy, well-seasoned 8-inch cast-iron skillet, melt 1 tablespoon of the butter over medium-high heat until foaming. Add the risotto mixture and spread it evenly in the pan with a large spoon, pressing down so it covers the bottom of the pan. Cook until the underside is well browned and crisp, 5 to 6 minutes. Shake the pan frequently to prevent the rice from sticking and press on it occasionally to help the pancake brown evenly.

2 cups leftover Creamy Risotto Milanese
   Style (page 155) or any other risotto, at
   room temperature
2 tablespoons freshly grated Parmigiano-
   Reggiano cheese
2 tablespoons unsalted butter

Remove the skillet from the heat. Place a plate large enough to hold the rice cake over the skillet. Carefully invert the risotto pancake onto the plate. Add the remaining 1 tablespoon butter to the pan and heat until foaming. Slide the pancake back into the pan uncooked side down. Cook until the second side is brown and crisp, about 4 minutes. Invert the pancake onto a serving plate and serve immediately.

Risotto Fritters

Suppli di Telefono

In my mind, the "*di telefono*" in the name of these *suppli* (fritters) is a reference to those little box telephones that we all played with as children. When you pulled the boxes apart, you were left with a string stretched between them. While eating the hot *suppli*, strands of hot mozzarella appear between your hands as you pull them apart. *Suppli* are wonderful to serve as hors d'oeuvres or accompaniments to braised or roasted meats.

MAKES ABOUT 25 PIECES

1 recipe Basic Risotto (page 153)

4 large eggs

½ cup very finely diced mozzarella cheese

½ cup very finely diced prosciutto di Parma (about 2 ounces)

½ cup freshly grated Parmigiano-Reggiano cheese

¼ cup minced fresh Italian parsley leaves

Pinch of freshly grated nutmeg

1 cup all-purpose flour

1½ cups plain dry bread crumbs, or as needed

1 cup vegetable oil

½ cup extra virgin olive oil

Prepare the risotto. Spread it on a tray or baking sheet and cool to room temperature.

In a medium-size bowl, beat 2 of the eggs together until blended. Add the mozzarella, prosciutto, Parmigiano, parsley, and nutmeg, and mix well. Beat the remaining 2 eggs together with a few drops of water in a shallow bowl. Place the flour and bread crumbs on two separate plates. Set a bowl of cool water nearby.

Take a ball made of 2 tablespoons of the cooled risotto, set it in the palm of your hand, and shape into a bowl. Make a small well in the center and add 1 teaspoon of the mozzarella mixture. Work the rice so that it encloses the stuffing and forms a smooth ball. Make sure the filling is completely enclosed in the rice. This may take a little practice, and you may find it easier to work with the rice if your hands are slightly wet. Dip them in the water from time to time. Continue until all the rice and filling are used up. These rice balls can be made ahead of time and refrigerated, but make sure that you return them to room temperature at least 30 minutes before breading them. Otherwise, the cheese in the center will not melt properly.

Bread the *suppli*: First roll each ball in the flour until completely coated, tapping off any excess. Then dip them into the beaten egg until coated. Let some of the excess egg drip off before rolling them in the bread crumbs. Let the coated *suppli* stand on a baking sheet as you coat the others. When all the *suppli* are breaded, reroll them one by one in the bread crumbs.

Heat the oils together in a wide, heavy casserole or skillet over medium heat until a sprinkling of bread crumbs sizzles on contact (about 350°F on a deep-fry thermometer). Add about one third of the *suppli* to the oil. Fry them, turning as necessary, until golden brown on all sides, about 8 minutes. The rice should be heated through and the cheese filling should be melted. Repeat with the remaining *suppli*. Set on paper towels to drain and serve hot. The fried *suppli* can be kept warm on a baking sheet in a 200°F oven for up to 20 minutes.

Rice Cooked with Olive Oil

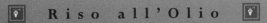 Riso all'Olio

This "medicinal" rice dish was best of all on days that I wasn't feeling well—because it was the ultimate in comfort food and because my mother made it especially for me.

MAKES 6 SERVINGS

In a heavy 4- to 5-quart pot, heat 5 cups of the water to boiling. Add ¼ cup of the oil and salt to taste. Stir in the rice and return to the boil, stirring constantly. Lower the heat to a simmer. Cook, uncovered, until the rice is al dente and the water evaporated, 12 to 14 minutes. Add the remaining cup of water if the water evaporates before the rice is tender.

5 to 6 cups water

6 tablespoons extra virgin olive oil

Salt

2 cups Arborio or Carnaroli rice

2 cups freshly grated Parmigiano-Reggiano cheese

Remove from the heat and stir in the remaining 2 tablespoons oil and the cheese. Serve immediately in warm shallow bowls.

Gnocchi

Every Sunday, the kneading board was brought out for making pasta or gnocchi. (It would make an appearance on other days too, but on Sundays it was a must.) The board was about two feet long by two feet wide, with a three-inch-high rim that ran along three of its sides and prevented flour and dough from spilling onto the worktable. On the fourth side—the side closest to you as you worked—a three-inch rim extended below the board, hugging the edge of the table so that as we kneaded, the board would not slide away under the pressure.

Because it was made of unfinished wood and would absorb water, the kneading board (or *tavola*) was never washed.

Rather, after the dough was made, it was scraped with a straight-edged metal dough scraper, brushed clean, and stored for its next use. My Grandmother Rosa would caution me in dialect *"Grata la tavola ben se no, non ti trovara un bon mari"* ("Scrape the board well, otherwise you will never find a good husband"). As the story goes, when a young man came courting a young lady, he would try to catch a glimpse of her kneading board: If the board was anything less than perfectly clean, it was a good indication that she was not diligent in her household duties, and therefore not a sought-after candidate for marriage. I still use a board at home when I make pasta or gnocchi and scrape it well when I am finished, even though I got married many years ago.

Gnocchi dough, which tends to stick to the kneading board more than pasta dough, is made of boiled potatoes, flour, and eggs. It's very versatile and can appear on an Italian table from first course straight through to dessert. Although you can find gnocchi in every region of Italy, they are more characteristic of the cuisine of Northern Italy (in the south, where hard wheat grows, dry pasta is more common).

I love the feeling of working gnocchi dough with my hands, but it is essential not to over-work the dough, since that is what gives gnocchi their notorious reputation for being "as heavy as lead." If made correctly—that is, kneaded lightly, using only enough flour to bind the dough together—gnocchi are feather-light.

In the fresh pasta chapter, I talk about how important it is to work and knead dough to form and develop gluten—the protein strands that give pasta dough its structure and strength. But the success of gnocchi dough lies in not developing the gluten: The dough should be soft and moldable, not tight and elastic like a well-kneaded pasta dough. To achieve this, you need to begin with a starchy potato such as a russet (also known as a baking or Idaho potato). The potatoes, whether boiled, baked, or cooked in a microwave oven, should be cooked in their jackets and peeled while still quite warm. The peeled potatoes are passed through a potato ricer, spread out on a marble or wooden working surface, and left to cool completely. Ricing the potatoes with a food mill will work in a pinch, but a food processor, blender, or hand mixer will render the potatoes gummy and not at all workable.

Once made, the dough should not be left to rest but rather should be shaped immediately into gnocchi. If the dough sits, the riced potatoes will begin to release water and the dough will become sticky and require additional flour. And more flour means heavy gnocchi. However, gnocchi can be prepared in advance in one of two ways: They can be frozen immediately after shaping or they can be cooked and cooled, to be reheated just before serving. Frozen gnocchi will keep for up to six weeks; cooked gnocchi should be reheated within three to four hours.

Vegetable purees such as carrot, spinach, squash, eggplant, mushroom, or tomato can be added to the basic gnocchi dough. However, you must cook the vegetables, puree them, and let them drain overnight in a cheesecloth-lined sieve until as much of the water as possible has drained off. Then knead the puree into the riced potatoes once about half the flour has been added.

Vegetable-Flavored Gnocchi Doughs
and Other Types of Gnocchi

Generally speaking, you will need about ½ cup of a very finely chopped or pureed vegetable to flavor one recipe of gnocchi dough. Whichever vegetable you choose, make sure as much of the liquid has been removed from it as possible and that it has been seasoned with salt before adding it to the dough. And remember, you will need extra flour when making vegetable gnocchi—possibly up to 1 cup more.

Spinach gnocchi: Remove any tough stems and thoroughly wash about ½ pound spinach leaves or leaves from other greens, such as Swiss chard or arugula. Cook the leaves in boiling water until tender. Drain the greens in a colander and, when cool, squeeze as much liquid as possible from the leaves with your hands. Finely chop the leaves in a food processor and again squeeze as much liquid as possible from them.

Carrot or beet gnocchi: Place about ½ pound peeled carrots or unpeeled beets in a roasting pan, coat with a little olive oil, and roast in a preheated 400°F oven until tender. Cool completely. Peel the beets, if using. Cut the beets or carrots into 1-inch pieces, place in a food processor, and process until smooth. (Alternatively, you can puree the vegetables in a blender. Make sure the vegetables are very tender, stop the motor often to push the vegetables closer to the blade, and resist the temptation to add water or other liquid.) Place the puree in a fine sieve set over a bowl, cover with plastic wrap, and let drain in the refrigerator overnight.

Tomato gnocchi: Add about ⅓ cup tomato paste to the basic gnocchi dough. It is not necessary to drain the tomato paste first.

Gnocchi made with ricotta instead of potatoes are quite good and easy to make, as are gnocchi made from bread—either bread crumbs moistened with milk or stale bread that has been soaked in milk and squeezed to remove most of the liquid.

The traditional way to shape gnocchi is to roll a thumbnail-size piece of dough into a ball, then press it against the tines of a fork or another ridged surface so that it ends up with an indentation on one side and a textured surface on the other. The indentation captures the sauce, while the texture is fun on the tongue.

Gnocchi dough can take on many forms, each with different feelings and textures.

- *Offelle*, typical of the Trieste region, are half-moons of gnocchi dough stuffed with Swiss chard and cheese (similar to the filling for the Spinach and Leek Gnocchi Roll on page 186) and dressed with butter, cheese, or meat sauce.

- *Strucolo*, typical of the Friuli-Venezia-Giulia region, is a roulade—that is, a jelly-roll shape—of gnocchi dough rolled with different fillings that can include vegetables, cheese, mushrooms, and meat. The *strucolo* is sliced, dressed with a butter and sage sauce and cheese, and baked until crisp.

- *Gnocchi dolci* are balls of gnocchi dough filled with sweetened fresh plums or chunky preserves. After boiling, they are tossed in toasted buttered bread crumbs with cinnamon and sugar—they're an all-time children's favorite.

- *Chifeletti* are horseshoe shapes made from gnocchi dough, fried and served with roasts to mop up the roasting juices. They can also be sprinkled with sugar and cinnamon and turned into a dessert, a dish I remember fondly from my childhood.

Making gnocchi is a wonderful family project. As children, we always got involved in shaping them, and when eating them, we would search our own plates for the ones we had shaped. The beauty of gnocchi is that—as simple as they might be—they have a lot of flavor. A little butter, a fresh sage leaf, and a sprinkle of grated Parmigiano-Reggiano cheese is all that is needed to make a simple plate of gnocchi into an exquisite dish.

Gnocchi

The basic gnocchi recipe and the recipes for saucing gnocchi that follow can be doubled easily if you have a larger crowd or if you would like to have some gnocchi to store in the freezer. However, as the dough must be shaped quickly, I suggest you make this quantity until you get the knack of forming the gnocchi.

MAKES 3 GENEROUS OR 4 SLIGHTLY SMALLER MAIN-COURSE OR 6 GENEROUS FIRST-COURSE SERVINGS

Place the potatoes in a large pot with enough cold water to cover. Bring the water to a boil and cook, partially covered, until the potatoes are easily pierced with a skewer but the skins are not split, about 35 minutes. (Alternatively, the potatoes can be baked in a preheated 400°F oven until tender, about 40 minutes.)

Drain the potatoes and let them stand just until cool enough to handle. (The hotter the potatoes are when they are peeled and riced, the lighter the gnocchi will be.) Working quickly and protecting the hand that holds the potatoes with a folded kitchen towel or oven mitt, scrape the skin from the potato with a paring knife. Press the peeled potatoes through a potato ricer. Alternatively, the potatoes can be passed through a food mill fitted with the fine disc, but a ricer makes fluffier potatoes and therefore lighter gnocchi. Spread the riced potatoes into a thin, even layer on the work surface, without pressing them or compacting them. Let them cool completely.

> 3 large baking (Idaho) potatoes (about 1¾ pounds), scrubbed
> 1 large egg
> 1 teaspoon salt
> ¼ teaspoon freshly ground white pepper
> Pinch of freshly grated nutmeg
> ¼ cup freshly grated Parmigiano-Reggiano cheese
> 2 cups unbleached all-purpose flour, or as needed

In a small bowl, beat the egg, salt, pepper, and nutmeg together. Gather the cold potatoes into a mound and form a well in the center. Pour the egg mixture into the well. Knead the potato and egg mixtures together with both hands, gradually adding the grated cheese and enough of the flour, about 1½ cups, to form a smooth but slightly sticky dough. It should take no longer than 3 minutes to work the flour into the potato mixture; remember, the longer the dough is kneaded, the more flour it will require and the heavier it will become. As you knead the dough, it will stick to your hands and to the work surface: Repeatedly rub this rough dough from your hands and scrape it with a knife or dough scraper from the work surface back into the dough as you knead.

Wash and dry your hands. Dust the dough, your hands, and the work surface lightly with some of the remaining flour. Cut the dough into six equal pieces and set off to one side of the work surface.

continued

Place one piece of dough in front of you and pat it into a rough oblong. Using both hands, in a smooth back-and-forth motion and exerting light downward pressure, roll the dough into a rope ½ inch thick, flouring the dough if necessary as you roll to keep it from sticking. (When you first begin making gnocchi, until your hands get the feel of the dough, you may find it easier to cut each piece of dough in half to roll it.)

Slice the ropes into ½-inch-thick rounds. Sprinkle the rounds lightly with flour and roll each piece quickly between your palms into a rough ball, flouring the dough and your hands as needed to prevent sticking. Hold the tines of a fork at a 45-degree angle to the table with the concave part facing up. Dip the tip of your thumb in flour. Take one ball of dough and with the tip of your thumb, press the dough lightly against the tines of the fork as you roll it downward toward the tips of the tines. As the dough wraps around the tip of your thumb, it will form into a dumpling with a deep indentation on one side and a ridged surface on the other. Set on a baking sheet lined with a floured kitchen towel and continue forming gnocchi from the remaining dough balls. Repeat the whole process with the remaining pieces of dough. At this point the gnocchi must be cooked immediately or frozen.

To cook gnocchi: Bring 6 quarts of salted water to a vigorous boil in a large pot over high heat. Drop about half the gnocchi into the boiling water a few at a time, stirring gently and continuously with a wooden spoon. Cook the gnocchi, stirring gently, until tender, about 1 minute after they rise to the surface. (You can cook the gnocchi all at once in two separate pots of boiling water. If you make a double batch of gnocchi, I strongly recommend cooking them in batches in two pots of water.)

Remove the gnocchi from the water with a slotted spoon or skimmer, draining them well, and transfer to a wide saucepan with some of the sauce to be used. Cook the remaining gnocchi, if necessary. When all the gnocchi are cooked, proceed according to the directions for saucing and serving in each recipe.

When saucing gnocchi, remember this tip: If the sauce is too dense or the gnocchi seem too dry, use some of the gnocchi cooking water to thin the sauce and moisten the gnocchi, as you would with pasta dishes.

To precook gnocchi: Cook the gnocchi as described above, remove them with a skimmer, and spread them out in a baking pan lightly coated with melted butter. When ready to serve, return the gnocchi to a large pot of boiling salted water until heated through, 2 to 3 minutes. Drain thoroughly and sauce and serve according to the particular recipe.

To freeze gnocchi: It is best to freeze gnocchi uncooked and as soon as they are shaped. Arrange the gnocchi in a single layer on a baking pan and place the pan in a level position in the freezer. Freeze until solid, about 3 hours. Gather the frozen gnocchi into resealable freezer bags. Frozen gnocchi can be stored in the freezer 4 to 6 weeks.

To cook frozen gnocchi: Frozen gnocchi must be cooked directly from the freezer in plenty of boiling water, or they will stick together. Bring 6 quarts salted water to a boil in each of two large pots. Shake any excess flour from the frozen gnocchi and split them between the two pots, stirring gently as you add them to the boiling water. It is important that the water return to a boil as soon as possible; cover the pots if necessary. Drain the gnocchi as described above and sauce and serve them according to the specific recipe.

Gnocchi with Tomato, Basil, and Olives

Gnocchi al Pomodoro, Basilico, ed Olive

MAKES 3 MAIN-COURSE OR 6 FIRST-COURSE SERVINGS

In a large, deep skillet, heat the butter over medium-high heat until foaming. Add the olives and cook, stirring, until sizzling, about 2 minutes. Add the tomato sauce and bring to a simmer. Remove from the heat and set aside.

Bring the salted water to a boil in a large pot over high heat. Cook and drain the gnocchi according to the directions on page 176.

Bring the tomato sauce back to a simmer over low heat. Add the gnocchi and stir gently with a wooden spoon until coated. Stir in the grated cheese and basil. Check the seasoning, transfer the gnocchi to a platter, and serve immediately.

2 tablespoons unsalted butter
½ cup pitted Gaeta olives or Cerignola or
    other large green olives
1½ cups Tomato Sauce (page 144)
6 quarts salted water
1 recipe Gnocchi (page 175)
½ cup freshly grated Pecorino Romano
    cheese
5 fresh basil leaves, washed, dried, and
    shredded
Salt and freshly ground black pepper

Gnocchi with Herb Pesto

Gnocchi al Pesto d'Erbe

This is a recipe that can be pulled together in twenty minutes by using frozen gnocchi and pesto that you have stored in the refrigerator.

MAKES 3 MAIN-COURSE OR 6 FIRST-COURSE SERVINGS

6 quarts salted water

1 recipe Gnocchi (page 175)

½ cup Chicken Stock (page 180), canned low-sodium chicken broth, or reserved gnocchi cooking water

3 tablespoons unsalted butter

1 cup string beans or haricots verts cut into 1-inch pieces, blanched in boiling water for 2 minutes and drained

6 tablespoons Herb Pesto (page 146)

Salt and freshly ground black pepper

½ cup freshly grated Parmigiano-Reggiano cheese

Bring the salted water to a boil in a large pot over high heat. Cook and drain the gnocchi according to the directions on page 176.

Meanwhile, in a large, deep skillet, bring the stock and butter to a boil over medium heat. Add the beans and pesto and season with salt and pepper to taste. Bring to a boil and remove from the heat.

Add the gnocchi to the pesto sauce and stir with a wooden spoon over low heat until the gnocchi are coated with sauce and heated through. Remove the skillet from the heat and stir in the grated cheese. Check the seasoning, transfer the gnocchi to a platter, and serve immediately.

Gnocchi with Sage Sauce and Dry Ricotta

Gnocchi alla Salvia con Ricotta Salata

A wonderful and simple dish can be made by saucing the gnocchi with just sage, butter, and grated Parmigiano-Reggiano cheese. A more complex version, offered here, adds ricotta—smoked or not—for a dish typical of the Friuli region.

MAKES 3 MAIN-COURSE OR 6 FIRST-COURSE SERVINGS

With a vegetable peeler or the slicing side of a box grater, shave the ricotta into thin shards. Place the shards, without pressing them together, in a covered bowl in the refrigerator.

In a large skillet, melt the butter over low heat. Add the sage and stir for 2 minutes. Add the stock and cream and bring to a boil. Season with pepper to taste and remove from the heat.

While you prepare the gnocchi, bring the salted water to a boil in a large pot over high heat. Cook and drain the gnocchi according to the directions on page 176.

Add the gnocchi to the sage sauce. Stir over low heat with a wooden spoon until the gnocchi are coated with sauce and heated through, 1 to 2 minutes. Remove the skillet from the heat and stir in the Parmigiano-Reggiano and pepper to taste. Transfer to shallow bowls, scatter the shaved ricotta over the gnocchi, and serve immediately.

4 ounces ricotta salata or ricotta affumicata cheese (see Note)

¼ cup (½ stick) unsalted butter

6 fresh sage leaves

½ cup Chicken Stock (page 80), canned low-sodium chicken broth, or reserved gnocchi cooking water

¼ cup heavy cream

Freshly ground black pepper

1 recipe Gnocchi (page 175)

6 quarts salted water

¼ cup freshly grated Parmigiano-Reggiano cheese

Note: Ricotta salata is a smooth, firm, pure white sheep's milk cheese imported from Italy. Ricotta affumicata is a lightly smoked version of the same cheese. Both are available in cheese and specialty stores and Italian grocers.

Gnocchi with Lentils and Garden Vegetables

Gnocchi all'Ortolana

Any choice of vegetables can be used for this recipe, but I always enjoy adding lentils. If you don't feel like cooking them, or if you find yourself preparing this dish during the summer, try adding toasted pine nuts instead.

MAKES 3 MAIN-COURSE OR 6 FIRST-COURSE SERVINGS

¼ cup finely diced carrots

¼ cup shelled fresh peas or ½ cup defrosted and drained frozen peas

¼ cup finely diced zucchini (see Note)

2 tablespoons extra virgin olive oil

½ cup chopped scallions

10 fresh sage leaves

¾ cup Chicken Stock (page 80), canned low-sodium chicken broth, or reserved gnocchi cooking water

¼ cup blanched and peeled shelled fava beans (see page 233)

¼ cup cooked lentils (see Note)

Pinch of peperoncino (crushed red pepper)

Salt and freshly ground black pepper

1 recipe Gnocchi (page 175)

6 quarts salted water

2 tablespoons unsalted butter

¼ cup freshly grated Parmigiano-Reggiano cheese

In a steamer insert set over boiling water, steam the carrots, fresh peas, and zucchini separately until each is tender but still firm, about 3 minutes for the carrots, 2 minutes for the peas, and 1 minute for the zucchini. Drain them and set aside. (It is not necessary to steam the frozen peas.)

In a large, deep skillet, heat the olive oil over medium heat. Add the scallions and sage leaves, reduce the heat to low, and cook, stirring, for 2 minutes. Add the chicken stock, fava beans, lentils, peperoncino, steamed vegetables, and frozen peas if using, bring to a simmer, and cook for 5 minutes. Season with salt and pepper to taste and remove from the heat.

While you prepare the gnocchi, bring the salted water to a boil in a large pot over high heat. Cook and drain the gnocchi according to the directions on page 176.

Meanwhile, bring the vegetable sauce to a simmer over low heat and check the seasoning.

Add the gnocchi and butter to the sauce and stir with a wooden spoon until the gnocchi are coated with sauce, 1 to 2 minutes. Transfer the gnocchi to shallow bowls, sprinkle with the grated cheese, and serve immediately.

Note: For the prettiest dish, trim the zucchini and cut it lengthwise into quarters. Cut away the skin and about ¼ inch of the white flesh in thick strips; discard the "seedy" center part. Cut these green and white strips into ¼-inch dice.

For ¼ cup cooked lentils, cook about 2 tablespoons lentils in a small saucepan of boiling water with 2 bay leaves until tender, about 20 minutes. Drain well.

Gnocchi with Butternut Squash Sauce

Gnocchi con Salsa di Zucca

Top this dish with shaved ricotta salata (dry ricotta) for a savory finish. For a sweet finish, sprinkle a few crumbs of crushed amaretti cookies over the sauce.

MAKES 3 MAIN-COURSE OR 6 FIRST-COURSE SERVINGS

One 2-pound butternut squash, halved lengthwise, half reserved for another use
¼ cup (½ stick) unsalted butter
¼ cup heavy cream
½ teaspoon salt
Pinch of freshly grated nutmeg
Freshly ground black pepper
1 recipe Gnocchi (page 175)
6 quarts salted water
½ cup freshly grated Parmigiano-Reggiano cheese

Preheat the oven to 350°F. Wrap the squash half loosely in aluminum foil and place it on a baking sheet. Bake until tender when pierced with a knife, about 1 hour.

Let the squash stand until just cool enough to handle. Scoop out and discard the seeds. With a large spoon, scoop the pulp from the skin into a fine sieve. Set the sieve over a bowl to catch the liquid and refrigerate, covered, for about 8 hours, or overnight.

Transfer the drained squash to a food processor (a blender will make the squash puree too dense) and process, scraping down the sides of the work bowl once or twice, until smooth. Pass the squash through a fine sieve, using a ladle to force it through.

In a small saucepan, heat 2 tablespoons of the butter over medium heat until foaming. Stir in the cream, salt, nutmeg, and squash puree. Bring to a boil and adjust the level of heat to a simmer. Simmer for 5 minutes. Season with pepper to taste and remove from the heat.

While you prepare the gnocchi, bring the salted water to a boil in a large pot over high heat. Cook and drain the gnocchi according to the directions on page 176 and transfer them to a large warm platter.

In a small saucepan, melt the remaining 2 tablespoons butter over low heat. Pour the melted butter over the cooked gnocchi and sprinkle them with the grated cheese. Spoon the gnocchi into shallow bowls, piling them in a little mound. Spoon the squash sauce over the top of the mounds, and let it run down the sides. Serve immediately.

Prosciutto di Parma "Purses" *(page 33)*, Steamed Vegetables with Warm Prosciutto Vinaigrette *(page 218)*, and Swiss Chard and Vegetable Crostata *(page 228)*

Montasio Cheese Crisp *(page 43)*,
Chickpea Puree *(page 235)*,
and Cannellini and
Olive Puree

(page 234)

Clockwise from the back: Bread, Potato, and
Arugula Soup *(page 75)*, Sauerkraut and Bean
Soup *(page 58)*, and Red Snapper and
Rice Soup *(page 66)*

Raviolacci Stuffed with Spring Herbs and Cheese

(page 108)

Left: Making the raviolacci

Skewer Maccheroni with
Green Olives and Capers *(page 117)*

Left: Forming the skewer maccheroni

Shrimp Risotto *(page 158)*

Gnocchi with Lentils and Garden Vegetables *(page 180)* and
Gnocchi with Venison Stew *(page 184)*

Left: Forming the gnocchi

Roasted Guinea Hen with
Balsamic Glaze *(page 240)*
and
Bread and Tomato Salad
(page 39)

Seared Rabbit Loin over Arugula with Truffle Dressing *(page 248)*

Roasted Veal Shanks *(page 280)* with Fried Potato Crescents *(page 183)*

Seared Lamb Chops with Rosemary and Mint Sauce *(page 294)*
and Braised Spring Legumes *(page 232)*

Baked Squid and Potatoes
(page 317)
and Stuffed Squid with
Borlotti Beans *(page 318)*

King Crab Salad with Citrus Fruit *(page 329)*

Whole Roasted Striped Bass *(page 336)*

Apple Strudel *(page 345)* and
Blueberry-Apricot Frangipane
Tart *(page 350)*

Chocolate Sponge Cake with Sour
Cherry and Chocolate Zabaglione
Mousse Filling *(page 378)*
and Zabaglione *(page 377)*

Fried Potato Crescents

Chifeletti di Patate

This recipe exemplifies the versatility of gnocchi dough. I usually make *chifeletti* with half a batch of gnocchi dough, the other half of which I shape into regular gnocchi. I then freeze the crescents and, when ready to make the *chifeletti*, allow them to defrost halfway on a kitchen towel before frying them.

A word of caution: Make sure the oil is not hotter than 350 °F when frying frozen *chifeletti*, or they will burn on the outside and remain raw on the inside. Serve *chifeletti* next to roasted or stewed meat to mop up the juices.

MAKES 6 SERVINGS

Prepare the gnocchi, adding the additional 1 teaspoon salt to the egg mixture.

> 1 recipe Gnocchi (page 175)
> 1 teaspoon salt
> 3 cups vegetable oil

Dust your hands and the work surface with flour. Take 1 tablespoon of the dough and roll it out with the palms of your hands on the floured surface to a cylinder about 3 inches long and ½ inch thick, with slightly tapered ends. Bend the cylinder into a U shape and set it on a baking sheet lined with a lightly floured kitchen towel. Repeat with the remaining dough.

Preheat the oven to 200°F. Pour the oil into a heavy, deep, medium-size skillet. Heat over medium heat until a deep-frying thermometer registers 350°F. Add just as many of the crescents as will fit in the skillet without touching and fry, turning once, until deep golden brown, about 4 minutes. Adjust the level of heat as necessary during frying to maintain a constant temperature. Remove with a slotted spoon and drain on paper towels. Keep the fried *chifeletti* warm on a baking sheet in the oven and repeat with the remaining crescents. Serve hot.

Gnocchi with Venison Stew

▣ Gnocchi con Guazzetto di Capriolo ▣

There is nothing that will stand up to a bitter winter day better than a plate of gnocchi with venison stew. I serve it as a main course with a nice salad and cheese afterwards, along with a good bottle of Barolo that will stand up to both. *"E lascia che soffia il vento,"* as Grandpa would say, "Let the wind blow, this dish will sustain us through it all."

MAKES 3 MAIN-COURSE OR 6 FIRST-COURSE SERVINGS

¼ cup dried porcini mushrooms
  (about 1½ ounces)

1 cup hot water

1 fresh or dried bay leaf

1 small sprig fresh rosemary or ½ teaspoon
  dried rosemary

1 clove

2 tablespoons extra virgin olive oil

1 small onion, minced

2 tablespoons minced pancetta or bacon

Salt and freshly ground black pepper to taste

1¼ pounds boneless venison from the leg or
  shoulder, trimmed of fat and cut into
  1-inch cubes

¼ cup dry red wine

1 tablespoon tomato paste

1¾ cups Meat Stock (page 78) or canned
  low-sodium beef broth

1 recipe Gnocchi (page 175)

6 quarts salted water

2 tablespoons chopped fresh Italian parsley
  leaves

½ cup freshly grated Parmigiano-Reggiano
  cheese

Soak the porcini in the hot water until softened, about 30 minutes. Drain the mushrooms and reserve the liquid. Rinse and chop the mushrooms, discarding any tough bits. Strain the soaking liquid through a coffee filter or a sieve lined with cheesecloth and set aside.

Tie the bay leaf, rosemary, and clove securely together in a small square of cheesecloth and set aside.

Meanwhile, in a large heavy pot or casserole, heat the oil over medium-high heat. Add the onion and pancetta and cook, stirring, until golden, about 6 minutes. Season lightly with salt and pepper. Increase the heat to high, add the venison, and cook, stirring occasionally, until all the meat juices have evaporated, about 15 minutes.

Add the wine, herb bundle, and chopped porcini and cook, stirring, until the wine has nearly evaporated, about 5 minutes. Stir in the tomato paste and season lightly with salt and pepper. Add the stock and the reserved mushroom liquid and bring to a boil. Reduce the heat to medium-low and simmer, partially covered, until the meat is tender, about 1½ hours. Remove the herb bundle. (The venison stew can be made up to 2 days ahead and refrigerated, covered.)

Meanwhile, prepare the gnocchi. Bring the salted water to a boil in a large pot over high heat. Cook and drain the gnocchi according to the directions on page 176.

Meanwhile, if necessary, bring the venison stew to a simmer over medium heat.

With a wooden spoon, gently stir the gnocchi and parsley into the venison stew over low heat. Stir in the grated cheese, transfer the gnocchi to a platter, and serve immediately.

Spinach and Leek Gnocchi Roll

Strucolo di Spinaci e Porri

If you like the texture and flavor of gnocchi but want to avoid the last-minute work for a larger dinner party, this is the ideal pasta course. (Make sure to allow time for the ricotta to drain.) If the *strucolo* is prepared completely in advance, the serving is easy and foolproof, and the results are delicious.

MAKES 10 SERVINGS

For the filling

1 pound fresh ricotta or one 15-ounce container ricotta

¼ cup (½ stick) unsalted butter

2 leeks, light green and white parts, well washed and finely chopped

1 pound fresh spinach, tough stems removed, well washed, and leaves cut into thin strips

Salt and freshly ground black pepper to taste

1 large egg

2 tablespoons chopped fresh marjoram leaves (sage or basil can be substituted)

1 recipe Gnocchi (page 175)

6 to 8 quarts salted water

For the sauce

¼ cup (½ stick) unsalted butter

10 fresh sage leaves

1 cup freshly grated Parmigiano-Reggiano cheese

Place the ricotta in a fine sieve over a bowl. Cover with plastic wrap and refrigerate for at least 8 hours or overnight.

In a large skillet, heat the butter over medium-high heat until foaming. Add the leeks and cook, stirring, until wilted, about 4 minutes. Stir in the spinach, season lightly with salt and pepper, and cook, stirring, until tender but still bright green, about 5 minutes. Scrape the spinach mixture into a sieve placed over a plate. Press lightly to remove excess liquid. Cool completely.

In a medium-size bowl, combine the drained spinach mixture and the drained ricotta. Add the egg and marjoram, season with salt and pepper to taste, and stir until well blended.

While you prepare the gnocchi, bring the water to a boil in a fish poacher (see Note). Cut three 12 × 18-inch pieces of cheesecloth and stack them one atop the other.

On a well-floured work surface, roll the dough with a floured rolling pin out to a 12 × 15-inch rectangle, lifting the dough once or twice with the help of a large metal spatula or dough scraper to flour the surface underneath. Spread the spinach mixture in an even layer over the entire surface of the dough rectangle.

Starting from one of the rectangle's longer sides and working with the metal spatula or dough scraper to help you, roll the dough into a tight cylinder as you would a jelly roll. Center the roll over the cheesecloth. Wrap the roll tightly in the cloth and tie the ends securely with kitchen string. Carefully lower the roll into the boiling water. Adjust the level of heat to a gentle boil and cook until a knife inserted in the center comes out clean, about 1 hour. Remove the *strucolo* from the water, drain, and allow to stand for about 15 minutes.

Meanwhile, preheat the oven to 375°F and prepare the sauce. In a small skillet, melt the butter over very low heat, swirling the skillet constantly until the butter is melted and creamy but not separated. Add the sage and cook for 1 minute. Keep the sauce in a warm spot.

Unwrap the *strucolo* and place on a cutting board. With a serrated knife, using a gentle back-and-forth motion, cut the roll into ½-inch-thick slices. Arrange the slices side by side in one large (about 18 × 12-inch) baking dish or two small (10-inch round or 8-inch square) buttered baking dishes. Drizzle the sage sauce and leaves over the slices. Bake for 20 minutes, then sprinkle with half of the grated cheese and bake until the top is golden brown and crisp, about 10 minutes. Serve with the remaining grated cheese.

Note: A fish poacher—a long, oval pan with a perforated removable rack—is the ideal vessel for cooking the *strucolo.* If you don't have one, use your widest, deepest pot or roasting pan, but measure it first to make sure it is wide enough to fit the finished roll (about 16 inches long) lengthwise and deep enough to keep the roll submerged in water during cooking. Make these arrangements in advance; once the gnocchi dough is rolled out and filled, the roll must be poached immediately.

To prepare the dish entirely in advance: Cook the *strucolo* as described above. Unwrap the cooling *strucolo* after 15 minutes and let it stand until completely cool. Cut the roll into ½-inch-thick slices and arrange the slices side by side in a buttered baking pan. Drizzle the sage sauce and leaves over the slices and cover the pan with aluminum foil. Refrigerate for up to 1 day. Let the pan of *strucolo* stand at room temperature for 1 hour. Preheat the oven to 350°F. Bake for 20 minutes, uncover the pan, sprinkle the slices with the grated cheese, and bake until the *strucolo* is golden brown and crisp on the surface, about 10 minutes.

Ricotta Gnocchi with Radicchio Trevisano

⊞ Gnocchi di Ricotta con Radicchio Trevisano ⊞

For this dish, *radicchio Trevisano*, the long red radicchio, is ideal. Round cabbage-like *radicchio di Chioggia*—which is easier to find—is a fair substitute, but it will not give you the same intensity of flavor the Trevisano will.

MAKES 3 MAIN-COURSE OR 6 FIRST-COURSE SERVINGS

For the gnocchi

1½ pounds ricotta (about 3 cups), preferably fresh

1 cup unbleached all-purpose flour, or as needed

2 large eggs, beaten

1 tablespoon chopped fresh Italian parsley leaves

1 teaspoon salt

½ teaspoon freshly ground black pepper

¼ teaspoon freshly grated nutmeg

6 quarts salted water

For the sauce

¼ cup finely chopped pancetta or bacon (about 1 ounce)

2 tablespoons extra virgin olive oil

3 garlic cloves, crushed

3 cups coarsely shredded *radicchio Trevisano* or *radicchio di Chioggia*

Salt and freshly ground black pepper

1 cup Chicken Stock (page 80) or canned low-sodium chicken broth

½ cup freshly grated Parmigiano-Reggiano cheese

Place the ricotta in a fine sieve over a bowl. Cover with plastic wrap and refrigerate for at least 8 hours or overnight.

In a medium-size bowl, stir the drained ricotta, 1 cup of the flour, the eggs, parsley, salt, pepper, and nutmeg together gently but thoroughly until a soft dough forms, adding a little more of the flour if the dough is sticky when poked.

In a large pot, bring the salted water to a boil over high heat.

Meanwhile form the gnocchi: Dip 2 tablespoons in cool water. Using one spoon, scoop up a heaping tablespoon of the ricotta mixture and use the other spoon to form it into a smooth, pointed oval. (Alternatively, you can roll the mixture into balls with well-floured hands, using about 2 tablespoons ricotta mixture for each ball.) Place the gnocchi on a baking sheet lined with a lightly floured kitchen towel.

Gently slip as many of the gnocchi at a time as will float freely into the pot of boiling water, stirring gently with a wooden spoon as you do. Cook until the gnocchi rise to the surface, about 7 minutes. (Test one for doneness by cutting into the center; the gnocchi should be the same color and consistency all the way through.) Scoop them out with a wire skimmer as soon as they are cooked and transfer to a platter. Cover loosely with aluminum foil to keep warm.

Meanwhile, cook the pancetta in a large, heavy skillet over medium heat until it is crisp and has rendered its fat, about 5 minutes. Discard the fat and add the olive oil and garlic to the skillet. Stir until the garlic begins to sizzle. Add the radicchio and season lightly with salt and pepper. Add the stock and bring to a simmer. Cook until the radicchio is wilted but still has some crunch to it, about 3 minutes. Remove the garlic cloves, check the seasoning, and keep the sauce warm over low heat.

Ladle the radicchio sauce into the bottom of six shallow soup bowls. Divide the hot ricotta gnocchi over the sauce in each and sprinkle them with the grated cheese. Serve immediately.

Plum Gnocchi

Gnocchi di Susine

As children, we loved sweet filled gnocchi, a dish we often had as our main course. While the adults enjoyed some sort of game sauce with their gnocchi, the kids were always happy with the sweet ones. They were even good cold. Today, you can simply put leftover plum gnocchi in the microwave, and they are as good as when first cooked.

For best results, use firm but ripe Italian prune plums in season, but this is also good made with chunky jam.

MAKES 24 GNOCCHI, ABOUT 6 SERVINGS

---

24 small Italian prune plums or 6 red or purple plums (or 2 cups chunky apricot or cherry jam)

¾ cup sugar

1 recipe Gnocchi (page 175), made without the pepper and Parmigiano-Reggiano cheese

6 quarts salted water

6 tablespoons (¾ stick) unsalted butter

2 cups coarse plain dry bread crumbs

2 teaspoons ground cinnamon

If using Italian prune plums, halve them lengthwise and remove the pits. Fill each cavity with ½ teaspoon of the sugar and re-form the plums by pressing the halves together. If using larger plums, halve them crosswise, separate the halves neatly, and remove the pits with a small melon baller. Cut them into ½-inch dice. In a small bowl, toss the diced plums with ¼ cup of the sugar.

While you prepare the gnocchi dough, bring the water to a boil in a large pot over high heat.

Flour your hands, the dough, and the work surface. Roll the dough under your palms to form a cylinder 2 inches in diameter and slice it evenly into 24 rounds. Flatten each round in the palm of one hand to a circle about 5 inches in diameter. Place an Italian plum or about 3 tablespoons of the sweetened diced plums (or 2 tablespoons of the jam) in the center of each dough circle. Carefully gather the dough up around the fruit (or jam), enclosing it completely without tearing the dough. Pat the dough between your hands to seal and even the gnocchi. Flour the dough and your hands lightly as you work and place the gnocchi on a lightly floured baking sheet as you form them.

Add as many of the gnocchi as will fit without touching (about half) a few at a time to the boiling water, stirring gently with a wooden spoon to prevent sticking. Cook until the dough is tender and the plums are very soft, about 8 minutes after they rise to the surface.

Meanwhile, in a heavy, medium-size skillet, melt the butter over medium heat. Add the bread crumbs and toast, stirring almost constantly, until golden brown, about 7 minutes. Remove from the heat, add the remaining ½ cup sugar and the cinnamon, and blend thoroughly. Transfer to a large baking dish.

Remove the cooked gnocchi with a slotted spoon, draining them well, and repeat with the remaining gnocchi. Roll the cooked and drained gnocchi while still warm in the bread-crumb mixture until all are well coated. Arrange on a serving plate and sprinkle with any bread crumbs remaining in the baking dish. Serve warm.

Polenta

Maize, the term used by West Indian natives for corn, and its cultivation can be traced back to 3,500 B.C. in Central America. Because of its attributes—corn bears fruit in a relatively short time, about ninety days, has a high yield per plant, and requires little care—corn spread and became the main food plant in the Americas.

In Europe, the first cultivation of corn was recorded about thirty years after Christopher Columbus brought the kernels from the Americas to Andalusia. By the end of the seventeenth century, the cultivation of corn had taken hold across Mediterranean Europe and had even extended into the Ukraine.

It is no wonder that corn was quickly assimilated into the Italian diet and became one of the main cereals of Italy; the people of the Italian peninsula have a long history of cooking with grains. The Romans prepared *pultes*, or porridges, from many different grains and water. And in Friuli-Venezia-Giulia, where I come from, there was a porridge made from spelt (whole kernels of emmer) that was known as *pultes julians*, meaning "coming from Juliani," the name for the indigenous people of the area. When corn was introduced to this region, it was a natural to make the *pultes* out of the cornmeal, hence the first polenta. In fact, the Italians of the North are often called *polentoni,* or "polenta eaters," since polenta was, and still is, a main staple.

On the land around our house in Busoler, we always had a cornfield. The cornfields were well known to the kids—we loved to play hide-and-seek there. Corn plants grow tall and are planted with quite a bit of space between stalks, which gave us ample room to run and plenty of cover to hide. Besides, it was always cooler between the wide corn leaves that blocked us from the hot August sun of the Mediterranean. When we tired of playing hide-and-seek, we would pluck the beards off the maturing cobs and make cascading hairdos or corn "mustaches," holding them in place above our puckered lips. The smell of the young corn was wonderful and fresh.

Some of the corn was harvested ear by ear as it matured for use in fresh corn soup, like the *bobici* mentioned on page 60. Some ears were boiled, or roasted right in their husks over hot coals, and eaten on the cob. But most of the corn was harvested, after the whole plant was dry, to be turned into meal. The stalks were cut at the base with all of the ears still attached, brought to the courtyard, and dealt with there by the women. After they removed the corn from the stalks, the stalks were burned and their ashes returned to the earth as fertilizer. The husks were pulled from each ear of corn, leaving a few of the larger leaves attached, and the beard, or silk, removed. The husk leaves that were left attached to the ear were tied into a knot that was used to hang the ears for complete drying. If you travel in Italy—especially the northeastern part—in the fall, you will still see rows of hanging corn drying outside the houses. Their bright yellow color is part of the autumnal harvest and landscape.

The husk leaves plucked from the ears of corn were sorted; the larger, coarser leaves were used as food for the animals and ground cover in their pens. The softer leaves from closer to the ear were spread out on the cement floor of the courtyard to dry under the summer sun. The best of these were selected and made into a *paion*, or mattress. These light mattresses were used in the summer while the woolen ones were washed and rethatched for the winter months. Little corn-husk mattresses—*paioni*—were made specifically for newborns. There were no disposable diapers or plastic bed covers in those days, and these natural mattresses would absorb the moisture when the baby wet itself. Every good mother had several of these little mattresses and would rotate them, putting a damp one to dry in the sun and replacing it with one that had been dried and aired out.

I loved sleeping on my *paion* in the summer. It smelled of corn, of summer, and of grass. As my head rested on it, there were rustling sounds. In the dark, my imagination would run wild with such noises, transforming them into roars, musical voices, gallops, and the sound of trains. Finally, the rustling would lull me to sleep.

In that same courtyard where the corn was sorted and dried, there was also a *casetta nera*, a little black house. The wood and coal were stored in one corner of the house, and in another corner stood a large *fogoler*, or hearth, made of solid terra-cotta and cement that stood about five feet square and two feet high. Over the hearth, there was a chimney flue covered with a *nappa*, or hood, that held a shelf of spices—salt, pepper, cloves, and others. On the side of the hearth there were always branches of rosemary, bay leaves, oregano, and thyme, tied with string and hung on a nail. Braids of garlic, shallots, and onions adorned other nails or hooks in the wall. A big wooden table filled the middle of the room, and along the wall there was a *cassella,* a long wooden chest for storing flour, polenta, and beans, and, when closed, for sitting.

Inside the chimney, there were two large chains from which the cauldron hung. There was also a *trepiede,* a big and sturdy tripod, in the fireplace, where pots were set to cook. Grandma had a kitchen in the main house too, but she did her cooking for crowds in the *casetta nera*. She also prepared the food for her pen animals there.

The polenta was always cooked in the *casetta nera*, since it was best when cooked in the heavy cast-iron or brass cauldron. With a long wooden spatula, Grandma would mix the perking polenta—it looked like exploding bubbles of lava in the mouth of a volcano. When the polenta was done, it was poured onto a wooden board like a pallet and brought to the table. It was then cut at 1½-inch intervals with a taut string anchored on both index fingers. The same action was then repeated perpendicular to the first cut, to make squares of shimmering polenta.

When the polenta was poured out of the cauldron, a thin layer always remained attached to the sides. With the heat of the cauldron, it would dry and turn into a kind of corn chip. We children would wait for Grandma to pour out the polenta, then peel away the corn chips while the cauldron was still hot. Our fingertips would occasionally pay a price, but it was well worth it.

When I go back to visit, the *casetta nera* is locked up and full of stored boxes. One of these days, I will open that lock and rekindle the fire.

The Different Types of Cornmeal for Polenta

The coarseness of the cornmeal is very important when cooking polenta, since it will determine the texture of the finished polenta. The traditional cornmeal for making polenta—and the one I prefer—is coarse, stone-ground yellow cornmeal. You should look for cornmeal imported from Italy, which is usually coarse, or domestic brands that say "stone-ground" on the label. Coarse cornmeal cooks into a wonderful dish and, even when completely tender, it still has lots of texture. I like polenta to have a little bite, especially when served with hearty dishes, like game and meats.

Fine yellow cornmeal and white cornmeal will give good results, but remember that they are finer and will make a very smooth polenta the texture of which is almost like that of a pudding. Smooth polenta made from fine cornmeal is especially good with fish sauces, vegetables, and cheese.

Many types of cornmeal give an approximate cooking time on the container. These times range from five to six minutes for "instant" polenta to twenty minutes for fine cornmeal all the way up to forty minutes for the coarsest cornmeals. If you are uncertain about the type of cornmeal you have, use these timings as a guide.

Coarse yellow cornmeal has the texture of fine sand, with distinct yellow and white grains. Many Italian and American brands (Baretta, Valsugana, Padana, and Goya Coarse) are available. Coarse cornmeal is also available sold in bulk in many health food and specialty stores. Coarse cornmeal requires about thirty minutes of cooking, but it will benefit from an additional five to ten minutes on the stove. Figure five parts water to one part cornmeal when preparing polenta with this type of meal. Start the polenta in about half the total amount of water, keeping the other half hot to add slowly during the cooking process, as described in the basic recipe on page 198.

Fine yellow cornmeal has the consistency of coarse flour and will clump together when pinched between your thumb and forefinger. Brands of fine cornmeal include Goya (Fine), Indian Head, and Quaker. Because of its texture, fine cornmeal tends to thicken faster and form lumps when it is added to the boiling water, but it may eventually absorb less water than coarse cornmeal. Start cooking the polenta in five cups of water instead of the four called for in the basic recipe. Use a wire whisk instead of a spoon when adding the cornmeal to the water, and you will reduce the chances of a lumpy polenta. Polenta made with fine cornmeal will be ready in fifteen to twenty minutes, but it will benefit from an extra five to ten minutes of cooking. Fine yellow cornmeal, and the white cornmeal discussed below, require a total of about four parts water to one part cornmeal.

White cornmeal is typical of the Veneto region and, generally speaking, is ground fine. You should follow the guidelines for making polenta with fine yellow cornmeal when using white cornmeal.

"Instant" polenta, imported from Italy, is ready in five to six minutes; you may cook it an extra few minutes, adding a little water, if you like. As for yellow and white cornmeal, use about four parts water to one part meal, starting with about three quarters of the total amount of water and adding the remaining water as necessary.

Tarragna is whole-grain cornmeal mixed with buckwheat (*grano turco*) meal, which accounts for the flecks of brown throughout. *Tarragna* is earthier-tasting and coarser still than the coarse cornmeal described above. It is a great favorite in the Valtellina area of Lombardy, but it is difficult to find in the United States. If you should find it, cook it as you would coarse yellow cornmeal, cooking it forty to forty-five minutes and giving it a little extra water during that time if necessary. As with polenta made from all other types of cornmeal, *tarragna* will be improved by cooking it for an additional five to ten minutes.

Polenta Cooking Tips

Making polenta requires patience, certain equipment, and a strong stirring arm. But I assure you, it is all well worth the effort; polenta is a food that hugs you and comforts you and earns you praise at the table.

The traditional cooking vessel for polenta is a cast-iron or brass cauldron, but in today's kitchens a wide cast-iron or enameled cast-iron saucepan with slightly sloping sides and a capacity of three to four quarts is ideal. Lacking that, any wide, sturdy pan with a heavy bottom will do. A sturdy metal whisk (for fine cornmeal) or a flat-nosed wooden stirrer (for coarse cornmeal) is best for mixing. Use an oven mitt to hold the handle or edge of the saucepan while you're mixing.

Add the cornmeal very gradually, sifting it through your open fingers and stirring constantly. It should take about five minutes to add all the cornmeal for a batch of Basic Polenta.

To cook polenta well is to cook it slowly. Whichever kind of cornmeal you are using, start it in enough of the water to make a smooth, dense mixture. Stir the polenta constantly as it thickens, then add the rest of the water gradually, letting the polenta thicken each time before adding more water. Continue like this until the cornmeal is tender. You will notice that the polenta takes less and less water each time to become smooth and loose again.

Tradition says that you mix the polenta always in the same direction; do not make "U-turns." Is this a bona fide concern? I can't answer for sure, but I still stir polenta that way. However you stir it, make sure to scrape along the bottom and around the edges of the pan, the two places where the polenta is most likely to stick and scorch.

The cooking temperature should always remain steady, with the cornmeal "perking"—that is, one or two big bubbles bursting on the surface at a time. Don't let the heat get too high, or the polenta will perk right out of the pot. Because of its density, polenta retains heat and can cause quite a burn. And keep your oven mitts on—the pot can get very hot while cooking polenta.

When polenta is ready, it will develop a shine and begin to gather around the spoon as you stir it. Unlike pasta and rice, which should be eaten al dente, polenta can be cooked for up to an additional fifteen minutes after it is tender. This extra cooking will enhance its flavor and digestibility.

Milk can be substituted for up to half of the water for a richer-tasting polenta, but it should be scalded first and added in the last stages of cooking (see the recipe for White Creamy Polenta with Fresh Plums, page 209).

Basic Polenta

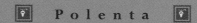 Polenta

Polenta is cornmeal cooked in water with seasonings until it reaches a dense, porridge-like texture. There is no secret to learn or difficult technique to master in cooking polenta. The one thing you do not want is *grumoli* (lumps) in your polenta; when cooked, polenta should be smooth on the tongue.

Polenta is very diverse in its uses. You can serve it hot, as a *contorno* (side dish) or first course. Any leftovers—or a whole freshly cooked batch—can be poured into a pan or mold and cooled until it sets. When polenta sets, it is quite firm and very easy to handle. It can then be cut into any shape and grilled, baked, panfried, or steamed. It can be served as an accompaniment to meats or fish, or topped with any condiment of choice.

Polenta is one of those neutral carriers of flavors like pasta and rice—and once you have mastered its method, it will become a reliable part of your culinary repertoire.

MAKES 6 SERVINGS

8 cups water, or as needed

2 fresh or dried bay leaves

1 tablespoon coarse salt (either sea or kosher), or as needed

1 tablespoon extra virgin olive oil

1½ cups coarse yellow cornmeal (see Note)

In a small saucepan, bring 4 cups of the water to a simmer; keep this "backup" water hot, covered, over medium-low heat. In a 3- to 4-quart cast-iron, enameled cast-iron, or other heavy saucepan, bring the remaining 4 cups water, the bay leaves, and salt to a boil over medium-high heat. When it is boiling, add the olive oil.

Place the cornmeal in a wide bowl in close reach of the stove. Scoop up a small handful of the cornmeal and, while stirring constantly with a wooden spoon or flat-nosed stirrer, let it sift slowly through your fingers into the seasoned boiling water. The cornmeal should fall *a poggia*—like rain—into the water. Sift the remaining cornmeal into the water a small handful at a time, stirring constantly and paying special attention to the edges of the pot. It should take about 5 minutes to add all the cornmeal.

When all the cornmeal has been added, the mixture should be smooth and thick and begin to "perk"—large bubbles will rise to the surface. Reduce the level of heat to medium-low—the polenta should continue to perk—and continue stirring until the mixture becomes too thick to stir easily, about 4 minutes. Add enough of the backup water—about 1 cup—to restore the mixture to a smooth stirring consistency. Stir until the mixture is again too thick to stir easily. Continue adding the backup water and stirring like this until the cornmeal is tender, about 20 minutes from the time the cornmeal was added. As the polenta cooks, you will need to add less water each time and stir longer between additions. It is possible that you will not need to add all the water.

When the cornmeal is tender, stir the polenta without adding water until it is shiny and begins to gather around the spoon as you stir it, 5 to 10 minutes. (The polenta should become thick enough to stand a spoon in.) The polenta is ready to serve at this point, or you can choose to cook it an extra few minutes to intensify the flavor and make the texture even smoother. To continue cooking, reduce the level of heat to low and stir the polenta constantly for 5 to 10 minutes. You may need to add a small amount of water during this extra cooking if the polenta begins to stick or become too thick.

To serve the polenta hot: Scrape the polenta away from you into a ceramic bowl. Let the polenta stand for 10 minutes before serving to cool a bit. Remove the bay leaves. To serve, scoop the polenta onto plates with a large spoon, dipping the spoon in water before each scoop. (An ice cream scoop can be used in the same fashion; it makes nice round mounds of polenta.)

You can also serve the polenta hot directly from a board in the traditional way: Scape the hot polenta onto the center of a wooden cutting board, keeping the polenta in a high mound. Let the polenta stand for a few minutes, until it is firm enough to cut. Cut the polenta with a string stretched taut between your index fingers or a thin knife. Gently transfer the slices to plates.

To chill the polenta for baking, grilling, or panfrying: You can begin to see the true versatility of polenta when it has been chilled until firm and cut into shapes for baking, grilling, or panfrying. To serve polenta this way, pour the hot polenta—either freshly made for this purpose or left over from a batch made to be eaten hot—into a baking dish or mold to a thickness of about ½ inch. (One whole recipe of Basic Polenta makes enough to fill two 13 × 9-inch baking dishes to this depth.) Cover with plastic wrap, pressing it directly to the surface of the polenta, and refrigerate until thoroughly chilled and very firm, 4 to 5 hours. Invert the polenta onto a cutting board and cut it into any desired shape.

To bake: Place the polenta shapes on a lightly oiled baking sheet and place in a preheated 375°F oven until lightly browned and crispy, about 20 minutes. Turn the polenta once about halfway through the cooking.

To grill: Lightly brush both sides of the polenta pieces with olive oil. Place on a hot grill and cook, turning once, until well marked and heated through, about 2 minutes per side.

To panfry: Heat a small amount of olive oil in a nonstick skillet over medium-high heat. Add the polenta slices and cook, turning once, until golden brown and crispy on both sides, 8 to 10 minutes.

continued

Note: The amount of water and the timing given in this recipe are for polenta made with coarse yellow cornmeal; if you are using fine yellow or white cornmeal, "instant" polenta, or *tarragna*—whole-grain cornmeal—please read The Different Types of Cornmeal for Polenta on page 195. (A description of coarse yellow cornmeal is also found there.)

Cold-Water Method for Making Lump-Free Polenta

Traditionally, polenta is made by adding cornmeal very slowly to boiling seasoned water as described in the recipe for Basic Polenta on page 198. Newcomers to making polenta may find it easier to make lump-free polenta by starting the process in cold water.

Read through the Basic Polenta recipe. Measure into the saucepan the amount of water specified for the type of cornmeal you are using; add the salt, bay leaf, and oil, but do not bring the water to a boil. Measure the "backup" water into a second pan and place it over low heat. Stir all the cornmeal into the cold, seasoned water until the mixture is smooth. Place the cornmeal mixture over medium heat and bring it to a boil, stirring constantly. This will take 10 to 15 minutes. From that point, follow the recipe for Basic Polenta, adding the backup water as described in the recipe.

Polenta with Anchovies

Polenta con Acciughe

The simplicity of this dish is, for those who love anchovies as I do, wonderful. You can add finely shredded Belgian endive or *radicchio Trevisano* to the pan when sautéing the anchovies and the dish will take on another dimension.

MAKES 6 SERVINGS

If using whole anchovies, rinse them under cool water. With a paring knife, scrape off any remaining salt and the skin. Pull off the tails. Wipe the anchovies clean. With the knife or your fingers, split them lengthwise into two fillets. Scrape out and discard the small interior bones. Taste the anchovies; If they are very strong, you may want to rinse them again—or even soak them briefly—in cool water; drain them thoroughly if you do. If using canned anchovy fillets, simply drain the oil from the can.

14 oil- or salt-packed whole anchovies, or
    two 2-ounce cans anchovy fillets, drained
1 recipe Basic Polenta (page 198)
1 tablespoon extra virgin olive oil
3 tablespoons water
2 tablespoons chopped fresh Italian parsley
    leaves

Prepare the polenta. Pour it away from you into a ceramic bowl. Let it stand for 10 minutes.

Meanwhile, in a small skillet, heat the olive oil over medium heat. Add the anchovies and stir until they begin to fall apart, 1 to 2 minutes. Add the water and parsley and bring to a boil. Remove from the heat. Spoon the polenta onto plates, dipping the spoon in cold water between spoonfuls, and top with the anchovy sauce.

Polenta as Served in Piedmont

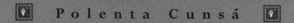 Polenta Cunsá

MAKES 6 SERVINGS

1 recipe Basic Polenta (page 198)

1¼ cups diced (½-inch) Fontina cheese (about ¼ pound)

1¼ cups diced (½-inch) Toma cheese (about ¼ pound; see Note)

¾ cup freshly grated Parmigiano-Reggiano cheese

5 tablespoons unsalted butter

Freshly ground black pepper

Prepare the polenta, but during the last 10 minutes of cooking—after all the water has been stirred into the polenta—add the Fontina, Toma, and about half of the Parmigiano-Reggiano, one cheese at a time and about a handful at a time, mixing continuously as you do. Pour the polenta away from you into a shallow ceramic bowl and let stand for 10 minutes.

Meanwhile, in a small skillet or saucepan over medium heat, cook the butter until the white flecks turn golden brown, about 4 minutes.

Pour the browned butter over the polenta and sprinkle with the remaining Parmigiano-Reggiano cheese and pepper. Serve immediately, spooning the polenta onto plates and dipping the spoon in cold water between spoonfuls.

Note: Toma is a 100 percent cow's milk cheese from the Piedmont region of Italy. It comes in rounds that measure approximately 4 inches across and is covered, when ripe, with a beige-speckled white rind. You can substitute Brie or Camembert for Toma.

Polenta as Served in Friuli

Polenta Cuinzada Friulana

This dish is wonderful as an accompaniment to roasted or braised meats, or served with a braised vegetable such as escarole or spinach for lunch. It can also be served as is for a pasta course.

MAKES 6 SERVINGS

Preheat the oven to 375°F. Using some of the butter, grease an 8 × 10-inch baking dish.

In a small skillet or saucepan, cook the remaining butter over medium heat until the white flecks turn golden brown, about 4 minutes. Remove the skillet from the heat and set aside in a warm place.

½ cup (1 stick) unsalted butter
1 recipe Basic Polenta (page 198)
1½ cups grated Montasio cheese
    (about 6 ounces; see page 42)
2 teaspoons ground cinnamon

Prepare the polenta.

Remove the bay leaves from the polenta. Pour about one third of it into the prepared dish and spread it into an even layer with a rubber spatula dipped in water. Pour one third of the browned butter over the polenta and sprinkle it with one third of the Montasio cheese and one third of the cinnamon. Repeat this process two more times, with the remaining polenta, butter, cheese, and cinnamon. (The polenta can be prepared to this point up to 4 hours in advance. Cover the baking dish and leave it at room temperature; do not refrigerate.)

Uncover the baking dish if necessary. Bake the polenta until the cheese is lightly browned and the edges are bubbling, about 30 minutes. Remove from the oven and let rest for 10 minutes. Cut the polenta into squares and serve immediately.

Polenta, Gorgonzola, and Savoy Cabbage Torte

⚏ Torta di Verza e Polenta ⚏

This dish makes an excellent appetizer, served in place of a pasta course. The polenta can be layered with any cheese—or combination of cheeses—you choose, or the cheese can be eliminated altogether. You may also use any vegetables you like, but in the Istrian tradition, Savoy cabbage and polenta are partners. Sometimes a grilled sausage is sliced and added to the dish and it becomes a main course.

MAKES 8 SERVINGS

1 recipe Basic Polenta (page 198)

4 quarts salted water

2 medium-size baking (Idaho) potatoes, peeled and cut into quarters

1 small head (2 pounds) Savoy cabbage

2 tablespoons extra virgin olive oil

4 garlic cloves, lightly crushed

Salt and freshly ground black pepper

1½ cups crumbled Gorgonzola or coarsely grated Fontina cheese, or a mixture of the two (about 6 ounces)

2 teaspoons unsalted butter, at room temperature

½ cup freshly grated Parmigiano-Reggiano cheese

Prepare the polenta. While it is still hot, pour it into a lightly buttered 2-inch-deep 9-inch round cake pan (see Note). Let stand until cool, then refrigerate until completely chilled, 4 to 5 hours.

In a large pot over high heat, bring the salted water to a boil. Add the potatoes and cook for 10 minutes.

Meanwhile, remove any wilted or yellow leaves from the cabbage and cut out the core. Cut the cabbage into 1-inch cubes.

Add the cabbage to the pot and cook until both vegetables are tender, about 15 minutes. Drain thoroughly.

In a large skillet, heat the oil over medium heat. Add the garlic and cook, stirring, until lightly browned, about 3 minutes. Add the cabbage-potato mixture and season to taste with salt and pepper. Cook, turning the vegetables occasionally, until the liquid has evaporated and the vegetables begin to sizzle. Mash the vegetables coarsely with the spoon as you turn them, leaving plenty of lumps. Be careful not to scorch the mixture—cook it just until the liquid is gone. Remove the garlic cloves and season again with salt and pepper, if necessary.

Preheat the oven to 400°F.

Invert the cooled polenta cake onto a cutting board. With a long, thin knife, slice the cake horizontally into three even layers. Place the top layer upside down in the bottom of a buttered 10 × 4-inch springform pan. Top with half of the potato-cabbage mixture and half of the Gorgonzola. Top the cheese with the center layer of polenta and top that with the remaining potato-cabbage mixture and Gorgonzola. Place the bottom layer of the polenta cake upside down over the torte and press gently. Melt the butter and brush the top of the torte with the butter and sprinkle with the grated Parmigiano.

Bake the torte until the top layer of cheese is lightly browned and the torte is heated through, about 40 minutes. Remove the torte from the oven and cool for 5 minutes. Remove the sides of the springform pan and cut the torte into slices to serve.

Note: If you do not have the necessary cake and springform pans, the torte can be made as follows: Pour the hot polenta out onto a cutting board and let it cool until very firm, about 30 minutes. Cut the cooled polenta into ½-inch-thick slices. Arrange one third of the slices to cover the bottom of a buttered 11-inch oval (or similar-size) baking dish. Arrange half of the potato-cabbage mixture over the polenta and sprinkle it with half of the Gorgonzola. Make another layer like the first, using half of the remaining polenta and all of the remaining potato-cabbage mixture and Gorgonzola. Top with the remaining polenta slices. Finish off and bake as directed above.

Polenta with Swiss Chard

Polenta con Bietola

This recipe can be very versatile—any vegetable, or combination of vegetables, can be added, as long as it is partially cooked and diced beforehand. You might want to prepare this polenta a day in advance and let it set in a baking pan or mold (see page 199); the vegetables become embedded in the polenta like a mosaic. Slice it and grill it or bake it to serve alongside grilled chicken, braised meats, or fish.

MAKES 6 SERVINGS

1 pound Swiss chard, beet greens, or kale

8 cups salted water

1 recipe Basic Polenta (page 198) prepared using the chard cooking water

2 tablespoons unsalted butter

1 cup freshly grated Parmigiano-Reggiano cheese

With a small knife, trim the stem ends and any wilted or yellow parts from the chard. Pull or cut off the stems. Cut the stems crosswise into ½-inch lengths. Cut the leaves lengthwise in half, then crosswise into ½-inch-wide strips. Swish the chard in a large bowl of cool water, then lift it with your hands to a colander to drain. Repeat the washing until there is no grit in the bottom of the bowl.

In a large saucepan, bring the salted water to a boil. Stir in the chard and cook until tender, about 15 minutes (other greens can be trimmed, cut, and washed in the same way as chard, but may require slightly more or less cooking time to become tender). Drain the Swiss chard, reserving the cooking liquid. Measure the liquid and, if necessary, add enough water to measure 8 cups. Set aside. Coarsely chop the chard.

Prepare the polenta, using the reserved chard cooking liquid in place of the water called for in the Basic Polenta recipe. During the last 10 minutes of polenta cooking time, after all the water has been added, add the cooked chard. During the last 5 minutes of cooking, add the butter.

Pour the polenta away from you into a ceramic bowl. Let stand for 10 minutes. Spoon the polenta onto plates, dipping the spoon in water between spoonfuls. Sprinkle the polenta with the grated cheese and serve.

Polenta Nest with Truffled Egg

Nido di Polenta con Uovo al Tartufo

This can be a wonderful breakfast or a first course. The truffles make this dish exceptional but sautéed mushrooms or buttered asparagus also work nicely.

MAKES 6 SERVINGS

In a small saucepan, heat the milk over medium heat until small bubbles form around the edges. Cover the pan and keep the milk warm over low heat.

In a small cast-iron or enameled cast-iron saucepan, bring the water, salt, and bay leaf to a boil over medium heat. Prepare the polenta according to the directions in the Basic Polenta recipe on page 198, using the hot milk in place of the backup water. Remove the polenta from the heat and stir in 3 tablespoons of the butter.

Meanwhile, preheat the oven to 425°F and place the rack in the center position. Use some of the remaining butter to lightly grease six 8-ounce ceramic ramekins or custard cups. In a small saucepan or skillet, melt the remaining butter over low heat.

Ladle the hot polenta into the ramekins, dividing it evenly and dipping the ladle in water between ladlefuls. Dip the back of the ladle in water and make an indentation in the center of each polenta serving large enough to hold an egg yolk. Set an egg yolk in each indentation. Sprinkle the yolks lightly with salt and drizzle them with the melted butter. Place the ramekins on a baking sheet and set in the oven. Bake until the yolks are set outside but very runny inside, 4 to 5 minutes.

Remove the ramekins to serving plates. With a truffle slicer or the coarse side of a box grater, shave the truffles (see page 6) to cover the eggs and polenta. Serve immediately.

2 cups milk

2 cups water, or as needed

1½ teaspoons coarse (sea or kosher) salt

1 fresh or dried bay leaf

¾ cup coarse yellow cornmeal (see page 195)

6 tablespoons (¾ stick) unsalted butter

6 large egg yolks

2 ounces fresh white truffle (see page 5), brushed clean

Polenta with Honey and Strawberries

Polenta Dolce con Miele e Fragole

Italians are not big breakfast eaters. Usually they have *caffè latte* (coffee with steamed milk) with bread, toast, *biscotti* (cookies), or *cornetti* (croissants). When breakfast does include something cooked, it is often polenta prepared in one of two ways: either *polenta con latte* (polenta made with hot milk and sugar) or leftover polenta cut into pieces (see page 199) and served in hot milk sprinkled with sugar. These two dishes are typical children's meals—even for lunch and dinner. When I was growing up, soft—freshly made, that is—polenta with milk and honey was also given to infants. Today I serve slices of chilled polenta, panfried and topped with strawberries in a honey syrup, in place of pancakes for breakfast, or for an unusual dessert.

MAKES 3 BREAKFAST OR 6 DESSERT SERVINGS

---

1 pint ripe strawberries, washed, hulled, and sliced ¼ inch thick, or other berries, rinsed and drained

3 tablespoons honey or pure maple syrup

12 slices (3 × 2 × ½ inch) chilled polenta (see Note)

2 tablespoons unsalted butter

Confectioners' sugar

3 to 6 sprigs fresh mint

Place the sliced strawberries in a small bowl and pour the honey over them. Let them stand, tossing once or twice, while preparing the polenta.

Preheat the oven to 200°F.

In a large, heavy, nonstick skillet, melt 1 tablespoon of the butter over medium heat. When the butter is foaming, add half the polenta slices in a single layer. Cook the polenta, turning once, until golden brown on both sides, 8 to 10 minutes. Transfer the polenta to a baking sheet and keep warm in the oven. Repeat with the remaining butter and polenta.

Divide the polenta slices among serving plates. Spoon some of the berries and their syrup over each serving and sprinkle with confectioners' sugar. Decorate the plates with the mint sprigs and serve.

Note: Three cups (half the Basic Polenta recipe, page 198) hot polenta poured into a 13 × 9-inch baking dish will make twelve slices of this size, with some scraps for the cook to nibble on.

White Creamy Polenta
with Fresh Plums

MAKES 6 SERVINGS

Wash the plums and dry them well. Cut them in half and remove the pits. In a large skillet, melt 2 tablespoons of the butter over medium heat. Add the plums, 1 cup of the water, the sugar, and cinnamon. Bring to a boil, then adjust the level of heat to a simmer. Cook, stirring occasionally, until the plums are very tender but still chunky and the liquid is syrupy, about 30 minutes. Remove the skillet from the heat and keep warm, covered.

Meanwhile, in a small pan, heat the milk over medium heat until small bubbles form around the edges. Cover the pan and keep the milk warm over low heat.

1 pound ripe Italian prune plums

5 tablespoons unsalted butter

7 cups water, or as needed

5 tablespoons granulated sugar

2 teaspoons ground cinnamon

2 cups milk

1 tablespoon coarse sea salt

2 cups white cornmeal

Confectioners' sugar

In a cast-iron, enameled cast-iron, or other heavy 3- to 4-quart saucepan, bring the remaining 6 cups water to a boil with the salt. Add the remaining 3 tablespoons butter. Prepare the polenta according to the instructions on page 198, adding the hot milk in place of the backup water. The cooking time after all the cornmeal has been added will be about 20 minutes—or longer if you decide to give it the extra cooking time mentioned in the Basic Polenta recipe. The polenta should be as dense as cooked oatmeal and begin to gather around the spoon as you stir.

Scoop the polenta into warm bowls, dipping the spoon in water between scoops. Spoon the plum mixture over the polenta and sprinkle with confectioners' sugar. Serve immediately.

Vegetables

Verdure

The Italian peninsula in the middle of the Mediterranean has a God-favored climate, from the sun-filled South to the rich valleys and hills of the North, from the grain basket of Puglia to the rich pastures of the Po Valley. As a result, Italy has a tremendous variety and diversity of vegetables, legumes, grains, and fruits such as few other countries have. This extensive availability gives the Italian cuisine its endless repertoire of vegetable-based recipes—from *antipasti* and salads to soups, pastas, and *contorni* (side dishes). There is no cuisine more colorful in its vegetables than the Italian.

The Italians still follow the rhythm of the seasons, and different vegetables are enjoyed year-round at their optimal times of flavor and nutrition. The culture of the open market is still alive and well, although the need for convenience food is slowly creeping into the mainstream. I pray to God that convenience foods won't replace seasonal cuisine, and I trust that they won't. I have faith in my fellow Italians—the pleasure and cognizance of true individual flavors is hard to forfeit. In fact, the Italians value vegetables as much as meat and other proteins, and it shows in the amount of attention Italians pay to their preparation—vegetables in Italian cuisine are not a sidekick but a protagonist.

If there is one single most exhilarating experience—something one must do while traveling in Italy—it is to see the open vegetable markets. Whether you visit the Campo dei Fiori market in Rome, the Ponte Rosso market in Trieste, or the Vucceria in Palermo, the Italian way of life unfolds in front of your eyes.

The *bancarelle* (vendor stands) beam with the splendor of local produce and vegetables. Every product is proudly displayed with artistic flair by women and men whose hands are cracked by the earth and sun. They caress their bundles of broccoli, artichokes, fennel, chicory, radicchio, and whatever else they have brought to offer to the shoppers. The *venderigole*, as they are called in Trieste, sing out the praises of their produce to lure their prospective buyers.

"*Signore, radichietto primo toio, tenero come la seda*" in dialect ("Ladies, radicchio, first cut, soft like silk").

"*Pesche dolci come il miele*" ("Peaches sweet like honey").

"*Qua, qua signore, la mia roba ze piu'bella*" ("Here, here ladies—my produce is better!").

The vegetables glisten, still covered by the morning dew, as they are placed in bags. During the transaction, there are always a few words of advice, words exchanged between the *venderigola* and the customer on the best way to prepare the vegetables. Recipes are offered too. Some of my favorite vegetable dishes have come from the recipes that the farmers and *venderigole* have shared with me at the markets.

One spring, we visited the Campo dei Fiori market in Rome. There were mounds of crisp fennel bulbs with their bright green fronds gathered as veils on top. There was a pudgy smiling man standing behind the *bancarella* whose weathered face was testimony to his life experiences. I knew this would be the man who would reveal to me the ultimate recipe for fennel. So I asked him how he enjoyed his fennel the most. "*Finocchio croccante in pinzimonio, condito con olio d'oliva buono è la fine del mondo*" ("Crispy fennel dipped in a condiment of good olive oil, garlic, and hot crushed pepper is the end of the world").

This I already knew, so I quickly followed with, "How about cooked fennel?" "*Finocchio cotto non vale un fico secco*" ("Cooked fennel is not worth a dry fig"). I left uninformed but smiling—fennel *is* best left uncooked.

The most important part of good cooking by far is the raw ingredients. Their quality and freshness determine the flavor of the finished dish. I love going to markets to shop for my restaurants and my home—there is nothing like the fresh products in the markets to inspire me.

As a child of seven or eight, I would go to the market with Nonna Rosa, my maternal grandmother, who lived in Busoler on the outskirts of Pola. The one road that led through the little town of Busoler was lined on both sides with small houses with red roofs. Each house had a large vegetable garden, which gave way to the vineyards and olive groves beyond.

I think my love and passion for food was instilled in those formative years I spent with my grandparents in Busoler. They were self-sufficient and grew most of what they needed. In the season of plenty, food was bottled, dried, or smoked and put by for leaner times. What they had in abundance was bartered or offered for sale by Grandma in the market.

The market was in the middle of Pola. Long rows of stalls were lined up under enormous chestnut trees. It smelled wonderful in the spring, when clusters of white chestnut flowers filled the trees. We would come from Busoler, pushing a laden hand cart that Grandma Rosa shared with our Aunt Ivana, as we called her (she was really my aunt's mother-in-law, whom we called aunt as a sign of respect). The night before we went to market, the vegetables would be washed in the large courtyard next to our house, then drained and set in wooden crates lined with burlap bags. In the morning, the crates were stacked on the cart and topped with baskets of herbs and fruits of the season.

The cart had two large wheels, a wide plank of wood for a body, and a long metal handle with a "T" at the end that Rosa and Ivana used to push or pull the cart. The front of the cart had one short leg to steady it when it was standing still. I loved going with them to the market, and we had a deal. "*Per su si sburta, per giu'se mena*" in dialect ("Uphill you push, downhill you can ride the cart"). I took that deal very seriously, and at the smallest decline in the road, I was up on top of the cart with the crates.

At the market, I had a great time. I loved playing with the balancing scale and weights, adding and subtracting leaves of spinach on one of the two trays until it balanced perfectly with the weights on the other. There were no plastic bags then—everyone came with canvas or rope shopping bags, and one of my important duties was to make cones out of newspaper that would hold the vegetables. I would twirl the sheets of newspaper around my arm and fold the tip over tightly a few times, then stack the cones one inside the other so Grandma would have them ready.

On market days, Grandma wore a very special apron with deep pockets in which to keep the money. The coins she left for me to play with, but the paper went deep in the pockets. Around ten o'clock, she would send me to buy *merenda* (snacks). Sometimes this would be a mortadella sandwich, sometimes a *krophen* (doughnut) or an ice cream cone. When just about everything was sold, Grandma left me alone and went to visit and chat with her friends down the line. I felt very important then, and I remember calling to the shoppers. I wanted to sell everything before she came back. I was a true little merchant.

Not all our vegetables were sold every time, but they certainly weren't wasted. On the way home, Grandma would knock on the kitchen doors of restaurants and trattorias and barter the unsold vegetables for stale bread, which she would bring home and feed the chickens, ducks, pigs, and pigeons. It was a complete food circle in which nothing was wasted.

Going to the market with my grandmother was a source of childhood excitement and lifelong culinary inspiration. My recollections of the flavors, aromas, sights, and sounds live on in recipes that I make today.

Arugula Salad with Shavings of Porcini Mushrooms and Parmigiano-Reggiano Cheese

Insalata di Rucola, Funghi, e Parmigiano-Reggiano

This salad can easily become an appetizer, a lunch, or a cheese course at the end of a meal. I use Parmigiano-Reggiano, but Montasio or Pecorino Romano can be substituted.

MAKES 6 SERVINGS

2 ounces Parmigiano-Reggiano cheese

2 tablespoons extra virgin olive oil

1 teaspoon fresh lemon juice

Large pinch of salt

¼ pound baby or hydroponic arugula (about 8 cups), washed and spun dry

2 ounces fresh porcini mushrooms, wiped clean, trimmed, and very thinly sliced (about 2 cups; see Note)

Freshly ground black pepper

Truffle oil

Make shards of Parmigiano-Reggiano cheese by scraping it with a vegetable peeler. You should have about 1¼ cups. Set the shards aside.

In a large bowl, whisk the olive oil and lemon juice together with the salt until blended. Add the arugula and mushrooms and sprinkle with salt and pepper. Toss until the salad is coated with the dressing. Fold the shaved Parmigiano-Reggiano into the salad and divide among serving plates. Drizzle the salads with truffle oil to taste.

Note: Shiitake or cremini mushrooms can be substituted for the porcini. Whichever type of mushroom you choose, make sure they are firm and as free of blemishes as possible. Before slicing, trim any tough parts from the stems—completely remove the shiitake stems—and wipe the caps clean with a damp paper towel.

Fennel, Olive, and Citrus Salad

 Insalata di Agrumi con Olive

My cousin Gianni and his friend Luciano have a little rooftop apartment overlooking the Pantheon in Rome. One warm summer afternoon, we had this salad with Pecorino Romano cheese for lunch while seated on a terrace full of hanging geraniums. *Le Rondini al Nido* sung by Pavarotti played in the background. It was magical. This salad is delicious with a piece of grilled fish.

MAKES 4 SERVINGS

Combine all the ingredients in a medium-size bowl. Toss to blend and let stand for 30 minutes, tossing once or twice, to let the flavors mingle before serving.

Note: Cut the lemon into ⅛-inch-thick slices with a very sharp serrated knife. Stack a few of the slices at a time and cut them into ⅛-inch-wide strips, then cut the strips crosswise into ⅛-inch cubes.

2 cups pitted oil-cured Gaeta olives

1 lemon, washed and cut into ⅛-inch cubes (including rind; see Note)

2 cups diced (⅜-inch) fresh fennel bulb (use only the tender inner layers)

2 tablespoons extra virgin olive oil

Juice of 1 lemon

Green Salad with Montasio Cheese and Green Apple

Insalata di Montasio con Mele

To vary this dish, try changing the mesclun salad to arugula, frisée, or tender, young fresh spinach leaves.

MAKES 4 SERVINGS

3 tablespoons extra virgin olive oil

1 tablespoon plus 1 teaspoon fresh lemon juice

1 Granny Smith apple

½ pound mesclun salad or assorted baby greens, such as arugula, spinach, or Lolla Rossa lettuce (about 6 cups), washed and spun dry

Salt and freshly ground black pepper

2 ounces Montasio cheese or other medium-soft cheese, such as Fontina or mild Vermont Cheddar

In a small jar with a tight-fitting lid, shake the olive oil and lemon juice together until blended. Pour the dressing into a large bowl.

Cut the apple into quarters, cut out the core, and slice the quarters very thin. Toss the apple with the dressing. Add the greens to the bowl, sprinkle them with salt and pepper, and toss until coated with dressing.

With a vegetable peeler, shave the cheese into thin strips over the salad. Toss again to mix the cheese into the greens. Divide the salad among four salad plates and serve immediately.

Red Cabbage and Shrimp Salad

Insalata di Cavolo Rosso con Gamberi

I love red cabbage. I don't understand why it is so underused a vegetable. It is readily available, inexpensive, and quite tasty and refreshing.

MAKES 6 SERVINGS

Stir the olive oil, vinegar, and salt and pepper to taste together in a large bowl. Remove any wilted or dark outer leaves from the cabbage. Cut the cabbage in half and cut out the core. Shred the cabbage as thin as you can and add it to the bowl with the dressing. Cut the endive in half lengthwise and cut out the cores. Cut the endive crosswise into ⅓-inch-wide pieces and add to the bowl. Toss the cabbage and endive with the dressing, adding more salt and pepper to taste. Let stand for 30 minutes, tossing once or twice, to let the flavors mingle before serving.

Meanwhile, in a 4- to 5-quart pot, bring the water, celery, carrots, and bay leaf to a boil and let boil for 20 minutes. With a skimmer or slotted spoon, remove the vegetables and discard. Add the shrimp and boil just until cooked through, about 2 minutes. Drain immediately.

¼ cup extra virgin olive oil

3 tablespoons red wine vinegar

Salt and freshly ground black pepper

1 medium-size head red cabbage
    (about 2 pounds)

2 heads Belgian endive

2 quarts water

1 celery stalk, cut crosswise into thirds

½ cup sliced carrots

1 fresh or dried bay leaf

1 pound small shrimp (about 45), shelled
    and deveined

Divide the cabbage mixture among six salad plates, arranging it in a mound in the center of the plates. Toss the shrimp in the dressing remaining in the bowl. Arrange the shrimp over the cabbage salad and serve.

Steamed Vegetables with Warm Prosciutto Vinaigrette

Insalata di Verdure Cotte al Prosciutto

This is a wonderful way to use leftover prosciutto as a condiment.

MAKES 4 SERVINGS

2 medium-size beets (about ½ pound with greens removed), trimmed and scrubbed

Salt

1 medium-size carrot, trimmed

1 small zucchini

¼ pound tender young string beans, ends trimmed

½ head cauliflower, cut or broken into florets (about 4 cups)

½ head broccoli, cut or broken into florets (about 3 cups)

4 small heads Lolla Rossa lettuce or other tender baby lettuces, washed and spun dry

1 tablespoon extra virgin olive oil

Four ⅛-inch-thick slices prosciutto di Parma (about ¼ pound), chopped medium-fine

¼ cup red wine vinegar

3 tablespoons Chicken Stock (page 80), canned low-sodium chicken broth, or water

Cook the beets in a medium-size saucepan of boiling salted water until easily pierced with a skewer or paring knife, 20 to 35 minutes, depending on the beets. Drain.

Meanwhile, set a vegetable steamer over boiling water in a large pot with a tight-fitting lid. Steam the vegetables until tender but still firm: about 15 minutes for the carrot, 8 minutes for the zucchini, 7 minutes for the string beans, and 6 minutes for the cauliflower and broccoli. (You can steam more than one vegetable at a time, depending on the size of the steamer.) Remove the vegetables and cool them completely.

Scrape the skins off the beets as soon as they are cool enough to handle. Cut the carrot, zucchini, and peeled beets into thick matchstick strips, about 2 × ¼ × ¼ inch. Arrange the lettuce leaves like a flower in the center of a platter. Arrange the vegetables in groups around the leaves.

In a medium-size skillet, heat the olive oil over medium heat. Add the prosciutto and cook, stirring a few times, until it begins to brown, about 3 minutes. Add the vinegar and cook until it has evaporated, about 3 minutes. Add the stock and bring to a boil. Spoon the hot dressing over the greens and vegetables and serve.

Asparagus Gratin with Parmigiano-Reggiano Cheese

Asparagi Gratinati al Parmigiano-Reggiano

There is no difficult technique involved in making this dish—it is just a simple and great classic Italian dish.

MAKES 6 SERVINGS

Bring the salted water to a boil in a large saucepan. Trim the woody ends from the asparagus stalks. With a vegetable peeler, peel the bottom half of the stalks. Add the asparagus to the boiling water and cook until tender but still crisp, about 6 minutes. Drain well.

Meanwhile, in a small bowl, toss the cheese, bread crumbs, and lemon zest together until blended.

Preheat the broiler. Arrange the asparagus stalks in a single layer in an 8-inch square or similar-size flameproof baking dish. Drizzle the asparagus with the melted butter and sprinkle an even layer of the bread crumb mixture over it. Broil about 4 inches from the heat until the bread crumb mixture is golden brown, about 3 minutes. Serve hot.

3 quarts salted water

24 medium-size asparagus spears (about 1½ pounds)

½ cup freshly grated Parmigiano-Reggiano cheese

2 tablespoons fine plain dry bread crumbs

½ teaspoon grated lemon zest (yellow part of the lemon skin only, not the underlying white pith)

3 tablespoons unsalted butter, melted

Marinated and Braised Turnips

🔸 Brovada 🔸

This is a typical Friulian dish made by marinating whole turnips in wine dregs (the skins, stems, and seeds left after crushing the grapes for wine). An excellent substitution for the dregs is a full-bodied wine. Serve this dish with a pork roast or grilled meats. In Friuli, it is traditionally served with *musetto*—also known as *cotechino*—a very gelatinous pork sausage made with pork snout.

MAKES 6 SERVINGS

3 pounds large, firm turnips (each about
    4 inches across)
1 cup red wine vinegar
1 to 2 bottles full-bodied wine, such as
    Merlot, Cabernet Franc, or Cabernet
    Sauvignon
2 tablespoons extra virgin olive oil
¼ cup finely chopped bacon
4 garlic cloves, peeled
Salt and freshly ground black pepper
1 cup Chicken Stock (page 80) or canned
    low-sodium chicken broth, or as needed

Cut off any stems and leaves and the root from the turnips. Scrub the turnips well and place them in a ceramic or glass container large enough to hold them all with about 2 inches of headroom. Pour in the vinegar and enough of the wine to completely cover the turnips. Cover the container and store in a cool (45° to 50°F) place for 30 days. (A cool cellar in winter is ideal. Alternatively, the turnips may be stored in the refrigerator, but increase the time to 40 days to allow them to marinate fully.)

Drain the turnips and peel them. Grate the turnips on the coarsest side of a box grater.

In a deep, heavy pot, heat the olive oil over medium heat. Add the bacon and garlic and cook, stirring, until golden, about 5 minutes. Add the turnips, season lightly with salt and pepper, and reduce the heat to low. Add ¼ cup of the stock and cover the pot. Cook the turnips, stirring often, until meltingly tender, about 1 hour. Add more stock a few tablespoons at a time if the turnips become dry. When finished, the turnips should be moist but not soupy. If there is too much liquid in the pot toward the end of cooking, uncover the pot to evaporate some of it. Check the seasoning and add more salt and pepper if necessary. Serve hot.

Braised Savoy Cabbage

Verze Stufate

This is one of my favorite recipes for Savoy cabbage. My grandma would make it and serve it with polenta and a grilled sausage on the side.

MAKES 6 SERVINGS

Remove any wilted or discolored leaves from the cabbage. Cut the cabbage in half and cut out the core. Cut the cabbage into ½-inch-wide strips. Wash and thoroughly drain.

In a deep, heavy casserole with a tight-fitting lid, heat the olive oil over medium heat. Add the onions and garlic and cook, stirring occasionally, until golden brown, about 8 minutes. Add the cabbage and rosemary and season lightly with salt and pepper. Stir until the cabbage is wilted, about 4 minutes. Reduce the heat to low, cover the casserole, and cook, stirring often, until all the water has been rendered, about 30 minutes.

1 medium-size head Savoy cabbage
    (about 2½ pounds)
¼ cup extra virgin olive oil
1 cup diced onions
4 garlic cloves, crushed
Sprig fresh rosemary
Salt and freshly ground black pepper
1 tablespoon red wine vinegar
1 cup Chicken Stock (page 80), canned
    low-sodium chicken broth, or warm
    water, or as needed

Add the vinegar and continue cooking until the cabbage is very tender and medium brown, about 45 minutes longer. Stir the cabbage often and add small amounts of stock or water if it begins to stick. The cabbage should be moist but not soupy and intense in flavor. Remove the garlic cloves and season with more salt and pepper if needed. Serve hot.

Tomato-Braised Cauliflower

Cavolfiore Affogato al Pomodoro

This is an excellent side dish, but it also makes a great sauce for pasta or, when topped with shaved Pecorino Romano cheese, a delicious appetizer. It is wonderful as a topping for *Bruschette* (page 21).

MAKES 6 SERVINGS

1 head cauliflower (about 2½ pounds)

3 tablespoons extra virgin olive oil

1 cup diced onions

4 garlic cloves, crushed

2 fresh or dried bay leaves

½ teaspoon peperoncino (crushed red pepper)

Salt

2 cups cored, peeled (see page 141), and seeded, vine-ripened plum tomatoes or one 16-ounce can Italian plum tomatoes, preferably San Marzano, drained and seeded

Pull off the cauliflower leaves and cut out the core. Break the cauliflower head into florets no larger than 1½ inches.

In a large casserole, heat the olive oil over medium heat. Add the onions and garlic and cook, stirring, until wilted, about 4 minutes. Add the cauliflower, bay leaves, and peperoncino and season lightly with salt. Cook for 5 minutes, stirring occasionally. Meanwhile, crush the tomatoes by hand.

Add the tomatoes to the cauliflower and cook, covered, until the cauliflower is very tender and most of the liquid has been absorbed, about another 30 minutes. Check the cauliflower after about 20 minutes: There should be just enough liquid to lightly coat it. If there is more, finish cooking the cauliflower, uncovered. Season with salt and serve hot.

Roasted Potato Wedges

Spicchi di Patate Arroste

Everybody has a favorite potato dish and this one is my brother's. He makes them taste so good and I love them too, because they are his project when cooking dinner at my house.

MAKES 6 SERVINGS

Preheat the oven to 475°F.

Pat the potatoes dry and cut them lengthwise in quarters. In a bowl, toss the potato wedges with 3 tablespoons of the olive oil, the salt, and rosemary. Arrange the wedges skin side down, without touching, in a heavy baking pan or two cast-iron skillets. Bake until the potatoes are tender and well browned, about 30 minutes. With long tongs, turn once or twice so they brown and cook evenly.

Meanwhile, in a small bowl, stir together the garlic, parsley, and the remaining 2 tablespoons olive oil.

4 medium-size Idaho (baking) potatoes, scrubbed

5 tablespoons extra virgin olive oil

1 teaspoon salt

1 tablespoon fresh rosemary or thyme leaves

6 garlic cloves, crushed

2 tablespoons chopped fresh Italian parsley leaves

Freshly ground black pepper

When the potatoes are done, press each wedge gently so that it cracks in the middle, then transfer them with tongs to a large bowl. Add the oil-and-garlic mixture and fresh pepper to taste. Toss gently but well until the potatoes are coated with the seasoned oil. Remove the garlic and serve hot.

String Beans and Potatoes

Fagiolini e Patate al Tegame

Greens and a starch all in one—when you serve this next to grilled meat or fish, you will need no other side dish.

MAKES 6 SERVINGS

2 medium-size to large Idaho (baking)
  potatoes
2 quarts salted water
1 pound fresh string beans, ends trimmed
3 tablespoons extra virgin olive oil
4 garlic cloves, sliced
Salt and freshly ground black pepper

Combine the potatoes and salted water in a large saucepan. Bring to a boil and cook for 20 minutes. Add the beans and cook until the potatoes are tender but still firm and the beans are tender, about 7 minutes. Drain the vegetables in a colander. Remove the potatoes and set them aside to cool. Refresh the beans under cold running water and drain well. When the potatoes are cool enough to handle, peel them and cut into ⅓-inch cubes.

In a large, deep skillet, heat the olive oil over medium heat. Add the garlic and cook until golden, about 1 minute. Add the potatoes and string beans and season with salt and pepper. Cook the vegetables, mashing the potatoes roughly as you stir them, until they are heated through. Add more salt and pepper if necessary and serve hot.

Swiss Chard and Potatoes

⬛ Bietola e Patate ⬛

The flavor of this dish actually improves when it is made in advance and reheated.

MAKES 6 SERVINGS

Trim the ends from the Swiss chard stems. Cut off and discard any wilted or yellow parts of the leaves. Strip the stems from the leaves and cut the stems into ½-inch-thick slices. Cut the leaves lengthwise in half, then crosswise into ½-inch-wide strips. Wash the leaves and stems thoroughly, then drain well.

Bring the salted water to a boil in a large pot. Add the potatoes and cook for 10 minutes. Add the Swiss chard and cook until the potatoes and chard stems are very tender, another 20 to 30 minutes. Drain in a colander.

> 2 pounds Swiss chard
> 4 quarts salted water
> 3 medium-size Idaho (baking) potatoes, peeled and each cut crosswise into 4 pieces
> ¼ cup extra virgin olive oil
> 4 garlic cloves, crushed
> Salt and freshly ground black pepper

In a large skillet, heat 2 tablespoons of the olive oil over medium heat. Add the garlic and cook just until it begins to brown, about 1 minute. Add the drained Swiss chard and potatoes and season them lightly with salt and pepper. Cook, stirring and mashing the potatoes, until the liquid has evaporated and the potatoes are coarsely mashed; if the potatoes begin to brown, reduce the heat to medium-low. Add the remaining 2 tablespoons olive oil, season to taste with salt and pepper, stir, and serve hot.

Rice and Zucchini Crostata

Crostata di Riso e Zucchini

This recipe belongs to Dante Laurenti, a dedicated captain at Felidia until his retirement. Besides being a talented captain, he is an excellent cook. We still cure pancetta and prosciutto, make wine vinegar, and cook other good things together on free weekends.

MAKES 6 SERVINGS

Crostata Dough (recipe follows)

2 cups Arborio rice

4 cups shredded small, firm zucchini (about 1 pound)

3 large eggs

3 cups ricotta, preferably fresh

2 cups chopped scallions (white and tender green parts; about 12 scallions)

1½ cups freshly grated Parmigiano-Reggiano cheese (about 6 ounces)

1½ cups half-and-half

Salt and freshly ground black pepper

1 large egg yolk, beaten with a few drops of water, or extra virgin olive oil, for the crust

Make the crostata dough.

In a large bowl, toss the rice and zucchini together until evenly distributed. Let stand for 30 minutes.

In a small bowl, whisk the eggs together until blended. Combine the egg mixture, ricotta, scallions, and Parmigiano-Reggiano in the bowl of an electric mixer. Add the rice and zucchini and mix at low speed until blended. (Alternatively, the mixture can be beaten by hand with a wooden spoon.) Add the half-and-half and mix thoroughly. Season to taste with salt and pepper.

Preheat the oven to 375°F. Lightly butter an 18 × 12-inch baking pan with sides about ½ inch high.

On a lightly floured surface, roll the dough out to a 22 × 16-inch rectangle. Flour the surface and rolling pin as necessary to prevent the dough from sticking. Fold the dough into quarters, center it over the prepared pan, and unfold it. The dough should overhang all the sides by about 2 inches.

Pour the rice mixture into the dough-lined pan and smooth it into an even layer. Fold the overhanging dough over the filling to form a 2-inch border on all sides. Brush the dough lightly with the egg yolk or olive oil. Bake until the filling is firm in the center and golden brown and the crust is a deep golden brown, about 45 minutes. Cool the crostata for about 30 minutes, then cut into squares and serve warm.

Crostata Dough

Pasta per Crostata

This dough is quite simple to make and freezes beautifully. Make a double batch and freeze half, securely wrapped in plastic, to make your next crostata even easier.

MAKES ENOUGH DOUGH FOR ONE 18 × 12-INCH CROSTATA

Process the flour, oil, and salt together in a food processor fitted with a metal blade until smooth, scraping down the sides of the work bowl once or twice. With the motor running, pour in enough water to make a smooth, very soft dough. Turn the dough out onto a lightly floured surface and knead, adding more flour if the dough begins to stick to your hands, until the dough is very smooth and no streaks of flour or oil remain, about 1 minute. Wrap the dough in plastic wrap and let it rest for 30 minutes at room temperature or for up to 1 day in the refrigerator. Allow refrigerated dough to stand at room temperature for 30 minutes before continuing.

2 cups all-purpose flour, or as needed

½ cup extra virgin olive oil

1 teaspoon salt

⅓ cup water, or as needed

Alternatively, pile the flour on your work surface and make a well in the center. Add the olive oil, ⅓ cup water, and the salt to the well. Mix the dough according to the instructions for making pasta dough by hand on page 89.

Swiss Chard and Vegetable Crostata

Crostata di Verdure

This is a favorite on the antipasto platter at our restaurant Becco, in Manhattan's theater district. It is wonderful as an appetizer or as a passed hors d'oeuvre at parties.

MAKES 6 SERVINGS

Crostata Dough (page 227)

3 pounds Swiss chard

3 tablespoons extra virgin olive oil

2 cups chopped leeks (white and light green parts only), well washed

2 cups chopped scallions (white and tender green parts; about 12 scallions)

2 tablespoons chopped fresh marjoram, basil, or thyme leaves

Salt and freshly ground black pepper

2 cups ricotta (about 1 pound), preferably fresh

1 cup freshly grated Parmigiano-Reggiano cheese (about 4 ounces)

½ cup heavy cream

3 large eggs

1 large egg yolk, beaten with a few drops of water, or extra virgin olive oil, for the crust

Make the crostata dough.

Prepare the chard according to the directions in the first step of Swiss Chard and Potatoes, page 225.

In a large, heavy casserole, heat the olive oil over medium heat. Add the leeks and cook, stirring, until softened, about 8 minutes. Add the chard, scallions, and marjoram and season lightly with salt and pepper. Reduce the heat to low and cook, stirring occasionally, until the vegetables are tender and most of the liquid has evaporated, about 20 minutes. Drain thoroughly and cool the mixture to room temperature.

Combine the ricotta, Parmigiano-Reggiano, and cream in the bowl of an electric mixer. Mix at low speed until blended. Add the cooled vegetables and mix thoroughly at low speed. Season to taste with salt and pepper. Beat in the eggs. (Alternatively, mix everything together by hand.)

Preheat the oven to 375°F. Lightly butter an 18 × 12-inch baking pan with sides about ½ inch high.

On a lightly floured surface, roll the dough out to a 22 × 16-inch rectangle. Flour the surface and rolling pin as necessary to prevent the dough from sticking. Fold the dough into quarters, center it over the prepared pan, and unfold it. The dough should overhang all the sides by about 2 inches.

Pour the chard mixture into the dough-lined pan and smooth into an even layer. Fold the overhanging dough over the filling to form a 2-inch border on all sides. Brush the dough lightly with the egg yolk or olive oil. Bake until the filling is firm in the center and lightly browned and the crust is a deep golden brown, about 45 minutes. Cool the crostata for about 30 minutes, then cut into squares and serve warm.

Nettle Flan with Fresh Tomato Coulis

Flan di Ortiche

This is a recipe made by Fortunato Nicotra, the executive chef at Felidia. He is a wonderful Sicilian who grew up and trained in Piedmont and now is with us in New York.

When older, the nettle is covered with irritating hairs, but when young, it can be cooked like spinach. Other greens, such as Swiss chard or spinach, can be substituted for the difficult-to-find nettle. By using the basic recipe and changing the vegetable according to what is available, you can make a flan for each season.

MAKES 6 SERVINGS

Prepare the flan. Preheat the oven to 275°F and place the rack in the center position. Butter six 8-ounce ceramic ramekins, glass custard cups, or disposable aluminum cups and set aside.

Cook the nettle leaves in a large pot of boiling salted water until tender, 3 to 4 minutes. Drain thoroughly. Rinse under cold water until cool enough to handle. With your hands, squeeze out as much water as possible.

In a small bowl, whisk the eggs, salt, pepper, and nutmeg together until blended. Combine the squeezed nettles, chives, and sage in a food processor and process until finely chopped. Add the egg mixture and grated cheese and process until the mixture is extremely smooth, 3 to 4 minutes. Add the cream and process until thoroughly incorporated, about 30 seconds.

Divide the nettle mixture among the prepared ramekins. Set the ramekins in a large baking dish so they don't touch each other. Place the dish on the oven rack and pour in enough hot water to come halfway up the sides of the ramekins. Bake until the centers are firm to the touch, about 1 hour.

Meanwhile, make the coulis. Blend the tomatoes at low speed in a blender or process in a food processor until finely chopped. With the motor running, slowly add the olive oil in a steady stream and blend until smooth. Pass the mixture through a sieve and season to taste with salt and pepper.

For the flan

Softened butter for the flan molds

1 pound fresh young nettle leaves (see Note)

4 large eggs

1 teaspoon salt

¼ teaspoon freshly ground black pepper

Pinch of freshly grated nutmeg

⅓ cup chopped fresh chives

4 fresh sage leaves

⅓ cup freshly grated Parmigiano-Reggiano cheese

2 cups heavy cream

For the coulis

2 cups cored, peeled (see page 141), and seeded vine-ripened tomatoes

2 tablespoons extra virgin olive oil

Salt and freshly ground black pepper

continued

Remove the baking dish from the oven and let the flans cool in the water for 10 minutes. Run a thin-bladed knife around the sides of the ramekins and invert the flans onto serving plates. Spoon the tomato coulis around the flans and serve immediately.

Note: A 1½-pound bunch of spinach—that is, spinach with the stems attached—can be substituted for the nettles. Remove the thick stems from the spinach and wash the leaves thoroughly before cooking it.

Braised Artichokes and Fava Beans
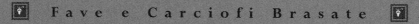 Fave e Carciofi Brasate

Fava beans are wonderful. They require you to shell them twice—once to remove them from the pod and once to remove the tough skin. To facilitate the second shelling, blanch them in boiling water, then "shock" them in ice water.

MAKES 6 SERVINGS

6 medium-size artichokes (about ¼ pound each)

1 lemon, cut in half

¼ cup extra virgin olive oil

½ cup chopped onions

1 cup chopped scallions (white and tender green parts; about 6 scallions)

2½ pounds fresh fava beans in the pod, shelled, blanched, and peeled (see page 233)

½ cup chopped celery

½ teaspoon peperoncino (crushed red pepper)

Salt

Prepare the artichokes for cooking according to the directions on page 231, using the lemon halves. Slice the artichoke halves into ¼-inch-wide wedges.

In a large, heavy casserole with a tight-fitting lid, heat the oil over medium heat. Add the onions and cook until wilted, about 4 minutes. Drain the artichokes well and add them, along with the scallions, fava beans, celery, and peperoncino, to the casserole. Stir the vegetables well and season lightly with salt. Reduce the heat to low, cover the pot, and cook, stirring occasionally, until the vegetables are very tender, about 45 minutes. (The vegetables should give off enough moisture during cooking to prevent sticking or burning. If you find they are sticking, you may add a few tablespoons of water. Make sure the heat is very low and the pot is tightly covered before continuing to cook. It is fine, however, if the vegetables do brown a little.) Season to taste with salt and serve hot.

How to Prepare Artichokes for Cooking

Even if you are serving artichokes whole—for guests to remove the leaves one by one and scrape the tasty pulp from the leaf bottom with their teeth—they should be trimmed: Cut the stem flush with the bottom of the artichoke so it stands steady on the plate. Cut a lemon in half and keep the halves handy. With a paring knife, cut off the smaller leaves around the base of the artichoke. Cut off the top third of the artichoke with a sturdy serrated knife. If you like, you can trim off the pointy tips of the outermost large leaves before cooking. Rub all cut surfaces with a lemon half as you work to prevent them from darkening. Bring a large pot of salted water to a boil. Add the lemon halves and the prepared artichokes and boil until the bottoms of the artichokes are tender when poked with the tip of a paring knife or a wooden skewer. Place a heatproof plate or smaller pot lid over the artichokes to keep them submerged during cooking.

Artichokes can also be trimmed further before cooking, making the pieces completely edible in the finished dish. Generally speaking, the larger the artichoke, the more it needs to be trimmed. Cut a lemon in half and squeeze the halves into a bowl of cool water. Drop the halves into the water. With a paring knife, cut off enough of the outer layers of leaves to expose the leaves that are pale yellow almost all the way to the tip. (In small artichokes, this will be one or two layers; in larger artichokes, you may have to remove several layers of leaves.) Cut off the top third of the artichoke leaves with a serrated knife. With a paring knife, trim the bases of the leaves, which can have an irregular appearance, flush with the artichoke bottom. With a vegetable peeler or a paring knife, trim the dark outer layer of the artichoke stem. Dip the artichoke in the lemon water as you go to prevent it from darkening. Cut the artichoke in half through the stem. With a small spoon—a grapefruit spoon is ideal—scoop out the fuzzy choke. Pull out the violet leaves that surround the choke if there are any—they are inedible. Place the trimmed artichoke halves in the lemon water. The artichoke halves can be cooked as is or cut into smaller pieces or wedges, as in the accompanying recipe.

Braised Spring Legumes

⚜ Scaffata ⚜

This is a wonderful Roman spring dish that can be made when peas and favas in their shells are young and sweet. The name comes from the word *scaffare*—"to shell" in Roman dialect. It is especially good when served with roasted spring lamb or goat. The outermost, less tender leaves of a head of romaine, which you may not want to use in a salad, are perfect for this dish.

MAKES 6 SERVINGS

3 tablespoons extra virgin olive oil

1 cup chopped scallions (white and tender
　　parts; about 6 scallions)

½ cup chopped onions

2½ pounds fresh peas in the pod, shelled

1¼ pounds fresh fava beans in the pod,
　　shelled, blanched, and peeled

1 cup finely diced zucchini

½ teaspoon peperoncino
　　(crushed red pepper)

Salt

2 cups thinly shredded romaine leaves

1 tablespoon finely shredded fresh
　　mint leaves

In a large, heavy casserole with a tight-fitting lid, heat the olive oil over medium heat. Add the scallions and onions and cook, stirring, until wilted, about 4 minutes. Add the peas, fava beans, zucchini, and peperoncino and season lightly with salt. Stir well, reduce the heat to low, and cover the casserole tightly. Cook for 15 minutes, stirring occasionally.

Add the romaine and mint, cover the casserole, and cook, stirring occasionally, until the vegetables are very tender, about 25 minutes more. (The vegetables should give off enough moisture during cooking to prevent sticking or burning. If you find they are sticking, you can add a few tablespoons of water. Make sure the heat is very low and the pot is tightly covered before continuing to cook. It is fine, however, if the vegetables do brown a little.) Season to taste with salt and serve hot.

How to Prepare Fresh Fava Beans

Fava beans grow side by side in dull to bright green insulated pods that can reach a foot in length. When you buy fava beans, look for sound pods with little discoloration and feel to make sure they are filled with firm, fully developed beans. Empty or partially filled pods, or pods that contain tiny beans, mean a lot of wasted labor and you may find yourself with fewer beans than you need for a specific recipe.

Before you begin to shell the beans, bring a large saucepan of water to boil. Snap the stem of each pod and use it to pull off the string that runs the length of the pod along the seam. Open the pod along this seam and brush the beans into a bowl.

Add the beans to the boiling water and cook them just until you can see a dark spot in the center of the bean's skin, about 3 minutes. Drain the beans and refresh them with cold water until they are cool enough to handle. Drain them well. With a paring knife, pull off the dark, crescent-shaped marking at one end of each bean. Squeeze the bean out through this opening. Discard the shell. The favas are now ready to eat or to use in a recipe.

It takes about 1¼ pounds fresh favas in the pod to yield ½ pound shelled (but not peeled) fava beans.

Cannellini and Olive Puree

Purè di Cannellini ed Olive

We serve two wonderfully tasty purees, this and the Chickpea Puree on page 235, in all three of our New York restaurants—Felidia, Becco, and Frico Bar. They are served with the bread basket in addition to butter and they also make excellent toppings for hors d'oeuvres.

MAKES ABOUT 6 CUPS

1½ pounds dried cannellini or other small white beans, such as baby lima or Great Northern, picked over and rinsed

2 fresh or dried bay leaves

Salt

2 cups pitted Gaeta olives or other large black olives, such as Calamata

6 garlic cloves, peeled

½ cup extra virgin olive oil

Freshly ground black pepper

Garlic Toasts (page 313; optional)

Place the beans in a medium-size bowl and pour in enough cool water to cover by 4 inches. Soak the beans in a cool place for at least 8 hours, or overnight.

Drain the beans and place them in a medium-size saucepan. Pour in enough cold water to cover generously and add the bay leaves. Bring the water to a boil over high heat. Reduce the heat to a simmer and cook until the beans are tender, 40 to 60 minutes. About 10 minutes before the end of cooking, season the beans with salt. Drain the beans, remove the bay leaves, and cool to room temperature.

Combine the beans, olives, and garlic in a food processor and process until the beans are coarsely chopped. With the motor running, add the olive oil in a thin stream. Continue processing until the mixture is very smooth, about 3 minutes, stopping once or twice to scrape down the sides of the work bowl. Pass the bean mixture through a fine sieve, pressing it through with a rubber spatula. Season to taste with salt and pepper. Transfer the puree to a crock and smooth the top. The puree can be stored in the refrigerator for up to 4 days.

Serve with garlic toasts or as a topping with bread and crackers.

Chickpea Puree

Purè di Ceci

Place the chickpeas in a medium-size bowl and pour in enough cool water to cover by 4 inches. Soak for at least 8 hours, or overnight.

Drain the chickpeas and place them in a medium-size saucepan. Pour in enough cold water to cover generously and add the bay leaves and 8 of the garlic cloves. Bring the water to a boil over high heat. Reduce the heat to a simmer and cook until the chickpeas are tender, about 1½ hours. About 10 minutes before the end of cooking, season with salt. If necessary, add water to keep the chickpeas covered completely throughout the cooking. Drain the chickpeas, remove the bay leaves, and cool to room temperature.

½ pound dried chickpeas, picked over and rinsed

2 fresh or dried bay leaves

10 garlic cloves, peeled

Salt

1 cup packed fresh basil leaves, washed and dried

½ cup freshly grated Parmigiano-Reggiano cheese

¼ cup pine nuts, toasted (see Note)

½ cup extra virgin olive oil

Freshly ground white pepper

Garlic Toasts (page 313; optional)

In a food processor, combine the cooked chickpeas and garlic cloves with the basil, grated cheese, pine nuts, and the remaining 2 garlic cloves. Process until the chickpeas are coarsely chopped. With the motor running, slowly add the olive oil. Continue processing until the mixture is very smooth, about 3 minutes, stopping once or twice to scrape down the sides of the work bowl. Pass the bean mixture through a fine sieve, pressing it through with a rubber spatula. Season to taste with salt and white pepper. Transfer the puree to a crock and smooth the top. The puree can be stored in the refrigerator for up to 4 days.

Serve the puree with the garlic toasts, as a bread and cracker topping or as an accompaniment to fish or chicken.

Note: Place the pine nuts in a small, heavy skillet over medium-low heat. Toss and stir them constantly until evenly golden brown, about 5 minutes. Remove the pine nuts from the skillet and cool them completely.

Game and Chicken

Selvaggina e Pollame

O ur family arrived in Trieste in 1956, eleven years after World War II ended. We had spent all our lives in Italy, on the peninsula of Istria in the northeast part of the country, but we suddenly found ourselves living in Yugoslavia when Istria and the surrounding territories were given to Yugoslavia as the spoils of war. My parents decided to leave Istria for Italy, but the Iron Curtain had descended along the border of Italy and Yugoslavia and, under the new regime, things had truly changed. The family could not journey all together to Italy, nor could it be known that we wanted to leave permanently. One member of the family had to remain to assure the Communist regime that the family would return. My parents formed a plan in which my mother, brother, and I would go to Italy as tourists, and my father would follow later by secretly passing over the border during the night. Our destination was Trieste, where my Great-Aunt Nina Rapetti lived with her family. She took us in and offered us refuge during this tumultuous period of our lives.

We children didn't know what was happening when we arrived in Trieste. I remember Zia Nina and my mother talking quietly together and my mother being more pensive as the days passed. When the date for our return to Istria had passed, we were told that we would not go back home, but that our dad would join us in our new home in Trieste. I still didn't understand the gravity of the situation until one night I was awakened by a rumbling at the door—my great-aunt's voice, my mother's sobbing, and my father's voice. I jumped up and there he was. He stood shaking—unshaven and dirty, with mud all over his shoes and pants, his clothes torn. He had just escaped over the border of Yugoslavia at Skofie, where border guards had shot at him and dogs had chased him until he found refuge in a barn on the Italian side of the border. We were finally reunited and safe, and ready to begin our journey towards a new life.

In Italy in the aftermath of World War II, life was very difficult. Italy had many wounds to heal; jobs and living quarters were hard to come by. My parents had a difficult time finding work and decided to migrate on. We became political refugees. Catholic Charities and the Italian government had set up camps that helped refugees reconstruct their lives. We moved to a *campo profughi* (refugee camp) called San Saba, named after the neighborhood in Trieste where it was located. Life there was quite different from the insulated environment we had enjoyed with Grandma Rosa back in Istria. There were many refugees from Istria in the camp—people who had decided that they could not live under the Communist regime. There were young people, families with children, and older people, all awaiting an opportunity to continue their lives.

The camp in San Saba was made up of big buildings with open floors like lofts. We lived on one of those big floors, separated from the others by partitions. Each family had a cubicle of space in which to sleep. There was a big mess hall on the main floor with long wooden tables where we ate. We waited in line for our food at mealtime, and I recall the food being decent and abundant. At night, in our cubicle, I remember staring at the ceiling in the darkness and listening to the noises of human existence—children crying, people snoring, coughing, sneezing, whispering, lamenting, and sighing.

Trieste was always a beautiful city—even when it was full of refugees. It has a magnificent natural *golfo* (bay) on the Northern Adriatic Sea, and it is flanked to the north by the Giulian Alps. The closeness of the two, and the exchange of hot and cold air, sometimes gave way to thunderous windstorms. The wind is called *La Bora*, and it sometimes blows up to 140 kilometers—or about 90 miles—per hour! *La Bora* is so strong that ropes are placed on crucial corners throughout the city for people to hold onto while walking.

The market in Trieste is called the Ponte Rosso (Red Bridge), and it always buzzed with activity and offered good produce and fruit. I loved going there—it reminded me of my days with

Grandma at the market in Pola. I went around the Ponte Rosso with Zia Nina, who, in her younger days, had been an apprentice cook in a noble household in Trieste, which at that time was a part of the Austro-Hungarian Empire. After her apprenticeship, she had become a sought-after personal chef. Zia Nina truly had the hands and palate of a *maestra*, with a special gift for harmonizing flavor.

I loved going to the Ponte Rosso with her. We inspected each stall together and returned to the ones with the best products before she bought anything. She gently touched each fruit, smelled them, turned the vegetables in her hands, and clipped leaves off the salad greens to taste them. She gently palpated the vegetables as if she were looking for a heartbeat, which was not much appreciated by the salesladies. But they were all friends, and food shopping was a serious endeavor. When the fruit and vegetable shopping was done, it was time for a little *merenda* (snack) in the corner trattoria—a *panino di prosciutto cotto* (baked ham sandwich with fresh horseradish) or *porcina cotta con krauti* (boiled meats, pork or beef, with sauerkraut). Zia Nina had her espresso and we went on to the *macelleria* (butcher shop) or *pescheria* (fish market). I didn't particularly like the *macelleria* and the sight of the chickens hanging by their feet, with their heads dangling, beaks and all. There were also always some furry white rabbits on display, as well as ducks with orange beaks and webbed feet that hung by their necks. As the fall began, the prized corner of the *macelleria* was the display of game—pheasants in all their plumage, hinds of deep ruby *capriolo* (venison), and the shorter, chubbier, pink-red hinds of *cinghiale* (wild boar). Small birds such as *quaglie* (quails) or *piccioni* (squab) hung in clusters of plumage. There were chops, loins, and sausages of all types. I couldn't tell the difference, but Zia Nina knew exactly what to buy and how to prepare it. There were no great quantities bought—she had one net bag and that would suffice—but the meals she prepared were delicious. I owe to her some of my first truly wonderful cooking experiences.

I recall being excited after our return from Ponte Rosso and opening the bags to display all we had bought on the table. Zia Nina would tie my apron on and we would cook—sometimes for hours, sometimes for just minutes. The results were many a memorable meal that we enjoyed at her table. Zia Nina was especially good at preparing game sauces. With one bird, a pheasant or duck, she could make a meal for twelve; a small piece of venison or boar would result in a feast. The spirit and flavors of Zia Nina's cooking still linger with me today.

I return yearly to Trieste—the city that embraced us and offered us refuge and many tasty memories. Many of my friends and family live there and still shop at Ponte Rosso. Trieste is now a prosperous border city, alive with culture and industry. Coffee is a major product—it is the home of Illy Caffè, one of the largest and most prestigious makers of espresso coffee in the world. Trieste is the capital of the region of Friuli-Venezia-Giulia and, like a giving mother, still continues to harbor refugees from Eastern Europe in their trek to the Western world for a better life.

Roasted Guinea Hen with Balsamic Glaze

Faraona Arrosta al Balsamico

The blend of balsamic vinegar and honey used to baste the guinea hen gives the bird a beautiful mahogany glaze and a delicious sweet-tart taste. This glazing technique can be used for most birds. I even use it on roasted lamb, pork, and veal and brush it on meats and poultry when I roast them on the spit. This is delicious served with Asparagus Gratin with Parmigiano-Reggiano Cheese (page 219).

MAKES 6 SERVINGS

Two 2½-pound guinea hens

Salt and freshly ground black pepper

4 sprigs fresh rosemary

8 fresh sage leaves

2 fresh or dried bay leaves

¼ cup extra virgin olive oil

2 medium-size onions, coarsely chopped

1 cup chopped celery

1 cup diced carrots

2 cups Chicken Stock (page 80) or canned low-sodium chicken broth, or as needed

3 tablespoons balsamic vinegar

1 tablespoon honey

Preheat the oven to 425°F. Remove the necks and giblets and all visible fat from the hens. Rinse the hens under cold water and pat them dry inside and out with paper towels. Season the birds generously inside and out with salt and pepper. Place 1 rosemary sprig, 2 sage leaves, and 1 bay leaf in the body cavity of each bird.

In a heavy, flameproof roasting pan or very large oven-proof skillet, heat the oil over medium heat. Add the onions, celery, carrots, and the remaining 2 sprigs rosemary and 4 sage leaves and cook, stirring, until the onions are wilted, about 5 minutes. Smooth the vegetables into an even layer and nestle the hens breast side up over them. Place in the oven and roast, basting with enough of the chicken stock to keep the vegetables well moistened, until the vegetables and hens are golden brown, about 1 hour. The leg joint should wiggle somewhat freely.

Spoon off enough of the roasting juices, not including fat, to measure 1 cup. Stir in the vinegar and honey until the honey is dissolved. Return the hens to the oven and roast, basting occasionally with the honey mixture, until the hens are a rich mahogany color and the leg joint moves easily when you wiggle it, about another 25 minutes. (If you are using a meat thermometer, it should register 180°F when inserted into the thickest part of the thigh, away from the bone.)

Remove the hens from the oven and cover them with a tent of aluminum foil to keep them warm. Strain the vegetables and pan juices through a sieve into a small saucepan, pressing as much of the vegetables through the sieve as possible. Skim the fat from the surface of the sauce and bring the sauce to a simmer while carving the birds.

To carve the birds, remove the wings by cutting through the joint that attaches them to the body. With a long, thin knife, carve thin slices of the breast meat parallel to the rib cage, including some of the skin with each slice. Arrange the breast slices on a platter. Separate the legs from the body by cutting through the joint that connects the legs to the backbone. This will be easier if you first hold each leg by the tip of the drumstick and pull it away from the body, allowing you to see the joint that connects it to the backbone. Cut the legs in half at the knee joints. Arrange the leg pieces on the platter. Spoon some of the sauce over the birds and pass the remaining sauce separately.

Pheasant in Guazzetto with Gnocchi

Fagiano in Guazzetto con Gnocchi

In this preparation, pasta can be substituted for the gnocchi. You can also replace the pheasant with other game birds, such as grouse, mallard duck, or any bird according to preference or availability.

MAKES 6 SERVINGS

4 cups hot Chicken Stock (page 80) or canned low-sodium chicken broth, or as needed

8 large slices dried porcini mushrooms (about ½ cup, loosely packed)

1 pheasant (about 3 pounds)

3 fresh or dried bay leaves

1 tablespoon fresh rosemary leaves

4 cloves

¼ cup extra virgin olive oil

2 cups minced onions

¼ cup minced pancetta

Salt and freshly ground black pepper

1½ tablespoons tomato paste

1 cup dry white wine

1 recipe Gnocchi (page 175) or 1 pound dry pasta, such as shells or rigatoni

¼ cup freshly grated Parmigiano-Reggiano cheese, plus more for serving

In a small heatproof bowl, pour 1 cup of the hot stock over the porcini mushrooms. Let them stand for 30 minutes. Drain the mushrooms, straining the soaking liquid through a coffee filter or a sieve lined with a double thickness of cheesecloth. Rinse the mushrooms briefly and remove any tough bits with your fingers. Finely chop the mushrooms.

While the mushrooms are soaking, prepare the pheasant. Remove the giblets and neck from the cavity. Finely chop the liver and set it aside; reserve the neck and remaining giblets. With kitchen shears, cut out the backbone, then cut the backbone in half crosswise with a heavy knife. Open out the pheasant and lay it skin side down on the cutting board. Cut the pheasant in half by cutting lengthwise through the breastbone. Cut each half into five pieces: Cut off the legs, then cut each leg into two pieces through the knee joint; remove the wing by cutting through the joint where it is connected to the breastbone; and cut the breast in half crosswise. Pat the pheasant pieces (including the backbone, neck, and giblets) dry with paper towels.

Tie the bay leaves, rosemary, and cloves securely together in a 4-inch square of cheesecloth.

In a large, deep skillet, heat the olive oil over medium heat. Add the onions and cook, stirring occasionally, until wilted, about 5 minutes. Add the pancetta and cheesecloth bundle of herbs. Cook until the pancetta has rendered its fat and the onions are just beginning to brown, 3 to 5 minutes.

Season the pheasant pieces (including the backbone), neck, and giblets generously with salt and pepper. Push the onions to one side of the skillet and add as many of the pheasant pieces, skin side down, to the skillet as will fit in a single layer. Cook, turning the pieces once, until browned on all sides, about 5 minutes. Stir the onions occasionally to keep them from burning. Repeat with the remaining pieces of pheasant if necessary. (If necessary, remove the onions from the skillet to prevent them from burning.)

Return all the pheasant pieces to the skillet if necessary. Add the porcini and liver to the skillet and cook for 3 minutes. Stir in the tomato paste and cook until it begins to deepen in color, about 3 minutes. Add the wine, stirring well, and bring to a boil. Boil until the wine has almost completely evaporated, scraping the skillet to loosen the particles stuck to the bottom. Add about 1 cup of the remaining stock and adjust the heat to a simmer. Simmer, partially covered, adding more hot stock as necessary to keep the level of liquid more or less the same, until the pheasant is tender, about 1 hour. Turn the pheasant pieces occasionally as they cook. (If you are serving the pheasant with gnocchi, cook and rice the potatoes at this point and allow them to cool while the pheasant is simmering.)

Remove the pheasant pieces to a baking pan and cool them completely.

Bring a large pot of water to a boil. Meanwhile, pick the pheasant meat from the bones including the neck, shredding it coarsely and discarding the skin and bones as you do. Chop the giblets finely. Return the meat to the sauce. (If you are serving the pheasant with gnocchi, prepare the gnocchi dough, then roll and form the gnocchi at this point.)

To serve, cook the gnocchi according to the directions on page 176 or cook the pasta according to the directions on page 123. Meanwhile, heat the pheasant sauce to a simmer and check the seasonings.

Drain the gnocchi or pasta and return to the pot over medium-low heat. Add about half of the liquid from the pheasant sauce. Stir until the sauce is simmering and the gnocchi or pasta is coated. Remove from the heat and stir in the grated cheese. Divide the gnocchi or pasta among serving plates and top each serving with some of the pheasant in sauce. Pass additional grated cheese at the table.

Wild Boar Braised in Barolo

🐗 Cinghiale Brasato al Barolo 🐗

Boar is one of those meats that home cooks tend to shy away from—don't you do that too! It is a wonderful meat to cook with, full of flavor. Most boar meat available at your butcher is from a young animal with a mellow flavor of game, but still possessing enough of the complexity of flavor that one expects from game meat. In this preparation, I use Barolo wine for its fruitiness and complexity, but any good full-bodied red wine will do. Remember that the end product is the sum of all its parts—the better the wine you use, the better the sauce will be.

MAKES 8 SERVINGS

½ cup extra virgin olive oil

1½ cups minced onions

2 tablespoons minced pancetta or bacon

Salt and freshly ground black pepper

1 cup shredded carrots

10 juniper berries

6 fresh or dried bay leaves

6 cloves

1 teaspoon fresh rosemary leaves

3½ pounds wild boar with bone (see Note)

3 tablespoons tomato paste

1 bottle (750 ml) good-quality Barolo wine

1 cup coarsely chopped, peeled (see page 141) Italian plum tomatoes, fresh or drained canned

6 to 8 cups Meat Stock (page 78) or canned low-sodium beef broth

In a heavy, deep, nonreactive casserole large enough to hold the boar comfortably, heat the olive oil over medium heat. Add the onions and pancetta and cook, stirring occasionally, until the onions are golden brown, about 8 minutes. Season the onions with salt and pepper and add the carrots, juniper berries, bay leaves, cloves, and rosemary. Stir well, then push the vegetable mixture to one side of the casserole.

Season the meat generously with salt and pepper and add it to the cleared side of the casserole. Brown the meat on all sides, turning it as necessary, about 15 minutes. Stir the vegetables often as the meat browns to prevent them from burning. Stir the tomato paste into the vegetable mixture and cook, stirring, for 5 minutes. Add the wine and bring to a boil. Reduce the heat to medium, distribute the vegetables around the boar, and simmer for 30 minutes, turning the boar occasionally.

Add the tomatoes and enough of the stock to cover the meat and bring the liquid to a boil. Partially cover the casserole and simmer, skimming frequently and stirring occasionally, until the meat is barely tender, about 3½ hours. Add more stock as necessary to keep the meat covered.

Remove the meat from the pot and set aside. Pass the sauce through a sieve, pressing the solids to extract as much liquid as possible and force some of the vegetables through the sieve. Discard the solids left in the sieve, return the meat and strained sauce to the casserole, and simmer, uncovered, until the boar is very tender and the liquid is reduced to about 3½ cups, about another 45 minutes. Turn the boar occasionally and skim any foam or fat from the surface as it cooks.

Remove the boar to a carving board and cut the meat parallel to the bone into ¼-inch-thick slices. (If you are preparing a boneless roast, simply cut it crosswise into even slices.) Arrange the slices on a platter and spoon some of the braising liquid over them. Pass the remaining sauce separately.

Note: Wild boar can be found in season at specialty butcher shops. For this recipe, use a 3½-pound bone-in cut from the leg or shoulder. If you prefer to carve a boneless cut, ask your butcher to bone and tie the boar for you. (Cooking time will remain the same.) However, leaving the bone in the meat will add a bit more flavor to the sauce.

Rabbit
(Il Coniglio)

The texture of rabbit meat is quite similar to that of chicken and, like chicken, it is light, low in fat, very tasty, and easy to prepare. Rabbit is wildly popular at our Manhattan theater district restaurant, Becco. People order it out and love it, so why not prepare it at home?

Rabbits can be bought in two sizes. "Fryers," which range from two and a half to three pounds, are good in preparations that call for cooking rabbit on the bones. "Roasters," on the other hand, range from four to six pounds and are good for roasting whole or in sections with the bone, or for boneless preparations.

Braised Rabbit in Balsamic Sauce
🔒 Coniglio al Balsamico 🔒

This preparation can also be made with boneless rabbit cut into pieces. Have your butcher debone the rabbit for you and keep in mind that boneless rabbit will take about twenty minutes less cooking time and about one cup less of stock than called for in the ingredients list. Either way, this dish is excellent served with Swiss Chard and Potatoes (page 225).

MAKES 6 SERVINGS

Two 3-pound rabbits, each cut into 6 pieces (see Note)
Salt and freshly ground black pepper
All-purpose flour for dredging
¼ cup extra virgin olive oil
8 garlic cloves, crushed
2 tablespoons unsalted butter
4 fresh sage leaves
3 tablespoons balsamic vinegar
1 cup lager or pilsner beer
2 cups Chicken Stock (page 80), Meat Stock (page 78), or canned low-sodium chicken broth, or as needed

Season the rabbit pieces generously with salt and pepper. Dredge them in flour until lightly coated, tapping off the excess flour.

In a very large (at least 14 inches), deep skillet or casserole, heat the olive oil over medium heat. Add the garlic cloves and cook until light golden brown on all sides, about 2 minutes. Add as many of the rabbit pieces as will fit in a single layer. Cook, turning as necessary, until the rabbit is golden brown on all sides, about 8 minutes. Remove the rabbit pieces as they brown and, if necessary, add any remaining pieces to the skillet. Remove the garlic cloves too if they begin to turn any darker than a rich golden brown. Return the rabbit to the pan, add the butter and sage leaves, and cook for 2 minutes, turning the rabbit pieces in the butter. Add the vinegar and let it sizzle until almost entirely evaporated, about 3 minutes. Add the beer and cook, turning the rabbit pieces occasionally, for 10 minutes.

Add the stock, season lightly with salt and pepper, and let simmer over medium-low heat until the rabbit is tender and the sauce is lightly thickened, about 40 minutes. If necessary, add small amounts of stock toward the end of the cooking time to prevent the sauce from becoming too thick. Remove the garlic and sage leaves and serve the rabbit, spooning some of the sauce over each serving.

Note: Ask your butcher to cut the rabbit into six pieces according to the following directions, or do it yourself with a boning knife or other sturdy, thin-bladed knife. Rabbit bones—especially the legs—are similar to chicken bones and can be thin and splintery. You should avoid whacking them with a heavy knife. Cutting the saddle in half as described below, is an exception.

Place the rabbit leg side up on a cutting board. Separate the forelegs and hind legs from the loin by cutting along the backbone where the leg joins the backbone. Pull each leg outward from the backbone to make it easier to see the joint. Then work the tip of the knife between the thigh joint and backbone and cut through the joint, separating the leg from the backbone. What remains is the loin, or saddle. Cut the loin in half crosswise with a heavy knife or cleaver.

Seared Rabbit Loin over Arugula with Truffle Dressing

Filetto di Coniglio con Rughetta e Tartufo

Truffle oil gives this dish an extra dimension, but the salad is still delicious without it. Truffle oil is available in specialty stores that carry French and Italian products.

MAKES 6 SERVINGS

½ cup golden raisins

6 large boneless loins of rabbit
(4 to 5 ounces each; see Note)

Salt and freshly ground black pepper

12 fresh sage leaves

½ cup extra virgin olive oil

2 tablespoons fresh lemon juice

1 pound arugula, well washed and dried

1 cup pine nuts or shelled "natural"
pistachios or walnuts, toasted
(see Note on page 235)

1 tablespoon truffle oil (optional)

Place the raisins in a small bowl. Pour in enough hot water to cover and let them soak for 20 minutes. Drain well.

With a paring knife, remove any white membranes from the surface of the loins. Season the loins generously with salt and pepper and press 2 sage leaves into the sides of each one.

In a large bowl, whisk 6 tablespoons of the olive oil together with the lemon juice. Season with salt and pepper and whisk until creamy. Set aside.

In a large, heavy cast-iron or nonstick skillet, heat the remaining 2 tablespoons olive oil over medium-high heat. Add the rabbit loins and cook, turning as necessary, until well browned on all sides and just a slight trace of pink remains at the thickest point, 5 to 7 minutes. (Do not overcook the rabbit; it will continue to cook a little after you remove it from the skillet.) Transfer the rabbit to a cutting board and let rest for 2 to 3 minutes.

Meanwhile, whisk the lemon dressing again, then add the arugula, pine nuts, and drained raisins to the bowl. (If you are not using the truffle oil, first remove a little of the lemon dressing for drizzling over the finished salad.) Sprinkle lightly with salt and pepper and toss until the greens are coated with dressing. Divide the dressed salad among six plates, placing it in the center.

Cut one of the rabbit loins on a slight angle into ¼-inch-thick slices. Arrange the sliced rabbit around the arugula. Repeat with the remaining rabbit and salads. Drizzle the truffle oil or reserved lemon dressing over the sliced rabbit and serve immediately.

Note: The rabbit loin is the long, round muscle that runs along the rabbit's backbone. This cut, when the bone is left in, is often called the saddle, and is much more tender then the fore or hind legs.

Venison

(Il Capriolo)

Venison is distinguishable by its dense, dark red, fine-textured meat that contains very little fat. Most of the venison meat sold in the United States is from farm-raised animals and that means it has a milder flavor and more tender texture than wild venison. In the wild, the animal has to work much harder to sustain itself and therefore builds tougher muscles. In addition, the diet of wild venison is much more varied—hence, the flavor of the meat is usually more intense and complex. The age of the animal also gives great variability to the texture and flavor. If the meat you are using for these recipes is from a wild or older animal, marinate it a bit longer and cook it a bit longer, adding a little more liquid as you do.

The recipe for Pheasant in Guazzetto with Gnocchi on page 242 can be made with venison stew meat. Just cook it for an additional thirty to forty minutes. It is an exceptional sauce for gnocchi or polenta.

Venison Ossobuco with Spaetzle

Ossobuco di Capriolo con Spaetzle

MAKES 6 SERVINGS

With a vegetable peeler, remove the zest (the bright orange part of the skin without the underlying white pith) from the oranges in wide strips. Do the same to the lemon. Cut the zest of one orange into very thin—about ⅛ inch wide—strips; set aside. With a paring knife, cut off the white pith from one of the oranges. Working over a bowl, cut the orange segments free of the membranes, letting them drop into the bowl as you work. Squeeze the juice from the remaining orange into another bowl. Set the wide orange and the lemon zest strips, the orange segments, and the orange juice aside separately.

Wrap the bay leaves, cloves, rosemary, and juniper berries securely together in a 4-inch square of cheese-cloth.

In a heavy nonreactive casserole or braising pan large enough to hold all the venison pieces, heat the olive oil over medium heat. Add the onions and cook, stirring, until wilted, about 5 minutes. Add the carrots, celery, and the cheesecloth bundle of herbs, season lightly with salt, and reduce the heat to low. Cook, stirring occasionally, until the vegetables are light golden brown, about 10 minutes.

Meanwhile, season the venison pieces generously with salt. Dredge them in flour until lightly coated, tapping off the excess flour. In a wide skillet, heat the vegetable oil over medium-high heat. Add as many of the venison pieces as will fit in a single layer and cook, turning as necessary, until well browned on all sides, about 10 minutes. Add the browned *ossobuchi* to the braising pan and repeat with the remaining shanks. (If the vegetables are browned before all the venison is browned, remove the casserole from the heat.)

2 oranges

1 lemon

2 fresh or dried bay leaves

4 cloves

1 sprig fresh rosemary

10 juniper berries

¼ cup extra virgin olive oil

2 cups finely chopped onions

½ cup shredded carrots

½ cup finely chopped celery

Salt

6 venison shanks (*ossobuchi*) (8 to 10 ounces each; see Note)

1 cup all-purpose flour

½ cup vegetable oil

2 teaspoons tomato paste

1 cup fruity red wine, such as Chianti

1 cup fresh carrot juice, available at many health food stores

1 cup canned crushed Italian plum tomatoes, preferably San Marzano, or peeled (see page 141) ripe plum tomatoes

5 cups hot Chicken Stock (page 80) or canned low-sodium chicken broth

1 recipe Tiny Spinach Dumplings (page 253)

Freshly ground black pepper

continued

Return the casserole to medium heat if necessary. Stir the tomato paste into the vegetable mixture and cook, stirring until it begins to caramelize, about 10 minutes. Add the wine and bring to a boil. Add the carrot juice, the wide strips of orange zest, the lemon zest, and orange juice, bring to a vigorous boil, and boil for 10 minutes. Add the tomatoes, adjust the heat to a simmer, and simmer, uncovered, for 30 minutes.

Add 2 cups of the hot chicken stock, stir well, and return to a simmer. Let cook, with the lid slightly askew, until the meat is tender at its thickest point, about 1½ hours. Add the remaining stock as necessary to keep the meat almost completely covered. Test for doneness with a cooking fork: The fork should pierce the meat all the way to the bone with only light resistance.

When the *ossobuchi* are tender, remove them from the casserole. Pass the sauce through a sieve, pressing on the vegetables to extract as much liquid from them and to force some of them through the sieve. Return the meat and sauce to the casserole and bring to a simmer. Cover the pan and keep the venison warm off the heat.

Meanwhile, prepare and cook the dumplings. Remove them with a wire skimmer to a large skillet. Spoon enough of the venison sauce over the spaetzle to coat them. Toss lightly over low heat until the spaetzle begin to absorb the sauce. Season with salt and pepper.

To serve, transfer the *ossobuchi* to a platter or plates. Spoon most of the sauce over the venison and sprinkle it with the finely sliced orange zest. Decorate the shanks with the orange segments and spoon the spaetzle around them. Serve at once.

Note: For this recipe, I prefer an ossobuco of venison cut from the thickest part of the shank, just below the knee. If this is not possible, and you are buying the whole shank, cut into one thick piece and thinner piece, you may want to figure on 1½ pieces per person. Either way, have the butcher tie the venison pieces around the perimeter with a length of sturdy kitchen twine to help them keep their shape during cooking when the gelatin that holds them together dissolves into the sauce, giving it that characteristic rich stickiness.

Tiny Spinach Dumplings

Spaetzle di Spinaci

Spaetzle, like the Angels' Kisses on page 352, are an example of the cross-cultural cuisine of the region of Istria where I grew up. Traditionally, spaetzle makers are made of wood, but recently a very inexpensive, simple-to-use metal spaetzle maker has become available. A movable square well holds the spaetzle batter over a flat piece of metal perforated with large holes. Sliding the well back and forth forces batter through the holes and into the boiling water. You can try making spaetzle by forcing the batter through a colander with large holes, but it is much simpler with a spaetzle maker.

These spaetzle lend themselves to many variations: You can make them without the spinach and with the addition of Parmigiano-Reggiano cheese, saffron, cinnamon, or nutmeg. Or you can substitute a puree of carrot, winter squash, or roasted red pepper for the spinach. (See the notes on gnocchi variations on page 173.) In any case, make sure you add the right amount of flour to make a stiff but supple dough.

MAKES 6 SERVINGS

In a large bowl, stir the flour, salt, pepper, and nutmeg together. Make a well in the center of the flour and pour in the eggs and all but 2 tablespoons of the milk. With a fork, incorporate the flour gradually into the egg mixture, adding enough of the remaining milk as necessary to make a stiff but supple dough. Beat in the spinach. Cover the bowl and let the dough rest for 1 to 2 hours at room temperature before cooking.

Bring a large pot of salted water to a boil. Transfer the dough to the well of a spaetzle maker and pass the dough into the boiling water. Cook the spaetzle until tender, 10 to 15 minutes, depending on the size of spaetzle your particular spaetzle maker produces. Scoop out the spaetzle with a skimmer and transfer to a large skillet. If you are serving the spaetzle with a stew, such as the ossobuco of venison above, dress the spaetzle with some of the sauce from the recipe, or simply melted butter, and toss over medium heat. Check the seasoning and serve hot.

> 2¼ cups all-purpose flour
> 1 teaspoon salt
> ¼ teaspoon freshly ground black pepper
> Large pinch of freshly grated nutmeg
> 2 large eggs, well beaten
> ½ cup milk
> ½ cup finely minced cooked fresh spinach
> (see Note)

Note: It is very important to squeeze out as much water from the spinach as possible. To end up with ½ cup minced cooked spinach, start with ½ pound fresh spinach leaves. Remove any tough stems, then blanch the spinach in a large pot of boiling salted water until it is tender, about 1 minute. Drain the spinach in a colander and rinse under cold water until cool enough to handle. With your hands, squeeze as much liquid as possible from the spinach, chop the spinach very fine, and then squeeze again to remove more water.

Braised Venison with Polenta

Capriolo alla Montanara con Polenta

This is a typical recipe from Friuli, where venison is hunted in the wild. The venison is marinated for quite a long time, which tenderizes the somewhat tough meat of wild deer. If you have a hunter in your family, this is the recipe to use in preparing the catch.

MAKES 6 SERVINGS

For the marinade

½ cup extra virgin olive oil

2 large onions, quartered

2 celery stalks, coarsely chopped

4 garlic cloves, crushed

4 sprigs fresh thyme

4 sprigs fresh marjoram

4 fresh or dried bay leaves

1 cinnamon stick

Salt and freshly ground black pepper

2 pounds lean venison stew meat, from the shoulder or leg, trimmed of fat and cut into 1½-inch pieces

1 bottle (750 ml) full-bodied red wine, such as Refosco or Cabernet

½ cup red wine vinegar

To finish the stew

2 tablespoons extra virgin olive oil

2 tablespoons unsalted butter

2 cups sliced onions

Salt and freshly ground black pepper

To serve the stew

Basic Polenta (page 198)

Prepare the marinade. In a large, heavy saucepan, heat the olive oil over low heat. Add the quartered onions, celery, garlic cloves, thyme, marjoram, bay leaves, and cinnamon stick and cook, stirring occasionally, until the vegetables are tender, about 25 minutes. Season with salt and pepper. Cool completely.

In a large bowl, toss together the venison with the wine, vinegar, and cooked vegetable mixture. Cover and marinate in the refrigerator for 2 days.

Remove the meat from the marinade and thoroughly pat it dry with paper towels. Strain the marinade and reserve the liquid. In a wide, heavy braising pan or casserole, heat the olive oil and butter together over medium heat until the butter is foaming. Add the sliced onions and cook until wilted, about 5 minutes. Add the venison pieces, season lightly with salt and pepper, and cook until all the liquid given off by the venison has evaporated and the meat has begun to brown, about 15 minutes.

Skim the oil from the surface of the strained marinade and add 1 cup of the marinade to the casserole. Adjust the heat to a simmer and simmer, with the lid slightly askew, until the venison is tender, about 1½ hours. Add additional marinade as needed during cooking to keep the level of liquid more or less even. When the venison is cooked, the sauce should be syrupy and savory.

Meanwhile, prepare the polenta.

To serve, spoon the polenta onto the center of plates or a large platter. Spoon the venison and liquid partially over the polenta and onto the plates. Serve hot.

Chicken

(Il Pollo)

Chicken is a staple in the cooking of every culture. And no wonder; it is one of the most versatile foods in the kitchen. You can cook it any way you like—by broiling, frying, roasting, boiling, sautéing, or stewing—and with the proper condiments and a little judgment, a good dish will emerge.

The chicken was domesticated as early as 2500 B.C., from the red jungle fowl of Southeast Asia. Through these ancient times and up until very recently, chicken was considered a special treat, but today's extensive chicken farming and modern methods have made chicken quite inexpensive and consistently available. These traits don't come cheaply, however. We have given up the flavor and the quality of "free-range" chickens in return. Gratefully, sources for organic and free-range chickens are increasing, and the flavor-conscious cook will not use anything but.

When shopping for chickens, the younger and most tender are the spring chickens or, as they are often called, poussins. They weigh about one pound whole. The meat is very tender and delicious grilled or panfried as it is in the following recipes that call for spring chickens.

Broiler or fryer chickens, which weigh two to four pounds, are best broiled, roasted, or braised. The roaster is a big bird of anywhere from four to seven pounds, and the best way to prepare it for, as we say in Italian, *"la sua morte"* (literally, its death but figuratively "the ultimate preparation"), is in the roasting pan. Roasters are also excellent for making chicken soup or boiled chicken.

Whatever the size of the chicken you choose, remember these few things: The color of the chicken is not usually an indication of the flavor of the bird, but rather of what the bird has been feeding on. Choose a chicken that has a textured and tough skin, not one that is slippery and wet. The meat should be firm and have a rosy pink color. Whenever possible, buy free-range chickens from certified organic farmers.

Chicken Bites with Sausages in a Vinegar Sauce

Bocconcini di Pollo all'Aceto con Salsicce

The sauce in this chicken dish should have a stick-to-the-finger quality when done. Chicken pieces on the bone can also be very good prepared this way—just keep in mind that they will need fifteen minutes additional cooking time and about a half cup more chicken stock than called for in this recipe. Serve the chicken with a nice big salad or a braised vegetable like escarole or broccoli.

MAKES 6 SERVINGS

¼ cup extra virgin olive oil

½ pound sweet Italian sausage, sliced (see Note)

2 pounds boneless, skinless chicken breasts, cut into 2-inch pieces

Salt

4 garlic cloves, finely chopped

2 teaspoons honey

2 tablespoons unsalted butter

¼ cup red wine vinegar

½ cup aromatic white wine, such as Gewürztraminer or Riesling

½ cup Chicken Stock (page 80) or canned low-sodium chicken broth

2 tablespoons chopped fresh Italian parsley leaves

In a wide (at least 12-inch), heavy, nonreactive skillet, heat 2 tablespoons of the oil over medium heat. Add the sausage and cook, stirring often, until the sausage is lightly browned on all sides, about 3 minutes for thinner sausages and 5 minutes for fatter sausages.

Pour off the fat from the pan and add the remaining 2 tablespoons oil. Season the chicken pieces with salt and add them to the skillet. Cook the chicken, turning the pieces often, until light golden brown on all sides, about 4 minutes. About halfway through the cooking time, clear a small area on one side of the skillet and add the garlic to it. When the garlic is light golden brown, about 1 minute, stir it into the chicken-and-sausage mixture. Drizzle the honey over the chicken and sausage and cook, stirring constantly, until the chicken is a rich mahogany color, about 1 minute. Add the butter and stir until melted. Pour in the vinegar and bring to a boil. Boil until the vinegar has almost entirely evaporated, about 2 minutes. Add the wine and bring to a boil, then add the chicken stock. Boil until the sauce is quite thick and there is just enough of it to barely coat the chicken pieces, about 2 minutes. Sprinkle the parsley over the chicken and serve.

Note: For this I prefer *luganica,* a thin (½-inch-wide) pork sausage seasoned only with salt and pepper and without seeds of any kind. If unavailable, use the wider (1-inch-thick) sweet pork sausages, preferably without seeds. Cut the *luganica* into 1-inch lengths, the wider sausages into ½-inch slices.

Seared Marinated Breast of Chicken with Tomato and Basil

Petto di Pollo in Padella con Pomodoro e Basilico

This is one of those simple, quick, and very flavorful recipes, especially good in the summer months when tomatoes are wonderful and plentiful. The sauce also pairs well with quickly sautéed seafood like scallops or cod.

MAKES 6 SERVINGS

For the chicken breasts

2 pounds boneless, skinless chicken breasts
   (about 6 breast halves)
½ cup extra virgin olive oil
1 tablespoon minced fresh rosemary leaves
1 tablespoon minced fresh sage leaves
4 garlic cloves, crushed
Salt and freshly ground black pepper

For the sauce

3 tablespoons extra virgin olive oil
8 garlic cloves, crushed
1½ pounds vine-ripened plum tomatoes,
   cored, peeled (see page 141), and
   seeded, juice reserved
Large pinch of peperoncino
   (crushed red pepper)
Salt
½ cup finely shredded fresh basil leaves

Cut each chicken breast half crosswise on the bias into three more or less even pieces. Place three of the chicken pieces between two sheets of plastic wrap and pound them lightly with a meat mallet or small, heavy skillet to a thickness of about ¼ inch. Repeat with the remaining chicken pieces.

Stir the olive oil, rosemary, sage, and garlic cloves together in a large bowl. Add the chicken pieces and toss to coat well. Season with salt and pepper and toss well again. Cover the bowl and refrigerate the chicken for at least 8 hours, or overnight. Remove the chicken to room temperature about 30 minutes before cooking.

Just before serving, make the sauce. In a medium-size saucepan, heat the olive oil over medium heat. Add the garlic and cook, shaking the pan occasionally, until it is light brown, about 2 minutes. Remove the pan from the heat and carefully add the tomatoes and their reserved juice. Return to the heat. Stir in the peperoncino, season with salt, and adjust the level of heat to a simmer. Simmer until the tomatoes are softened and the sauce is pink and thick, about 5 minutes. Stir in ¼ cup of the basil leaves and keep the sauce warm, covered, off the heat.

Heat one or two large, nonstick or well-seasoned cast-iron skillets over medium-high heat. Add as many of the chicken pieces as will fit in a single layer. Cook until well browned on the underside, about 2 minutes. Turn the chicken and cook until the second side is browned and no trace of pink remains in the center, 1 to 2 minutes. If necessary, keep the first batch of chicken warm on a baking sheet in an oven turned to the lowest setting and cook the remaining chicken in batches.

Divide the chicken pieces among serving plates, overlapping them in a circular pattern in the center of the plates. Spoon the sauce into the center of each circle, drizzling some of it over the chicken pieces. Sprinkle with the remaining ¼ cup shredded basil and serve.

Merlot-Braised Chicken Thighs

Fagottini di Pollo al Merlot

When it comes to home cooking, chicken breasts always seem to get top billing—and that makes the legs and thighs a great buy. Many people don't know how to prepare chicken thighs, and for them I offer this delicious dish made from simple ingredients and very rich in flavor. I guarantee that if you try it once, it will make a chicken-thigh lover out of you.

MAKES 6 SERVINGS

2 tablespoons unsalted butter

3 tablespoons extra virgin olive oil

1 cup chopped onions

1 cup chopped leeks (white and light green parts only), well washed

1 cup finely chopped carrots (both the carrots and celery can be chopped in a food processor)

1 cup finely chopped celery

Salt and freshly ground black pepper

1 cup freshly grated Parmigiano-Reggiano cheese

¼ cup chopped fresh Italian parsley leaves

12 boneless, skinless chicken thighs (about 4 pounds; see Note)

12 small sprigs fresh rosemary

12 fresh sage leaves

6 garlic cloves, crushed

1 cup Merlot or other soft, dry red wine

1 cup Chicken Stock (page 80) or canned low-sodium chicken broth

In a medium-size skillet, heat the butter and 1 tablespoon of the olive oil together over medium heat until the butter is foaming. Add the onions and leeks and cook, stirring occasionally, until wilted, about 5 minutes. Add the carrots and celery and season lightly with salt and pepper. Reduce the heat to low and cook, stirring occasionally, until the vegetables are tender, about 10 minutes. Transfer the vegetables to a large bowl and cool completely. Stir in the grated cheese and parsley.

Cut twenty-four 4-inch lengths of kitchen twine. Place a chicken thigh, skin side down, on a work surface. With a small sharp knife, cut out any traces of bone or fat from the meat. Spread about ¼ cup of the vegetable mixture in an even layer over the chicken thigh. Roll the thigh around the filling into a tight cylinder. Place the stuffed thigh, seam side down, and tie it securely with two pieces of twine. Tuck a rosemary sprig under the twine on one side of the thigh and a sage leaf on the other side. Set aside and repeat with the remaining thighs, vegetable mixture, rosemary sprigs, and sage leaves.

In a nonreactive skillet large enough to hold the thighs in a single layer, heat the remaining 2 tablespoons olive oil over medium heat, then add the chicken bundles and garlic. Cook, turning the chicken thighs often and rotating them in the skillet so they cook evenly, until golden brown on all sides, 7 to 10 minutes. Tilt the skillet and spoon off the fat. Season the chicken with salt and pepper, add the wine, and bring it to a boil. Add the stock and bring to a boil, then adjust the level of heat down to a lively simmer. Cook, uncovered, turning the chicken pieces occasionally, until the chicken is pierced easily with a skewer and the sauce is reduced to a syrupy consistency, about 20 minutes. Turn the chicken often as it simmers.

Cut and remove the strings and discard the herbs. Spoon the sauce over the chicken and serve immediately.

Note: If you cannot find boneless chicken thighs, you can easily debone them yourself: Lay a chicken thigh, skin side down, on the work surface. You will see a line of yellow fat that runs more or less down the center of the thigh. Cut along this line down to the bone using the tip of a small, sharp knife. Once the length of the bone is exposed, use the tip of the knife to scrape the meat away from the bone until the bone is completely free. Check the thigh for pieces of bone and cartilage, especially where the ends of the bone were. Trim the thighs of fat as described above.

Country-Style Spring Chicken with Olives and Potatoes

Pollastrella alla Campagnola con Cipolle, Patatine Rosse, ed Olive

This is a favorite at my home, especially when my daughter, Tanya, and her husband, Corrado, come and visit from Prato, a town right outside Florence known for its textiles. In our restaurants, patrons love it, and I am sure that it will be a favorite in your home. You will need two large skillets to hold all the ingredients, or the recipe can be easily halved and prepared in one skillet.

MAKES 6 SERVINGS

4 spring chickens (poussins), about 1 pound each (see Note)

¼ cup extra virgin olive oil

Salt and freshly ground black pepper

1½ pounds small (about 1½-inch) new red potatoes, halved

3 small onions (about 6 ounces)

2 sprigs fresh rosemary

20 pitted Calamata olives

1 whole peperoncino (dried hot red pepper), broken in half, or ½ teaspoon peperoncino (crushed red pepper)

2 tablespoons chopped fresh Italian parsley leaves

In a large bowl, toss the chicken pieces together with the olive oil. Season with salt and pepper and toss again. Heat two large (at least 12-inch) nonstick or well-seasoned cast-iron pans over medium heat. Add the chicken pieces, skin side down, and cover the skillets. Cook the chicken, turning it once, until golden brown on both sides, 5 to 7 minutes.

Move the chicken pieces to one side of each skillet. Add the potato halves, cut side down, to the cleared sides of the skillets and cook over medium heat for 15 minutes, turning them and the chicken pieces often, until evenly browned. (At this point, both the chicken and potatoes should be crisp and brown.)

Meanwhile, peel the onions and cut them in quarters through the core, leaving the core intact to hold the quarters together while they cook. Reduce the heat to medium-low, divide the onions, rosemary, olives, and peperoncino between the skillets, and cook, covered, until the onions have softened and the flavors have blended, about 15 minutes. Stir the contents of the skillets gently several times as they cook.

Drain the oil from the skillets, sprinkle the chicken and potatoes with the chopped parsley, and serve.

Note: Cut each spring chicken into four pieces: 2 breasts/wings and two legs. You can substitute two large (about 1¾ pounds each) Cornish hens for the spring chickens. Cut the hens into 8 pieces each: 2 wings, 2 breasts, 2 thighs, and 2 legs. Cooking time will be approximately the same.

Griddle-Crisped Spring Chicken

Galletto alla Piastra

The secrets to the success of crispy-skinned and moist chicken are a hot cooking surface and a weight that will ensure maximum contact between the chicken and the cooking surface. Although a griddle is ideal—inexpensive cast-iron ones that fit over two stovetop burners are widely available—two wide cast-iron skillets give equally good results. To weight the chicken down, another skillet will do the job; otherwise, bricks or half-bricks can be wrapped in aluminum foil and used as weights.

Quail can also be delicious prepared in this manner. The cooking time will be about half that of the spring chicken.

MAKES 6 SERVINGS

6 spring chickens (poussins)
    (about ¾ pound each; see Note)
Coarse salt and freshly ground black pepper
¾ cup extra virgin olive oil
6 garlic cloves, crushed
Leaves from 6 sprigs fresh rosemary or
    10 fresh sage leaves

With poultry shears, cut along both sides of the backbone of each chicken to remove it. Lay the chicken out flat, skin side down. With a small, sharp knife, make an incision along both sides of the breastbone, then use your fingers to pry the keel-shaped breastbone out. With the knife, cut away the small rib bones and the wishbone, which runs along the front and thickest part of the breastbone.

Pat the chickens dry with paper towels and season them generously with coarse salt and pepper. In a large bowl, combine the olive oil, garlic cloves, and rosemary. Turn the chickens gently in this marinade until coated. Cover with plastic wrap, then refrigerate, turning the chickens once or twice in the marinade, for at least 8 hours, or overnight.

Heat a griddle over medium-high heat until a drop of water evaporates almost immediately on contact, or place one or more heavy stovetop griddles or large cast-iron skillets over medium-high heat. Place the chickens on the griddle or skillet, skin side down, and weight them down with a clean skillet or bricks wrapped in aluminum foil. The weights should be applied so they press the greatest amount of skin down in contact with the cooking surface as possible. Cook until the skin is deep golden brown and crispy, 7 to 10 minutes. Resist the temptation to peek at the skin for at least the first 3 or 4 minutes: The longer the chicken cooks undisturbed, the less likely it will be to stick. Turn the chickens over, gently releasing the skin with a metal spatula if it sticks in places. Weight the chickens again and continue cooking until the other side is deep golden brown and crispy and the chicken is cooked through, with no trace of pink, about 7 minutes. The chicken should be crispy but still juicy. Serve immediately.

Note: Most spring chickens weigh about one pound, but it is possible to find this smaller size. The size of the chickens, and the means you have to cook them, will determine how many chickens you can serve. In other words, you should estimate how many chickens, when deboned and lying flat, will fit on your griddle or portable griddle or in your cast-iron skillet(s). If you don't have the room for 6 chickens, decrease the proportions of the other ingredients accordingly. Also, this recipe is delicious when prepared on a charcoal grill. Make sure the grill is clean and free of residue and resist the temptation to peek at the skin for the first several minutes. Most foods will stick to the grill at first, but will release themselves after a few minutes.

Roasted Chicken with Pomegranate

🔆 Pollo Arrosto al Melograno 🔆

Pomegranate is one of the fruits mentioned in the Bible, and it is still a favorite fruit of the Mediterranean. It is revered almost as much as the olive tree, signifying good luck and fertility. Making your own pomegranate juice is slow going at first, but becomes quicker once you get the knack of freeing the seeds from the fruit's membranes. If you live near a Middle Eastern specialty shop, look for bottled unsweetened pomegranate juice.

If you cannot find two-pound chickens, or if you don't have two very large cast-iron skillets, prepare this dish with two three-pound chickens, using slightly smaller (about 12-inch) cast-iron skillets. Moving the hot skillets in and out of the oven requires caution: Make sure you have strong hands and thick oven mitts.

MAKES 6 SERVINGS

Three 2-pound chickens

1 teaspoon salt

¼ teaspoon freshly ground black pepper

Extra virgin olive oil

1 cup fresh pomegranate juice (from about 3 pomegranates; see Note)

1 cup Chicken Stock (page 80) or canned low-sodium chicken broth

6 tablespoons Grand Marnier

¼ cup (½ stick) unsalted butter

3 tablespoons extra virgin olive oil

2 tablespoons fresh rosemary leaves

2 tablespoons brandy

Heat the oven to 425°F.

With poultry shears, cut the backbone from each chicken, starting at the neck and cutting along both sides of the backbone. Lay each chicken flat, skin side down, on the work surface. Cut the chicken in half through the breastbone. Remove the central breastbones and the smaller attached ribs using your fingers and a paring knife. Season both sides of the chicken halves with the salt and pepper and rub them with olive oil.

Place two very large (about 14-inch) well-seasoned cast-iron or other heavy, ovenproof skillets over medium-high heat. When hot, place the chicken halves, skin side down, in the skillets—they should fit comfortably side by side without overlapping. Cook until the skin is well browned, 5 to 7 minutes. Resist the temptation to peek for at least the first few minutes—the skin is much less likely to stick if it is allowed to brown and crisp. Turn the chicken halves over, freeing the skin with a metal spatula if it sticks in places, and cook until the other side is brown, about another 5 minutes.

Place the skillets in the oven and roast, turning the chickens twice, until no trace of pink remains at the knee joint, about 20 minutes. Remove the skillets from the oven and spoon off all the rendered fat. Divide the remaining ingredients between the two skillets and return them to the oven. Cook for 10 minutes, basting the chickens frequently and turning them once until no trace of pink remains at the knee joint. Transfer the chickens to plates.

Combine the sauce from both skillets in one pan, place over medium heat, and simmer until syrupy. Strain the sauce through a fine sieve and spoon the sauce over the chicken. (If the skillets are too heavy or hot for you to pick up comfortably, spoon the sauce from one skillet into the other, then spoon the sauce into the sieve to strain it.)

Note: To make pomegranate juice, cut one of the pomegranates in half. Break each half into several large pieces. Working over a sieve placed over a bowl, scrape the red seeds free of the membranes into the sieve. Continue until all the seeds from the pomegranate are in the sieve, breaking the pomegranate into smaller pieces if necessary to free all the seeds. With a pestle or small ladle, crush the seeds against the sieve to extract as much juice as possible. Remove the seeds from the sieve and repeat with the remaining pomegranates until you have the amount of juice called for in the recipe (plus a little more for the cook, if you like).

Meat

Le Carni

I loved going with Grandma and Grandpa to the *fiera-samanj* (animal fair). The fair was a big event that was held in the town of San Vincenti—an hour's ride from Busoler in the horse-drawn cart. On the far end of San Vincenti, there was a square studded with large trees. Between the trees, there were cement poles with metal rings to which the animals were tied. There were also stone slabs used as tables where merchandise and food would be displayed.

The people came to the *fiera* from the surrounding towns with their goods to sell, barter, or exchange. Livestock was the main merchandise. Most clearly, I remember the large white

Istrian oxen, resembling the Chiannina breed from Tuscany with their stubby legs and drooping chins. They usually had two brass spheres stuck on the points of their long and impressive horns so that they couldn't hurt each other. I also recall magnificent horses with large black manes and shiny brown bodies with clusters of hair around each hoof, whisking the summer flies away with their long tails. There were also colts, donkeys, sheep, and lots of goats.

Wooden pens held squealing suckling pigs that my Grandpa came to buy. We would make the rounds of the suckling pig vendors—it was easy to locate them by the raucous sound that came from their pens. The owners were often yelling louder than the squealing piglets as they tried to make a sale. Grandpa would pick the little sucklings up by the hind legs and raise them into the air. He would check their hind legs, snouts, eyes, and weight. He wanted them healthy with large bones so they would grow up to be big. When it came time to make the prosciutto, Grandpa wanted the hind legs and pancetta (belly bacon) nice and large. With their back legs tied, the piglets were weighed and, after some negotiation as to price, they ended up in a burlap bag. Each time we went to the *fiera* we brought at least two or three of them home. Grandpa had a wooden crate lined with straw where he would put them for the trip home. I played with the piglets through the cracks of the crate—they were so warm and pink and had soft, floppy ears and very inquisitive snouts. As I fed them fruit, I would giggle every time their warm snouts would catch my fingers. Even the sweetest fruits would not appease them, and they would squeal all the way home.

The *fiera* was also a socializing event, with grills set up everywhere. There were lambs grilled on the spit, grilled suckling pig, sausages, prosciutto, and salads of ripe tomatoes, cucumbers, and onions. There was always a demijohn (a fifty-four-liter bottle or jug in a wicker sheath) of homemade wine, and in the center there was a big *vasca* (tub) filled with drinking water for the animals.

Toward the end of the day, the solitary music of the *meh* (bagpipes) accompanied the voices of contented men and women singing folk songs that had been sung for generations before them. There were always other children my age at the *fiera*, and we would play hide-and-seek, with plenty of hiding places behind the trees and the animal pens to choose from. Once I was found, I would hop on the blanket that was waiting for me in the back of the cart and play and tease the little pink snouts of the pigs until it was time to go home.

The Italian style of eating is quite different from the American, most significantly in the amount of meat or other protein that is eaten at the meal: In the Italian diet, meat, fish, or poultry is only a part of a meal that typically includes a pasta, soup, or rice first course as well as an assortment of fresh vegetables served along with the main course, and fresh fruits for dessert. This is a key point—along with the use of olive oil—in making the Italian (and what has come to be known as the Mediterranean) diet so healthful.

Veal is the most esteemed meat in Italy, with pork and lamb taking an honored second place. Far less appreciated is beef, which may come as a surprise to most steak-loving Americans. Whatever the animal in question, two things hold true: In general, the animal is butchered—and appreciated more—when younger (hence the preference of veal over beef). And, secondly, all parts of the animal—tripe, liver, kidneys, sweetbreads, heart, and brain—are eaten.

The technique chosen for cooking meats varies according to the type and cut of meat in question and, to some extent, the age and species of the animal, what the animal has been fed, and how the animal has been butchered. It is important to have a reliable butcher who can share this information with you and prepare cuts of meat most appropriate for your recipes. Generally speaking, more tender cuts of meat can be cooked more quickly, using dry-heat methods like roasting, grilling, panfrying, or broiling. Tougher cuts of meat, from the legs and shoulders, should be cooked slowly in liquid, as for the *Guazzetto* on page 284 and Braised Beef in Barolo Wine on page 297. I love these long, slow-cooked dishes with their rich harmony of flavors. A bonus is that the cuts used for these recipes, such as muscles, shanks, necks, and oxtails, are usually cheaper and, when cooked for a long time, easier to digest.

Cooking in a Skillet

You will notice I am including a lot of recipes—especially in this and the Game and Chicken chapter—that call for cooking in a skillet. Some of these dishes have vegetables added during the cooking, sometimes they are finished in the oven, and sometimes a quick sauce is made in the skillet after the meat or poultry is removed. Whatever the case, there are certain principles that apply to cooking in a skillet and I have outlined them below. Also, I use a restaurant skillet and a commercial range, even when cooking at home. I know that isn't practical for most people, so I offer the following suggestions to help you cook these dishes successfully in your kitchen.

- Choose the widest, heaviest skillets available, preferably made of a nonreactive material. A nonreactive material is one that doesn't interact with certain foods—most typically wine, tomatoes, vinegar, and other acidic ingredients—that are being cooked in it. Nonreactive materials include stainless steel, nonstick coatings, Calphalon, and, for the recipes in this book, a well-seasoned cast-iron skillet (but even seasoned cast iron will discolor pale sauces and can lend an "off" flavor to delicate sauces). Unseasoned iron and unlined aluminum are highly reactive and should be avoided.

- Add only enough food to the skillet at one time as will fit comfortably, leaving a little space between each piece. If the pieces of meat or poultry touch—or worse, overlap—they won't come in touch with the hot cooking surface and will steam rather than brown. Overcrowding also lowers the temperature of the skillet, defeating the whole purpose of searing.

- Many of the recipes call for dividing the ingredients between two large skillets. If you don't have two large skillets, cook the ingredients in batches. Turn the oven to the lowest setting before you begin and keep the first batch warm on a baking pan loosely covered with aluminum foil while preparing the remaining batch(es).

- Let the skillets heat up sufficiently before you add any food to them. The flavor of these dishes depends in large part on searing and caramelizing the ingredients. Generally speaking, the oil and pans are hot enough to begin cooking if when you dip a corner of whatever you are cooking—a chicken thigh, for example—into the oil, it gives off a lively, but not violent, sizzle.

- These large skillets can be heavy, especially when filled with food. Be cautious: If the recipe calls for spooning off the fat, for example, get a firm grip on the handle using a double thickness of pot holder and tilt the skillet away from you at a slight angle. If it helps, remove some of the food from the skillet first.

- If the recipe calls for making a sauce in the skillet and you are using two skillets, pour the pan juices from one into the other first. If you are directed to "deglaze" the skillet, that is, to pour wine or another liquid into the skillet to release the flavorful bits that cling to the bottom, pour the liquid into one skillet and scrape up the bits, then pour the liquid into the second skillet and do the same.

Pork

(*Maiale*)

Domesticated from its cousin the wild boar, the pig is one of the most useful animals to man and has long been a main dietary staple in both Western and Asian cultures. There is a recorded recipe from about 500 B.C. in China for roasting a suckling pig. The pig is easy to care for, feed, and keep. It is a prolific animal and has at least two litters a year with an average of seven sucklings in each. For a minimal investment, it gives a good yield in quantity of meat when slaughtered. In certain areas—where the climate or terrain were not conducive to growing olives for oil or raising cows for butter—the rendered fat of the pig was traditionally used for cooking and was valued as much as the meat.

Today, in the United States, the pig is raised primarily for its tasty pink meat and has been bred with a lower fat content. Pork is a savory meat with a sweet finish, quite versatile and rather inexpensive compared to other meats, and an excellent source of protein. It is slaughtered under tightly controlled FDA (Food and Drug Administration) conditions and divided into "primal sections" that are bought by butchers and ultimately cut into retail cuts or cured. When buying pork, look for lovely pink meat with a uniform texture and bright white fat.

Basically, any recipe that is prepared with veal can be prepared instead with pork. A pork scallop or thin slice of boneless pork can be a very quick and tasty answer to the question of what to make for a meal; just make sure not to overcook it! Because of the danger of trichinosis, there has always been a concern about undercooking pork, which has led to the belief that pork must always be cooked to extremely high temperatures. In fact, today pork that is cooked to 150°F is well past the safety point but not at all dry—a fact that is especially important when cooking the lean pork that is bred today in the States. If you do not have a meat thermometer, pierce the thickest part of the meat—the juices will run clear, with no traces of pink, when the meat is fully cooked. Roast pork cooked much beyond this temperature will dry. Braised pork, especially chops like the Spicy Pork Chops on page 277, will reabsorb some of the cooking juices if simmered over low heat and be tender and tasty.

Boneless Pork Loin

Both of the following pork roast recipes call for a boneless center rib roast that weighs about three pounds and comes from a center loin roast (bone-in) weighing about five pounds. You can ask your butcher to bone the center rib roast, or you can do it yourself: Stand the meat on the backbone with the rib bones pointing upwards. With a sharp boning knife, start from the far end and work toward you, separating the meat from the rib bones by pressing—almost scraping—the knife along the rib bones. Use a series of small, easy strokes and cut all along the bones, following the rib bones along the curve to the backbone until the meat is free of the bones. You will have a compact "eye" of the roast, with a small flap attached to the side. If there is a stuffing for the roast—as there is in both of these recipes—it is helpful to make a cut about halfway through and along the entire length of the eye. Place the filling in this cut and fold the small flap over the opening before tying the roast to secure the filling. Whether you bone the roast yourself or let the butcher do it, always reserve the bones. Cut them into smaller pieces with a cleaver and add them to the roasting pan along with the vegetables—they will add much flavor. The rib roast will come with a layer of fat on the outside. With a sharp knife, shave most of it off, leaving a thin layer that will protect the meat from drying out while cooking.

Rosemary-Roasted Loin of Pork

Arista di Maiale

MAKES 8 SERVINGS

Preheat the oven to 450°F. Place the fennel, garlic, and the leaves from 2 of the rosemary sprigs on a cutting board and chop them together until minced. Transfer the mixture to a mortar and add 1 tablespoon of the olive oil. Grind the mixture to a paste with a pestle. Season with salt and pepper. (Alternatively, the mixture can be ground fine in a blender, stopping often to scrape down the sides of the jar.)

Spread half the fennel mixture into the entire length of the cut in the roast. Fold the flap over the opening and tie the roast securely with kitchen twine at 2-inch intervals. Thread the 2 remaining sprigs of rosemary through the twine on either side of the roast. Make holes in the top and sides of the roast with a paring knife or thick skewer and force the remaining vegetable mixture into the holes. Season the outside of the roast generously with salt and pepper, then rub with the remaining 2 tablespoons olive oil. Set the roast in an 18 × 14-inch roasting pan.

Roast for 15 minutes, then reduce the oven temperature to 400°F. Tilt the roasting pan and spoon off excess fat from the bottom. Scatter the carrots, celery, and onions around the roast. Roast for another 15 minutes. Pour the stock into the pan and continue cooking, basting the roast occasionally with the pan juices, until a meat thermometer inserted into the thickest part of the roast registers 155°F, 40 to 50 minutes.

Remove the roast to a platter. Pass the vegetables and pan juices through a food mill fitted with the fine disc into a small bowl. (Alternatively, strain the liquid through a sieve, pressing on the vegetables to extract as much liquid as possible and force some of the vegetables through the sieve.) Skim all fat from the surface of the sauce. The sauce should be thick enough to lightly coat a spoon. If not, transfer the sauce to a small saucepan and bring to a simmer. Simmer until thick enough to lightly coat a spoon. Season the sauce with salt and pepper, if needed. Cut the meat into ¼-inch-thick slices and serve with the sauce.

1 cup diced fresh fennel bulb and fronds

2 garlic cloves, peeled

4 sprigs fresh rosemary

3 tablespoons extra virgin olive oil

Salt and freshly ground black pepper

One 3-pound boneless center rib roast of pork, prepared according to the directions on page 274

½ cup diced (¼-inch) carrots

½ cup diced (¼-inch) celery

½ cup roughly chopped onions

2½ cups Chicken Stock (page 80) or canned low-sodium chicken broth

Roasted Loin of Pork Stuffed with Prunes

Arrosto di Maiale alle Prugne

Grappa can be used instead of bourbon for this recipe, but I love the mellow caramel flavor the bourbon imparts to the meat and the sauce.

MAKES 8 SERVINGS

½ pound pitted prunes

½ cup bourbon

One 3-pound boneless center loin of pork roast, prepared according to the directions on page 274

10 fresh sage leaves

Salt and freshly ground black pepper

2 tablespoons extra virgin olive oil

½ cup diced (¼-inch) carrots

½ cup diced (¼-inch) celery

½ cup roughly chopped onions

4 garlic cloves, crushed

2½ cups Chicken Stock (page 80) or canned low-sodium chicken broth

In a small bowl, soak the prunes in the bourbon for 1 hour.

Preheat the oven to 450°F. Drain the prunes and reserve four of them along with the soaking liquid. Arrange the remaining soaked prunes along the entire length of the slit in the roast. Fold the flap over the opening and tie the roast securely with kitchen twine at 2-inch intervals. Thread the sage leaves in two rows through the twine on either side of the roast. Season the roast generously with salt and pepper and rub it with the olive oil. Place the roast in an 18 × 14-inch roasting pan.

Roast for 15 minutes. Reduce the oven temperature to 400°F. Tilt the roasting pan and spoon off excess fat from the bottom. Scatter the carrots, celery, onions, and garlic around the roast. Roast for another 15 minutes. Add the reserved prunes and soaking liquid and roast for another 10 minutes.

Pour the stock into the pan and continue cooking, basting the roast occasionally with the pan juices, until a meat thermometer inserted into the thickest part of the roast registers 155°F, 30 to 40 minutes.

Remove the roast to a platter. Pass the contents of the pan through a food mill fitted with the fine disc into a small bowl. (Alternatively, strain the liquid through a sieve, pressing on the vegetables to extract as much liquid as possible and to force some of the vegetables through the sieve.) Skim all fat from the surface of the sauce. The sauce should be thick enough to lightly coat a spoon. If not, transfer the sauce to a small saucepan and bring to a simmer. Simmer until thick enough to lightly coat a spoon. Season the sauce with salt and pepper, if needed. Cut the meat into ¼-inch-thick slices and serve with the sauce.

Spicy Pork Chops

Costolette di Maiale Piccanti

For this *piccante* recipe I recommend rib chops, although loin chops can also be very good. Have your butcher cut the chops for you, if possible. If not, look for chops of equal thickness and size, so the cooking time is the same for all.

MAKES 6 SERVINGS

Pat the pork chops dry with paper towels and sprinkle both sides of each lightly with salt. Coat the chops with flour and shake off any excess flour. Divide the oil between two large, heavy skillets—cast iron is ideal—and place the skillets over medium heat, letting them heat up. Add the chops and cook, turning once, until golden brown on both sides, about 10 minutes total.

Tuck the garlic into the skillet around the chops and cook until golden, about 3 minutes. Reduce the heat to low. Tilt the skillets and spoon off as much of the fat as possible. Divide the cherry peppers and marjoram between the skillets. (Be careful—the fumes can be irritating.) Add half of the vinegar to each skillet and cook, shaking the skillets, until evaporated. Pour half of the wine into each skillet and cook until reduced by half, about 5 minutes.

Six ¾-inch-thick lean rib or loin pork chops (about 3 pounds)

Salt

All-purpose flour for dredging

5 tablespoons extra virgin olive oil

12 garlic cloves, crushed

3 bottled cherry peppers in vinegar, halved and stems and seeds removed

2 sprigs fresh marjoram or rosemary

3 tablespoons red wine vinegar

¼ cup dry white wine

1 cup Chicken Stock (page 80) or canned low-sodium chicken broth

Add ½ cup of the chicken stock to each skillet, cover them, and simmer for 15 minutes, turning occasionally. Remove the chops to plates. The sauce should be slightly syrupy. If not, increase the heat to high and boil for 1 to 2 minutes. Spoon the sauce over the chops. If you like, you can strain the sauce first, but it is more interesting with the pieces of pepper and garlic still in it.

Sauerkraut with Pork

Capucci Garniti

There is not one holiday that goes by at our house where a pot of *capucci* is not bubbling away on the stove. It is an Istrian tradition—especially for weddings where the first course would be Istrian Wedding Pillows (page 106).

MAKES 8 SERVINGS

One 1-pound piece smoked pork butt, cut lengthwise in half

1 pound smoked pork sausages (see Note)

1 pound smoked pork ribs, cut apart between the ribs

4 smoked ham hocks

4 pounds sauerkraut, preferably the kind sold loose or in plastic bags

2 tablespoons extra virgin olive oil

2 garlic cloves, sliced

6 fresh or dried bay leaves

Freshly ground black pepper

Salt

2 cups water

Bring a large (at least 8-quart) pot of water to boil. Add the pork butt to the water and bring back to a boil. Boil for 5 minutes. Remove to a colander and drain. Repeat with the remaining meats. Discard the water.

Meanwhile, drain the sauerkraut in a colander. Rinse it briefly under cold water and drain. Taste the sauerkraut; if it is unpleasantly salty or acidic, rinse it a little more thoroughly and drain it well.

Pour the olive oil into a large (about 8-quart), heavy casserole or Dutch oven with a lid. Add half the sauerkraut and strew the garlic, bay leaves, pepper to taste, and, if necessary, salt over it. Arrange the pork butt and ham hocks over the sauerkraut, cover with the remaining sauerkraut, and add the water. Bring to a boil, reduce the heat to medium, and simmer, covered, for 30 minutes.

Tuck the sausages and ribs into the sauerkraut and continue cooking until the pork butt and hocks are tender and the liquid is almost completely absorbed, about 30 minutes. Stir the contents of the pot occasionally from the bottom up.

Cover the pot and let stand off the heat for 15 minutes.

Cut the sausages and pork butt into ½-inch-thick slices. Pile the sauerkraut in the center of a very large platter and arrange the sliced meats, ribs, and hocks around it.

Note: There are many kinds of smoked sausages available. If you live near a German or Eastern European pork store that specializes in smoked pork products, choose a freshly made smoked pork sausage for this recipe. If not, any smoked pork sausage will do.

Veal

(*Vitello*)

Generally speaking, veal is the meat of a calf slaughtered between the age of three and five months. Milk-fed veal—from calves three to four months old that have fed only on milk—has powder pink meat with creamy white fat and a fine, tender texture. Grass-fed veal, on the other hand, comes from calves that have been weaned from milk and have started to feed on grass and are four to five months old. The meat of grass-fed veal is redder in color, and the fat has a yellow tinge. Also, the meat is a bit tougher because of the muscular activity involved in grazing. What grass-fed veal lacks in tenderness it makes up for in a more pronounced flavor. Whenever I use long-cooking techniques for veal, I try to buy grass-fed veal.

What gives flavor and moistness to any cut of meat is the amount of fat it contains. Since veal is quite lean, be conscious of adding flavor with herbs and spices when cooking and be sure not to let the meat dry out through overcooking. Veal can be kept moist by quick cooking, as in the recipe for Veal Scaloppine with Tomato and Basil on page 285, or through long, moist cooking, as in the Guazzetto on page 284.

The veal carcass is similar to beef—it's just younger and therefore smaller. The most tender and therefore most sought-after and expensive cuts come from along the backbone. They are the rib chops, loin chops, and sirloin chops. Scallops and cutlets, as well as the rump and round roasts, come from the hind leg, the shanks of which can be roasted whole (as in Roasted Veal Shanks on page 280) or cut crosswise into thick pieces and used for ossobuco (literally, "bone with a hole," a reference to the central bone and its bounty of marrow). The shoulder is used for roasting, and the breast for stuffing whole or making savory sauces, such as Guazzetto, for gnocchi or pastas. The remnants and smaller pieces can be made into ground veal.

Veal is best prepared when freshly bought, although it keeps well in the freezer for a month or two. But as with any meat that has been frozen, it will lose a substantial amount of its natural juices when defrosted.

Roasted Veal Shanks

Stinco di Vitello Arrosto

I love this dish when made with fresh—that is, unsmoked—pork shanks. For some reason they are extremely difficult if not impossible to find in this country, so I have adapted my favorite recipe for them to veal shanks.

When brought to the table, bone and all, this dish makes an impressive presentation. The shanks are quite easy to carve in front of your guests. The bones should be left at the table for your guests to pick on—the gelatin that has caramelized on the bone is a special treat.

MAKES 6 SERVINGS

2 whole veal shanks (3 to 3½ pounds each)

Salt and freshly ground black pepper

6 tablespoons extra virgin olive oil

1 large carrot, chopped

1 small onion, sliced

2 garlic cloves, crushed

2 tablespoons fresh rosemary leaves, chopped

6 fresh sage leaves

1 cup dry white wine

3 cups Meat Stock (page 78), Chicken Stock (page 80), or canned low-sodium chicken broth, or as needed

Preheat the oven to 425°F.

Pat the shanks dry with paper towels and season them generously with salt and pepper. In a flameproof roasting pan large enough to hold the shanks comfortably, heat ¼ cup of the olive oil over medium heat, using two burners if necessary. Add the shanks and cook them, turning often, until well browned on all sides, about 12 minutes. Transfer the roasting pan to the oven and roast for 30 minutes, turning the shanks occasionally with a pair of sturdy tongs.

Meanwhile, in a small skillet, heat the remaining 2 table-spoons olive oil over medium heat. Add the carrot, onion, garlic, rosemary, and sage, season lightly with salt and pepper, and cook until the vegetables are softened, about 10 minutes.

Tilt the roasting pan and spoon off the excess fat. Add the sautéed vegetable mixture and pour in the wine and 2 cups of the stock. Return the pan to the oven and roast, turning and basting the shanks occasionally, until the meat is very tender and its surface nicely caramelized, about 2 hours. Add some or all of the remaining stock as needed to prevent the vegetables from drying out.

Remove the shanks from the roasting pan. Strain the contents of the roasting pan into a bowl. With a wooden spoon or ladle, mash the vegetables in the sieve and force as much of them as possible through the sieve. (Alternatively, you may pass the vegetables and liquid through a food mill fitted with the fine disc.) Skim all the fat from the surface of the liquid. Return the shanks and liquid to the pan. Roast, basting the meat with the sauce occasionally, until the sauce is syrupy and forms a rich glaze on the meat, 10 to 15 minutes. There should be about ¾ cup of sauce.

To serve, hold each shank by the bone with a kitchen towel and, with a carving knife, cut ¼-inch-thick slices parallel to the bone, turning the bone until all the meat is removed. Arrange the slices on a platter and drizzle the sauce over them.

Veal Ossobuco with Barley Risotto

I'm sure you already have ten recipes for ossobuco. But please try my rendition—the orange juice and carrot juice keep it light and fresh but still very comforting.

MAKES 6 SERVINGS

For the ossobuco

1 sprig fresh rosemary

1 sprig fresh thyme

2 fresh or dried bay leaves

4 cloves

1 lemon

1 orange

¼ cup extra virgin olive oil

1 cup finely chopped onions

1 cup shredded carrots

1 cup finely diced celery

Salt

3 whole veal shanks (3 to 3½ pounds each), each cut into 4 pieces

Freshly ground black pepper

All-purpose flour, for dredging

½ cup vegetable oil

1 tablespoon tomato paste

1 cup dry white wine

½ cup carrot juice (available in many health food stores or at juice bars)

½ cup celery juice (available at many health food stores or at juice bars)

2 cups canned crushed Italian plum tomatoes

Prepare the ossobuco. Tie the rosemary, thyme, bay leaves, and cloves together securely in a 4-inch square of cheesecloth. With a vegetable peeler, remove the zest (yellow part of the peel only) from the lemon in wide strips. Do the same to the orange. Squeeze the juice from the orange and reserve separately.

In a wide, heavy nonreactive casserole large enough to hold the veal shanks, heat 2 tablespoons of the olive oil over medium heat. Add the onions and cook, stirring occasionally, until wilted, about 5 minutes. Add the carrots, celery, and the cheesecloth bundle of herbs. Season lightly with salt. Reduce the heat to low and cook, stirring occasionally, for about 10 minutes.

Meanwhile, pat the veal shanks dry with paper towels. Tie a piece of kitchen twine securely around the perimeter of each piece of shank to hold them together during cooking. Season with salt and pepper and coat with the flour, shaking off any excess. Divide the vegetable oil between two large, heavy skillets and heat over medium heat. Add the shanks to the skillets and cook, turning once, until well browned on both sides. (Alternatively, the shanks can be browned in batches in a single skillet.)

Add the browned ossobuco to the casserole with the vegetables. Add the tomato paste, stir it into the vegetables, and cook, stirring occasionally and turning the shanks once or twice, for 10 minutes. Add the wine and bring to a boil, then add the reserved orange juice, the carrot juice, celery juice, and the orange and lemon zest. Bring to a vigorous boil over high heat and boil for 10 minutes. Add the crushed tomatoes, reduce the heat to low, and simmer, covered, for 30 minutes.

Stir in 1 cup of the stock. Cover and simmer over low heat, adding stock to keep the level of liquid in the casserole the same, until the shanks are tender, about 1½ hours longer. Rotate the veal shanks in the casserole as they cook.

Meanwhile, prepare the barley and the gremolata. In a large saucepan, bring the water, carrots, onions, celery, bay leaves, and olive oil to a boil. Stir in the barley and cook until tender but still firm, about 20 minutes. Drain the barley and set aside.

To make the gremolata, toss the lemon zest, parsley, and garlic together in a small bowl until blended and set aside.

When the veal is tender, remove it from the casserole and cut off the strings. Pass the cooking liquid through a sieve, pressing hard on the solids to remove as much liquid as possible. Return the meat and sauce to the casserole and bring to a boil. Check the seasoning and keep the veal warm over low heat.

To finish the barley, heat the butter in a large, heavy skillet over medium-low heat. Add the barley and cook, stirring often, until it is heated through and coated with butter. Season with salt and pepper.

Serve some barley and two pieces of the veal on each plate, sprinkling the veal with the gremolata.

4 cups Chicken Stock (page 80) or canned low-sodium chicken broth

For the barley risotto
2 quarts water
1 cup diced (¼-inch) carrots
1 cup diced (¼-inch) onions
1 cup diced (¼-inch) celery
2 fresh or dried bay leaves
1 teaspoon extra virgin olive oil
1½ cups pearl barley
3 tablespoons unsalted butter
Salt and freshly ground black pepper

For the gremolata
Zest of 2 lemons (yellow part only, without the underlying white pith), finely chopped
¼ cup fresh Italian parsley leaves, finely chopped
1 garlic clove, finely chopped

Veal in Guazzetto
Vitello in Guazzetto

This dish is very savory on its own, or it can be served with a side dish like Swiss Chard and Potatoes (page 225). But I like it best served as a sauce for fresh or dry pasta or for Gnocchi (page 175), which are especially good dressed with this. To enhance the flavor and richness of the *guazzetto*, I like to add some veal neck, rib, or shank bones, which are full of gelatin. When they are cooked, pick the meat off the bones and return the meat to the sauce.

MAKES 6 SERVINGS

½ ounce dried porcini mushrooms
  (about 8 slices)
1 cup hot water
4 fresh or dried bay leaves
2 sprigs fresh rosemary
2 sprigs fresh marjoram
2 cloves
⅓ cup extra virgin olive oil
1 large onion, minced
3 pounds boneless veal stew meat (from the
  shoulder or leg), trimmed of fat and cut
  into 1-inch cubes
Three or four 2-inch pieces meaty veal
  shank, breast, or neck bones (optional)
1½ cups dry white wine
2 tablespoons tomato paste
4 cups Chicken Stock (page 80) or canned
  low-sodium chicken broth
Salt and freshly ground black pepper

Soak the dried porcini in the hot water in a small bowl until softened, about 30 minutes. Strain the soaking liquid through a coffee filter or a sieve lined with a double layer of cheesecloth. Trim any hard bits from the mushrooms and rinse them briefly under cold water. Reserve the mushrooms and strained liquid separately.

Tie the bay leaves, rosemary, marjoram, and cloves securely together in a 4-inch square of cheesecloth.

In a large, wide casserole, heat the oil over medium-high heat. Add the onion and cook, stirring often, until translucent, about 5 minutes. Add the veal and the veal bones, if using, and stir until the liquid the veal gives off has evaporated and the meat is beginning to brown, 10 to 15 minutes. Add the cheesecloth bundle of herbs and stir, then pour in the wine, increase the heat to high, and cook until the wine is reduced by half, about 10 minutes. Add the tomato paste and mushrooms. Stir slowly until the tomato paste is evenly distributed, then stir in the reserved mushroom liquid. Simmer for 5 minutes. Add half of the chicken stock and bring to a boil. Reduce the heat to a simmer and cook, uncovered, adding the remaining stock a small amount at a time to keep the level of liquid more or less the same, until the veal is tender and the sauce has thickened, about 45 minutes.

When the *guazzetto* is finished, the sauce should be syrupy. If not, increase the heat to medium-high and boil, stirring often to prevent sticking, until the sauce is thickened. Season with salt and pepper. Serve hot.

Veal Scaloppine with Tomato and Basil

Scaloppine di Vitello al Pomodoro e Basilico

This dish can be made with pork scaloppine or with chicken breasts. It is simple but has been a favorite among my restaurants' customers for years.

MAKES 6 SERVINGS

Place the scallops two at a time between sheets of plastic wrap and pound them with a meat mallet or small, heavy saucepan to a thickness of about ¼ inch. Pat the veal scallops dry with paper towels and season them with salt and pepper. Coat the scallops with the flour, shaking off any excess.

In a large, nonreactive skillet, preferably nonstick, heat the oil over medium heat. Add as many of the veal pieces as will fit without touching. Cook, turning once, until lightly browned on both sides, about 3 minutes. Remove the veal and drain on paper towels. Repeat with the remaining veal.

Add the garlic to the pan and cook until lightly browned, about 2 minutes. Pour off any excess oil from the skillet, then add the tomatoes, butter, and peperoncino. Season lightly with salt and pepper and bring to a simmer. Tuck the veal scallops into the sauce and simmer until the sauce is slightly thickened, about 4 minutes. Stir half of the basil into the skillet and cook for 1 minute.

Divide the veal among serving plates. Remove the garlic cloves from the sauce and adjust the final seasoning. Spoon the tomato sauce over the veal and sprinkle some of the remaining basil over each serving.

Eighteen 2- to 3-ounce thin veal scallops (about 2½ pounds total)
Salt and freshly ground black pepper
All-purpose flour for dredging
¼ cup extra virgin olive oil
6 garlic cloves, crushed
1½ pounds ripe tomatoes, cored, peeled (see page 141), seeded, and cut into ½-inch dice (about 3 cups)
2 tablespoons unsalted butter
1 teaspoon peperoncino (crushed red pepper)
10 fresh basil leaves, washed, dried, and shredded just before using

Veal Chops with Spinach and Pecorino Romano

Costolette di Vitello agli Spinaci e Pecorino

If the *contorno* of lightly sautéed cherry tomatoes seems like too much trouble to do at the last minute, or if you find yourself without beautiful cherry tomatoes, these spinach-topped veal chops still make a lovely dish. Serve the chops with mashed potatoes.

MAKES 6 SERVINGS

6 loin veal chops, each 1 to 1½ inches thick and about ¾ pound

Salt and freshly ground black pepper

7 tablespoons olive oil

4 garlic cloves, crushed

1½ pounds fresh spinach, tough stems removed, well washed and drained

1 cup freshly grated Pecorino Romano cheese

1 pint red or yellow cherry tomatoes, stems removed and cut in half

4 fresh basil leaves, washed, dried, and cut into thin strips

Prepare a charcoal grill or heat two large grill pans or cast-iron skillets over medium heat for 10 minutes.

Pat the veal chops dry with paper towels and season generously with salt and pepper. Rub 2 tablespoons of the olive oil over the chops. Grill the chops or cook them in a skillet or grill pan, turning once, until both sides are well marked (or well browned if using a skillet) and just a slight trace of pink remains in the thickest part of the chop near the bone, 15 to 18 minutes, depending on the heat of the grill or pan and the thickness of the chops. Transfer the chops to a broiler pan or sturdy baking pan and preheat the broiler.

Meanwhile, divide 3 tablespoons of the olive oil between two large, heavy skillets. Add 1 garlic clove to each skillet and cook over medium heat until golden, about 3 minutes. Add half the spinach to each skillet and season very lightly with salt and pepper. Cook, stirring, until the spinach is wilted and tender, 3 to 4 minutes. Season again with salt and pepper. (Alternatively, the spinach can be prepared in one skillet in two batches.) Drain the liquid from the skillets and remove the garlic cloves.

Arrange the spinach evenly over the veal chops. Sprinkle the spinach with the grated cheese and set aside.

In a large skillet, heat the remaining 2 tablespoons olive oil over medium heat. Add the remaining 2 garlic cloves and cook until lightly browned, about 2 minutes. Add the tomatoes and basil and season lightly with salt and pepper. Cook, tossing the tomatoes in the skillet, just until wilted, about 2 minutes. Season with salt and pepper and remove the garlic cloves. Remove the skillet from the heat and cover it to keep the tomatoes warm.

Meanwhile, broil the chops until the cheese is lightly browned and crisp, about 3 minutes. (If a broiler is not available, set the baking pan in a preheated 475°F oven for about 5 minutes.) Transfer the veal chops to plates. Spoon the tomatoes alongside the veal chops and serve hot.

Calf's Liver Venetian Style

⬛ Fegato alla Veneziana ⬛

Whenever we put calf's liver on the menu in any of my three Manhattan restaurants—Felidia, Becco, and Frico Bar—it is a big seller. People like calf's liver, but maybe they are too intimidated to prepare it at home and that is why they frequently order it out. The truth is, liver is quite easy to prepare—use high heat initially to sear the outside, then cook it just lightly enough for a pink interior. This is my rendition of calf's liver *alla veneziana*—slowly browned onions tossed with quick-seared liver.

MAKES 6 SERVINGS

2 pounds calf's liver (see Note)
½ cup olive oil
1 pound white onions, cut into ¼-inch-thick
    slices
4 fresh or dried bay leaves
Salt
1 teaspoon red wine vinegar
Freshly ground black pepper
Basic Polenta (page 198; optional)

If you bought the liver in one piece, trim it of its outer covering membrane, blood vessels, and any blemishes. Cut the liver into ½-inch-thick slices. (Your butcher may do this for you.) Pat the slices dry with paper towels and cut them into 2 × ½ × ½-inch strips. Set them aside. (Liver, because of its texture, can be a little tricky to cut into even strips; if in doubt, it is better to cut the liver into thicker, rather than thinner, pieces.)

In a large skillet, heat ¼ cup of the oil over medium-high heat. Add the onions, bay leaves, and a pinch of salt and cook, stirring and tossing often, until the onions begin to brown, about 8 minutes. Reduce the heat to medium-low and continue cooking, stirring often, until the onions are golden brown, about another 12 minutes. Add the vinegar and cook until the onions are tender and the vinegar has evaporated, about 3 minutes. Season with salt and pepper, cover the skillet, and set aside.

Prepare the polenta, if using. Finish the liver while the polenta is standing. In a heavy, preferably nonstick, skillet large enough to hold the strips of liver in a single layer, heat the remaining ¼ cup olive oil over high heat. (Use two skillets or cook the liver in two batches if you do not have a skillet large enough.) Add the liver and cook, stirring and tossing the liver strips constantly, until browned on the outside but still quite pink in the center, 1 to 2 minutes. (Cooking the liver like this will give you medium-rare liver. For more well-done liver, increase the cooking time by

1 minute.) With a slotted spoon, transfer the liver strips to the skillet containing the onions (repeat with the remaining liver if necessary).

Place the skillet of onions and liver over medium heat and toss gently until combined and warmed through, about 2 minutes. Check the seasoning and serve alongside soft polenta if desired.

Note: If possible, ask your butcher to trim the liver of its outer membrane, blood vessels, and blemishes before slicing it into ½-inch-thick slices. The liver will then be very easy to work with. If not, simply follow the directions above for preparing the liver.

Spicy Seared Veal Kidneys

Rognoni Trifolati

When buying veal kidneys, make sure they are from a young calf three to four months old. The color should be an even purplish pink with no blotches. There is no skin to remove—just the outer and inner fat, and that is quite simple to do.

MAKES 6 SERVINGS

2 pounds veal kidneys

2 quarts cool water

1 cup red wine vinegar

Salt and freshly ground black pepper

1 teaspoon all-purpose flour

6 tablespoons extra virgin olive oil

6 garlic cloves, crushed

3 cherry peppers, fresh or bottled in vinegar, cut in half and stems and seeds removed

¼ cup dry white wine

2 fresh or dried bay leaves

½ cup Meat Stock (page 78) or canned low-sodium beef broth

2 tablespoons chopped fresh Italian parsley leaves

Basic Polenta (page 198) or Swiss Chard and Potatoes (page 225)

Turn the kidneys fat side up and with a small knife cut along the line of fat to reveal the interior fat. Remove as much of this interior fat as possible. Don't worry about removing it all, as small pieces can be removed later. Combine the water and vinegar in a large bowl and add the trimmed kidneys. Let soak for 30 minutes.

Drain the kidneys, pat them dry with paper towels, and cut into ¼-inch-thick slices. Trim any remaining fat from the slices. Cut the slices into ¾-inch pieces. Place the kidneys in a medium-size bowl and season them lightly with salt and pepper. Sprinkle the flour over the kidneys and toss well.

Pour 2 tablespoons of the olive oil into each of two large, heavy, preferably nonstick, skillets and place them over high heat. When the oil is very hot—a piece of the kidney dipped in the oil should give off a very lively sizzle—add as many of the kidney pieces as will fit in a single layer and cook, stirring and tossing constantly, until the kidneys are well browned, about 3 minutes. (Alternatively, the kidneys can be cooked in one skillet in batches. Most important is to sear the kidneys well. If necessary—even if you are using two skillets—cook the kidneys in batches, using some of the oil for each batch.) Remove the kidneys to a plate and repeat with the remaining kidneys if necessary.

Wipe out one of the skillets, add the remaining 2 tablespoons olive oil, and heat over medium heat. Add the garlic and cherry peppers and cook, shaking the skillet occasionally, until the garlic is golden brown, about 2 minutes. Remove the skillet from the heat and pour in the wine, then increase the heat to high and bring the wine to a boil. Add the kidneys and bay leaves and return the liquid to a boil. Add the stock, season lightly with salt, and cook vigorously until the liquid is reduced by half and the kidneys are tender but still have a trace of pink, about 3 minutes.

Remove the garlic and bay leaves, stir in the parsley, and check the seasoning. Serve with polenta or Swiss chard.

Lamb and Goat

(*Agnello e Capretto*)

The best lamb and goat come from milk-fed—that is, not-yet-weaned—animals between the ages of six and eight weeks. The whole dressed carcass of either baby lamb or kid goat should weigh between fourteen and twenty pounds. At this size, the meat is powder pink, with hardly a trace of fat, and will be quite sweet and tender when cooked. Generally speaking, I wouldn't buy a goat that weighed more than twenty pounds, but an older lamb—one that has begun feeding on grass and may weigh up to thirty pounds—can be quite delicious. Roasting is an ideal way to cook kid goat, baby lamb, and the hind leg from older, grass-fed lamb. Chops and racks from older lambs can be grilled, sautéed, or roasted, and any small pieces of either lamb or goat are delicious *in guazzetto*—slowly simmered with herbs, wine, and tomato—and used as a sauce for pasta or gnocchi.

Braised Lamb Shanks in Guazzetto

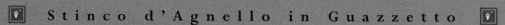

Stinco d'Agnello in Guazzetto

MAKES 6 SERVINGS

8 slices dried porcini mushrooms
    (about ½ cup, loosely packed)

2 cups hot water

2 oranges

4 fresh or dried bay leaves

2 sprigs fresh rosemary

4 cloves

6 lamb shanks (about 1 pound each;
    see Note)

Salt and freshly ground black pepper

¼ cup extra virgin olive oil

2 cups minced onions

Soak the porcini in the hot water in a medium-size bowl until softened, about 20 minutes. Strain the porcini and the soaking liquid through a coffee filter or a sieve lined with a double thickness of cheesecloth. Rinse the mushrooms and cut off any tough bits. Reserve the mushrooms and soaking liquid separately.

Meanwhile, with a vegetable peeler, remove the zest (the orange part of the skin, without any of the underlying white pith) from the oranges in long strips. Cut enough of the orange zest into very thin strips to measure 1 tablespoon. Squeeze the juice from the oranges. Reserve the thick strips of zest and juice separately from the thin strips.

Tie the bay leaves, rosemary, and cloves together securely in a 4-inch square of cheesecloth. Season the shank pieces generously with salt and pepper.

¼ cup minced pancetta or bacon
1 cup dry red wine, such as Barolo
¼ cup tomato paste
6 cups Chicken Stock (page 80) or canned low-sodium chicken broth
Spaetzle (page 253; optional)

In a wide, heavy nonreactive casserole large enough to hold the shanks, heat the oil over medium-high heat. Add the onions and pancetta, season lightly with salt and pepper, and cook, stirring, until golden brown, about 8 minutes. Remove the onion mixture with a slotted spoon, leaving as much of the oil in the casserole as possible, and set aside. Add as many of the lamb pieces as will fit in a single layer. Cook, turning the lamb pieces occasionally, until all the liquid has evaporated and the lamb is beginning to brown, about 15 minutes. Remove the lamb and repeat with the remaining pieces if necessary.

Return the onion mixture to the casserole. Add the porcini, the cheesecloth bundle of seasonings, the thick strips of orange zest, and the orange juice. Cook for 5 minutes. Add the wine and cook, stirring occasionally, until it has almost completely evaporated, about 10 minutes.

Stir in the tomato paste and season lightly with salt and pepper. Add the reserved mushroom soaking liquid and enough of the chicken stock to cover the shanks. Bring the liquid to a boil, reduce the heat to medium-low, and simmer, partially covered, until the lamb is tender and the sauce lightly thickened, about 1½ hours. Turn the shanks in the sauce occasionally and replenish with more stock as needed to keep the shanks covered.

If serving the shanks with spaetzle, prepare the spaetzle batter once the lamb begins to simmer. Bring the water to a boil and cook the spaetzle about 10 minutes before the lamb is finished cooking.

Remove the lamb shanks to a serving platter. Strain the sauce into a wide skillet and bring to a boil over high heat. Boil the sauce until thickened enough to lightly coat a spoon. Spoon the sauce over the shanks and sprinkle the thin orange zest strips over the bone end of the shanks. Or, if serving the spaetzle, leave about ½ cup sauce in the skillet and transfer the spaetzle from the boiling water to the sauce with a slotted spoon. Boil the spaetzle in the sauce until the sauce is reduced enough to coat the spaetzle. Spoon the spaetzle onto one side of each serving plate. Prop the shanks against the spaetzle, exposed bone side up.

Note: The best shanks for this recipe are foreshanks, preferably cut so as to include a little of the leg above the knee joint. Because of their size and shape, they are a little more difficult to work with than smaller shanks and you will probably have to brown them in two or three batches. If you cannot find these larger shanks, use six of the more commonly found foreshanks cut below the knee.

Seared Lamb Chops with Rosemary and Mint Sauce

Costatine d'Agnello alla Menta

For this dish, rib chops cut from a rack of lamb are best because of the length of the bones. Look for a bright red color a few shades lighter than beef and a big "eye" of meat—about 2½ inches wide.

MAKES 6 SERVINGS

For the chops

12 "frenched" rib lamb chops
   (about 3 pounds; see Note)
1 tablespoon fresh rosemary leaves
2 teaspoons extra virgin olive oil
1 teaspoon salt
1 teaspoon freshly ground black pepper

For the sauce

1 orange
1 pound meaty lamb bones
3 tablespoons extra virgin olive oil
1 tablespoon all-purpose flour
½ cup chopped onions
¼ cup sliced carrots
¼ cup sliced celery
1 tablespoon chopped fresh sage leaves
1 tablespoon chopped fresh rosemary leaves
1 tablespoon chopped fresh mint leaves
Salt and freshly ground black pepper
3 cups Chicken Stock (page 80) or canned
   low-sodium chicken broth
1 cup water
½ cup dry white wine

Rub the chops with the rosemary, oil, salt, and pepper and let them stand at room temperature for up to 2 hours or refrigerate, covered, for up to 1 day.

Make the sauce. Preheat the oven to 425°F. Remove the zest—the orange part of the peel without the underlying white pith—from the orange with a vegetable peeler. Squeeze the juice from the orange. Reserve the zest and juice separately. Trim the lamb scraps of all fat and combine them with the lamb bones in a roasting pan. Pour 1 tablespoon of the olive oil over the trimmings and bones and toss to coat. Roast for 30 minutes. Sprinkle the flour over the bones and roast until the bones are well browned, about another 15 minutes.

Meanwhile, in a large nonreactive saucepan, heat the remaining 2 tablespoons oil over medium heat. Add the onions and cook, stirring occasionally, until softened, about 5 minutes. Add the carrots, celery, sage, rosemary, mint, and orange zest. Season lightly with salt and pepper and cook, stirring occasionally, until the vegetables are lightly browned, about 15 minutes. If the vegetables begin to stick, add a small amount of the stock and stir well.

Transfer the browned bones and meat scraps to the saucepan. Pour off and discard all the fat from the roasting pan. While the roasting pan is still hot, add the water, wine, orange juice, and the remaining chicken stock and scrape the bottom of the pan to release all the browned drippings. Pour the liquid into the saucepan and bring to a boil over high heat. Reduce the heat to a simmer and cook, skimming the foam and fat frequently from the surface, until the liquid is reduced to about 1½ cups, about 1¼ hours.

To serve

Braised Spring Legumes (page 232; optional)

Roasted Potato Wedges (page 223; optional)

Sprigs fresh mint

Discard the bones and strain the sauce through a fine sieve, pressing down hard on the solids to squeeze as much liquid as possible from them. Return the sauce to the saucepan and simmer over low heat until reduced to the consistency of gravy. Cover and keep warm in a warm place.

Heat a heavy griddle or large cast-iron pan over high heat. Add as many chops as will fit without touching. Cook the chops, turning them once, until well browned outside and rosy pink in the center, about 3 minutes. (For more well-done chops, add 1 to 2 minutes to the cooking time.) Repeat with the remaining chops, if necessary.

Spoon the sauce onto plates and arrange the chops over the sauce, with the bones crossing. Arrange the *scaffata* and potatoes next to the lamb and decorate with mint sprigs.

Note: Ask the butcher to french the chops, or do it yourself: Cut the meat and fat away from each rib bone, starting at the point where the "eye" of meat meets the bone. Scrape the bone clean with the back side of a knife. There should be from 1½ to 3 inches of bone protruding. Save all trimmings from the chops to use in the sauce.

Roasted Kid Goat

◉ Capretto Arrosto ◉

Lamb or kid goat is the traditional Easter meal at our house, and it is served with spring vegetables, peas, and roasted spring potatoes. (Use the recipe for Roasted Potato Wedges on page 223 as a guide for making roasted spring potatoes with the skin on.)

For this dish, ask the butcher to cut a forequarter of a young goat, which will weigh about five pounds, into neat two-inch cubes. If possible, buy milk-fed kid, and always look for meat with a creamy pink color and very little fat.

MAKES 6 SERVINGS

1 kid goat forequarter (including shoulder, legs, and rib sections, about 5 pounds), cut into 2-inch cubes
2 celery stalks, coarsely chopped
2 medium-size carrots, coarsely chopped
1 large onion, sliced
1 cup dry white wine
½ cup extra virgin olive oil
4 sprigs fresh rosemary
¼ teaspoon freshly ground black pepper
½ teaspoon salt
2 cups Meat Stock (page 78) or canned low-sodium chicken or beef broth

In a very large bowl, toss all the ingredients except the stock together until well blended. Cover and refrigerate for 24 hours, tossing occasionally.

Preheat the oven to 425°F. Transfer the contents of the bowl to a flameproof roasting pan, placing the vegetables in the bottom of the pan and the pieces of goat over them. Add the stock and roast, basting and turning the kid frequently, until the meat is very tender, about 1 hour.

Reduce the oven temperature to 350°F. Transfer the goat to a smaller roasting pan in which it can fit in a single layer (the meat will have shrunk). Skim and discard as much fat as possible from the pan liquid. Place the pan over high heat on the stovetop and boil until the liquid is reduced to about 1¼ cups. Strain the reduced sauce over the goat, pressing on the vegetables to squeeze out as much liquid as possible. Return the goat to the oven and roast, turning the meat every 10 minutes, until the meat is extremely tender and caramelized, about 30 minutes.

Transfer the kid to a serving platter. If necessary, boil the cooking liquid in a small saucepan until reduced to ½ cup. Check the seasoning and pour the sauce over the kid.

Beef

(*Manzo*)

As beef is not a major staple of the Italian diet, most cattle are raised for veal, which is favored by Italians. Traditionally, older—and much tougher—work animals are slaughtered for beef. Therefore, Italian recipes for preparing beef usually use long, moist cooking techniques such as braising and boiling.

Braised Beef in Barolo Wine

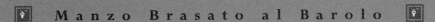 Manzo Brasato al Barolo

Braising is a wonderful technique because all the flavors of the ingredients—in this case, porcini, rosemary, cloves, and the essence of violets and blackberries in the Barolo—are absorbed by the meat, resulting in a velvety complexity of rich flavors. This dish is wonderful served with polenta (page 198) or carrot and potato puree and, of course, a good Barolo.

MAKES 6 SERVINGS

Soak the dried porcini in 1 cup of the hot stock until softened, about 30 minutes. Strain the soaking liquid through a coffee filter or a sieve lined with a double layer of cheesecloth. Trim any hard bits from the mushrooms and rinse them briefly under cold water. Reserve the mushrooms and strained liquid separately.

In a large, deep, nonreactive casserole or stockpot, heat the olive oil over medium heat. Add the onions and pancetta and cook, stirring, until the onions are golden and soft, about 7 minutes. Season lightly with salt and pepper. Add the carrots, bay leaves, cloves, and rosemary and stir well. Remove the mixture from the pot with a slotted spoon and set aside.

Season the beef generously with salt and pepper and add it to the fat remaining in the pot. Increase the heat to medium-high and cook the beef, turning as necessary,

½ ounce dried porcini mushroom (about 8 slices)

6 to 8 cups hot Meat Stock (page 78) or canned low-sodium beef broth

½ cup extra virgin olive oil

1½ cups minced onions

2 tablespoons chopped pancetta or bacon

Salt and freshly ground black pepper

1 cup shredded carrots

6 fresh or dried bay leaves

6 cloves

2 sprigs fresh rosemary

One 3½-pound beef eye of round

3 tablespoons tomato paste

1 bottle (750 ml) Barolo wine

1 cup drained and coarsely chopped canned Italian plum tomatoes

until lightly browned on all sides, about 15 minutes. Reduce the heat to medium-low. Return the onion mixture to the pot, add the tomato paste, and stir it into the vegetables. Add the wine and simmer over medium-low heat for 30 minutes, turning the beef occasionally.

Add the tomatoes, the porcini and their soaking liquid, and 5 cups of the remaining stock. Bring to a simmer and simmer, covered, skimming the foam and fat from the surface frequently and stirring occasionally, until the meat is tender, about 2½ hours. Add the remaining 2 cups of stock as needed to keep the meat covered, and turn the meat regularly as it simmers so it cooks evenly and does not scorch. Remove the meat from the pot and set aside.

Pass the sauce through a sieve, pressing on the solids with a spoon to extract as much liquid as possible. (Alternatively, the liquid and vegetables can be passed through a food mill fitted with a fine disc.) Discard the solids and return the meat and strained sauce to the pot. Bring to a simmer and simmer, uncovered, until the liquid reduces to about 3½ cups and the meat is very tender, skimming any foam from the surface as it forms, 30 to 60 minutes.

Transfer the meat to a cutting board and cut it into ¼-inch-thick slices. Arrange the slices on a serving platter and spoon the sauce over them.

Minute Steak as Served in Trieste

Bistecca alla Triestina

Traditionally in Italy, with the exception of the *bistecca fiorentina*, there has never been a large steak culture as there is in the United States. The cow was not raised for its meat but as a working animal. Therefore, when a full-grown cow was slaughtered, the meat would be tough and so was usually simmered slowly in soups, stews, or braised dishes. Sometimes steaks were pounded thin and sautéed in a pan with lots of garlic and parsley. Here is one rendition of that dish, which features the lovely flavor of browned garlic and has been adapted to American tastes by using a slightly thicker steak and cooking it to medium-rare rather than well-done as it is traditionally cooked. Feel free to substitute a tougher steak, like a chuck steak, which can be tenderized by pounding it thin.

MAKES 6 SERVINGS

6 boneless top loin steaks, each about ½ pound and ¾ inch thick
Salt
6 tablespoons extra virgin olive oil
8 garlic cloves, very finely chopped
1 cup Meat Stock (page 78) or canned low-sodium beef broth
1 teaspoon freshly ground black pepper
3 tablespoons finely chopped fresh Italian parsley leaves

Remove all the fat from the steaks and pound them with a meat mallet or a small, heavy saucepan to a thickness of about ½ inch. Season both sides of the steaks generously with salt.

Choose two large, heavy, preferably cast-iron, skillets in which the steaks fit comfortably in a single layer. Pour 2 tablespoons of the oil into each skillet and place them over medium heat. Divide the garlic between the two skillets and cook, shaking the skillets, until the garlic is light brown, about 1 minute. With a spoon, push the garlic to the sides of the skillets. Increase the heat to medium-high and add the steaks. Cook the steaks, turning them once, until browned on both sides, about a total of 3 minutes. (Spoon the garlic out of the skillet if it begins to scorch.) Divide the stock, pepper, and the remaining 2 tablespoons olive oil between the skillets. Bring to a boil and boil vigorously for 1 minute, then stir in the parsley. Remove the steaks to a hot plate. The sauce should be syrupy; if not, cook for an additional minute. Check the seasoning and spoon the sauce over the steaks. Serve hot.

Mixed Boiled Meats

❦ Bollito Misto ❦

The traditional *bollito misto* is made with beef, capon, tongue, *cotechino* (a gelatinous pork sausage made of the cartilage and snout skin plus the meat), and *testina* (calf's head, including the meaty part of the cheeks). The meats are usually served with vegetables that are cooked along with them and dressed with different sauces, such as *salsa verde* (green sauce—a fresh-tasting, tangy herb-and-vegetable sauce), *salsa di kren* (horseradish sauce—a very pungent fresh horseradish-and-cream sauce), and *mostarda di Cremona* (fruit marinated in sugar syrup and hot dry mustard—a delightful play on flavor, it's both sweet and spicy). *Bollito misto* is best made in substantial amounts, for ten to twelve people. It is ideal for a dinner party, as both first and second courses are all in one pot. Serve the broth with pastina or rice as the first course. The *bollito misto* with its vegetables accompanied by the sauces is a wonderful second course.

Here follows the traditional version, but you can enjoy just one or two kinds of boiled meat served in the *bollito misto* fashion.

A word about calves' heads: The calves' heads in the United States are quite large. If you decide to use one, search for a small one. Or, if they aren't available, try instead calf's cheeks, which are meaty, succulent, full of gelatin, and, generally speaking, underappreciated. These tasty, hidden treats are found in all kinds of animals and fish: Ask New England fishermen about cod cheeks or Chinese cooks about the strip of rich flesh that runs along the top of fish heads. Or do a little digging for yourself to find the "oysters"—those little nuggets nestled near where the thigh bones meet the backbone—in turkey and chicken.

MAKES 10 SERVINGS

8 quarts water

1½ pounds eye round of beef or
     bone-in short ribs

Fresh (not smoked) veal tongue
     (about 1½ pounds)

1 *cotechino* sausage (about 7 × 2 inches
     and 1 pound)

1½ pounds veal shank or bone-in breast

1½ pounds calf's head and/or
     cheeks (optional)

In a 12-quart pot, bring the water to a boil. Wash all the meats, including the chicken, under cold running water and drain them well.

Add the beef, celery, carrots, onions, bay leaves, peppercorns, parsley, and 3 tablespoons of the salt to the boiling water. Bring back to a boil, then adjust the heat to a gentle boil. Cook for 45 minutes, regularly skimming off the foam that forms on the surface.

Meanwhile, combine the tongue and salted water in a large (at least 8-quart) pot and bring to a boil. Adjust the heat to a simmer and cook for 30 minutes. Add the *cotechino* and continue cooking until the tongue is tender when poked with a skewer and the *cotechino* is cooked through, about 1 hour. Place the *cotechino* in a bowl of cold water so it does not burst, then return it to the pot with the tongue to keep it warm.

If the contents of one pot are done before the other, don't worry: The meats and vegetables in both pots can be kept warm in their broth in covered pots off the heat for up to 30 minutes. Longer than that, you should keep them warm over very low heat.

While the meats are cooking, prepare the leeks: Trim off the root ends and dark green leaves. Split the leeks lengthwise, leaving the layers still attached at the root ends, and wash them well under cold water to remove sand and grit from between the layers. Tie the split leeks securely together in one bundle with three pieces of kitchen twine.

One 1½-pound breast of capon or roaster chicken breast (on the bone)

4 celery stalks, cut into 3-inch pieces

3 medium-size carrots, cut into 2-inch pieces

2 medium-size onions, halved

2 fresh or dried bay leaves

6 black peppercorns

3 sprigs fresh Italian parsley

¼ cup coarse sea salt

5 quarts salted water

2 leeks

4 large baking (Idaho) potatoes, peeled

1¼ cups pastina or rice, or as needed

Add the veal shank, calf's head, capon, leeks, and potatoes. Bring back to a gentle boil. Taste the broth and season with salt if necessary. Cook until the meats are tender, about 1 hour.

Drain the *cotechino* and tongue and discard the cooking liquid. To prepare the tongue for slicing, first remove the outer layer—it should peel off easily. Cut away any little bones and cartilage from the underside. Wrap the *cotechino* and tongue in aluminum foil to keep them warm.

To serve the broth as a first course: Strain about 10 cups of the broth into a large saucepan. Skim off any fat from the surface and bring the broth to a boil. Adjust the heat to a simmer and stir in the pastina or rice. Cook until the pasta or rice is tender but firm. Check the seasoning and ladle the broth into warm bowls.

To serve the meats and vegetables: I like to serve *bollito misto* family-style so that everyone can take what they like. Slice and arrange the meats according to what you have included in your *bollito misto*. Cut all boneless meats—tongue, sausage, and eye round of beef, for example—on a bias into ¼-inch-thick slices. Meat on the bone, like veal breast, veal shank, short ribs, and capon breast, should be carved into thin slices as the bone structure allows. As you prepare the meats, keep the unsliced meats warm in the broth and cover the sliced meats with aluminum foil to keep them warm. Just before serving, arrange all the sliced meats and the vegetables on a large hot platter and ladle a small amount of the hot broth over the meats and vegetables.

continued

Serve the sauces (see Note and recipes that follow) on the side and let everyone help themselves.

Note: *Mostarda di Cremona* are candied fruits, whole or cut into pieces, that are preserved in a white wine and honey syrup highly flavored with spices and mustard. It is produced and widely used around the area of Cremona—as the name indicates—but one can find it all over Italy and now in many specialty shops in the States. Speri is a good producer. The flavor of *mostarda di Cremona* is quite intense: Cutting the larger pieces of fruit into smaller pieces may be a better way to enjoy its flavor. When serving *mostarda* as a *contorno* (side dish), as here with the *bollito misto,* serve the fruits at room temperature.

Horseradish and Cream Sauce

Salsa di Kren

MAKES ABOUT 1½ CUPS

2 tablespoons unsalted butter
1 tablespoon fine plain dry bread crumbs
Large pinch of sugar
2 ounces fresh horseradish, peeled and
    grated (about ½ cup lightly packed),
    or 2 tablespoons bottled horseradish,
    well drained
¼ cup Chicken Stock (page 80),
    Meat Stock (page 78), or
    reserved *bollito misto* broth
½ cup heavy cream
Salt

In a small skillet, melt the butter over medium heat. Add the bread crumbs and cook, stirring, until golden brown, about 4 minutes. Add the sugar and horseradish, mix well, and add the stock. Bring to a boil, add the cream, and season with salt. Bring to a boil again, reduce the heat to medium-low, and simmer until lightly thickened, 1 to 2 minutes. Serve warm. (The sauce can be made up to a day in advance and rewarmed gently over low heat.)

Vegetable and Herb Sauce

Salsa Verde

MAKES 3 CUPS

In a medium-size mixing bowl, stir together all the ingredients except the salt and pepper until thoroughly mixed. Season with salt and pepper. Serve at room temperature.

Note: To prepare a properly cooked hard-boiled egg with no discoloration around the yolk, start the egg in a small saucepan of cold water. Bring to a boil over high heat, then immediately reduce the heat to a simmer. Cook the egg for 12 minutes, then plunge it into cold water until completely cool. Peel the egg and separate the yolk and white before mincing.

¾ cup extra virgin olive oil

½ cup finely minced roasted red bell peppers, freshly prepared or bottled

½ cup minced fresh Italian parsley leaves

½ cup minced red onions

¼ cup finely diced gherkin pickles

¼ cup red wine vinegar

1 hard-boiled egg, shelled and minced (keep the yolk and white separate; see Note)

2 tablespoons capers, drained and minced

Salt and freshly ground black pepper

Fish and Shellfish

Pesce e Frutti di Mare

Pola is a city on the tip of Istria, a peninsula situated in what I think is the world's most beautiful sea—the Northern Adriatic. If you row westward, you arrive in Venice; eastward, you reach the numerous islands in the Kvarner on the Dalmatian coast. The sea is a turquoise green, reflecting the lush vegetation of its rocky bottom. It is a rich pasture for a multitude of mollusks, shellfish, and finfish.

The Istrian coastline is rocky, with stretches of pebble beach shaded by the branches of the *pino marittimo* (maritime pine), which spread their branches like umbrellas. As young-sters, we spent day after day in the heat of the summer on those pebbled beaches or on the rocks, which were like smooth slabs of terrazzo. We were always in groups—friends and cousins—and usually accompanied by an adult. We would play and lie on the rocks like seals, absorbing the heat of the Mediterranean sun, and by the end of the summer our olive skin had a golden mocha glow. While frolicking in the water, the only dangers were the sea urchins—a sting of their needles would have us limping for days, but we got even by eating them.

Depending on which beach we chose, there was always some kind of mollusk to be collected. We would find *pedoci-cozze* (mussels), *boboli* (periwinkles), *patelle* (limpets, which looked like small half clams stuck to the rocks), *pinna* (fan mussels), *ricci di mare* (sea urchins), and *datteri di mare* ("sea dates"). Catching *datteri* was a serious game, because they were sought after and expensive—if sold at the market, they could fetch good money. *Datteri* are mollusks with oval brown shells that resemble dates that burrow into a rock—in fact, they spend their whole lives buried in one rock. The boys would usually dive for the rocks, which were easy to recognize because of their multitude of holes and their light weight. With a hammer or another rock, we would gently break the rock open and collect these precious mollusks.

The *pinna* had beautiful large orange shells that looked like mother-of-pearl. We would dry the shells in the sun, then paint the inside with flowers or landscapes and hang them on walls as decorations. The smaller ones were used as ashtrays or bowls for fruits.

The mollusks we children brought home always ended up in the pot to be enjoyed by the family. But the true family fisherman was my Uncle Emilio, who was married to my mother's sister Lidia. Zio Milio, as we called him, was an electrician by profession, but his true passion was fishing. Zio Milio was a very gentle soul. He loved children, and I liked fishing, so sometimes he would take me along with him in his little *barca* (boat) called *Bella*. One particular evening we went fishing for calamari. My aunt had packed mortadella panini and bottles of water and wine for my father, Vittorio, my brother, Franco, Zio Milio, and me. As we took off in the *barca*, I was given the chore of ripping an old piece of white cloth into long strips.

When we arrived at the spot that Uncle Emilio was familiar with, we shut off the motor. It was a cloudy night and in the distance we could see the shimmering lights of the harbor and hear the fading sound of music. The smell and taste of the sea was so intense on my tongue that I still can recall it. Zio Milio lit a big *feral* (light in our dialect) at the back of the boat and tied the pieces of white cloth onto different lines. He gave me one to hold and as it trailed behind the boat under the light, he threw out two more lines that my brother was holding. My father was slowly rowing the *barca* as Zio Milio prepared a line with a snag—three or more hooks on a single stem—and we were ready. Soon the first calamari appeared, waving their tentacles and looking like puffs of pink smoke floating in the water. My uncle quickly threw the snag in like a lasso, and then with a splash, the calamari were landed in the boat. The colored dots on their bodies changed from deep red to light pink—up and down like goose pimples. I felt sorry for the calamari, but before I knew it, into the bucket they went. The calamari kept coming to the surface, their tentacles spread wide, like fireworks exploding in the sky, with Zio Milio lassoing them as as they rose into view. The bucket was full when we pulled alongside the pier—it was a good night.

Zio Milio would go fishing often, especially when the *granzevole* (spiny crab in dialect) season arrived in February and March. *Granzevole* resemble Alaskan king crabs, but they are smaller. We lived near the market in Pola, not far from the *riva* (shore) and the piers where my uncle docked his boat. He would bring his catch to our house in the wee hours of the morning to await the opening of the fish market. One particular morning, I got up to go to school and went to the bathroom to wash myself. The tub was full of *granzevole*, long, spiny orange legs climbing onto each other trying to get out. I played with them with the end of a broom for a while, then brushed my teeth and went to school. I knew dinner would be good that day.

For the sake of simplicity, I will divide the fish into three categories: mollusks, crustaceans, and finfish. It is not so important to remember specifically which family each type of seafood belongs to, but it is helpful to know which are similar. For example, if you know that squid and cuttlefish are related, you might be less hesitant to substitute one for another in a favorite recipe. I have given you some basic information on some of the members of each of the three groups, followed by a recipe or two for each.

Mollusks

(*Molluschi*)

Mollusks are divided into three classes: gastropods, bivalves, and cephalopods.

Bivalves (Bivalvi)

Bivalves are sea creatures that live between two shells, such as scallops, clams, mussels, and oysters. All members of this group should be especially fresh when bought and prepared as soon as possible. When they are fresh, the shells should be shiny and of a vivid color, not dry and dull. The shells should be shut tight, or close tightly when handled. Hold a few in the palm of your hand: They should feel full and heavy. (If they seem unusually heavy, this may mean the shells are full of mud.) When opened, they should have a fresh, briny aroma; the body should be shiny, and the color bright. The body should be attached firmly to the shell.

Scallops (Capesante) There are two main kinds of scallops: sea scallops, which are by far the most prevalent, with shells from six to ten inches across, and bay scallops, with shells about four inches across. The shells of both are fan-shaped, with small protrusions that extend from the pointed end of the fan. The two shells are joined and hinged along these protrusions. Scallops of either kind rarely make it to the markets in the United States in their shells; rather, they are shucked while the scallop boat is still out at sea. Typically, the only part of the scallop that reaches the market in the States is the round, thick muscle that connects the shells. In Europe, the pale- or bright-orange roe attached to this muscle is also saved. (Occasionally you will find scallops with the roe attached; if you do, take advantage and cook them as you would ordinary scallops.)

Because scallop boats stay out at sea for quite a while, usually the shucked scallops are put into a liquid that helps preserve their freshness and also adds quite a bit of weight to the scallops.

The overwhelming majority of scallops sold in retail markets are these "wet" scallops. "Wet" scallops are easy to identify—they are uniform milky white in color, are shiny, and tend to lose their individual shape when piled together. Because they have absorbed so much liquid, it is difficult to get these wet scallops to brown. They start to give up liquid as soon as they are heated. They also shrink quite a bit when cooked. If you have the opportunity to sample "dry" scallops—that is, scallops that have been shucked but not soaked in liquid—you should. Dry scallops are easy to tell from wet ones—they range in color from off white to very pale pink and even creamy orange. They keep their individual shapes even when piled in a mound, and they feel slightly sticky to the touch. These scallops are ideal for sautéing or broiling; their dry surface will caramelize and intensify the natural sweetness of the scallops. You may also come across the expression "diver's scallops" at the market. This term is used to describe scallops that are harvested individually in the wild, rather than cultivated or dredged.

If you do find scallops in their shells in the market, here's how to deal with them: Pry them open with a clam knife at the back joint and slide the blade along both shells to disconnect the scallop muscles, first on one side and then on the other; press the knife against the shell as you go to prevent cutting the scallop in half. Remove the muscle, with the roe attached (if present), and discard the rest of the scallop. Scrub out the shells and reserve them—for use in Scallops Baked in Their Shells (page 311) or another recipe.

Mussels (Cozze) Mussels are one of the most abundant mollusks. They are found all around the world in one form or another. The most common mussel found in our markets is the blue mussel, which lives in the waters off the eastern coast of North America and throughout European waters. They are inexpensive, quite versatile, and delicious.

Mussels start their lives as free swimmers, but soon attach themselves in clusters to rocks, pieces of wood, metal, or ropes near the shore. (If you harvest them yourself, do not harvest or eat any that have anchored themselves to metal.) It is this trait that makes mussels such an ideal seafood to cultivate. Mussels have long been cultivated by several methods in Europe, and today mussels are being farmed very effectively here in the States, especially in Maine. These farmed mussels are usually small—about two inches in length—and are almost completely free of sand or dirt. Most blue mussels in the market range in size from two to four inches. I prefer the small to medium sizes, those with shells two to three inches in length.

Whatever the size, the most important thing is that the mussels are fresh and the meat is plump and fills the shell. Set a mussel in the palm of your hand to sense its fullness. If it feels heavy for its size, it is possible that the shell is full of mud. A simple test will determine if this is the case—or if the shell is empty or the mussel dead: Try to slide the two halves of the shell in opposite directions. If the shell is full of mud, or the mussel is dead, the halves will slide apart; if not, the shells will remain firmly closed. If the mussel feels light but stays firmly closed, it is possible that the mussel is spawning. This usually happens in warmer months and during this process mussels can lose a considerable part of their body weight and be somewhat bland. They are still fine to eat.

Purging Shellfish

All shellfish—clams, mussels, and oysters among them—can contain quite a bit of sand and grit. They can be purged of their sand as follows: Mix 2 teaspoons salt into 2 quarts water. Stir in a handful of bread crumbs or fine cornmeal and place the shellfish in this solution. Refrigerate for 1 to 2 hours. Drain and rinse the shellfish before using.

Of all the shellfish, mussels will let your nose know immediately if they are not fresh. Pick up a mussel and smell it: It should smell briny and clean. Don't be alarmed if the shell is slightly open. If fresh mussels are kept very cold, or experience a change in temperature, their shells will open slightly. When you squeeze the two shells lightly between your fingers, however, the mussel should respond by clamming up—if not, it isn't fresh.

To clean mussels, scrape the shells clean of any barnacles or other attached objects (this is not necessary with cultivated mussels) and scrub clean under running water. With your fingers, pluck off the "beards," the wiry fibers that stick out from between the flat side of the shells. (The beards are secreted by the mussel and are what keep them anchored in their natural habitat.) Keep in mind that the mussels should be cooked soon after the beards are removed.

You cannot pry open the shells of a mussel as you can a clam or oyster; heat should always be used to open the shells and get at the delicacy within.

Hard-shell Clams (Vongole) Hard-shell clams, also called quahogs, are found all along the East Coast of North America. These clams are sold according to size, and it is their size that determines how they are eaten. Littleneck clams are the smallest of the hard-shell clams that come to market. The shells of littlenecks measure about two inches or less across, and they number about 480 per bushel. They are my favorite to use for clam cocktail, for serving raw on the half-shell, or for steaming or baking.

The cherrystone clam, which is slightly larger—about 2½ inches across and about 400 per bushel—is good for clam sauce. I prefer top necks, which are slightly larger still, when making soups and chowder. Hard-shell clams with shells larger than three inches across are usually referred to simply as chowder clams, and they are the least expensive of all.

The shells of hard-shell clams should be closed tight, or "clam up" when you press them together. All hard-shell clams need a good scrubbing with a stiff brush under cold running water before they are ready to be used. They can be purged as described above.

Razor Clams (Cannolicchi) These clams have golden-brown shells four to five inches long and as wide as a finger. The shells are golden to dark brown and slightly curved, like the straight razor that gave them their name. Razor clams are found along almost the entire length of the eastern coast of North America, but they rarely come to commercial markets here, probably because they are so dif-

Shellfish Shucking Tip

To facilitate the shucking of an oyster, clam, or scallop, set it in the freezer for 20 minutes, then proceed to shuck. The low temperature will make the muscle that keeps the shell shut dormant so that it will be easier to shuck.

ficult to gather. They are much more common in the markets of Europe, where they are found in just about every sea, including the Aegean. If you do see razor clams in the market, expect their shells to be gaping at both ends and their bodies to be hanging out from the gaping shells. They should be alive when bought, and they are often quite sandy. Soak them for two to three hours in lightly salted water, then rinse them thoroughly and proceed to cook. The shells are fragile and can break as they cook. To keep the shells intact, stir the clams gently with a wooden spoon or just shake the pan gently.

Oysters I have not included recipes for cooking oysters, as I prefer to eat them raw, on the half shell. It is particularly important when buying oysters you plan to eat raw to do so from a reputable dealer who can vouch for the cleanliness of the waters where the oysters were gathered.

Clam and Mussel Cooking Tips

- Even though you have thoroughly scrubbed and purged mussels or clams before cooking, there is still a chance that some grit will work its way into the cooking liquid. After steaming mussels or clams, remove them with a slotted spoon and slowly pour off the cooking liquid, leaving the last half cup or so—which will contain any grit—in the bottom of the pot.

- Any steamed mussel or clam dish will benefit from a drizzle of olive oil just before serving. Pour about 1 tablespoon very fruity extra virgin olive oil over the shellfish, bring them to a quick, hard boil, and then remove from the heat.

- Any clam or mussel that doesn't open along with the others should be discarded before serving.

- The addition of chopped fresh Italian parsley toward the end of cooking is very traditional; it adds color and a refreshing taste to any clam or mussel dish.

Scallops Baked in Their Shells

🔆 Capesante al Forno 🔆

This dish makes an excellent appetizer. For a main course, double the quantities. The scallops are best in their shells, but if these are unavailable you can set the scallops in clamshells reserved from a previous meal, in store-bought scallop shells or small baking dishes (see Note), or even directly on a baking sheet.

MAKES 6 SERVINGS

Preheat the oven to 425°F.

In a small bowl, mix the bread crumbs, parsley, garlic, and lemon zest until blended. Season with salt and pepper to taste. Stir in the wine and 3 tablespoons of the olive oil until evenly blended.

In a medium-size bowl, toss the scallops with the remaining 3 tablespoons olive oil and season lightly with salt and pepper. Place 1 scallop in each scallop half-shell, if using, or place 3 scallops in each of eight large (5-inch) store-bought shells or 4- to 5-inch ceramic baking dishes, and place on one or more baking sheets. (Alternatively, the scallops can be placed directly on a baking sheet.) Sprinkle the bread crumb mixture over the scallops, dividing it evenly.

1 cup coarse plain dry bread crumbs

½ cup lightly packed chopped fresh Italian parsley leaves

2 garlic cloves, finely chopped

Grated zest of 1 lemon (yellow part only, without the underlying white pith)

Salt and freshly ground black pepper

½ cup dry white wine, such as Pinot Grigio

6 tablespoons extra virgin olive oil

24 sea scallops in their shells, shucked and shells reserved, or 24 shucked medium-size sea scallops (about 1 pound)

Lemon wedges

Bake until the bread crumb mixture is golden brown and crisp on top, 10 to 15 minutes. Serve immediately, with wedges of lemon.

Note: Natural or ceramic scallop shells and small ceramic baking dishes of the size described above can be purchased in specialty cookware stores.

Mussels in Saffron Broth

▣ Cozze allo Zafferano ▣

Mussels are so versatile that they can be substituted for clams and razor clams in the recipes I offer in this chapter, but the following recipe is one of my favorites for mussels. Make sure that you purge the mussels according to the instructions on page 309 if you are not using cultivated mussels.

MAKES 6 SERVINGS

1 teaspoon saffron threads

1 cup hot water

5 tablespoons extra virgin olive oil

4 garlic cloves, crushed

1 cup chopped onions

3 pounds mussels, cleaned according to the directions on page 309

1 cup dry white wine, such as Tocai

4 sprigs fresh thyme or 1 teaspoon dried thyme

2 fresh or dried bay leaves

Freshly ground black pepper

3 tablespoons chopped fresh Italian parsley leaves

Garlic Toasts (recipe follows)

In a small bowl, sprinkle the saffron threads over the hot water and let stand for 30 minutes.

In a deep, heavy, nonreactive pot, heat 3 tablespoons of the olive oil over medium heat. Add the garlic and cook until lightly browned, about 2 minutes. Add the onions and cook, stirring, until wilted, about 4 minutes. Add the mussels, wine, thyme, bay leaves, and the saffron water. Season lightly with pepper. Cover the pot and bring to a boil. Cook, shaking the pot occasionally to cook the mussels evenly, just until the mussels open, 3 to 4 minutes.

Remove the mussels with a wire skimmer or slotted spoon to warm shallow bowls, discarding any that do not open. Strain the cooking liquid through a cheesecloth-lined sieve or coffee filter into a large skillet over high heat. Bring to a vigorous boil, then add the remaining 2 tablespoons olive oil and the parsley and boil until slightly reduced and thickened, about 4 minutes. Ladle the sauce over the mussels and serve hot, with the garlic toasts.

Garlic Toasts

Bruschetta all'Aglio

Serve these simple, crispy, garlicky toasts with any steamed shellfish dish to soak up the wonderful juices.

MAKES 12 TOASTS

Heat the oven to 375°F. Arrange the bread slices in a single layer on a baking sheet and bake until very lightly golden brown, about 10 minutes. Brush one side of the toasts with olive oil, then rub them with the garlic cloves—once or twice for a mild garlic flavor, more times for a more assertive flavor. Serve at room temperature.

Twelve ½-inch-thick slices Italian bread
Extra virgin olive oil
2 large garlic cloves, peeled

Razor Clams in Broth

Brodetto di Cannolicchi

Razor clams are best when four to five inches long. Like mussels, they sometimes have sand in them, but don't let that discourage you. Soak them for one to two hours according to the instructions on page 309 and they will purge themselves. If you cannot find razor clams in your market, substitute an equal amount of mussels, preferably the cultivated type.

MAKES 6 SERVINGS

5 tablespoons extra virgin olive oil

3 garlic cloves, crushed

2 pounds razor clams with shells,
    4 to 5 inches long, purged (see page 309)

1 cup dry white wine, such as Tocai

3 sprigs fresh thyme

½ cup finely chopped onions

1 tablespoon tomato paste

2 tablespoons fine plain dry bread crumbs

3 tablespoons chopped fresh Italian parsley
    leaves

Garlic Toasts (page 313; optional)

In a large, heavy pot, heat 3 tablespoons of the olive oil over moderate heat. Add the garlic and cook until lightly browned, about 2 minutes. Add the clams, wine, and thyme. Bring to a boil over high heat and cover the pot. Cook, shaking the pot occasionally, until the clams open, about 10 minutes.

Remove the clams with a slotted spoon or skimmer, reserving as much of the cooking liquid as possible. Discard any clams that do not open. Strain the cooking liquid through a cheesecloth-lined sieve or a coffee filter and reserve.

In a large skillet, heat the remaining 2 tablespoons olive oil over medium heat. Add the onions and cook, stirring, until wilted, about 4 minutes. Add the tomato paste and stir well, then add the strained cooking liquid, the bread crumbs, and parsley. Bring to a boil.

Meanwhile, remove the top shells from the clams.

When the sauce comes to a boil, add the clams and shake gently until heated through, 2 to 3 minutes. Arrange the clams on a warm platter. Spoon any sauce remaining in the skillet over the clams and serve with garlic toasts, if you like.

Cephalopods (Cefalopodi)

Cephalopods are creatures that do not have a spinal structure, or any bones at all. They have tentacles attached to their heads, and their bodies are loose and soft like a sac. Cephalopods include *calamari* (squid), *seppie* (cuttlefish), and *polipo* (octopus). When fresh, cephalopods should have shiny, clear-looking skin. Their color should be light, with the pigment spots quite visible. The eyes should be black and vivid, and the odor pleasant and sweet.

Squid (Calamari) The squid has ten arms, two of which have developed into longer tentacles, attached to the head. The head in turn joins the innards that are contained in, and protected by, the tubular body sac. Running along the innards is the silvery sac that contains the ink used in some recipes. Also inside the body sac is a transparent, cartilage-like "quill," so called because it is shaped exactly like the quill pens of old. When squid are fresh, the color pigments of the thin, mottled skin that cover the body range from reddish to violet. Squid can grow quite large—up to sixty feet in length—but the smaller they are, the sweeter and more tender they are. *Fragole di mare,* or sea strawberries, are thumbnail-size squid popular around Venice.

   To clean squid, hold the body in place while gently pulling the head and tentacles out. The innards should come out following the head. Cut off the tentacles just above the eyes. Pull out the "quill." The skin can be left on or peeled off, depending on the preparation or your preference. Cut off the pointed tip of the body sac and run cold water through the body to wash out any sand or debris. If the tentacles are large, they can be cut in half.

Octopus (Polipo) The octopus has a round sac for a body and head, with eight tentacles (arms) that spread out from the sac, each with a double row of suction cups. The color is gray pink.

   To clean octopus: Most octopus available in the market has been defrosted and is already cleaned. If you should need to clean an octopus, turn the sac inside out without detaching it. Scrape out everything from the sac and turn it right side out. Remove both eyes by cutting them out in a wedge shape with a small, sharp knife. Turn the octopus over and feel at the center of the tentacles for the "beaks," a pair of hard, round spheres located behind the mouth area. Press from behind with your thumbs to push out the beaks.

Clams with Tomato and Basil

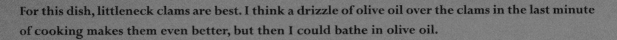 Vongole al Pomodoro e Basilico

For this dish, littleneck clams are best. I think a drizzle of olive oil over the clams in the last minute of cooking makes them even better, but then I could bathe in olive oil.

MAKES 6 FIRST-COURSE SERVINGS OR
3 MAIN-COURSE SERVINGS

5 tablespoons extra virgin olive oil

3 garlic cloves, peeled

½ teaspoon peperoncino (crushed red pepper)

3 pounds littleneck clams, cleaned according to the directions on page 309

½ cup dry white wine, such as Pinot Grigio

2 tablespoons fresh lemon juice

2 medium-size ripe tomatoes, cored, seeded, and cut into ½-inch cubes

2 scallions, chopped

10 fresh basil leaves, washed, dried, and cut into very thin strips

Salt

Garlic Toasts (page 313; optional)

In a wide, heavy casserole, heat 2 tablespoons of the olive oil over medium heat. Add the garlic and cook, stirring, until golden brown, about 2 minutes. Add the peperoncino and stir well, then add the clams and wine. Cover the pot, increase the heat to high, and cook, shaking the pot occasionally, until the clams open, about 7 minutes.

In the meantime, whisk the remaining 3 tablespoons olive oil and the lemon juice together in a small bowl. Add the tomatoes, scallions, and basil, stir well, and add salt to taste.

Transfer the clams with a wire skimmer or slotted spoon to a large serving bowl, discarding any with unopened shells. Carefully pour out 1 cup of the cooking liquid, leaving any grit behind in the casserole. Add this cooking liquid to the tomato mixture, stir, and pour over the clams. Toss lightly and serve with garlic toasts, if desired.

Baked Squid and Potatoes

Teglia di Calamari con Patate

This is one of those dishes that in its simplicity has all the complexity of a great meal. Serve hot with a salad and nothing else, or at room temperature as a first course in warmer weather.

MAKES 6 SERVINGS

Preheat the oven to 475°F.

Cut the bodies of the calamari crosswise into three pieces. In a large bowl, toss the calamari pieces and tentacles with the parsley, olive oil, salt, and pepper to taste until evenly coated. Add the potatoes and onions and toss well.

Transfer the mixture to a 14 × 12-inch baking pan, spreading it in an even layer. Pour the water over the top and cover the pan tightly with aluminum foil. Perforate the foil in several places with a fork and bake for 30 minutes.

Uncover the baking pan, turn the potatoes and calamari with a spatula, and cook, uncovered, turning the potatoes and calamari twice more, until golden brown and tender, about 20 minutes longer. Serve hot.

2 pounds medium-size calamari (about 12), cleaned according to the directions on page 315, with skin left on
1 cup lightly packed chopped fresh Italian parsley leaves
⅓ cup extra virgin olive oil
2 teaspoons fine sea salt
Freshly ground black pepper
1½ pounds baking (Idaho) potatoes, peeled and cut into ¼-inch-thick rounds
1 cup sliced onions
1 cup water

Stuffed Squid with Cannellini Beans

Calamari Ripieni Affogati con Cannellini

When filling the calamari, use an espresso spoon or a teaspoon and resist the temptation to over-fill the bodies—when cooked, the calamari shrink and so a small amount of filling will suffice.

MAKES 6 SERVINGS

For the beans

½ pound dried white beans, such as baby lima beans or cannellini beans, picked over and rinsed

2 fresh or dried bay leaves

Salt

2 tablespoons extra virgin olive oil

2 garlic cloves, crushed

Freshly ground black pepper

For the calamari

6 tablespoons extra virgin olive oil

3 tablespoons finely chopped onions

3 tablespoons finely chopped shallots

4 garlic cloves, finely chopped

12 squid with bodies 3 to 4 inches long (2½ pounds total), cleaned according to the directions on page 315, skin removed, and tentacles finely chopped

3 tablespoons shredded carrots

3 tablespoons finely diced zucchini

2 teaspoons chopped fresh thyme leaves or ½ teaspoon dried thyme

Salt and freshly ground black pepper

2 tablespoons Cognac

Place the beans in a medium-size bowl and pour in enough cool water to cover by 4 inches. Soak the beans for at least 8 hours, or overnight.

Drain the beans and place them in a medium-size saucepan. Pour in enough cold water to cover generously, then add the bay leaves. Bring the water to a boil over high heat. Adjust the heat to a simmer and cook the beans until tender, about 40 minutes. Add a pinch of salt about 30 minutes into the cooking time. Drain well.

In a large skillet, heat the olive oil over medium-high heat. Add the garlic, and cook until lightly browned, about 2 minutes. Add the beans to the skillet and stir for a few minutes, then season with salt and pepper. Discard the bay leaves and set the beans aside.

Prepare the squid. In a medium-size skillet, heat ¼ cup of the olive oil over medium heat. Add 2 tablespoons each of the onions and shallots and half of the chopped garlic and cook, stirring, until lightly golden, about 4 minutes. Add the chopped squid tentacles, the carrots, zucchini, and thyme, season lightly with salt and pepper, and cook until the squid and vegetables are lightly browned and the liquid has evaporated, about 10 minutes. Add the Cognac and bread crumbs and cook, stirring, for 5 minutes. Stir in ¼ cup of the parsley. Remove from the heat.

Using a small spoon—an espresso spoon is ideal—divide the bread crumb mixture among the calamari bodies. Seal the open end of each with a toothpick.

In a large skillet, heat the remaining 2 tablespoons olive oil over medium heat. Add the remaining onions, shallots, and garlic and cook until wilted, about 1 minute. Add the stuffed calamari, season with salt and the peperoncino, and cook, turning the calamari occasionally, until golden on all sides, about 6 minutes. Add the wine, reduce the heat to medium-low, and cook until the liquid is reduced by half, about 10 minutes. Add ½ cup of the fish stock and the butter and simmer, turning the calamari occasionally, until tender, about 10 minutes.

Add the cooked beans and the remaining ½ cup fish stock and ¼ cup parsley and simmer for 5 minutes. There should be enough liquid to coat the beans generously. If not, add water as needed. Check the seasonings and serve, ladling the bean mixture into warm shallow bowls and topping with the stuffed calamari, removing the toothpicks first.

2 tablespoons fine plain dry bread crumbs

½ cup loosely packed chopped fresh Italian parsley leaves

Pinch of peperoncino (crushed red pepper)

½ cup dry white wine, such as Pinot Grigio

1 cup Fish Stock (see Note on page 333) or Vegetable Broth (page 81)

2 tablespoons unsalted butter

Simply Braised Octopus
🐙 Polipo in Umido 🐙

When freshly caught, octopus can be tough. I remember that the fishermen would beat the octopus with a wooden mallet or against the sea rocks to render them tender. The defrosted octopus you buy at the fishmonger has been tenderized by the freezing process and is quite good. Some of the best octopus I have found in the market comes from Mexico and weighs sixteen to twenty ounces each. At this size, they are meaty enough but tender.

MAKES 6 SERVINGS

3 tablespoons extra virgin olive oil

8 garlic cloves, peeled

4 sprigs fresh Italian parsley

2 fresh or dried bay leaves

½ teaspoon peperoncino (crushed red pepper)

Two 1¼-pound octopus, cleaned according to the directions on page 315

Basic Polenta (page 198; optional)

Combine the olive oil, garlic, parsley, bay leaves, and peperoncino in a wide, heavy casserole. Place the octopus head side down in the casserole and place the casserole over medium heat. When the liquid in the casserole begins to simmer, adjust the heat to very low. Cover the casserole and cook, shaking gently occasionally, until a fork senses a little resistance but slides out easily when poked into the thickest part of an octopus tentacle, 45 minutes to 1 hour. The cooking liquid should be syrupy, purple-reddish in color, and flavorful.

Meanwhile, prepare the polenta, if using.

Place the octopus side by side on a large platter and spoon the cooking liquid around them. With scissors, cut each octopus in three somewhat equal body parts with some tentacles attached to each. Spoon some polenta, if using, onto each plate and top with a portion of octopus and some of the juices, or serve the polenta family-style separately.

Gastropods (Gasteropodi)

Gastropods are creatures living in single shells, such as *patella* (limpets), *chiocciola marina* (sea snails), *ricci di mare* (sea urchins), and *murice sconciglio* (sea conch).

Sea Urchins (Ricci di Mare) Freshness is an absolute must with sea urchins—they should taste like a mouthful of ocean. To clean an urchin, line the palm of one hand—not your knife-wielding hand—with a folded damp kitchen towel. Set the urchin in the center of your palm with its mouth facing up. With a pair of sharp scissors, cut out a circular opening around the mouth. Drain out and reserve the liquid and, with a teaspoon, clean out the viscera. All that should be left is the five-pointed orange coral attached to the top part of the shell. Scoop out the coral gently with a teaspoon. Strain the liquid to use it in the recipe.

Sea Conch (Murice Sconciglii) Sea conch can be found occasionally at the fishmonger in its shell and still alive. The shell measures about four inches long and is similar in shape to the large conch shells found in the Caribbean, but it has a thin "tail" protruding from its narrower end. Live *sconciglio* in the shell can be easily removed after cooking. More common are *sconciglii,* which have been removed from their shells, parboiled, and frozen. In both cases, the end result is quite good.

Directions for preparing both types of sea conch are given in the recipe for Sea Conch Salad (page 232).

Note: Neither of these creatures is commonly found in the market; sea urchins can be found occasionally in large urban centers with ethnically diverse populations and sea conch can be found in Italian neighborhoods, either in the shell or shelled, partially cooked, and frozen. Or, if you are lucky, you may be able to gather them yourself. Either way, I have included recipes for these creatures here in the hope that they will intrigue you enough to seek them out. They are an integral part of the Italian culinary repertoire, and I couldn't have left them out.

Capellini with Sea Urchins

⚿ Capellini con Ricci di Mare ⚿

The beauty and flavor of this dish lie in the brininess of the sea urchin—to cook it is to alter that. Heat the sauce only by tossing it with the pasta, never directly over the flame. To make sure the pasta is warm when you serve it, warm the plates beforehand and serve it quickly.

MAKES 6 SERVINGS

24 sea urchins

½ cup extra virgin olive oil

3 garlic cloves, crushed

½ teaspoon peperoncino (crushed red pepper)

6 quarts salted water

3 tablespoons chopped fresh Italian parsley leaves

Freshly ground black pepper

2 medium-size vine-ripened tomatoes, cored, peeled (see page 141), seeded, and finely diced

1 pound capellini (angel hair) pasta

Clean the sea urchins as described on page 321. (You should have about 2 to 2½ cups coral.) Filter the liquid through a cheesecloth-lined sieve or coffee filter and set aside.

In a large skillet, heat 2 tablespoons of the olive oil over medium heat. Add 2 of the garlic cloves and the peperoncino. Cook, stirring, until the garlic is lightly browned, then remove the skillet from the heat.

In a large pot, bring the salted water to a boil.

Meanwhile, in a bowl, whisk the sea urchin coral, parsley, the remaining clove of garlic, and salt and pepper to taste together until blended. Beat in the remaining 6 tablespoons olive oil and the reserved sea urchin liquid. Stir in the tomatoes.

Stir the capellini into the boiling water. Cover the pot and reheat to boiling, stirring occasionally. Partially cover the pot and cook, stirring once or twice, until the pasta is al dente—tender but firm to the bite—about 3 minutes. Reserve ½ cup of the pasta cooking water and drain the pasta.

Return the skillet containing the garlic and peperoncino to medium heat. Add the capellini and the reserved cooking water, toss well for 1 to 2 minutes, and remove from the heat. Add the sea urchin mixture, toss the capellini well with the sauce, and serve on warm plates.

Sea Conch Salad

Insalata di Murice (Sconciglii)

Sconciglii—with their spiral shell that tapers to a fine point—may intrigue you as you are choosing your daily catch. Don't be intimidated by the shell; sea conch are quite easy to prepare and make a delicious appetizer salad or main course. This recipe makes six appetizer portions; double it for six main-course servings.

MAKES 6 FIRST-COURSE SERVINGS

Add the bay leaves to a large pot of water and bring to a boil. Add the sea conch in the shell and cook for 30 minutes; if using shelled parboiled conch, cook them for 15 minutes. Reserve ¼ cup of the cooking liquid and drain the conch. Cool completely.

To remove the sea conch from their shells, insert a skewer into each shell and through the meat, then pull the conch from the shell. Each conch will have a fingernail-shaped cartilage-like seal at the opening that should be cut away and discarded.

To clean *sconciglii* after cooking, cut along the outer curved side of each conch until you reach the digestive sac, which is about one inch long and the diameter of a thin pencil and runs from the middle of the body to the tail. Scrape out the sac. The rest is all good to eat. With a sharp knife, slice the body lengthwise into very thin slivers, like corn chips.

In a medium-sized bowl, combine the sliced conch with the remaining ingredients except the salt and toss well. Add the reserved cooking liquid and salt to taste and toss again. To serve, spoon the salad into mounds in the center of serving plates. Spoon any remaining dressing in the bowl over the salad.

2 fresh or dried bay leaves

1½ pounds sea conch in the shell (about 12) or 1 pound (about 10 pieces) shelled parboiled sea conch, defrosted if frozen, and washed

1 cup chopped tender inner celery stalks without leaves

½ cup sliced pitted green olives, such as Cerignola or Picholine

½ cup sliced pitted black olives, such as Gaeta or Calamata

3 tablespoons chopped fresh Italian parsley leaves

3 tablespoons extra virgin olive oil

2 tablespoons red wine vinegar

1 garlic clove, finely chopped

½ teaspoon peperoncino (crushed red pepper)

Salt

Crustaceans

(*Crostacei*)

Crustaceans, or shellfish, are creatures that live in a calciferous shell, usually have ten legs for crawling, and antennas. For our purposes, there are basically three categories: prawns and shrimp, lobsters, and crabs.

The meat of shellfish is sweet and tasty and quite sought after. For best results, buy either shellfish that is still alive (crabs and lobsters) or that has been frozen immediately after being caught and processed (most shrimp and prawns). When shellfish is fresh, the shell will be shiny and clean, and the eyes black and bright. An opaque hue to the shell and eyes is an indication that the shellfish is less than fresh. Let your sense of smell be your guide when choosing shellfish, as it should be with all fish. If there is any odor of ammonia, do not buy it.

Shellfish does not require a long cooking time; in fact, it gets tougher with long cooking.

Prawns and Shrimp (Gamberoni e Gamberi)

These can be found fresh with their heads attached, but in most instances your fishmonger will have headless defrosted shrimp, which are very good if they've been handled properly. Look for the ones that are white or light pink in color—these are the best quality. Their price is usually tied to their size—the larger the shrimp, the higher its price. Most shrimp in retail markets are labeled "jumbo," "large," "medium," etc., which can be vague or confusing. A better system is to ask specifically what size the shrimp are: At the time of processing, all shrimp are sorted according to size and the boxes are marked with the correct size. "U/6," or "under six," for example, means that there are six shrimp or fewer to a pound, and each shrimp will be about 2½ ounces—a large shrimp indeed. Shrimp marked "U/16" contain sixteen or fewer shrimp per pound, with each shrimp weighing about an ounce, and so on. Shrimp sizes are often marked with two numbers: "21/25," for example, meaning that there are between twenty-one and twenty-five shrimp per pound. For sauces, pasta, and risotto 31/35 (or U/35) shrimp are fine. Larger shrimp are perfect for sautéing, stuffing, grilling, or broiling.

When you buy shrimp, choose shrimp that have been recently defrosted, smell clean and fresh, and have no trace of ammonia odor. Store them in the coldest part of the refrigerator for no more than a day.

To prepare shrimp: Peel off the shell a couple of segments at a time, removing the small legs along with it. Leave the tail attached or peel it off, depending on the recipe. To devein the shrimp, make a shallow cut with a paring knife down the outer curved side of the shrimp and pull out the vein that runs the length of the shrimp. This vein can be faint and barely noticeable, or dark and quite thick.

Lobsters (Aragosta)

American lobsters, sometimes called Maine lobsters—those with two large claws of different sizes—are some of the best in the world. The lobster should be alive and kicking—waving its claws and flicking its tail. Here's a good test for quality you can perform if the lobster's claws are secured: With your fingers, grasp the lobster just behind the head and squeeze. The shell should be firm and not buckle under your touch. When you pick it up, it should feel heavy and full, and the claws should be tight and close to the body, not limp and hanging. The 1- to 1¼-pound lobsters are considered small, but they are quite sweet and excellent for pasta sauces or soups. The 1½- to 2½-pound lobsters are ideal for grilling or broiling. Beyond these weights, they can be impressive and sweet but sometimes tough.

To clean a lobster: Place the lobster in the freezer until its movements have become very slow, about 30 minutes to 1 hour. Position the lobster firmly on a cutting board with the tail flippers down and the claws and tail stretched out. Hold the lobster firmly by the tail and cut the head section lengthwise in half by inserting a heavy, sharp knife where the tail meets the head section and bringing the knife down through the head to the cutting board in a swift motion. Turn the lobster around and do the same to the tail. The lobster should be completely split in half. Near each of the eye sockets, there is a digestive sac. Scrape it out, then pull out the dark vein that runs along the tail. (The female lobsters caught just before spawning contain a dark green roe in both the body cavity and tail. The liver, called the tomalley, is a paler green color, but turns pink when cooked. Both are very good, either cooked in a whole lobster and eaten as is, or forced through a sieve and stirred into a sauce at the last possible moment.) Separate the tail pieces from the head pieces and, with scissors, cut off the claws and the legs. The lobster is ready to be cooked.

King Crab

King crab is similar to, but larger than, the *granzevole* my Uncle Emilio was so happy to catch. King crab legs are usually sold frozen or defrosted, rarely fresh. The larger they are, the more meat they contain in proportion to the shell, and the juicier that meat will be. Larger legs are more expensive. When buying frozen king crab legs, look at the end of the leg that was attached to the body. It should be solid and white, not straw-like and yellow, which can be a sign of freezer burn. Bring the crab to your nose and take a sniff. If it smells fishy, it most likely has been defrosted for a while, or has been refrozen.

King crab can be eaten warm after a quick cooking in a vegetable-seasoned broth, as described in the recipe for King Crab Salad with Citrus Fruit on page 329, or chilled and turned into any number of cold salads.

Shrimp and Melon Salad

Coda di Gamberi con Melone

This is a refreshing and simple appetizer that can also be served in larger portions as a main course.

MAKES 6 FIRST-COURSE SERVINGS

2 quarts water

1 medium-size onion, sliced

1 celery stalk, cut into pieces

2 fresh or dried bay leaves

1 pound medium-size shrimp (about 36)

8 cups diced (¾-inch) peeled ripe
  cantaloupe or honeydew melon

2 tablespoons fresh lemon juice

2 tablespoons extra virgin olive oil

Salt

1 teaspoon freshly ground black pepper, or
  more to taste

6 sprigs fresh mint

In a large saucepan, bring the water to a boil with the onion, celery, and bay leaves. Boil for 20 minutes. Add the shrimp and cook for 3 minutes. Immediately drain the shrimp and let cool.

Meanwhile, combine 3 cups of the melon, the lemon juice, and olive oil in a blender. Blend at low speed until completely smooth. Pass the melon puree through a fine sieve to remove the fibers, season lightly with salt, and set aside.

Remove the shells and tails from the shrimp. Cut down the outer curved side of the shrimp to expose the dark vein that runs along the back and scrape away the vein.

In a large bowl, gently toss the remaining 5 cups diced melon, the shrimp, and pepper together.

To serve, ladle some of the melon puree into the center of each of six salad plates. Set the shrimp and melon salad on top and decorate each plate with a mint sprig.

Lobster in Zesty Tomato Sauce

☙ Aragosta in Brodetto ☙

Lobster cooked slowly with tomato, vinegar, and onions is delicious on its own, with polenta (page 198), or with pasta—either freshly made *garganelli* or store-bought spaghetti.

The vinegar in this recipe comes from an old technique used by Venetian sailors to preserve their food—it actually gives a nice balance to the sweetness of the lobster.

MAKES 6 SERVINGS

Cut the live lobsters into pieces according to the directions on page 325. If you plan to serve the lobster with pasta, bring the salted water to a boil.

In a large skillet, heat the vegetable oil over medium-high heat. Meanwhile, lightly coat the exposed meat of the lobster tails with flour, shaking off any excess. The oil is hot enough when a corner of a lobster tail dipped in it gives off a lively sizzle. Add the lobster tails, meat side down, and cook, shaking the skillet occasionally, until golden brown, about 2 minutes. Remove the tails from the skillet and set them aside.

In a large, wide, nonreactive saucepan or small stockpot, heat ⅓ cup of the olive oil over medium heat. Add the onions and scallions and cook, stirring, until translucent, 3 to 4 minutes. Add the lobster body pieces and cook, stirring, until they turn bright red, about 5 minutes. Stir in the tomato paste and cook for 5 minutes. Blend the vinegar with the hot water, add to the pan, and bring to a full boil. Add the tomatoes, parsley, and salt, bring to a boil, and cook for 3 minutes. Season with peperoncino.

Six 1¼-pound lobsters
6 quarts salted water (optional)
⅓ cup vegetable oil
All-purpose flour for dredging
½ cup extra virgin olive oil
1½ cups diced onions
1 cup diced scallions
6 tablespoons tomato paste
½ cup red wine vinegar
3 cups hot water
4 cups canned crushed Italian plum
    tomatoes
½ cup loosely packed chopped fresh
    Italian parsley leaves
½ teaspoon salt
Peperoncino (crushed red pepper)
1 recipe *garganelli* (page 92) or
    1 pound spaghetti (optional)

Remove the lobster bodies with tongs, allowing all the juices to drain back into the sauce. (The bodies should be reserved for another use or, if the meal is informal, they can be served on a communal platter in the center of the table. The most delicate meat is in the bodies and should not be wasted.) Add the claws to the pan and cook for 7 minutes. (If you plan to serve the *brodetto* with pasta, add the pasta to the boiling water at this point.)

Add the reserved lobster tails and the remaining olive oil. Adjust the heat as necessary and simmer until the lobster tails are fully cooked, 3 to 5 minutes longer, skimming off all surface foam. Remove the tails and claws and keep warm under a sheet of aluminum foil. Bring the sauce to a boil and boil until slightly thickened.

Arrange the lobster pieces on a warm platter and spoon the hot sauce over them or, to serve the *brodetto* with pasta, drain the pasta and return it to the pot. Add half the lobster sauce and toss to coat over low heat. Transfer the pasta to a platter and flank with the lobster pieces. Spoon the remaining sauce over the lobster.

King Crab Salad with Citrus Fruit

 Insalata di Granzevola con Agrumi

Traditionally the spiny crab found in the Adriatic is used to make this salad, but king crab is readily available here and makes a delicious substitute. About one pound of the meat from Dungeness or blue claw crabs is also a good substitute but requires some work freeing it from the shell. The fresh lump or jumbo lump crabmeat sold in containers by your fishmonger is the easiest alternative, but also the most expensive.

These quantities are for appetizer servings; double them for main-course servings.

MAKES 6 FIRST-COURSE SERVINGS

Choose a pot large enough to hold the crab legs comfortably and fill it to about 3 inches from the top with water. Bring to a boil, add the onion, celery, carrots, and bay leaves, and boil for 15 minutes. Add the crab legs and cook for 5 minutes. Remove the crab and let cool. Discard the cooking liquid.

Meanwhile, in a small bowl, whisk the olive oil, lemon and orange juices, and salt together until the dressing is golden yellow and emulsified. Whisk in the parsley.

With sturdy kitchen scissors, cut apart the crab legs between their joints and pull out the meat with a cocktail fork or skewer. Cut each leg segment open with the kitchen shears if you have difficulty removing the meat from the shell. Cut the crabmeat into 2-inch pieces, removing any cartilage as you go. Divide the crabmeat evenly and place in small mounds in the center of six salad plates. Place a cluster of salad leaves next to each. Arrange the grapefruit and orange segments decoratively around the crabmeat. Grind some fresh pepper and drizzle the citrus dressing over the crabmeat and salad leaves and serve.

Note: To remove grapefruit and orange segments from the fruit, cut away all the peel and white pith with a small sharp knife. Hold the fruit over a bowl and, with the knife, cut along each membrane to free the citrus segments, allowing the juice to drip into the bowl. Reserve some of the orange juice for the dressing and the rest as a reward for the cook.

1 small onion, cut into quarters

2 celery stalks, cut into 2-inch pieces

2 medium-size carrots, cut into ½-inch-thick slices

2 fresh or dried bay leaves

2 pounds king crab legs (2 to 3 whole legs), defrosted if frozen

¼ cup extra virgin olive oil

3 tablespoons fresh lemon juice

2 tablespoons fresh orange juice

Pinch of salt

2 tablespoons chopped fresh Italian parsley leaves

6 ounces young salad leaves, such as baby arugula or tender baby lettuces, or mesclun greens, washed and dried

12 grapefruit segments without membranes (see Note)

12 blood orange or navel orange segments without membranes (see Note)

Freshly ground black pepper

Finfish

(Pesce di Spina)

With regard to finfish, I will talk about only one category—those with some sort of spinal cord and scales. The most important issue here is the freshness of the fish you buy; it is more important than the actual preparation.

Fresh fish should be firm to the touch and have shiny bulging eyes and a glow to the body. The gills should be bright red. When buying fillets or fish steaks, look for the firmness, follow your nose, and make sure that the blood lines in fish like swordfish, tuna, and shark are bright red, not brown.

Fillet of Halibut with a Savory Tomato Sauce

❦ Rombo al Sugo ❦

Halibut is not found in the Mediterranean; however, its Italian cousin, the *rombo*—what the French call *turbot*—is. All are in the same family of flatfish that includes flounder and sole.

MAKES 6 SERVINGS

In a medium-size skillet, heat 6 tablespoons of the oil over medium heat. Add the celery and 4 of the garlic cloves and cook, stirring, until the celery is wilted, about 3 minutes. Add the tomatoes and parsley, season with salt and pepper, and cook until the sauce is lightly thickened, about 10 minutes. Keep warm.

Meanwhile, in a large skillet, heat 2 tablespoons of the remaining oil over medium heat. Add the remaining 2 garlic cloves and cook, stirring, until golden brown, about 3 minutes. Add about half the spinach and the peperoncino and cook, tossing, until the spinach is wilted. Add the remaining spinach a handful at a time, adding more as each handful in the skillet wilts. Cover the skillet and cook, stirring occasionally, until the spinach is tender but still bright green. The whole process should take about 5 minutes. Cover and keep warm.

Pat the halibut fillets dry with paper towels. Season them generously with salt and pepper and coat them with the remaining ¼ cup oil. Heat a large skillet, preferably nonstick, over medium-high heat. Add the halibut and cook, turning once, until well browned on both sides and barely opaque in the center, about 8 minutes. Drain any oil from the pan.

Drain any liquid from the spinach and divide the spinach among six serving plates. Top with the pieces of halibut. Remove the garlic cloves from the tomato sauce and spoon the sauce over and around the fish. Serve immediately.

¾ cup extra virgin olive oil

2 celery stalks, diced

6 garlic cloves, crushed

One 28-ounce can peeled Italian plum tomatoes, crushed lightly and passed through a food mill or coarse sieve

½ cup loosely packed minced fresh Italian parsley leaves

Salt and freshly ground black pepper to taste

1½ pounds fresh spinach, tough stems removed, thoroughly washed and drained

Pinch of peperoncino (crushed red pepper)

Six 5- to 6-ounce pieces halibut fillet

Pan-Roasted Monkfish with Thyme, Potatoes, Leeks, and Truffle Oil

Rospo con Porri al Timo e Olio Tartufato

The intense aroma of truffle oil is best enjoyed when it is uncooked, drizzled over a finished dish, as it is here. You can buy truffle oil in specialty food stores, especially those that carry Italian and French products.

MAKES 6 SERVINGS

2 large baking (Idaho) potatoes, (about 1 pound)

Salt

1 pound (about 3 medium-size) leeks, white and light green parts, cut into thin rounds, well washed and drained

2 pounds monkfish fillets

¾ cup extra virgin olive oil

3 garlic cloves, sliced

Freshly ground black pepper

All-purpose flour for dredging

1 cup dry white wine

½ cup fish stock (see Note) or Vegetable Broth (page 81)

3 tablespoons unsalted butter

4 sprigs fresh thyme

2 tablespoons truffle oil

2 tablespoons chopped fresh Italian parsley leaves

Place the potatoes in a large saucepan and cover generously with water. Add salt and bring to a boil. Continue to boil until the potatoes are tender, about 30 minutes. Drain the potatoes and let stand just until cool enough to handle. Peel and slice the potatoes ½ inch thick while still quite warm.

Blanch the leek slices in a medium-size saucepan of boiling salted water for 3 minutes. Drain thoroughly.

With a paring knife, remove the outer mottled gray membranes and any dark red portions from the fillets. Slice the fish on a slight angle into ½-inch-thick medallions. Place the medallions a few at a time between two sheets of plastic wrap and pound them lightly with the flat side of a meat mallet or the bottom of a small heavy saucepan to flatten them slightly.

In a large skillet, heat 3 tablespoons of the olive oil over medium-high heat. Add the blanched leeks and sliced potatoes, season them with salt and pepper, and cook, turning often, until golden brown, about 12 minutes. Remove the skillet from the heat and cover to keep the vegetables warm.

Meanwhile, sprinkle the monkfish slices with salt and coat them lightly with flour, tapping off any excess. In a large skillet, heat the remaining 9 tablespoons olive oil and the garlic over medium heat. Add as many of the monkfish slices as will fit in a single layer and cook, turning once, until golden brown on both sides, 5 to 7 minutes. Remove the monkfish to a plate and cover to keep warm; repeat with the remaining monkfish.

Drain the oil from the skillet. Add the wine and bring to a boil, scraping the sides and bottom of the skillet to remove any browned bits from the skillet. Add the fish stock, butter, and thyme and season lightly with salt and pepper. Simmer until the sauce is reduced by about half and lightly thickened, about 7 minutes. Strain the sauce through a sieve and check the final seasoning.

Divide the potatoes and leeks among six warm dinner plates. Drizzle the vegetables with the truffle oil and top with the slices of monkfish. Spoon the sauce over the fish and vegetables and sprinkle with the parsley.

Note: To make a quick fish stock, see step 1 of the Red Snapper and Rice Soup recipe on page 66 or follow the instructions in step 1 of the following recipe, using the frames from two 4-pound fish such as grouper, snapper, bass, or blackfish.

Grouper in White Sauce Served with a Side Dish of Pasta

Cernia di Scoglio alla Siciliana

Fortunato Nicotra is the Executive Chef at our restaurant Felidia. He has been with us for two years, and he brought with him his own personality and flavors. In all three of our restaurants, I believe in combining young Italian talent with American talent to maintain the authenticity of the original culture within its new home. Fortunato is splendid in exalting the pristine flavors of seafood—his appreciation for less fuss always results in more honest flavor. This is a recipe from his native Sicily.

Grouper is a fish that thrives in tropical and subtropical waters. In the States, it is abundant in the Caribbean waters off Florida and can be found as far north as the Carolinas. In the Mediterranean, it is well known to the French and Italians for its deliciously flavored, firm, white flesh. It is also a specialty of the cuisines of North Africa. This recipe is one of the few Italian dishes where pasta is served as a side dish.

MAKES 6 SERVINGS

Two 4-pound groupers, filleted,
    frames and heads reserved
8 quarts water
1 medium-size onion, quartered
2 cups diced celery (about 2 stalks)
2 cups diced carrots (about 3 medium-
    size carrots)
1 tablespoon extra virgin olive oil
2 garlic cloves, sliced
2 medium-size vine-ripened tomatoes,
    cored, seeded, and chopped
⅓ cup small (nonpareil) capers, drained
1 sprig fresh Italian parsley
Salt
1 pound linguine

In a large pot, combine the heads and fish frames—tails, and bones—with 2 quarts of the water, the onion, celery, and carrots. Bring to a boil over high heat, then adjust the level of heat to a simmer. Skim off any foam that rises to the surface as the broth comes to a boil. Simmer the broth for 40 minutes, skimming the surface occasionally. It should be very light in color and clear. Strain the broth through a very fine sieve or cheesecloth and set aside.

Meanwhile, cut each of the fillets into three equal pieces. Trim any bones or scales from the fillet pieces. In a wide, deep pan, heat the olive oil over medium heat. Add the garlic and cook, stirring, until golden, about 1 minute. Add the tomatoes, capers, and parsley and cook until the tomatoes are very soft, about 15 minutes.

Add the strained fish broth to the tomatoes and bring to a boil. Adjust the level of heat to a simmer, cover the pan, and cook for 15 minutes. Season to taste with salt. Meanwhile, bring the remaining 6 quarts water to a boil in a large pot and salt generously.

Arrange the pieces of grouper, skin side up, in a single layer in the sauce. (If necessary, divide the sauce between two large skillets.) Cover and cook over very low heat until the fish is cooked through, about 10 minutes.

Meanwhile, stir the linguine into the boiling water and cook, stirring occasionally, until al dente— tender but firm—about 8 minutes. Drain the linguine and return it to the pot.

Remove the fish fillets to a baking pan or platter and cover to keep warm. Add about half the sauce to the cooked pasta and toss for 1 to 2 minutes over low heat. Divide the pasta among six shallow bowls and place one piece of grouper on top. Spoon the remaining sauce over the pasta and serve immediately.

Note: If you prefer to serve the grouper without the skin, it is easier to remove after the fish is cooked: Simply peel the skin off with the help of a fork after removing the fish from the sauce.

Whole Roasted Striped Bass

Branzino al Forno

Cooking fish whole—on the bone with the head and tail attached—is the best way to eat fish. To my taste, the meat around the bones is always sweeter and tastier. American striped bass—like its Mediterranean counterpart *branzino*—is a rockfish, thriving near shores. The texture of the meat of striped bass is juicy, flaky, tasty, and very delicate. With a drizzle of good virgin olive oil and lemon, it is sublime in its simplicity.

MAKES 6 SERVINGS

For the garlic-infused oil

1½ cups extra virgin olive oil

8 garlic cloves, sliced

1 teaspoon salt

½ teaspoon freshly ground black pepper

For the fish

12 small red potatoes (about 1 pound)

6 whole striped bass (each about 1¼ pounds), cleaned and scaled

6 fresh or dried bay leaves

6 sprigs fresh rosemary

3 medium-size red onions, cut into ⅓-inch-thick slices

6 small, firm vine-ripened tomatoes, cut in half

Salt and freshly ground black pepper

1½ cups dry white wine

¼ cup fine plain dry bread crumbs

1 teaspoon fresh thyme leaves

About half an hour before roasting the fish, prepare the garlic-infused oil. In a small bowl, blend the olive oil, garlic, salt, and pepper. Allow the sauce to steep for 30 minutes.

In a large pot of boiling salted water, cook the potatoes until almost completely tender, about 10 minutes. Drain and let stand until cool enough to handle. Cut the potatoes in half, then cut a thin sliver from the round part of each potato half so it will sit flat during roasting.

Preheat the oven to 475°F. Use some of the garlic-infused oil to grease two large (at least 22 × 18 inches), heavy roasting pans, preferably with low sides. Brush each fish on both sides with the garlic oil and wrap the tails in aluminum foil. Place 1 bay leaf and 1 sprig of rosemary in the cavity of each fish. Arrange the fish in the prepared pans, leaving as much space between them, and between the sides of the pans, as possible. Arrange the potato halves, cut side up, the onion slices, and tomato halves around the fish so as not to overlap each other.

Season the fish and vegetables with salt and pepper and divide the wine between the pans. Bake until the fish and vegetables begin to brown, about 20 minutes, drizzling occasionally with about ½ cup of the garlic-infused oil. Rotate the roasting pans in the oven if necessary to cook the fish evenly.

To serve

5 tablespoons fresh lemon juice

3 tablespoons minced fresh
Italian parsley leaves

Salt and freshly ground black pepper

Meanwhile, in a small bowl, toss the bread crumbs with 1 tablespoon of the remaining garlic-infused olive oil and the thyme and set aside. (The rest of the garlic oil will be used as the base of a sauce to be served with the fish.)

Sprinkle all the vegetables with the seasoned bread crumbs and return to the oven until the fish is flaky and completely cooked along the backbone and the vegetables are golden, about 10 minutes longer. (If the vegetables are not golden brown at this point, remove the fish from the baking pans and combine the vegetables in one of the pans. Broil the vegetables under a preheated broiler, about 4 inches from the heat, until the bread crumbs are golden brown, about 2 minutes. You don't want to overcook the fish for the sake of browning the vegetables.)

Stir the lemon juice and parsley into the remaining garlic-infused oil and season with salt and pepper. Place one fish on each plate and flank with the vegetables. Spoon any juices from the baking pans over each serving, then stir the lemon-parsley sauce well and spoon a little over each serving. Set the rest of the sauce on the table for passing as the fish is being enjoyed.

Swordfish in Sweet-and-Sour Sauce

Pesce Spada in Agrodolce

This dish is a marriage of Sicily and the great Modenese product, balsamic vinegar. Balsamic vinegar is made in the area of Modena from the juice of the Trebbiano grape. Traditional balsamic vinegar must spend at least five years in wooden barrels before being bottled. It continues to age after bottling—in some cases for a century or longer—and with the passage of time, it can transform from a condiment to a digestif and finally to a medicinal remedy.

MAKES 6 SERVINGS

Six 6-ounce skinless swordfish steaks, each about ⅓ inch thick

Salt and freshly ground black pepper

All-purpose flour for dredging

¼ cup vegetable oil

2 teaspoons extra virgin olive oil

2 teaspoons unsalted butter

1 cup dry white wine, such as Pinot Grigio or Tocai

½ cup balsamic vinegar, preferably aged at least 6 years

3 tablespoons small (nonpareil) capers, drained

Season both sides of the swordfish steaks lightly with salt and pepper. Dredge each piece in flour to coat both sides and shake off any excess.

In a large, nonreactive skillet, heat the vegetable oil over medium-high heat. Add the steaks and cook, turning once, until browned and cooked through, about 1½ minutes on each side. (If the steaks do not fit into the skillet in a single layer, cook them in batches.) Transfer the steaks to a platter and cover with aluminum foil to keep warm.

Discard the vegetable oil and carefully wipe out the skillet with several thicknesses of paper towels. Add the olive oil, butter, and a pinch of flour to the skillet. Place over medium heat, shaking the pan occasionally, until the butter is lightly browned, about 2 minutes. Add the wine and vinegar and bring to a boil. Boil, shaking the pan, until reduced and thickened to a light syrup, about 4 minutes. Stir in the drained capers, then spoon the sauce over the swordfish on the platter and serve immediately.

Note: If you like your fish well done, return the steaks to the finished sauce in the skillet and cook for an additional minute before serving.

Sweets

Dolci

I believe the Italians must have the largest repertoire of dessert recipes. It is no wonder; we are credited with spreading the art of pastry making to the rest of Europe. During the Renaissance, the cuisine of Italy—along with its art, music, and literature—flourished, and the Italian pastry cooks quickly positioned themselves as leaders in the art of pastry making. The Venetians were the first to introduce sugar to Europe and they used it in lavish productions of desserts and confections at state dinners, grand banquets, and feasts during the period when they dominated the spice trade.

Dolci, or desserts, always represent a special moment or

occasion in Italy—an extra indulgence to celebrate a religious holiday, private celebration, or special occasion. As in many cultures, most Italian dessert recipes are tied to religious observances. More than any other category of food, desserts recall special memories for all of us.

The dessert-making ritual is one that we Italians like best—maybe because desserts were so special to us as children growing up. Often, desserts were made for important occasions at my house. I remember most fondly the ritual of making *pinza* (Easter bread) at Grandma Rosa's house. The communal oven was in the courtyard in the middle of town. Maria was the official keeper, and it would be lit every second day. The townswomen would knead their breads according to their places in line, each one having to bring her own supply of wood in advance—always enough to bake her own bread.

We kids would run from house to house to advise our mothers and grandmothers of the readiness of the ovens for the next batch. Between batches the oven was brushed with a broom made out of *bussolo,* or branches tied to a long stick with wire. Their leaves would crackle like popcorn under the intense heat of the oven.

The women came—one by one—with the kneading boards lined with the puffy loaves of bread wrapped like babies. If it was cool, they would cover them with a blanket. "Risen bread should never 'catch a cold' or be in a draft," said Grandma. The women used the same board to take the baked bread home. If the loaves were well risen and high, they would carry them home uncovered, for everyone to see and praise. If the bread was not perfect, you can bet it was wrapped tightly, and taken home quickly.

The day before Easter Sunday was the best day to be near the oven—everybody was baking their Easter bread and the children made little dough dolls called *titole* or *puppa con uova,* with a colored boiled egg for the head surrounded by dough that was braided into a body. We played "mommy" with our *puppa* dolls, wrapping them in blankets and caring for them, but slowly our maternal instincts gave way to hunger and we would begin to nibble the *puppa* doll under its little blanket, beginning at the feet, until we were left with just the egg.

When Istria was given to what was then Yugoslavia after Italy's defeat in World War II, Communism was implemented. There were no private enterprises; everyone worked for the state. And if you worked for the state, you could not practice religion. But in the small towns, the people who worked the land still followed their religion and attended church secretly, my grandparents among them. I went to church with my grandmother and Santola Maria, my grandfather's sister, and the others, mostly older people and children. I did not go all that often, but I remember the Easter Sunday masses. Grandma would prepare two loaves of the *pinza* and tie them up in a kitchen towel along with hard-boiled eggs and scallions. At the end of mass, we would line up the gifts that we had brought at the altar, and they would be blessed. When we came home, the whole family sat at the table and recited our prayers before *merenda* (brunch). The *pinze* were sliced, the scallions were cut at the tips like brushes, and the boiled eggs were peeled. There was always a plate of coarse sea salt on the table too.

We dipped the scallions and the eggs lightly in the salt and ate them with slices of *pinza*. There was symbolism in this ritual besides good food. The salt signified the basic necessities of life, the scallions represented the land, and the eggs symbolized rebirth and continuation. *Pinze* were the sign of well-being and prosperity. We thanked God for his gifts that fed us and asked Him to bless us for another year.

Easter Bread

Pinza

Most of the Christian Mediterranean cultures have some form of rich, festive egg bread that they prepare for the Holy Week before Easter. This is when *pinze* were made at our house. It is a tradition that is still strong in the Veneto region of Italy. The *panettone* and *colomba* cakes often found today in the country are derivatives of *pinza*.

Making good *pinza* requires some understanding of leavening and bread making, which I have described carefully below. It also requires patience, because the dough, rich with eggs and butter, requires several long risings.

Serve slices of *pinza* with espresso, tea, or, in the morning, with *caffè latte*. For a richer dessert, top with whipped cream or mascarpone and berries, or enjoy it as is on a wonderful festive table or for brunch on Easter Sunday. The loaves keep well for one week at room temperature if sealed in plastic wrap or for six to eight weeks in the freezer. For the effort, it pays to make a larger quality and enjoy for weeks after.

MAKES 3 LOAVES

1½ cups golden raisins

½ cup dark rum

1 cup milk

1 cup granulated sugar plus 2 tablespoons

Four ⅗-ounce cakes fresh yeast, crumbled (⅓ cup), or four 1-ounce packages instant dry yeast

9 cups unbleached all-purpose flour, or as needed, sifted

3 large eggs, at room temperature

6 large egg yolks, at room temperature

½ cup (1 stick) unsalted butter, at room temperature, plus more for the bowl of dough

½ cup Vin Santo, Verduzzo, or other sweet white wine

Combine the raisins with the rum in a small bowl and toss to mix. Let soak, tossing occasionally, while preparing the bread.

In a medium-size saucepan, heat the milk over medium heat to lukewarm, about 100°F. Pour the warmed milk into a large bowl and add ½ cup of the sugar and the yeast. Stir until they are dissolved. Add 1 cup of the flour and stir until the mixture is smooth. Cover the bowl with a kitchen towel and let it rise in a warm, draft-free place (such as on top of the refrigerator or in a gas oven with the pilot light on) until frothy. (If it doesn't get frothy, that means the yeast is no longer active and you will have to start again with fresh yeast.)

Stir the dough with a fork to deflate it, then let it rise and froth two more times, stirring it down thoroughly and covering it again after each time. Depending on the environment, these three risings can take from 20 minutes to 45 minutes each.

In the bowl of a heavy-duty electric mixer fitted with the paddle attachment, whip 2 of the whole eggs, 2 of the yolks, and the remaining ½ cup sugar together at medium speed until foamy and pale yellow. Add ¼ cup (½ stick) of the butter, the wine, zests, salt, and vanilla. Beat until only small pieces of butter remain. Scrape the yeast mixture into the mixer bowl and beat until blended.

Grated zest (yellow part only, without the underlying white pith) of 2 large lemons
Grated zest (orange part only, without the white pith) of 1 orange
1½ teaspoons salt
2 teaspoons pure vanilla extract
2 tablespoons water

Change to the dough hook attachment of the mixer and reduce the speed to low. Add 5 cups of the remaining flour, 1 cup at a time, beating until the mixture forms a sticky dough. Wait for each cup of flour to be incorporated before adding the next and stop the machine occasionally to scrape any unmixed ingredients from the sides and bottom of the bowl into the dough. The dough will be quite sticky; form it into a rough ball, clean the sides of the bowl, and cover the bowl with a kitchen towel. Let the dough rise in a warm, draft-free place until doubled in bulk, 1 to 2 hours.

Return the bowl of dough to the mixer fitted with the dough hook. Mix the dough at medium-low speed until deflated. Add the remaining 4 egg yolks and ¼ cup (½ stick) butter and beat until incorporated. Gradually add enough of the remaining flour—about 2 cups—to form a firm but slightly sticky dough, stopping the mixer occasionally to scrape any unmixed ingredients from the sides and bottom of the bowl into the dough. Add the raisins and rum and mix until incorporated. The dough will be quite wet and sticky at this point.

Turn the dough out onto a well-floured surface. Knead the dough, adding as much of the remaining 1 cup flour as necessary to prevent the dough from sticking to your hands and to the table, until the dough is smooth, soft, and only very slightly sticky if left to rest a minute. (See notes on kneading pasta, page 90.)

Place the dough in a large lightly buttered bowl and turn the dough to butter all sides of it. Cover the bowl with a kitchen towel and set the dough to rise in a warm, draft-free place until doubled in bulk, ½ to 2 hours, depending on the environment.

Turn the risen dough out onto the floured work surface and knead until deflated. Cut the dough into three equal pieces and knead each into a ball, gathering and pinching the seam side of the dough together to form as smooth a ball as possible. (These formed loaves can be tightly wrapped in plastic wrap and refrigerated overnight. Allow extra time for refrigerated loaves to rise in the following step.)

Line two baking sheets with parchment paper. Place two loaves on one of the baking sheets, leaving as much space between them and the edges of the pan as possible. Place the third loaf in the center of the other baking sheet. With a pair of kitchen scissors, make three 1½-inch-deep, 3-inch-long intersecting cuts that meet at the center to form a six-pointed star pattern on the rounded top of each loaf. The cuts should be quite deep—at least halfway through the loaf—to allow the dough to rise up from the center and form the traditional crests on the loaf. Cover the loaves lightly with kitchen towels and let rise in a warm draft-free place until doubled in bulk, 1 to 2 hours.

Preheat the oven to 325°F. Bake the bread for 35 minutes. Whisk the remaining whole egg with the remaining 2 tablespoons sugar and the water until very smooth and the sugar is dissolved. Brush the *pinze* with this egg mixture, return them to the oven, and continue baking until very deep golden brown and a knife inserted into the center of the loaves comes out clean, about another 20 minutes.

Cool the *pinze* completely on a wire rack before slicing.

Apple Strudel

🔲 Strudel di Mele 🔲

Strudel is a Middle European dessert that is very common in the Italian region of Friuli-Venezia-Giulia and on the peninsula of Istria, where I grew up. In both of these areas, the crossing of cultures—and the wonderful cooking that results—is quite evident. But strudel is loved everywhere, especially at our restaurant Frico Bar, where it is served warm with vanilla sauce and cinnamon ice cream. A simpler way to serve this strudel at home is with a "sauce" made of melted vanilla ice cream spooned around the slices.

MAKES 10 SERVINGS

Make the strudel dough and let it rest.

In a small bowl, toss the raisins with the rum. Let them stand, tossing occasionally, while preparing the strudel.

With a fine grater, remove the zest—the bright yellow part of the skin without the underlying white pith—from the lemon. Squeeze the juice from the lemon through a strainer and combine the juice and zest in a medium-size mixing bowl.

In a medium-size skillet, melt ¼ cup (½ stick) of the butter over medium heat. Add the bread crumbs and toast, stirring constantly, until lightly browned, about 5 minutes. Remove the skillet from the heat and stir in ½ cup of the granulated sugar and the cinnamon.

1 recipe Strudel Dough (recipe follows)
1 cup golden raisins
2 tablespoons dark rum
1 lemon
½ cup (1 stick) unsalted butter, softened
1 cup fine plain dry bread crumbs
1½ cups granulated sugar
½ teaspoon ground cinnamon
3 pounds tart green apples, such as
    Granny Smith
Olive oil
Confectioners' sugar

Add the remaining cup of granulated sugar and the rum and raisins to the bowl with the lemon juice and zest.

With a paring knife, peel the apples and cut them into quarters. Cut away the seeds and cores and cut the apple quarters into ½-inch-thick wedges. As you work, add the apple wedges to the bowl containing the lemon-sugar mixture to keep them from darkening. Let the apples stand, tossing them occasionally, until the sugar begins to dissolve and the apples are coated with the syrup.

Preheat the oven to 450°F and brush a large (about 18 × 12-inch) baking sheet with olive oil.

continued

Lightly flour a large, smooth wooden or marble surface. With a rolling pin—preferably a long, dowel-shaped pin—roll out the dough from the center to the edges into a very thin rectangle that measures about 36 × 24 inches. The dough will fight you a little at first, but it will relax more the more you roll it. As it gets thinner, you should be able to pull and stretch the dough gently with your hands to coax it into the shape you want. Don't worry if the dough tears a little in spots—you can patch it later—or if it doesn't form a perfect rectangle. Flour the rolling surface and pin lightly as you work to keep the dough from sticking.

If necessary, turn the dough so one of the longer sides is facing you. Place a kitchen towel or length of double-thick cheesecloth so it is under the entire far side of the dough rectangle by about 4 inches. (This will help you move the strudel to the baking sheet once it is formed.) Spread the bread crumb mixture evenly over the dough, leaving a clean 1½-inch-wide border on all sides of the rectangle. Dot the bread crumbs with small pieces of the remaining ¼ cup (½ stick) butter. Arrange the apple mixture in a long mound along the side closest to you. The mound of apples should be about 4 inches wide and as long as the bread crumb mixture, leaving the 1½-inch-wide border clean.

Fold the clean border closest to you over the apples. Begin rolling the strudel into a fairly tight roll, starting at one end of the apple mound, giving it a half roll, and gradually working your way down the roll. Repeat as necessary, gradually working your way down the roll each time. Don't worry if the roll is uneven or tears in places. You should end up with a fairly even, lumpy-looking roll that is centered, seam side down, on the kitchen towel. Use the towel to transfer the strudel to the prepared baking sheet, bending the strudel into a crescent shape if necessary to fit it on the pan.

Cut off any excess dough from the ends. Seal the ends of the strudel by folding the ends of the roll underneath and pressing them firmly with your fingers. Brush the strudel lightly with olive oil and place in the preheated oven. Immediately reduce the oven temperature to 375°F. Bake for 30 minutes. Check the strudel: The top should be light golden brown. If it is deeper in color than that, reduce the oven temperature to 350°F. Rotate the baking sheet in the oven so the strudel cooks evenly and continue baking until the strudel is deep golden brown and the crust firm, about another 30 minutes.

Remove the strudel from the oven and let cool for 30 minutes. With two metal spatulas, carefully lift the strudel to a wire cooling rack and let stand until completely cooled.

To serve, cut the strudel into 1-inch-thick slices and sprinkle them with confectioners' sugar.

Strudel Dough

Impasto per Strudel

MAKES ENOUGH DOUGH FOR 1 STRUDEL

To make the dough in a food processor: Combine the flour, oil, and salt in the work bowl of a food processor fitted with the metal blade. With the motor running, add the water and process until the mixture forms a smooth, silky dough. If the mixture is too dry, add more water, 1 tablespoon at a time, stopping the motor after each addition, until the dough is the proper consistency.

> **2 cups sifted unbleached all-purpose flour, plus more for kneading the dough**
> **3 tablespoons extra virgin olive oil**
> **½ teaspoon salt**
> **½ cup tepid water, or as needed**

Turn the dough out onto a lightly floured work surface and knead, adding flour as necessary to prevent the dough from sticking to your hands and the work surface, until it is very smooth and elastic, about 3 minutes. Wrap the dough in plastic wrap and let it rest at room temperature for 2 to 3 hours or in the refrigerator for up to 2 days. (Let the refrigerated dough sit at room temperature for at least 1 hour before rolling it.)

To make the dough by hand: Pile the flour in a mound in a medium-size mixing bowl. Make a deep well in the center of the mound and add the oil, salt, and water. Beat the wet ingredients with a fork while gradually incorporating the flour from the sides of the well. When the dough is too stiff to mix with the fork, begin kneading in the flour with your hands. If the mixture is too dry, add more water 1 tablespoon at a time, mixing well after each addition, until the dough is the proper consistency. Turn the dough out onto a lightly floured work surface and knead and let rest as instructed above.

Ricotta-Filled Strudel

🔸 Strudel di Ricotta 🔸

Ricotta is extremely versatile in the Italian cuisine. It shows up in everything from appetizers and pasta sauces to pasta fillings and desserts. It represents very much an Italian *gusto,* or taste. I use it often in my desserts, and I especially like it in my strudel. It is essential to use fresh ricotta here, with large curds and a somewhat dry texture. Store-bought ricotta—no matter how long you drain it—will retain some moisture.

MAKES 10 SERVINGS

3 pounds fresh large-curd ricotta

1 recipe Strudel Dough (page 347)

3 tablespoons Maraschino liqueur or
    Cointreau or other orange liqueur

1 cup golden raisins

¾ cup (1½ sticks) unsalted butter, softened

1 cup fine plain dry bread crumbs

1 cup sliced blanched almonds, toasted
    (see Note)

3 cups granulated sugar

4 large eggs

Grated zest (yellow part only, without the
    underlying white pith) of 3 lemons

Grated zest (orange part only, without the
    white pith) of 1 orange

Olive oil

Confectioners' sugar

Place the ricotta in a large fine-mesh sieve or a colander lined with a double thickness of cheesecloth. Place the sieve over a large bowl and cover the ricotta with plastic wrap. Drain the ricotta in the refrigerator for at least 12 hours or for up to 24 hours.

Make the strudel dough and let it rest.

Pour the liqueur over the raisins in a small bowl and let stand, tossing once or twice, while preparing the filling.

In a large skillet, melt ¼ cup (½ stick) of the butter over medium heat. Add the bread crumbs and toast, stirring constantly, until lightly browned, about 5 minutes. Stir in the almonds, remove the pan from the heat, and stir in ½ cup of the granulated sugar.

In a large mixing bowl, beat ¼ cup (½ stick) of the remaining butter and the remaining 2½ cups granulated sugar together with an electric mixer until blended. Beat in the eggs one at a time and continue beating until the mixture is smooth and pale yellow. Add the drained ricotta and zests and beat at low speed just until blended. Fold in the raisins and liqueur. Refrigerate the filling while preparing the dough.

Preheat the oven to 450°F. Brush an 18 × 12-inch baking pan lightly with olive oil.

Lightly flour a large, smooth wooden or marble surface. With a rolling pin—preferably a long, dowel-shaped pin—roll out the dough from the center to the edges into a very thin rectangle, about 36 × 24 inches. The dough will fight you a little at first, but it will relax the more you roll it. As it gets thinner, you should be able to pull and stretch it gently with your hands to coax it into the shape you want. Don't worry if the dough tears a little in spots—you can patch it later—or if it doesn't form a perfect rectangle. Flour the rolling surface and pin lightly as you work to keep the dough from sticking.

Turn the dough so one of the longer sides is facing you. Place a kitchen towel or length of double-thick cheesecloth so it is under the entire far side of the dough rectangle by about 4 inches. (This will help you move the strudel to the baking sheet once it is formed.) Spread the bread crumb-almond mixture evenly over the dough, leaving a clean 1½-inch-wide border on all sides of the rectangle. Dot the bread crumbs with small pieces of the remaining ¼ cup (½ stick) butter. Arrange the ricotta mixture in a long mound about 4 inches wide and as long as the bread crumb mixture along the side closest to you, leaving the 1½-inch-wide border clean.

Fold the clean border closest to you over the ricotta filling. Begin rolling the strudel into a fairly tight roll, starting at one end of the filling, giving it a half roll and gradually working your way down the roll. Repeat as necessary, gradually working your way down the roll each time. Don't worry if the roll tears in places. You should end up with a roll of fairly even thickness that is centered, seam side down, on the kitchen towel. Use the towel to transfer the strudel to the prepared baking sheet, bending the strudel into a crescent shape if necessary to fit it on the sheet.

Seal the ends of the strudel by folding the ends of the roll underneath and pressing them with your fingers. Brush the strudel lightly with olive oil and place in the preheated oven. Immediately turn the oven temperature down to 375°F and bake for 30 minutes. Check the strudel: The top should be light golden brown. If it is deeper in color than that, reduce the oven temperature to 350°F. Rotate the baking pan in the oven so the strudel cooks evenly and continue baking until the strudel is deep golden brown and the crust firm, about another 30 minutes.

Remove the strudel from the oven and cool for 30 minutes. With two metal spatulas, carefully lift the strudel to a wire cooling rack and let stand until completely cooled.

To serve, cut the strudel into 1-inch-thick slices and sprinkle them with confectioners' sugar.

Note: To toast almonds, preheat the oven to 350°F. Spread the almonds out on a baking pan and bake, shaking the pan once or twice, until the almonds are uniformly golden brown, about 12 minutes. Remove them from the baking pan and cool them completely.

Blueberry-Apricot Frangipane Tart

Crostata di Mirtilli ed Albiccoche al Frangipane

Frangipane is a batter made of almond flour that, when baked, takes on a cakelike texture.

MAKES ONE 10-INCH TART; 8 SERVINGS

For the shell

1½ cups unbleached all-purpose flour

¼ cup granulated sugar

½ teaspoon baking powder

Pinch of salt

½ cup (1 stick) unsalted butter, cut into
cherry-size pieces and chilled

1 large egg yolk

Zest from 1 lemon

Ice water as needed

For the filling

½ cup (1 stick) unsalted butter, softened

⅓ cup granulated sugar

2 large eggs

1 cup finely ground blanched almonds
or almond flour

1 teaspoon pure vanilla extract

½ cup apricot glaze (see Note), warmed

1 cup fresh blueberries, picked over
for stems

1 pound ripe apricots, halved and pitted

Sift the flour, sugar, baking powder, and salt together into a bowl. Add the butter, egg yolk, and lemon zest and work the ingredients together with your fingers until the butter resembles cornflakes and is distributed evenly throughout the flour mixture. Sprinkle 3 tablespoons ice water over the mixture and toss lightly just until the dough holds together when lightly pressed. If necessary, add a little more ice water. Wrap the dough in plastic wrap and let rest in the refrigerator for 1 hour.

Butter a 10-inch tart pan with a removable bottom. Roll out the dough to a 12-inch circle of even thickness. Center the dough over the tart pan, fit the dough well into the edges with your fingers, and trim off any excess overhanging dough. Prick the bottom of the tart shell with a fork, and set on a baking sheet in the freezer for 10 minutes.

Meanwhile, preheat the oven to 350°F.

Make the filling. With an electric mixer at medium speed, cream the butter with the sugar until fluffy, about 3 minutes. Add the eggs one at a time, beating well after each addition. Add the ground almonds or almond flour and vanilla and mix until a smooth batter forms.

Brush the tart shell with ¼ cup of apricot glaze, then spread the blueberries over the bottom. Pour the almond mixture over the blueberries and, with a spatula, spread it evenly. Arrange the apricot halves over the almond mixture, cut side down. Bake until the almond mixture and the edges of the tart shell are golden brown, about 40 minutes.

Let the tart cool for 30 minutes, then brush with the remaining ¼ cup warm apricot glaze.

Note: Apricot glaze is available at some specialty food stores. To make your own, warm apricot jam in a small saucepan over low heat. If the jam is very chunky, add a tablespoon or two of water and strain before using.

Angels' Kisses

Baci d'Angelo

This is a "border-case" dessert, from the Austro-Hungarian territories that at one time included Istria. In the cafés of Vienna, these angels' kisses are quite popular. Instead of sandwiching the filling between two cookies as described below, you may want to fold each cookie around some of the filling, taco-style. This can come in handy at buffets or in other situations when finger food, rather than knife-and-fork food, is the rule.

MAKES 6 SERVINGS

4 large eggs, separated

¾ cup granulated sugar

Grated zest (yellow part only, without the underlying white pith) of 1 lemon

Grated zest (orange part only, without the white pith) of 1 orange

5 tablespoons unbleached all-purpose flour

3 large egg yolks

½ cup plus 2 tablespoons Vin Santo, Malvasia, Verduzzo, or other sweet white wine

1½ cups heavy cream

1 cup chopped toasted hazelnuts (see Note)

Confectioners' sugar

Preheat the oven to 350°F and place one rack in the top third and the other in the lower third of the oven.

In the top of a double boiler or a large heatproof bowl placed over a saucepan of simmering water, whisk 4 of the egg yolks and 3 tablespoons of the granulated sugar together until very smooth and doubled in volume, about 3 minutes. Stir in the zests, remove from the heat, and whisk until cool.

In a medium-size bowl, whip the egg whites with an electric mixer at medium speed until foamy. Add 5 tablespoons of the remaining granulated sugar 1 tablespoon at a time and continue beating until the whites are glossy and hold stiff peaks when the beaters are lifted.

Sprinkle the flour over the yolk mixture and mix gently until incorporated. Add about one fourth of the egg whites to the egg yolk mixture and, with a rubber spatula, fold them in, scraping the egg yolk mixture from the bottom of the bowl over the whites until just a few streaks of white remain. Fold in the remaining whites in the same way.

On each of two nonstick baking sheets, or baking sheets lined with parchment paper, form six 3½-inch circles, using 3 tablespoons of batter for each. (A simple way to make nice, even rounds is to trace six 3½-inch circles onto each sheet of parchment paper. Turn the sheets, marked side down, and use the circles as a guide, pushing the batter to the edges of the circle and smoothing the top flat with a small rubber spatula or icing spatula.) Bake until the cookies are golden brown and very light when lifted from the baking sheet, about 12 minutes. Rotate the baking sheets—rack to rack and back to front—about halfway through the baking for even browning. Remove the cookies to a wire rack to cool completely.

Meanwhile, in the top of a double boiler or in a heatproof bowl, beat the remaining 3 egg yolks, the remaining ¼ cup granulated sugar, and the Vin Santo together until blended. Place over simmering water and continue beating (switching to a handheld electric mixer at medium speed, if you like) until the mixture is pale yellow and fluffy and falls back on itself in thick ribbons when the whisk or beaters are lifted, about 8 minutes if you are whisking by hand, or 4 minutes if you are using an electric mixer. Remove the top of the double boiler or bowl from the heat, set it in a large bowl of ice water, and whisk until the zabaglione is completely chilled.

In a medium-size chilled bowl, whip the heavy cream with an electric mixer until it holds stiff peaks when the beaters are lifted. With a rubber spatula, fold the whipped cream into the cooled egg yolk mixture, scraping the egg yolk mixture from the bottom of the bowl over the whipped cream. Fold in the hazelnuts.

Place six of the cookies bottom side up on a work surface. Top each with ½ cup of the zabaglione filling and spread into an even layer to cover the whole surface of the cookie. Top with the remaining cookies and place a dollop of the remaining filling on each cookie sandwich. Sprinkle the tops with confectioners' sugar. Serve at room temperature.

Note: To toast hazelnuts, spread them out in a baking pan. Toast in a preheated 350°F oven until the skins begin to separate from the nuts and the nuts are deep golden brown, 8 to 10 minutes. Cool the hazelnuts to room temperature.

Remove as much of the skins from the nuts as possible by rubbing them together inside a clean kitchen towel. Particularly stubborn skins can sometimes be removed by placing the nuts a handful at a time in a coarse sieve and rubbing them against the sieve with a kitchen towel to protect your hands. In either case, it is unlikely you will remove all the skins from all the nuts; just remove as many as you can.

Zucchini Cake

Torta di Zucchini

At our restaurants, Felidia, Becco, and Frico Bar, we regularly welcome students from the culinary schools into our kitchens to serve their externships. It is particularly rewarding to share with young eager minds one's knowledge of and passion for a profession. This recipe, with slight modifications, was shared with me by Sally Posmentier, the grandmother of Ross Posmentier, who apprenticed with us at Felidia for several months. He was an enthusiastic, talented young man who should excel in our profession.

I particularly like this recipe because it reminds me of the olive oil–based cakes my grandmother used to make. Olive oil can be used as the shortening in many baked goods, where it adds flavor as well as tenderness.

MAKES 1 LOAF; ABOUT 8 SERVINGS

1 cup extra virgin olive oil, plus more
    for the loaf pan
2 cups unbleached all-purpose flour,
    plus more for the loaf pan
2 teaspoons ground cinnamon
1 teaspoon salt
1 teaspoon baking soda
3 large eggs
1⅔ cups granulated sugar
2 teaspoons pure vanilla extract
2 cups shredded trimmed small, firm
    zucchini
1 cup chopped walnuts
¾ cup golden raisins
Grated zest (yellow part only, without the
    underlying white pith) of 1 lemon

Place the rack in the center position in the oven and preheat the oven to 325°F. Lightly brush a 9 × 5 × 3-inch loaf pan with olive oil. Sprinkle the inside of the pan with flour and tap the pan to coat evenly and remove any excess.

Sift the 2 cups flour, the cinnamon, salt, and baking soda together into a small bowl.

In a large bowl, with an electric mixer at medium speed, beat the eggs and 1 cup olive oil together until well blended. Gradually add the sugar while continuing to beat, then beat until the mixture is foamy and pale yellow and the sugar dissolved. Beat in the vanilla.

Add the dry ingredients to the egg mixture and beat at low speed just until blended. Don't overmix. Add the zucchini, ¾ cup of the walnuts, the raisins, and lemon zest and fold in with a rubber spatula until evenly distributed. Transfer the batter to the prepared loaf pan, scraping all the batter out of the bowl with a rubber spatula. Spread the batter evenly in the pan and sprinkle the remaining ¼ cup walnuts over the top.

Bake until the cake has risen above the sides of the pan and a wooden skewer or cake tester inserted into the center comes out clean, about 1 hour and 10 minutes. Cool the cake on a wire rack for 20 to 30 minutes.

Remove the cake from the pan by inverting it onto a kitchen towel. Continue cooling the cake, right side up, on the wire rack until completely cool before slicing. The cake can be wrapped tightly in plastic wrap and stored in the refrigerator for up to 5 days.

Crepes

🔅 Crespelle 🔅

This recipe makes enough for any of the three filled *crespelle* recipes that follow. If this is the first time you have made crepes, you may want to double the amount of ingredients below to allow for a margin of safety. The finished crepes are best when served warm, but you can hold the batter in the refrigerator for up to two days.

For a very simple dessert or snack, crepes can be sprinkled with sugar or spread with marmalade and folded into quarters, then drizzled with a little Grand Marnier and sprinkled with confectioners' sugar. Or, in berry season, serve the crepes warm, topped with a spoonful of whipped cream and some fresh berries.

MAKES ABOUT 18 CREPES

1 large egg

1 cup milk

¼ cup club soda

2 tablespoons granulated sugar

1½ teaspoons dark rum

½ teaspoon pure vanilla extract

Large pinch of salt

1 cup unbleached all-purpose flour

1½ tablespoons extra virgin olive oil

Grated zest (yellow part only, without the underlying white pith) of 1 lemon

Grated zest (orange part only, without the white pith) of 1 orange

Vegetable oil

In a medium-size bowl, whisk the egg well. Add the milk, club soda, sugar, rum, vanilla, and salt and whisk gently until the sugar has dissolved. Gradually sift in the flour while stirring constantly to form a smooth batter. When the flour is incorporated, stir in the olive oil and zests.

In a 6- or 7-inch crepe pan (see Note), heat 1 tablespoon vegetable oil over medium-high heat. Pour off all but a very thin film of oil. Pour 2 tablespoons of the crepe batter into the pan and immediately tilt and swirl the pan to distribute the batter as evenly as possible and form a thin, even pancake. The secret to tender, even crepes is in the wrist, and this takes some practice. Even if this is not the first time you have made crepes, it may take a few attempts to get nicely formed crepes.

Return the pan to the heat, reduce the heat to medium, and cook the crepe until the underside is lightly browned in a lacy pattern, 30 to 40 seconds. Flip it carefully with a spatula and cook until brown spots appear on the second side. (The second side won't have the lacy pattern of the first.) Transfer the crepe to a warmed platter and repeat the process with the remaining batter, re-oiling the pan only as necessary to prevent sticking. Stack the finished crepes as you make them and keep them warm under a large mixing bowl.

Note: Traditional crepe pans are made of black steel that becomes seasoned with constant use. If you don't own one of these pans, a nonstick skillet of the same size will give you excellent results. Also, a heatproof rubber spatula is very helpful for turning crepes in a nonstick pan.

Sweet Crepes with Chocolate Walnut Filling

Crespelle Farcite con Noci e Cioccolato

Almost every culture has some form of crepes in its cuisine. I ate them as a child, sometimes filled with just marmalade—rose-hip marmalade was my favorite. On special occasions, we filled warm crepes with chocolate. Two or three *crespelle* and a glass of goat's milk was my supper on many an evening.

MAKES 6 SERVINGS

Make the crepes and keep them warm according to the directions on page 356.

Melt the chocolate in the top of a double boiler or in a heatproof bowl placed over a saucepan of hot (not boiling) water. Stir the chocolate often so it melts evenly. Remove the chocolate from the heat and stir in ½ cup of the walnuts.

18 Crepes (page 356)
6 ounces milk chocolate, chopped
1 cup coarsely chopped walnuts
Whipped cream
Confectioners' sugar

Place a crepe, lacy side down, on a work surface. Spread a generous tablespoon of the chocolate mixture over half of the crepe. Fold the other half over the chocolate, then fold the filled crepe in half again to form a triangle. Repeat with the remaining crepes and chocolate mixture.

Arrange three crepes overlapping on each serving plate and top with a dollop of whipped cream. Sprinkle the crepes evenly with the remaining ½ cup walnuts and confectioners' sugar. Serve at once.

Baked Crepes with Ricotta

Crespelle Farcite con Ricotta al Forno

The preparation of these *crespelle* is especially convenient for a dinner party. They can be made in advance, set in the refrigerator, and baked just before serving. Top with an assortment of juicy fresh berries and confectioners' sugar if desired.

MAKES 6 SERVINGS

1 pound ricotta, preferably fresh
12 Crepes (page 356)
6 tablespoons (¾ stick) unsalted butter, melted
1 cup granulated sugar
2 large eggs
Grated zest (yellow part only, without the underlying white pith) of 2 lemons
Pinch of freshly grated nutmeg
1½ cups golden raisins
¼ cup Limoncello or other lemon liqueur
Confectioners' sugar

Place the ricotta in a fine-mesh sieve or a colander lined with cheesecloth. Place the sieve over a bowl, cover with plastic wrap, and let the ricotta drain in the refrigerator for at least 12 hours, or up to 24 hours.

Make the crepes.

Preheat the oven to 350°F. Brush an 11 × 8-inch baking dish with some of the melted butter.

In a large bowl, whisk the granulated sugar and eggs together until pale yellow and smooth. Add the ricotta, lemon zest, and nutmeg and beat lightly until blended. Fold in the raisins.

Place a crepe, lacy side down, on the work surface. Spread about ¼ cup of the ricotta mixture over the crepe and roll the crepe up like a jelly roll. Place the crepe, seam side down, in the buttered baking dish. Repeat with the remaining crepes and filling, arranging them side by side in the dish.

In a small bowl, whisk the remaining melted butter and the liqueur together until blended and pour over the crepes. Bake until the filling is warmed through and the liquid in the dish is bubbling, about 20 minutes. Transfer the crepes to serving plates, spooning some of the butter sauce over each serving. Sprinkle with confectioners' sugar and serve immediately.

Fluffy Ricotta Pancakes

Crespelle di Ricotta

When they were young, my children, Joseph and Tanya, loved these ricotta pancakes. But that didn't stop them from asking, "Mom, why can't we have normal pancakes like all of our friends?" They didn't appreciate the ethnic flavors of our home kitchen at that age. Only after they were grown up did they tell me how they would skip their lunch because Nonna Erminia, my mother, who still lives with us, gave them fried eggplant or prosciutto sandwiches, or other such alien food. No other friend would bring anything like that for lunch at school! They have certainly come around, though, especially Joe, who helps to run—and gets involved in the kitchens of—all three of our restaurants.

MAKES 6 SERVINGS

Place the strawberries in a medium-size bowl and drizzle them with the honey. Toss gently and let them stand, tossing them once or twice.

In a large bowl, beat the milk, egg yolks, flour, baking powder, salt, and lemon zest together until well blended. Add the ricotta and blend gently, leaving some of the curds whole.

In a medium-size bowl, beat the egg whites with an electric mixer at high speed until they hold stiff peaks when the beaters are lifted. Add about one fourth of the whites to the ricotta mixture and, with a rubber spatula, gently fold them in, scraping the ricotta mixture from the bottom of the bowl over the whites. Fold in the remaining whites in the same way.

> 1 pint ripe strawberries, washed, hulled, and sliced ¼ inch thick
> ¼ cup acacia or other flavorful honey
> 1 cup milk
> 4 large eggs, separated
> ⅔ cup unbleached all-purpose flour
> 1½ teaspoons baking powder
> 2 pinches of salt
> Grated zest (yellow part only, without the underlying white pith) of 2 lemons
> 2 cups ricotta, preferably fresh
> Whipped cream
> Confectioners' sugar

Grease a griddle (see Note) and heat it over medium-high heat until a drop of water dances quickly across the surface. Pour the batter by quarter cupfuls onto the griddle and cook until the underside is a lacy golden brown, about 2 minutes. Flip the pancakes and cook until the second side is light brown, about 1 minute. Stack the pancakes on a plate and keep them warm, covered with a kitchen towel, while cooking the remaining batter.

Serve the pancakes warm, topping each serving with some of the strawberries and their juices, a dollop of whipped cream, and a sprinkling of confectioners' sugar.

continued

Sweets   359

Note: There are many options available if, like most kitchens, yours doesn't have a built-in griddle. Many housewares stores stock oval or rectangular cast-iron griddles long enough to fit over two stovetop burners. In addition to cooking pancakes like these, they come in very handy for other things, like the Griddle-Crisped Spring Chicken on page 264. If you cannot find this type of griddle, try the square, nonstick type and cook the pancakes in smaller batches.

Rice Soufflé

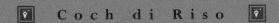 C o c h   d i   R i s o

Rice is commonly used to make desserts in Italy. It gives a flavor to the desserts that is typically Italian—whether in a *crostata di riso* (rice custard tart), *gelato di riso* (rice ice cream), or this *coch de riso* from Trieste. These individual soufflés are delicious eaten warm sprinkled with a little confectioners' sugar and even better when served with berries and whipped cream. If you like, you can go a little further and serve them with the Chocolate Sauce on page 362 or a sauce made from fresh seasonal fruit—like strawberries, peaches, or plums—whirled in the blender with a little sugar and lemon juice and then strained.

MAKES 6 SERVINGS

4 cups milk

⅔ cup long-grain rice

¾ cup granulated sugar

½ cup golden raisins

¼ teaspoon salt

3 tablespoons extra virgin olive oil,
   plus more for the ramekins

Fine plain dry bread crumbs

4 large eggs, separated

Grated zest (yellow part only, without the
   underlying white pith) of 1 lemon

Whipped cream

Confectioners' sugar

Fresh berries (optional)

Sprigs fresh mint (optional)

In a medium-size, heavy saucepan, bring the milk, rice, and ½ cup of the granulated sugar to a simmer over medium heat. Cook the rice, stirring often, for 10 minutes. Add the raisins and about half the salt and continue cooking, stirring often, until the rice is very tender and plump, about another 20 minutes. The more milk the rice absorbs, the more important it becomes to stir the rice to prevent scorching. Remove the rice from the heat and cool completely.

Place a rack in the center position and preheat the oven to 425°F. Brush six 6-ounce ceramic ramekins or glass baking cups with olive oil. Coat the insides with bread crumbs, rotating the ramekins to coat the sides and bottoms evenly. Tap out the excess crumbs.

In a large bowl, with an electric mixer at medium speed, beat the egg yolks with the remaining ¼ cup sugar until the mixture is pale yellow and falls back on itself in thick ribbons from the beaters. Add the 3 table-spoons olive oil and beat until thoroughly incorporated.

Clean the beaters well and dry them. In a medium-size bowl, beat the egg whites with the remaining salt until they hold stiff peaks when the beaters are lifted up.

Fold the cooled rice mixture into the egg yolk mixture. Add the lemon zest and mix well. Add about one fourth of the whites to the rice mixture and, with a rubber spatula, gently fold them in, scraping the rice mixture from the bottom of the bowl over the whites. Fold in the remaining whites in the same way.

Divide the rice mixture among the ramekins—the ramekins should be almost full. Set the ramekins in a deep baking pan and place the pan in the oven. Pour in enough warm water to come halfway up the sides of the ramekins. Bake until the soufflés have risen above the sides of the ramekins and are deep golden brown, about 35 minutes. Carefully remove the ramekins from the pan of water and let them stand for 15 to 20 minutes. They may fall slightly—that is fine.

Run a thin-bladed knife around the inside edge of the ramekins. Invert the soufflés onto serving plates and top with whipped cream. Sprinkle with confectioners' sugar and garnish with fresh berries or sprigs of fresh mint, if you like.

Chocolate Sauce

Salsa di Cioccolato

MAKES 1½ CUPS

8 ounces sweet chocolate, finely chopped

1 cup light cream or half-and-half

2 tablespoons dark rum

In a medium-size, heavy saucepan over medium heat, bring the chocolate and cream to a boil, stirring often. Reduce the heat to a simmer and simmer until the sauce is thickened enough to coat a spoon heavily, about 3 minutes. Remove from the heat and stir in the rum. Serve the sauce warm or at room temperature. The sauce can be stored, covered, in the refrigerator for up to 1 week. Reheat the sauce in a double boiler over simmering water.

Heavenly Cake

Torta Angelica

This flavorful, light sponge cake can be the base for many desserts. It can be topped with sweetened mascarpone cheese and fresh berries or soaked with Malvasia or Torcolato—two wonderful, sweet Italian dessert wines named for the grape varietals from which they are made—and topped with whipped cream. Cut the cake into portion sizes and, with a pastry brush, soak well with the dessert wine, then top with berries and whipped cream or with warm or chilled zabaglione. Sprinkle with confectioners' sugar and serve.

MAKES ONE 8-INCH CAKE; 10 SERVINGS

Preheat the oven to 350°F. Lightly grease an 8-inch springform cake pan with olive oil. Sprinkle the inside of the pan with flour and rotate the pan to coat the sides and bottom evenly. Tap out any excess flour.

Sift the 1½ cups flour and baking soda together into a small bowl.

In a large bowl, whisk the whole eggs and confectioners' sugar together until creamy, smooth, and doubled in volume. Add the zests and about half the salt and beat well. Alternately add the olive oil and flour mixture to the sugar mixture, stirring gently after each addition.

In a medium-size bowl, using an electric mixer at high speed, whip the egg whites with the remaining salt until they hold stiff peaks when the beaters are lifted up. Add about one fourth of the whites to the batter and, with a rubber spatula, gently fold them in, scraping the batter from the bottom of the bowl over the whites. Fold in the remaining whites in the same way.

Pour the batter into the prepared pan and bake until the top is deep golden brown and springs back quickly when pressed with your finger, about 50 minutes. Cool the cake on a wire rack for about 20 minutes.

Run a thin-bladed knife around the edges of the pan and release the sides of the pan. Cool the cake completely on the rack before serving.

½ cup extra virgin olive oil, plus more
   for the cake pan
1½ cups unbleached all-purpose flour,
   plus more for the cake pan
2 teaspoons baking soda
2 large eggs
2 cups confectioners' sugar
Grated zest (orange part only, without the
   underlying white pith) of 1 orange
Grated zest (yellow part only, without
   the white pith) of 1 lemon
¼ teaspoon salt
4 large egg whites

"Cooked Cream" with Fresh Berries

Panna Cotta con Frutta di Bosco

This is a traditional Italian dessert that is always welcome, everybody's favorite, and quite easy to make. This rendition is one that Fortunato Nicotra, chef at Felidia, shared with us. It is perfect for dinner parties because it can be made a day or two in advance and kept refrigerated until you serve it.

MAKES 6 SERVINGS

For the cooked cream

1½ teaspoons unflavored powdered gelatin

5 tablespoons water

1 cup milk

½ cup plus ⅓ cup granulated sugar

½ vanilla bean, split lengthwise

2 cups heavy cream

For the frutta di bosco (see Note)

1 cup fresh raspberries, gently washed and drained

1 cup strawberries, washed, hulled, and sliced ¼ inch thick

1 cup fresh red or black currants, gently washed and drained

6 sprigs fresh mint

Sprinkle the gelatin over 2 tablespoons of the water in a small bowl and let stand until the gelatin is softened, about 5 minutes.

In a medium-size saucepan, bring the milk, ½ cup of the sugar, and the split vanilla bean half to a boil. Immediately remove the saucepan from the heat. Scrape the gelatin mixture into the milk and stir until dissolved. Remove the vanilla bean and, with a paring knife, scrape the seeds into milk. Strain the milk mixture through a fine-mesh sieve into a medium-size bowl and let cool to room temperature.

Meanwhile, prepare the caramel-lined molds. Have six 8-ounce ceramic ramekins close at hand before starting the caramel. In a small, heavy saucepan, make a caramel with the remaining ⅓ cup sugar and the remaining 3 tablespoons water according to the directions on page 366. Immediately pour the caramel into the ramekins, dividing it evenly. Set the prepared ramekins aside, remembering that they will retain the heat for several minutes.

In a medium-size bowl, beat the heavy cream with an electric mixer until it holds stiff peaks when the beaters are lifted. Add the whipped cream to the milk mixture and fold the two together with a rubber spatula. Divide the whipped cream mixture among the caramel-lined ramekins and place in the refrigerator. Chill until firm, at least 2 hours, or up to 1 day.

To serve, invert the ramekins onto serving plates. Wait a moment until the caramel sauce begins to seep onto the plate, then lift the ramekins. Decorate with the *frutta di bosco* and mint sprigs and serve immediately.

Note: *Frutta di bosco* can be any assortment of fresh, seasonal fruit, but berries are especially nice with *panna cotta*. To use other ripe, soft fruits, such as cherries, peaches, or apricots, just remove the stones and peels as necessary and cut them into thin slices or bite-size pieces.

Making Caramel

A few of the recipes in this chapter call for lining a large mold or several smaller ramekins with hot caramel. You may have noticed that the size of the saucepan or skillet changes from recipe to recipe: I have suggested the size that is best for each quantity in each recipe. Whatever the amount of caramel you are making, the procedure remains the same, as outlined below. But first, read these pointers before making the caramel.

Caramel is extremely hot (over 325°F) and can cause severe burns. Make sure you are working with sturdy, heavy pots and thick pot holders or oven mitts.

Once a sugar syrup begins to darken and turn into caramel, it is difficult to stop the process, so you should only make caramel when you are guaranteed of having a few uninterrupted minutes. You can, however, dip the bottom of the pot in cool water to stop the transfer of heat to the caramel if it begins to color too quickly.

When you pour the caramel into the mold(s), some will remain in the pot and harden almost immediately. To clean, simply fill the pot with water and bring to a boil. Then stir until the caramel is dissolved.

A candy thermometer is helpful when making caramel, but the quantities of caramel called for in these recipes are not really large enough to allow you to get an accurate reading. Judge by color and remember to remove the pan from the heat a little before you reach the desired color—the heat retained in the bottom of the pan is sufficient to keep cooking the caramel.

To make caramel: Combine the sugar and water in the appropriate-size skillet or saucepan. Place over medium heat and cook, stirring occasionally, until the sugar is melted and the syrup is boiling. Don't stir the syrup after it comes to a boil, as this will most likely form crystals in the syrup. Cook, swirling the pan occasionally to prevent the syrup from hardening on the sides of the pan, until the syrup begins to turn a very pale golden brown. You will be able to tell when the syrup is about to change color—the bubbles will be larger and move a little more slowly. When the syrup begins to change color, reduce the heat to low and continue cooking and swirling until the syrup is a medium amber color (about 340°F on a candy thermometer). If the caramel begins to color too quickly, dip the bottom of the skillet or saucepan in a basin of cool water for a second or two.

Chocolate Amaretto Custard

🔯 Bonet 🔯

This typical Piemontese dessert is easy to prepare and delightfully tasty and smooth. It can be prepared several days in advance and is best when served with some plain whipped cream.

You may be wondering about the French word *bonet*. Since Piedmont borders France, the culinary culture and some of the words overlap.

MAKES 8 SERVINGS

Prepare the caramel-lined mold. Before you begin the caramel, have near at hand a 12 × 4 × 3-inch ceramic or steel pâté mold or a 9 × 5 × 3-inch loaf pan and a pair of heavy oven mitts. Make a caramel with 1 cup of the sugar and the water in a medium-size, heavy saucepan according to the directions on page 366. Immediately remove the caramel from the heat—it will continue to darken from the heat retained in the pan. Put on the oven mitts and, working quickly and carefully—the caramel is extremely hot—pour the caramel into the mold or pan. Tilt the mold or pan so the caramel covers the entire bottom and about halfway up the sides. You will see the caramel thicken and move more slowly as it begins to cool—make sure at least the bottom is entirely covered before it solidifies completely. Set the mold aside, remembering that it will stay quite hot for several minutes.

Place a deep baking dish or roasting pan on the center rack of the oven and pour in enough warm water to fill it halfway. Preheat the oven to 375°F.

In a small, heavy saucepan over medium heat, heat the milk until bubbles form around the edges. Remove from the heat and set aside.

Meanwhile, in a large bowl, whisk the eggs and the remaining 2 cups sugar together until smooth and pale yellow. Add the espresso, cocoa, crumbled amaretti, and amaretto and whisk until blended.

Slowly add the hot milk, whisking constantly until the sugar is dissolved.

3 cups granulated sugar
½ cup water
2½ cups milk
10 large eggs
½ cup strong brewed espresso
¼ cup unsweetened cocoa powder
¼ cup crushed amaretti cookies
(about 6 cookies)
¼ cup amaretto or other almond liqueur
1 cup heavy cream
Whipped cream, if desired

continued

In a chilled medium-size bowl, beat the heavy cream with an electric mixer at medium-high speed until it holds stiff peaks when the beaters are lifted. Add about 2 cups of the egg-milk mixture to the whipped cream and stir gently to blend. Fold the whipped cream mixture into the egg-milk mixture until evenly blended.

Pour the custard mixture into the caramel-lined mold and place the mold in the water bath. Bake until a thin-bladed knife inserted into the center of the custard comes out clean, about 40 minutes if baked in a pâté mold and about an hour if baked in a loaf pan.

Remove the mold from the water bath and cool the custard to room temperature. Refrigerate the custard until thoroughly chilled, at least 4 hours, or up to 2 days.

To unmold, run a thin-bladed knife around the edge of the custard. (It should already be loose or loosen very easily.) Place an oval, flat platter at least a couple of inches longer than the mold face down over the *bonet*. Holding the mold and platter firmly together, invert them with one quick motion. Wait a moment for the melted caramel to begin to seep onto the platter, then gently lift off the mold; the *bonet* should unmold very easily. Serve the *bonet* cold, cut into 1-inch-thick slices, with additional whipped cream, if desired.

Amaretti Pudding

🔖 Budino di Amaretti 🔖

Almond, like rice, is a favorite flavor for desserts among the Italians, especially in Sicily, which is a major source of almonds. The most beautiful time to go to Sicily is in late February, when *il mandorle in fiore* (the almond trees are in bloom). The whole countryside is in flower, perfumed with the sweet, buttery smell of almonds. From these almonds comes marzipan—so it is no wonder Sicily has a tremendous repertoire of marzipan-based sweets. *Latte di mandorle* (almond milk)—made by steeping crushed almonds in water—is sold in the *pasticcerie* of Sicily and is a refreshing way to wash sweets down.

MAKES 8 SERVINGS

In a small bowl, stir ¼ cup of the milk, the crushed amaretti, and the liqueur together until blended. Set aside for 1 hour.

Prepare the caramel-lined molds. Before making the caramel, have eight 8-ounce ceramic ramekins or heat-proof glass baking dishes and a pair of heavy oven mitts near at hand. Make a caramel with ½ cup of the sugar and the water in a medium-size, heavy skillet according to the directions on page 366. Immediately remove the caramel from the heat—it will continue to darken from the heat retained in the pan. Put on the oven mitts and, working quickly and carefully—the caramel is extremely hot—pour the caramel into the ramekins, dividing it evenly. Tilt the ramekins so the caramel coats the entire bottom. Set the ramekins aside, remembering they will retain heat for several minutes.

4 cups milk
½ cup crushed amaretti cookies (about 12 cookies)
½ cup amaretto or other almond liqueur
½ cup plus ⅔ cup granulated sugar
3 tablespoons water
¼ cup cornstarch
¼ cup (½ stick) unsalted butter, softened
3 large eggs, separated

Combine the amaretti mixture and the remaining ⅔ cup sugar in a blender or a food processor fitted with the metal blade and process at low speed until smooth.

In a medium-size, heavy saucepan, stir the remaining 3¾ cups milk and the cornstarch together until the cornstarch is dissolved. Scrape the amaretti mixture into the saucepan and place over low heat. Cook, stirring constantly, until the mixture is simmering. Simmer until thickened enough to coat a spoon, 1 to 2 minutes. Remove the saucepan from the heat and cool to body temperature, stirring often to prevent a skin from forming on the surface.

continued

Meanwhile, place a deep baking dish or roasting pan on the center rack of the oven and pour in enough warm water to fill it halfway. Preheat the oven to 400°F.

Add the butter and egg yolks alternately to the cooled milk mixture, whisking well until each addition is incorporated before adding another.

In a medium-size bowl, beat the egg whites with an electric mixer at high speed until they hold stiff peaks when the beaters are lifted. Add about one fourth of the egg whites to the amaretti mixture and, with a rubber spatula, fold them in, scraping the amaretti mixture from the bottom of the bowl over the whites until just a few streaks of white remain. Fold in the remaining whites in the same way.

Pour the pudding mixture into the prepared ramekins and place them in the water bath. Bake until the puddings are evenly set—that is, when you shake them, they jiggle evenly, rather than appearing firm around the edges and still liquid in the center—about 40 minutes. Remove the puddings from the water bath and cool completely before serving. (The puddings can be refrigerated for up to 1 day before serving.)

To serve, invert the puddings onto serving plates. Wait a moment for the caramel sauce to seep onto the plates, then lift off the ramekins. The puddings should unmold very easily. Serve the pudding with Chocolate Sauce (page 362) or Zabaglione (page 377).

Caramelized Tomatoes

❧ Pomodori Caramelizati ❧

Don't think you'd like tomatoes for dessert? I'll bet you're wrong! Try this simple, unusual, and delicious sweet spooned over vanilla ice cream—there is nothing better in the middle of summer after a light meal.

MAKES 6 SERVINGS

If the ice cream is frozen solid, let it stand at room temperature while preparing the tomatoes.

With a vegetable peeler, remove the zest (orange part of the peel only, not the underlying white pith) from the orange in wide strips. Cut the zest into very thin strips. Squeeze the juice from the orange and reserve the strips of zest and juice separately.

In a medium-size, heavy, nonreactive skillet, make a caramel with the sugar and water according to the directions on page 366. Just as the caramel turns a medium amber color, remove the skillet from the heat and carefully add the orange zest and orange juice. Return the skillet to the heat and bring to a boil, stirring constantly to dissolve any caramel that has hardened. Add the tomatoes and Grand Marnier. Stand back from the range and ignite the Grand Marnier with a long fireplace match. (If you do not have a long match, let the sauce boil an extra minute or two.) Continue cooking, shaking the skillet vigorously, until the flames subside and the sauce is thickened, about 2 minutes.

Scoop the ice cream into coupes or shallow dishes and spoon some of the tomatoes and the hot syrup over each serving. Garnish with mint sprigs.

1 pint vanilla ice cream

1 orange

6 tablespoons granulated sugar

2 tablespoons water

6 vine-ripened plum tomatoes, cored, peeled (see page 141), cut in half lengthwise, and seeded

¼ cup Grand Marnier or other orange liqueur

Sprigs fresh mint

Soft Ice Cream with Hazelnuts

🍶 Semifreddo alla Nocciola 🍶

The beauty of this ice cream preparation is that, although you do not need an ice cream machine to make it, the texture is as rich and creamy as the best of ice creams.

MAKES 8 SERVINGS

½ cup grated semisweet chocolate
   (about 3 ounces)

8 amaretti cookies, finely crumbled
   (about ⅓ cup)

1 tablespoon brandy

1 cup whole hazelnuts, toasted (see Note
   on page 353) and coarsely chopped
   to the size of rice grains

5 large eggs, separated (see Note)

1 cup superfine sugar

½ cup sweet Marsala wine

2 cups heavy cream

In a small bowl, stir the chocolate, crumbled amaretti, brandy, and chopped hazelnuts together until blended.

In the top of a double boiler or a medium-size heatproof bowl, whisk the egg yolks, ½ cup of the superfine sugar, and the Marsala together until smooth. Place over barely simmering water and continue beating (switching to a handheld electric mixer at medium speed, if you like) until the mixture is pale yellow and fluffy and falls back on itself in thick ribbons when the whisk or beaters are lifted, about 8 minutes if you are whisking by hand, or 4 minutes if using an electric mixer. It is important to whisk continuously, or the egg yolks will cook and the mixture will appear curdled. Remove the top of the double boiler or the bowl from the heat and set it in a large bowl of ice water. Whisk constantly until cold.

In a large bowl, whip the heavy cream with the electric mixer at medium speed until it holds stiff peaks when the beaters are lifted. Clean the beaters well and dry them.

In a medium-size bowl, beat the egg whites with the electric mixer at medium speed until foamy. While continuing to beat, gradually add the remaining ½ cup sugar and beat until the whites are glossy and hold stiff peaks when the beaters are lifted.

Add about one fourth of the beaten egg whites to the chilled Marsala mixture and, with a rubber spatula, gently fold them in, scraping the Marsala mixture from the bottom of the bowl over the whites. Fold in the remaining whites in the same way. Fold the Marsala mixture into the whipped cream in the same way.

Line a 9 × 5 × 3-inch loaf pan snugly with plastic wrap. Sprinkle the bottom with an even layer of the hazelnut mixture. Spoon one third of the egg-cream mixture over that and tap the bottom of the pan on a hard surface to settle the mixture in an even layer. Sprinkle half of the remaining hazelnut mixture in an even layer over the egg-cream mixture. Repeat the sequence, finishing with the last third of the egg-cream mixture. Smooth the surface with a spatula, cover with plastic wrap, and freeze until solid, at least 8 hours or up to 2 days. (*Semifreddo,* if tightly wrapped, will keep for up to 1 week in the freezer.)

To serve, remove the top layer of plastic wrap and invert the pan onto a platter large enough to hold the *semifreddo.* Tap the bottom of the pan sharply to loosen the frozen mixture and lift off the pan. Remove the plastic wrap and, with a long, thin knife, slice the *semifreddo* into ¾-inch-thick slices.

Note: Although only an extremely small percentage of eggs contain salmonella bacteria—which, if the eggs are improperly handled, can multiply and cause salmonellosis—it is worth noting that desserts and other dishes that call for uncooked eggs or eggs that are cooked below a temperature of 160°F can possibly cause illness. To greatly reduce this risk, buy only very fresh eggs in uncracked shells, refrigerate them immediately, and use them as quickly as possible. Wash your hands and all work surfaces and utensils thoroughly before and after working with eggs. It is best to avoid these dishes altogether if you will be serving children, elderly people, or those with compromised immune systems or if you live in an area that has experienced outbreaks of salmonellosis.

Soft Ice Cream with Nougat

Semifreddo al Torrone

Torrone, or nougat, which the Italians love, gives this *semifreddo a gelateria* (traditional Italian ice cream shop) quality and taste. Be sure to buy hard *torrone* for this dessert—the soft kind is impossible to chop and won't give the crunch that makes this such a treat.

MAKES 8 TO 10 SERVINGS

5 large eggs, separated (see Note on page 373)

1 cup superfine sugar

½ cup dry white wine

1 tablespoon brandy

2 cups heavy cream

1 cup finely chopped *torrone* or other hard nougat candy with nuts

In the top of a double boiler or in a medium-size, heat-proof bowl, whisk the egg yolks, ½ cup of the superfine sugar, and the wine together until smooth. Place over barely simmering water and continue beating (switching to a handheld electric mixer at medium speed, if you like) until the mixture is pale yellow and fluffy and falls back on itself in thick ribbons when the whisk or beaters are lifted, about 8 minutes if you are whisking by hand, or 4 minutes if using an electric mixer. It is important to whisk continuously, or the egg yolks will cook and the mixture will appear curdled. Remove the top of the double boiler or the bowl from the heat and set it in a large bowl of ice water. Whisk constantly until cold, then beat in the brandy.

In a large bowl, whip the heavy cream with an electric mixer at medium speed until it holds stiff peaks when the beaters are lifted. Clean the beaters well and dry them.

In a medium-size bowl, beat the egg whites with the electric mixer at medium speed until foamy. While continuing to beat, gradually add the remaining ½ cup sugar and beat until the whites are glossy and hold stiff peaks when the beaters are lifted.

Add about one fourth of the beaten egg whites to the chilled wine mixture and, with a rubber spatula, gently fold them in, scraping the wine mixture from the bottom of the bowl over the whites. Fold in the remaining whites in the same way. Fold the lightened wine mixture and *torrone* into the whipped cream in the same way.

Line a 9 × 5 × 3-inch loaf pan snugly with plastic wrap. Transfer the *torrone* mixture to the pan and smooth the surface with a spatula. Cover securely with plastic wrap and freeze until solid, at least 8 hours or up to 2 days. (*Semifreddo*, if tightly wrapped, will keep for up to 1 week in the freezer.)

To serve, remove the top layer of plastic wrap and invert the pan onto a platter large enough to hold the *semifreddo*. Tap the bottom of the pan sharply to loosen the frozen mixture. Remove the pan and the plastic wrap and, with a long, thin knife, slice the *semifreddo* into ¾-inch-thick slices.

Cornmeal Raisin Cookies

❦ Zaletti ❦

These are very typical Venetian cookies made with cornmeal flour—hence the name *zaletti*, which means "yellow-colored ones" in Venetian dialect.

MAKES ABOUT 6 DOZEN COOKIES

Combine the raisins with the water in a small bowl and let stand, tossing once or twice, while preparing the cookies.

In a medium-size bowl, stir the 1½ cups flour, cornmeal, baking powder, and salt together until blended.

In a large bowl, beat ¾ cup of the butter and the sugar together with an electric mixer at medium-high speed until fluffy. Add the egg, lemon zest, and vanilla and beat until thoroughly incorporated. Add the dry ingredients to the butter mixture and stir until blended. Add the raisins and water and stir until combined and the raisins are evenly distributed. Form the dough into a compact ball and wrap it in plastic wrap. Chill until very firm, at least 1 hour, or up to 2 days.

¾ cup golden raisins

¼ cup warm water

1½ cups unbleached all-purpose flour, plus more for the baking sheets

1 cup fine yellow cornmeal

1 teaspoon baking powder

½ teaspoon salt

¾ cup (1½ sticks) unsalted butter, softened, plus more for the baking sheets

⅔ cup granulated sugar

1 large egg

2 teaspoons grated lemon zest (yellow part only, without the underlying white pith)

1 teaspoon pure vanilla extract

Preheat the oven to 375°F. Butter and flour two large baking sheets, tapping off any excess flour. (This isn't necessary if you are using nonstick baking sheets.)

On a lightly floured surface, roll out the dough to a ¼-inch thickness. Cut the dough into diamond shapes 1½ inches long on each side. Place the cookies on the prepared baking sheets, leaving about ½ inch between them. Reroll the scraps and cut out more cookies until all the dough is used.

Bake until the undersides of the cookies are golden brown, 12 to 15 minutes. Transfer to wire racks to cool. The cookies can be stored in an airtight container for up to 1 week.

About Zabaglione

To say that zabaglione is an unset custard laced with a fortified wine—Marsala—is akin to saying that Venice is a city on the water. Zabaglione is the apotheosis of custard—light, airy, and rich, ethereal as a sauce or on its own.

To make zabaglione properly requires an understanding of its chemistry as well as of its poetry. As the egg yolks are heated and whisked, their fat molecules expand, and it is into these stretched fatty molecules that the evaporating wine and sugar are absorbed, thereby imparting a fluffy creaminess to the custard.

The proper ratio of ingredients is all-important to the success of the finished zabaglione. That basic ratio—which can be altered slightly—is one egg yolk to one tablespoon sugar to one tablespoon Marsala. If you choose a nonfortified wine, such as the Barolo I suggest or a Riesling, you can double the proportion of wine to yolks and sugar, because these wines contain less alcohol. Also, if you plan to make a large batch of zabaglione with, say, six or more yolks, you may want to add a little less Marsala and sugar.

Specially designed zabaglione makers are available but costly. They resemble double boilers but have a wider, shallower inset bowl, which is usually made of unlined copper. It is easy to improvise a zabaglione-making setup: Choose a 2- to 3-quart heatproof bowl—unlined copper is ideal, but any heatproof bowl will do—and a saucepan with an opening wide enough to nest the bowl in comfortably. Pour about 3 inches of water into the saucepan and place the empty bowl over the opening. The bottom of the bowl shouldn't touch the water and enough of the bowl should fit into the opening so all the ingredients will be in contact with the heat when they are added to the bowl.

All the ingredients in a zabaglione must be thoroughly blended before being subjected to heat and, once the heating has begun, the temperature must remain constant and moderate, a state that can be achieved by cooking the zabaglione in a bowl over—not sitting in—barely simmering water. Never rest the bowl directly in the water or let the water come to a boil; the zabaglione mixture is delicate and the proteins in the egg yolks will coagulate in contact with excessive heat. When coagulation takes place, your zabaglione becomes more like an unwanted dish of scrambled eggs. (If this should happen to you, there is no solution but to toss the curdled zabaglione and begin again.) Moreover, if the heat is too high, all the evaporating alcohol will escape, leaving the fat molecules empty and the custard heavy.

Although other wines of comparable or lesser alcohol content can be blended with or substituted for Marsala, as in the Zabaglione with Barolo Wine on page 380, cordials or liqueurs of higher alcoholic content should generally be avoided. The alcohol in these stronger spirits will escape immediately, leaving a flat zabaglione in the bowl. It is possible to use these higher-alcohol liqueurs to make a zabaglione if you reduce the ratio of sugar to egg yolks and start the zabaglione over slightly cooler water and increase the heat only very gradually, in minute increments. But these adaptations require more experience and dexterity that will only come with practice.

Zabaglione

In a medium-size copper or other heatproof bowl, whisk the egg yolks, Marsala, and sugar together until smooth. Place over, not in, barely simmering water and continue beating (switching to a hand-held electric mixer at medium speed, if you like) until the mixture is pale yellow and frothy and falls back on itself in thick ribbons

**6 large egg yolks, at room temperature
    (see Note on page 373)
¼ cup dry Marsala wine
¼ cup granulated sugar**

when the whisk or beaters are lifted, about 8 minutes if you are whisking by hand, or 4 minutes if using an electric mixer. It is important to whisk continuously, or the egg yolks will cook and the mixture will appear curdled. Remove the sauce from the heat and serve immediately, spooned either into individual coupes or over fresh fruit or berries.

Chocolate Zabaglione: In a small heatproof bowl set over a pan of gently simmering water, melt 3 ounces chopped semisweet chocolate, stirring often so the chocolate melts evenly. Remove the pan from the heat but leave the bowl of chocolate over the water to keep it warm. Prepare the zabaglione according to the directions above. Remove from the heat and fold in the warm, melted chocolate. Serve immediately.

Chocolate Sponge Cake with Sour Cherry and Chocolate Zabaglione Mousse Filling

Torta Rigojancsi

This dessert of Hungarian origin takes its name from the famous violinist Rigo Jancsi, who seduced his Belgian wife with this dessert.

MAKES ONE 10-INCH CAKE; 8 TO 10 SERVINGS

For the chocolate sponge cake

Unsalted butter, softened, for the cake pan

2 cups unbleached all-purpose flour, plus more for the cake pan

½ cup unsweetened cocoa powder

¼ teaspoon baking powder

¼ teaspoon baking soda

6 large eggs

1½ cups granulated sugar

For the cherry syrup

½ cup sweet Marsala wine

2 tablespoons confectioners' sugar

1 cup Amerene cherries, with their liquid (see Note)

For the filling

½ pound very good quality semisweet or bittersweet chocolate, chopped

1 teaspoon unflavored powdered gelatin

2 tablespoons cold water

7 large egg yolks, at room temperature (see Note on page 373)

Make the sponge cake. Place the rack in the center position of the oven and preheat the oven to 375°F. Butter the sides and bottom of a 10-inch by 3-inch-high round cake pan or springform pan. Sprinkle the sides and bottom with flour, making sure to coat the entire surface, and tap out the excess. To make the cake easier to remove, cut a piece of parchment paper the size of the bottom of the pan, insert it into the bottom of the buttered cake pan (you don't need to flour the pan if you're using parchment), and butter and flour that too.

In a small bowl, sift together the 2 cups flour, the cocoa, baking powder, and baking soda.

In a medium-size bowl set over a large saucepan of simmering water, beat the eggs and granulated sugar together until the mixture has warmed and most of the sugar has dissolved, about 3 minutes. Using a handheld electric mixer, beat the mixture at high speed until doubled in volume, about 5 minutes. Remove the bowl from the heat. With a rubber spatula, fold the dry ingredients into the egg mixture, scraping the egg mixture from the bottom of the bowl over the dry ingredients.

Pour the batter into the prepared cake pan and bake until a wooden skewer or cake tester inserted into the center of the cake comes out clean and the cake's surface springs back when lightly pressed, about 25 minutes. Let stand on a wire rack until completely cool, 1 to 2 hours, before removing from the pan.

Meanwhile, make the cherry syrup. In a small saucepan, stir the Marsala and confectioners' sugar together over low heat until the sugar is completely dissolved. Remove from the heat, add the cherries and their liquid, and set aside.

⅓ cup superfine sugar
½ cup dry Marsala wine
1½ cups heavy cream

1 tablespoon unsweetened cocoa powder
Chocolate Zabaglione (page 377), optional

Make the filling. In a small heatproof bowl set over a pan of gently simmering water, melt the chocolate, stirring often to melt it evenly. Remove the pan from the heat but leave the bowl of chocolate over the water to keep it warm.

Meanwhile, sprinkle the gelatin over the cold water in a small bowl. Let stand until softened, about 10 minutes.

In the top of a double boiler or in a medium-size heatproof bowl, whisk the egg yolks, superfine sugar, and the Marsala together until smooth. Place over barely simmering water and continue beating (switching to a handheld electric mixer at medium speed, if you like) until the mixture is pale yellow and fluffy and falls back on itself in thick ribbons when the whisk or beaters are lifted, about 8 minutes if you are whisking by hand, or 4 minutes if using an electric mixer. It is important to whisk continuously, or the egg yolks will cook and the mixture will appear curdled.

Scrape the softened gelatin into the egg yolk mixture and stir until the gelatin is dissolved. With a rubber spatula, fold in the chocolate mixture. Let the mixture stand until cool, about 10 minutes.

Meanwhile, in a medium-size bowl, beat the heavy cream with an electric mixer at medium speed until it holds stiff peaks when the beaters are lifted.

With a rubber spatula, fold the whipped cream into the chocolate-egg mixture until no traces of white are visible.

Assemble the cake. With a long, thin, serrated knife, slice the chocolate sponge cake horizontally into three even layers. Set the bottom layer in a 10-inch springform pan and brush it with about one third of the cherry syrup—it should be quite moist. Scatter half the cherries over the cake layer. Spoon half the chocolate zabaglione filling over the cherries. Moisten one side of the center layer with cherry syrup and place it, moistened side up, over the filling. Scatter the remaining cherries over the center layer and spoon the remaining chocolate zabaglione filling over the cherries.

continued

Moisten the cut side of the top cake layer with the remaining syrup and place it, cut side down, over the filling. Press very gently to even out the layers. Cover the pan securely with plastic wrap and refrigerate until the filling is firm, at least 6 hours, or up to 1 day.

To serve, release the side of the springform pan and remove it. Sift the cocoa over the cake. Cut the cake into wedges with a thin, serrated knife and serve with Chocolate Zabaglione (page 377), if you like.

Note: Amarene are wild cherries preserved in syrup. Fabbri is a very good brand.

Zabaglione with Barolo Wine
⬛ Zabaglione al Barolo ⬛

This zabaglione is good by itself, piled high in a coupe or wineglass, or as a topping for berries, especially blueberries and blackberries.

MAKES ABOUT 2 ½ CUPS; 6 DESSERT SERVINGS

¾ cup superior-quality Barolo wine

6 large egg yolks, at room temperature
(see Note on page 373)

6 tablespoons granulated sugar

In a medium-size copper or other heatproof bowl, whisk the Barolo, egg yolks, and sugar together until smooth. Place over, not in, barely simmering water and continue beating (switching to a handheld electric mixer at medium speed, if you like) until the mixture is light and frothy and falls back on itself in thick ribbons when the whisk or beaters are lifted, about 6 minutes if you are whisking by hand, or about 3 minutes if using an electric mixer. It is important to whisk continuously, or the egg yolks will cook and the mixture will appear curdled. Remove the sauce from the heat and serve immediately.

Index